T0268580

Praise for *Doppelganger*

"I've been raving about Naomi Klein's *Doppelganger*."
—Michelle Goldberg, *The New York Times*

"Dazzling and erudite . . . A deft and intricate investigation of online culture and political doubling . . . On her highbrow romp through this disturbing underworld, Klein's writing is clear, dynamic, ruthlessly honest, imbued with a rare integrity."
—Katie Roiphe, *The New York Times Book Review* (Editors' Choice)

"*Doppelganger* is an in-depth critique of what late-stage capitalism hath wrought. But it's also much more. Klein wields her polymathic expertise like a sword, slicing through the mirror world . . . There's a lot going on in *Doppelganger*, yet somehow Klein ties it all together into what we seem to be lacking as individuals: a cohesive whole. *Doppelganger* is both timely and timeless, a work in a grand tradition."
—Chris Vognar, *Los Angeles Times*

"A compelling and far-reaching political detective story . . . Especially when it comes to the political fallout from the pandemic, no other book I know of has been this intellectually adventurous, this loopily personal, or this entertaining . . . As a writer and a theorist, Klein is particularly talented at knitting together the sweep of history and the banalities of the present. She's equally attuned to what doppelgängers can mean in a more transhistorical sense."
—Laura Kipnis, *The Nation*

"[*Doppelganger* is] a very, very good book . . . An ambitious, wide-ranging exploration of this very frightening moment of polycrisis and systemic failure . . . Klein has produced a first-rate *literary* work just as much as this is a superb philosophical and political tome . . . An essential read."
—Cory Doctorow, *Pluralistic*

"Insightful . . . [*Doppelganger* is] the most introspective and whimsical of Klein's books to date, but it is also one of surprising insights, unexpected connections and great subtlety." —William Davies, *The Guardian*

"For nearly a quarter century, Klein's work has offered clarifying conceptual frameworks to understand the workings of power . . . [Klein] has a canny knack for capturing the zeitgeist, crystalizing ideas attuned to a given historical moment that serve to galvanize activists as much as scholars." —Nico Baumbach, *Bookforum*

"This story of mistaken identity would on its own be gripping and revealing enough, both as a psychological study and for its explorations of the double in art and history, the disorienting effects of social media, and the queasy feeling of looking into a distorted mirror. But the larger subject of *Doppelganger* turns out to be a far more complex and consequential confusion . . . A uniquely astute account of the scrambled political formations that have come out of the pandemic."

—Laura Marsh, *The New Republic*

"[Klein] is famous for the calm and poise with which she mainstreams a clear, solidly leftist political-economic critique . . . *Doppelganger* is both more literary and more personal than Klein's other books . . . Klein's purpose is to use her doppelganger adventures as 'a narrow aperture' into . . . an alternative-media ecosystem."

—Jenny Turner, *London Review of Books*

"[*Doppelganger*] stands alongside Klein's bestsellers *No Logo* and *The Shock Doctrine* as a crucial study of the ways that identity, image, ideology and economics become intertwined in the bewildering conditions of twenty-first-century consumer capitalism, and is in many ways a subtler and more challenging work than either of those."

—Andrew O'Hehir, *Salon*

"[A] brave new book . . . By the end [of *Doppelganger*], I wondered if maybe Klein had come closer than ever to cracking the code that reveals what, really, is at the heart of our collective dysfunction . . . Klein brings her analytical prowess and keen wit to an exploration of the concept of doubles . . . [She] blends the personal and the political so seamlessly that it's hard to imagine they could ever be apart."

—Bill Lueders, *The Progressive*

"[A] striking meditation . . . Klein's writing is perceptive and intriguingly personal . . . By articulating such an expansive view of the uncanny, Klein's mesmerizing narrative reflects the unique anxieties and modes of analysis that have come to dominate the online era. Like Klein's previous books, it's a definitive signpost of the times." —*Publishers Weekly*

"Klein's prose is tight and urgent . . . evoking both laughter and dismay and entrancingly matching the mounting frenzy of seeing your public self morph into someone else . . . [Klein's] comprehensive and nuanced treatments of these issues are valuable and compelling . . . A disarming and addictive call to solidarity." —*Kirkus Reviews*

"[Naomi Klein's] provocative thought exercise illuminates the myriad ways taken-for-granted balances can be upended and calls for heightened awareness of the dangers of identity erosion on both large and small scales." —Carol Haggas, *Booklist* (starred review)

"It seems ever more possible that our society might collapse under the sheer weight of nonsense and performance and crazy misinformation that overwhelm our infoworld. With her trademark clarity and perception, and with chemo-level doses of wit and common sense, Naomi Klein goes further than anyone has so far in helping us understand that buzzing and confounding mess, and to see some ways out. If ever a book was necessary, it's this one."

—Bill McKibben, author of *The Flag, the Cross, and the Station Wagon* and *Falter*

"Naomi Klein's thoughtful and honest inquiry into the troubling duplication of her name and the distorted appropriation of her views becomes the occasion for an incisive account of how the Right has appropriated Left discourses, producing a nightmarish doubling that has plunged some of us into silence. Klein moves her reader toward the truer grounds of solidarity in these times, showing us how to resist the lures of Fascism with militant humility and connection, letting ourselves be upended by what we thought we could not bear to see so that we can face and build an affirmative future."

—Judith Butler, author of *Who's Afraid of Gender?*

"Naomi Klein never disappoints. *Doppelganger* swirls through the bewildering ideas of the ultra-right that often appear as a distorted mirror of left-wing struggle and strategy. With her always incisive analysis of the systems and structures linked to global capitalism, Klein now fiercely and brilliantly urges that our justice movements be prepared to follow the quest for new meaning into dimensions where we might least expect to find it: in injury and vulnerability."

—Angela Y. Davis, author of *Freedom Is a Constant Struggle*

"If you want to make sense of a world upside down, this staggering masterpiece will show you how—and then it blazes a path to a more loving and caring future."

—V (formerly Eve Ensler), author of *Reckoning* and *The Vagina Monologues*

"Naomi Klein is one of our most important intellectuals, distilling the political economies of corruption and crisis in our time. Here she plunges into the topsy-turvy world of doubles and mirrors to show that the growth of the right is not a case of malignancies infecting our otherwise pure societies; rather, it's a matter of our own fears, insecurities, and defense mechanisms, all of them rooted in a savagely unequal and violent society. Klein writes with humor, enormous bravery, and humbling vulnerability. This is an extraordinary book."

—Keeanga-Yamahtta Taylor, author of *From #BlackLivesMatter to Black Liberation*

"Once a decade, Naomi Klein writes a book that prompts us to completely rethink the moment we're in. *Doppelganger* helps us to understand, in a deep and tectonic way, why our society is becoming unrecognizable to us—and why so many people we know are changing in disturbing ways. It's a book about going down a rabbit hole that becomes about the nature of the rabbit hole itself. If you want to understand where we are now—and how to find our way back to sanity—you have to read this totally brilliant book."

—Johann Hari, author of *Stolen Focus*

"This book is as foreboding as a guide through the maze of mirrors of the modern right should be. But it's not only that: Naomi Klein has made *Doppelganger* gripping and scintillating, too. The result is a reckoning with the present moment that's as insightful as all of Klein's indispensable work, and as suspenseful as a novel."

—China Miéville, author of *The City & The City* and *A Spectre, Haunting: On "The Communist Manifesto"*

"A dazzling, hallucinatory tour de force that takes the reader through shadow selves and global fascism, leaving them gasping by the end."

—Molly Crabapple, author of *Drawing Blood*

"Naomi Klein's books have been building one on the next to create a powerful cognitive mapping of our time. This new book takes a personal turn, then opens out into an analysis of our shared global dilemma that is as incisive and fascinating as anything she has ever written—which is saying a lot. As always, my first thought on finishing one of her books is *Thank you.*"

—Kim Stanley Robinson, author of *The Ministry for the Future*

"I finished this book and nearly cried with relief. Klein gave me the gift of being calm. She explores and diagnoses with empathy, warmth, and searing precision the confusion and utter madness of what it is to be alive right now. This is a big book with big ideas which poses the most direct questions for our times. Everyone needs to read it as a matter of urgency."

—Sheena Patel, author of *I'm a Fan*

Sebastian Nevols

NAOMI KLEIN

DOPPELGANGER

Naomi Klein is an award-winning journalist and documentary filmmaker, and a *New York Times* bestselling author of books including *No Logo*, *The Shock Doctrine*, *This Changes Everything*, *No Is Not Enough*, and *On Fire*, which have been translated into more than thirty-five languages. She is an associate professor in the department of geography at the University of British Columbia, the founding codirector of UBC's Centre for Climate Justice, and an honorary professor of Media and Climate at Rutgers University. She is the recipient of numerous honorary degrees and doctorates, was awarded the Sydney Peace Prize in 2016, and was nominated for an Emmy. *The Guardian* picked *No Logo* as one of its top 100 nonfiction books of all time, and *Time* chose *No Logo* as one of its top 100 nonfiction books published since 1923.

She speaks and lectures widely, writes a syndicated column for *The Guardian*, and appears in leading publications around the world. *Doppelganger* is her ninth book.

naomiklein.org

Also by Naomi Klein

No Logo

Fences and Windows

The Shock Doctrine

This Changes Everything

No Is Not Enough

The Battle for Paradise

On Fire

How to Change Everything

DOPPELGANGER DOPPELGANGER

A Trip into the Mirror World

NAOMI KLEIN

Picador
Farrar, Straus and Giroux
New York

Picador
120 Broadway, New York 10271

Copyright © 2023 by Naomi Klein
All rights reserved
Printed in the United States of America
Originally published in 2023 by Farrar, Straus and Giroux
First paperback edition, 2024

Grateful acknowledgment is made for permission to reprint a stanza of Stephen Mitchell's translation of "Jerusalem," by Yehuda Amichai, from *The Selected Poetry of Yehuda Amichai*, copyright © 2013 by Chana Bloch and Stephen Mitchell. Reprinted by permission of the publisher, University of California Press.

Library of Congress Control Number: 2023940122
Paperback ISBN: 978-1-250-33814-3

Designed by Abby Kagan

Our books may be purchased in bulk for promotional, educational, or business use. Please contact your local bookseller or the Macmillan Corporate and Premium Sales Department at 1-800-221-7945, extension 5442, or by email at MacmillanSpecialMarkets@macmillan.com.

Picador® is a U.S. registered trademark and is used by Macmillan Publishing Group, LLC, under license from Pan Books Limited.

For book club information, please email marketing@picadorusa.com.

picadorusa.com • Follow us on social media at @picador or @picadorusa

3 5 7 9 10 8 6 4

IN MEMORIAM:

Mike Davis,

Barbara Ehrenreich,

bell hooks,

Leo Panitch

A terrible multitude of duplicates had sprung into being.

—Fyodor Dostoyevsky, *The Double*, 1846

How many of everybody is there going to be?

—Jordan Peele, *Us*, 2019

CONTENTS

PART FOUR: FACING THE REAL

DOPPELGANGER

INTRODUCTION: OFF-BRAND ME

In my defense, it was never my intent to write this book. I did not have time. No one asked me to. And several people strongly cautioned against it. Not now—not with the literal and figurative fires roiling our planet. And certainly not about this.

Other Naomi—that is how I refer to her now. This person with whom I have been chronically confused for over a decade. My big-haired doppelganger. A person whom so many others appear to find indistinguishable from me. A person who does many extreme things that cause strangers to chastise me or thank me or express their pity for me.

The very fact that I refer to her with any kind of code speaks to the absurdity of my situation. For a quarter of a century, I have been a person who writes about corporate power and its ravages. I sneak into abusive factories in faraway countries and across borders to military occupations; I report in the aftermath of oil spills and category 5 hurricanes. I write books of Big Ideas About Serious Subjects. And yet in the months and years during which this text came into being—a time when cemeteries ran out of space, and billionaires blasted themselves into outer space—everything else that I had to write or might have written appeared only as an unwanted intrusion, a rude interruption. Would I participate in events leading up to a key United Nations Climate Summit? No, I'm sorry, I am overcommitted. Comment on the U.S. withdrawal from Afghanistan? The twentieth anniversary of 9/11? The Russian invasion of Ukraine? No, no, and no again.

In June 2021, as this project began to truly spiral out of my control, a strange new weather event dubbed a "heat dome" descended on the southern coast of British Columbia, the part of Canada where I now live with my family. The thick air felt like a snarling, invasive entity with malevolent intent. More than six hundred people died, most of them elderly; an estimated ten billion marine creatures were cooked alive on our shores; an entire town went up in flames. It's rare for this out-of-the-way, sparsely populated spot to make international headlines, but the heat dome made us briefly famous. An editor asked if I, as someone engaged in the climate change fight for fifteen years, would file a report about what it was like to live through this unprecedented climate event.

"I'm working on something else," I told him, the stench of death filling my nostrils.

"Can I ask what?"

"You cannot."

There were plenty of other important things I neglected during this time of feverish subterfuge. That summer, I allowed my nine-year-old to spend so many hours watching a gory nature series called *Animal Fight Club* that he began to ram me at my desk "like a great white shark." I did not spend nearly enough time with my octogenarian parents, who live a mere half hour's drive away, despite their statistical vulnerability to the deadly pandemic that was rampaging through the globe and despite that lethal heat dome. In the fall, my husband ran for office in a national election; though I did go on a few campaign trips, I know I could have done more.

I engaged in all of this neglect so that I could . . . what? Check her serially suspended Twitter account? Study her appearances on Steve Bannon's livestreams for insights into their electric chemistry? Read or listen to yet another of her warnings that basic health measures were actually a covert plot orchestrated by the Chinese Communist Party, Bill Gates, Anthony Fauci, and the World Economic Forum to sow mass death on such a scale it could only be the work of the devil himself?

My deepest shame rests with the unspeakable number of podcasts I mainlined, the sheer volume of hours lost that I will never get back. A master's degree's worth of hours. I told myself it was "research." That if I was going to understand her and her fellow travelers who are now in open warfare against objective reality, I had to immerse myself in the archive of several extremely prolific and editing-averse weekly and twice-weekly shows with names like *QAnon Anonymous* and *Conspirituality* that unpack and deconstruct the commingling worlds of conspiracy theories, wellness hucksters, and their various intersections with Covid-19 denial, anti-vaccine hysteria, and rising fascism. This on top of keeping up with the daily output from Bannon and Tucker Carlson, on whose shows Other Naomi had become a regular guest.

This listening devoured nearly every interstitial moment in my life: laundry folding, dishwasher unloading, dog walking, school-drop-off driving (return-only). In another life, many of these were pockets of time when I listened to music or the actual news, or when I called people I love. "I feel closer to the hosts of 'Conspirituality' than to you," I whimpered one night into my best friend's voice mail.

I told myself I had no choice. That this was not, in fact, an epically frivolous and narcissistic waste of my compressed writing time or of the compressed time on the clock of our fast-warming planet. I rationalized that Other Naomi, as one of the most effective creators and disseminators of misinformation and disinformation about many of our most urgent crises, and as someone who has seemingly helped inspire large numbers to take to the streets in rebellion against an almost wholly hallucinated "tyranny," is at the nexus of several forces that, while ridiculous in the extreme, are nonetheless important, since the confusion they sow and the oxygen they absorb increasingly stand in the way of pretty much anything helpful or healthful that humans might, at some point, decide to accomplish together.

Like grounding those space-faring billionaires and using their ill-gotten wealth to pay for housing and health care and getting off fossil fuels before the future is one protracted heat dome. Or, more modestly, sending your shark-identified child to elementary school without fearing that they will come home with a highly contagious and potentially lethal virus that they contracted from a classmate whose parents believe that vaccines are part of a plot to commit genocide and enslave humanity because some lady on the internet named Naomi convinced them it was so.

"Doppelganger" comes from German, combining *Doppel* (double) with *Gänger* (goer). Sometimes it's translated as "double-walker," and I can tell you that having a double walking around is a profoundly unsettling experience. Uncanny, a feeling Sigmund Freud described as "that species of the frightening that goes back to what was once well known and had long been familiar"—but is suddenly alien. The uncanniness provoked by doppelgangers is particularly acute because the thing that becomes unfamiliar is you. A person who has a doppelganger, Freud wrote, "may identify himself with another and so become unsure of his true self." He wasn't right about everything, but he was right about that.

And here's an extra twist: My doppelganger is a person who has undergone such a dramatic political and personal transformation that many have commented that she seems like a doppelganger of her former self. Which, in a way, makes me a double of a double, an uncanny state of affairs even Freud did not anticipate.

I am hardly the only one to grapple with a sense that reality is somehow warping. Almost everyone I talk to tells me about people they have lost "down the rabbit hole"—parents, siblings, best friends, as well as formerly trusted intellectuals and commentators. People, once familiar, who have become unrecognizable. Altered. It began to feel as if the forces that have destabilized my world are part of an expansive web of forces that are destabilizing our larger world—and that understanding these forces could hold a key to getting to firmer ground.

For more than twenty years, ever since those jetliners flew into the glass and steel of the World Trade Center, I have been preoccupied with the ways that large-scale shocks scramble our collective synapses, lead to mass regression, and make humans easy prey for demagogues. In the years that it took to research and write *The Shock Doctrine*, my 2007 book on this topic, I delved deeply into how post-shock states of discombobulation have been opportunistically exploited in many different contexts: 9/11, the collapse of the Soviet Union, the invasion of Iraq, Hurricane Katrina, and events significantly further back in time. With the public terrified and distracted, power-hungry players were able to move in and ram through policies that benefited corporate elites without debate or consent—not unlike the brutal methods deployed by torturers who use isolation and stress to soften up and break their prisoners. As I conducted this research, tracking the attacks on political rights as well as the auctioning off of public lands and services, I always imagined myself to be immune to these shock tactics, since I knew how they worked. I was not scrambled by unprecedented events, my sight was clear during crises, and I would help others see clearly as well. Or so I thought.

Looking back now, I cringe at how easy I had it. If I felt immune to shock, it was mainly because of my distance from its sources. It wasn't my family members who were killed from the air. It wasn't my neighborhood that was in line for demolition, nor was it my kid's teachers who were getting fired so that public schools could be converted to private ones.

But Covid . . . Covid was different. It scrambled my personal world, as it did all of our worlds. For the first four months, while I was still living in New Jersey, I was confined to our home with our neuroatypical son, trying in vain to help him learn online, and, more important, to soothe his porous soul, which could not help but absorb the terror that surrounded us. Ambulances picked up our neighbors, the virus tore through our friend group. I was still lucky—I wasn't on the front lines in the Covid wards, but neither was I protected from the pandemic with my usual reportorial distance. I woke up every morning exhausted and stared at my various screens in a stultified daze. For the first time, this was not someone else's shock. And then the shocks kept coming.

A state of shock is what happens to us—individually or as a society—when we experience a sudden and unprecedented event for which we do not yet have an adequate explanation. At its essence, a shock is the gap that opens up between event and existing narratives to explain that event. Being creatures of narrative, humans tend to be very uncomfortable with meaning vacuums—which is why those opportunistic players, the people I have termed "disaster capitalists," have been able to rush into the gap with their preexisting wish lists and simplistic stories of good and evil. The stories themselves may be cartoonishly wrong ("You are either with us or with the terrorists," they told us after September 11, along with "They hate our freedoms"). But at least those stories exist—and that alone is enough to make them better than the nothingness of the gap.

"Gather together, find your footing and your story." That is the advice I have been giving for two decades about how to stay out of shock during moments of collective trauma. Metabolize the shock together, I would tell people, create meaning together. Resist the tin-pot tyrants who will tell you that the world is now a blank sheet for them to write their violent stories upon.

It was solid advice. But Covid made it so very hard to act on. Controlling the virus forced on many of us, including me, the very conditions that make humans most vulnerable to states of shock: prolonged stress and isolation. My own isolation grew more extreme when, four months into the pandemic, we returned to Canada. It was supposed to be a temporary trip to be close to my parents. But, like so many others, we got stuck. We now live full-time up on a rock at the dead end of a street that is three hours, including a less than dependable ferryboat, from the closest city. Only occasionally do I regret giving up restaurant delivery, reliable electrical power, and subways in favor of a reliably open country school, easy access to forest trails, and the slim but nonetheless real chance of glimpsing the black dorsal fin of an orca slice the steely waters of the Salish Sea. It's good here—when it isn't choked by heat and wildfire smoke or lashed by storms for which we keep having to learn new names ("bomb cyclone," "atmospheric river," and "pineapple express" all in one long, wet winter). But it is isolated. So maybe that's what finally pushed me to (or is it "over"?) the edge. The months and months without humans in bodies to feel and think with.

That, and going online to try to find some simulation of the friendships and communities I missed, and finding, instead, The Confusion: a torrent of people discussing me and what I'd said and what I'd done—

only it wasn't me. It was her. Which raised an alarming question: Who, then, was I?

In an attempt to make sense of my predicament, I began reading and watching everything I could find about doubles and doppelgangers, from Carl Jung to Ursula K. Le Guin; Fyodor Dostoyevsky to Jordan Peele. The figure of the double began to fascinate me—its meaning in ancient mythology and in the birth of psychoanalysis. The way the twinned self stands in for our highest aspiration—the eternal soul, that ephemeral being that supposedly outlives the body. And the way the double also represents the most repressed, depraved, and rejected parts of ourselves that we cannot bear to see—the evil twin, the shadow self, the anti-self, the Hyde to our Jekyll. From these stories, I quickly learned that my identity crisis was likely unavoidable: the appearance of one's doppelganger is almost always chaotic, stressful, and paranoia-inducing, and the person encountering their double is invariably pushed to their limits by the frustration and uncanniness of it all.

Doppelgangers, however, are not only forms of torment. For centuries, doubles have been understood as warnings or harbingers. When reality starts doubling, refracting off itself, it often means that something important is being ignored or denied—a part of ourselves and our world we do not want to see—and that further danger awaits if the warning is not heeded. That applies to the individual but also to entire societies that are divided, doubled, polarized, or partitioned into various warring, seemingly unknowable camps. Societies like ours.

Alfred Hitchcock called the tumultuous state of living in the presence of doppelgangers "vertigo" in his 1958 classic of the same name, but from my experience, an even more resonant term is one used by the Mexican philosopher Emilio Uranga in 1952: *zozobra*. A Spanish word for existential anxiety and deep gloom, *zozobra* also evokes generalized wobbliness: "a mode of being that incessantly oscillates between two possibilities, between two affects, without knowing which one of those to depend on"—absurdity and gravity, danger and safety, death and life. Uranga writes, "In this to and fro the soul suffers, it feels torn and wounded."

Philip Roth explored this push and pull in his doppelganger novel

Operation Shylock: "It's too ridiculous to take seriously and too serious to be ridiculous," he wrote of a duplicate Roth. That sentence has become my mantra during this uncanny period. Are the political movements Other Naomi helps lead ridiculous, unworthy of attention—or are they part of a serious shift in our world that needs our urgent reckoning? Should I be laughing or crying? Am I sitting still on this rock, or is everything moving very fast?

If doppelganger literature and mythology is any guide, when confronted with the appearance of one's double, a person is duty bound to go on a journey—a quest to understand what messages, secrets, and forebodings are being offered. So that is what I have done. Rather than push my doppelganger away, I have attempted to learn everything I can about her and the movements of which she is a part. I followed her as she burrowed deeper and deeper into a warren of conspiracy rabbit holes, places where it often seems that my own *Shock Doctrine* research has gone through the looking glass and is now gazing back at me as a network of fantastical plots that cast the very real crises we face—from Covid to climate change to Russian military aggression—as false flag attacks, planted by the Chinese Communists/corporate globalists/Jews.

I tracked her new alliances with some of the most malevolent men on the planet, the ones sowing information chaos on a mass scale and gleefully egging on insurrections in country after country. I investigated their rewards—political, emotional, and financial—and explored the deep racial, cultural, and historical fears and denials off of which they feed. Most of all, I tried to figure out what kind of responses might drain these heavily armed, anti-democratic forces of their fast-growing power.

I felt justified in this pursuit. I have been confused with Other Naomi for so long and so frequently that I have often felt that she was following me. It seemed only right that I should follow her back.

In stories about doubles, twins, and imposters, it is often the case that the doppelganger acts as an unwelcome kind of mirror, showing the protagonist a vain and venal version of themselves. It will not give too much away to say that, while watching my doppelganger, I have felt that unwelcome wince of recognition more than once. Yet what drove me to write this book, sticking with it against all good judgment, is that the more I looked at her—her disastrous choices and the cruel ways she was often treated by others—the more I came to feel as if I were seeing not only undesirable parts of myself but a magnification of many undesirable aspects of our shared culture as well. The ambient and all-pervasive hunger for ever-more-fleeting relevance; the disposability with which we treat people who mess up; the trivialization of words and displacements of responsibility, and much else. In the end, looking at her helped me see myself more clearly, but it also, oddly, helped me better see the dangerous systems and dynamics we are all trapped inside.

This, then, is not a biography of Other Naomi, nor does it offer a psychoanalytic diagnosis of her behaviors. It is an attempt to use my own doppelganger experience—the havoc wreaked and the lessons learned about me, her, and us—as a guide into and through what I have come to understand as our doppelganger culture. A culture crowded with various forms of doubling, in which all of us who maintain a persona or avatar online create our own doppelgangers—virtual versions of ourselves that represent us to others. A culture in which many of us have come to think of ourselves as personal brands, forging a partitioned identity that is both us and not us, a doppelganger we perform ceaselessly in the digital ether as the price of admission in a rapacious attention economy. And all the while, tech companies use these data troves to train machines to create artificial simulations of human intelligence and human functions, lifelike doubles that carry their own agendas, their own logics, and their own threats. What, I have kept asking myself, is all of this duplication doing to us? How is it steering what we pay attention to and—more critically—what we neglect?

As I shadowed my double further into her world—a place where soft-focus wellness influencers make common cause with fire-breathing far-right propagandists all in the name of saving and protecting "the children"—I found myself confronting yet more forms of doubling and doppelganging, these ones distinctly more consequential. Like the way that all of politics increasingly feels like a mirror world, with society split in two, and each side defining itself against the other—whatever one says and believes, the other seems obliged to say and believe the exact opposite. The deeper I went, the more I noticed this phenomenon all around me: individuals not guided by legible principles or beliefs, but acting as members of groups playing yin to the other's yang—well versus weak; awake versus sheep; righteous versus depraved. Binaries where thinking once lived.

At first, I thought what I was seeing in my doppelganger's world was mostly grifting unbound. Over time, though, I started to get the distinct impression that I was also witnessing a new and dangerous political formation find itself in real time: its alliances, worldview, slogans, enemies, code words, and no-go zones—and, most of all, its ground game for taking power.

And all of this, it quickly became clear, was enmeshed in another, more ominous kind of doubling: the age-old way that race, ethnicity, and gender create dangerous doubles that hover over whole categories of people—the ones cast as Savage. Terrorist. Thief. Whore. Property. This raises the most chilling part of my doppelganger journey: it is not only an individual who can have a sinister double; nations and cultures have them, too. Many of us feel and fear a decisive flip. Democratic to authoritarian. Secular to theocratic. Pluralist to fascistic. In some places, the flip has already taken place. In others it feels as close and as intimate as a warped reflection in the mirror.

As my investigation has worn on, this is the form of doppelganger that increasingly preoccupies me: the fascist clown state that is the ever-present twin of liberal Western democracies, perpetually threatening to engulf us in its fires of selective belonging and ferocious despising. The figure of the doppelganger has been used for centuries to warn us of these shadow versions of our collective selves, of these monstrous possible futures.

Are we there yet? Not all of us, at least not quite yet. But the pandemic, layered on top of so many other long-repressed emergencies, has taken humanity somewhere we have not been before, somewhere close but different. That difference is what accounts for the strangeness so many of us have been trying to name—everything so familiar, and yet more than a little off. Uncanny people, upside-down politics, even, as artificial intelligence accelerates, a growing difficulty discerning who and what is real. That feeling of disorientation we tell one another about?

Of not understanding whom we can trust and what to believe? Of friends and loved ones behaving like strangers? It's because our world has changed, but, like a collective case of jet lag, most of us are still attuned to the rhythms and habits of the place left behind. It's past time to find our bearings in this new place.

In his novel *The Double*, José Saramago includes an epigraph: "Chaos is merely order waiting to be deciphered." Here is my attempt to decipher the chaos of doppelganger culture, with its maze of simulated selves and digital avatars and mass surveillance and racial and ethnic projections and fascist doubles and the studiously denied shadows that are all coming to the surface at once. It's going to take some wild turns—but rest assured that the point of this mapping is not to stay trapped inside the house of mirrors, but to do what I sense many of us long to do: escape its mind-bending confines and find our way toward some kind of collective power and purpose. The point is to make our way out of this collective vertigo, and get somewhere distinctly better, together.

PART ONE

Double Life

(Performance)

I have found a way to live to the side of my name. That has proven to be very helpful.

—Judith Butler, 2021

1

OCCUPIED

The first time it happened I was in a stall in a public bathroom just off Wall Street in Manhattan. I was about to open the door when I heard two women talking about me.

"Did you see what Naomi Klein said?"

I froze, flashing back to every mean girl in high school, pre-humiliated. What had I said?

"Something about how the march today is a bad idea."

"Who asked her? I really don't think she understands our demands."

Wait. I hadn't said anything about the march—or the demands. Then it hit me: I knew who had. I casually strolled to the sink, made eye contact with one of the women in the mirror, and said words I would repeat far too many times in the months and years to come.

"I think you are talking about Naomi Wolf."

That was November 2011, at the height of Occupy Wall Street, the movement that saw groups of young people camp out in public parks and squares in cities across the United States, Canada, Asia, and the United Kingdom. The uprising was inspired by the Arab Spring and youth-led occupations of squares in southern Europe—a collective howl against economic inequality and financial crimes that would, eventually, birth a new generational politics. That day, the organizers of the original Manhattan encampment had called for a mass march through the financial district, and you could tell by all the black clothing and heavy liquid eyeliner that no one in that bathroom was on break from derivative trading.

I could see why some of my fellow marchers had their Naomis mixed up. We both write big-idea books (my *No Logo*, her *Beauty Myth*; my *Shock Doctrine*, her *End of America*; my *This Changes Everything*, her *Vagina*). We both have brown hair that sometimes goes blond from over-highlighting (hers is longer and more voluminous than mine). We're both Jewish. Most confusingly, we once had distinct writerly lanes (hers being women's bodies, sexuality, and leadership; mine being corporate assaults on democracy and climate change). But by the time Occupy happened, the once-sharp yellow line that divided those lanes had begun to go wobbly.

At the time of the bathroom incident, I had visited the Occupy plaza a couple of times. I was mainly there to conduct interviews about the relationship between market logic and climate breakdown for what would become *This Changes Everything*. But while I was there, organizers asked me to give a short talk about the shock of the 2008 financial crisis and the raging injustices that followed—the trillions marshaled to save the banks whose reckless trades had caused the crisis, the punishing austerity offered to pretty much everyone else, the legalized corruption that all of this laid bare. These were the seeds of discontent that right-wing populists in dozens of countries would eventually exploit for a fiercely anti-immigrant and anti-"globalist" political project, including Donald Trump, under the tutelage of his chief advisor, Stephen K. Bannon. At the time, however, many of us still held out hope that the crash could catalyze a democratic revival and a new era of left power, one that would discipline corporate might and empower flailing democracies to address our many surging emergencies, including the climate emergency. That's what my speech at Occupy was about. You could look it up and weep at how naïve I was.

Naomi Wolf, once a standard-bearer of 1990s feminism, had intersected with the protests as well, and I suppose that's where the confusion began. She had written several articles arguing that the crackdown on Occupy demonstrated that the United States was tipping into a police state. This was the subject of her book *The End of America*, which outlined "ten steps" she claimed every government takes on its way to outright fascism. Her evidence that this evil future was now upon us was the aggressive way that Occupy demonstrators were having their freedom restricted. The city was not allowing megaphones and sound systems to be used in the park, and there had been a series of mass arrests. Wolf, in her articles, argued that activists should defy restrictions on their freedom of speech and assembly in order to prevent the coup she insisted was unfolding under their noses. Not wanting to give the police an excuse to clear the protest camp, the organizers took a different tack, using what became known as the "human microphone" (where the crowd repeats the speaker's words so that everyone can hear them).

That was not the only point of disagreement between Wolf and the organizers. For better or worse, the Occupiers had been very clear that the movement did not have a policy agenda—two or three political demands lawmakers could meet that would send them all home satisfied. Wolf insisted this was not true: she claimed the movement actually had specific demands and that she, improbably, had figured them out. "I found out what it was that OWS actually wanted," she wrote in *The Guardian*, explaining, "I began soliciting online 'What is it you want?' answers" from self-identified Occupy activists. Disregarding the movement's commitment to radical, participatory democracy, Wolf then turned the results of her haphazard surveying into a short list of demands and took it upon herself to deliver it to New York governor Andrew Cuomo at a black-tie event organized by *Huffington Post*, where she and Cuomo were both guests.

It got stranger. Failing to connect with Cuomo inside, Wolf left the event to spontaneously address Occupy Wall Street demonstrators on the sidewalk outside and, while informing the crowd what their demands were and telling them that they were demanding them wrong because "they had a first amendment right to use a megaphone," managed to get herself arrested in a burgundy evening gown, a melee documented by a bank of cameras. This is what the women in the bathroom were referring to when they talked about how "Naomi Klein" did not understand their demands.

I had paid only peripheral attention to Wolf's antics as they unfolded—they were just one of many bizarre things swirling around Occupy during that eventful fall. One day the camp buzzed with rumors that Radiohead was about to perform a free concert—only to discover that it was an elaborate prank and the band was still in England. The following day, Kanye West and Russell Simmons actually did drop by, entourages in tow, bearing gifts for the campers. Next it was Alec Baldwin's turn. In this circus atmosphere, a midcareer writer getting handcuffed while unsuccessfully ordering around protesters half her age was barely a blip.

After the bathroom incident, though, I started paying closer attention to what Wolf was doing, newly aware that some of it was blowing back on me. And it kept getting weirder. After police across the United States cleared the parks and plazas of Occupy encampments, she wrote a piece claiming, without any evidence, that the orders had come directly from Congress and Barack Obama's White House.

"When you connect the dots," Wolf wrote, it all made sense. The crackdowns on OWS were "the first battle in a civil war . . . It is a battle in which members of Congress, with the collusion of the American president, sent violent, organized suppression against the people they are supposed to represent." This, Wolf declared, marked a definitive tip into totalitarian rule—a claim that she had made before, under George W. Bush, confidently predicting he would not allow the 2008 election to take place (he did), and that she would make many more times in the years to come. "Sadly, Americans this week have come one step closer to being true brothers and sisters of the protesters in Tahrir Square," she wrote. "Like them, our own national leaders . . . are now making war upon us."

The logical leaps were bad enough. What made it worse for me was that, with Wolf's new focus on abuses of corporate and political power during states of emergency, something she touched on only briefly in *The End of America*, I felt like I was reading a parody of *The Shock Doctrine*, one with all facts and evidence carefully removed, and coming to cartoonishly broad conclusions I would never support. And while I was not yet confused with my doppelganger all that often, I knew that some people would credit me with Wolf's theories. It was an out-of-body feeling. I went back and took a closer look at the articles about her eveningwear arrest, and a line in *The Guardian* jumped out at me: "Her partner, the film producer Avram Ludwig, was also arrested."

I read the sentence to my partner, the film director and producer Avram Lewis (who goes by Avi).

"What the actual fuck?" he asked.

"I know," I said. "It's like a goddamned conspiracy."

Then we both burst out laughing.

In the decade since Occupy, Wolf has connected the dots between an almost unfathomably large number of disparate bits of fact and fantasy. She has floated unsubstantiated speculations about the National Security Agency whistleblower Edward Snowden ("not who he purports to be," hinting that he is an active spy). About U.S. troops sent to build field hospitals in West Africa during the 2014 Ebola outbreak (not an attempt to stop the disease's spread, but a plot to bring it to the United States to justify "mass lockdowns" at home). About ISIS beheadings of U.S. and British captives (possibly not real murders, but staged covert ops by the U.S. government starring crisis actors). About the arrest of Dominique Strauss-Kahn, the former managing director of the International Monetary Fund, on allegations that he sexually assaulted a housekeeper in a New York City hotel room (the charges were eventually dropped and a civil suit settled but Wolf wondered if the whole thing had been an "intelligence service" operation designed to take Strauss-Kahn out of the running in French elections where he had been "the odds-on favorite to defeat Nicolas Sarkozy"). About the results of the 2014 Scottish referendum on independence, which the "no" vote won by a margin of more than 10 percent (potentially fraudulent, she claimed, based on an assortment of testimonies she collected). About the Green New Deal (not the demands of grassroots climate justice movements, she said, but yet another elite-orchestrated cover for "fascism").

In our era of extreme wealth concentration and seemingly bottomless impunity for the powerful, it is perfectly rational, even wise, to probe official stories for their veracity. Uncovering real conspiracies is the indispensable mission of investigative journalism, a subject I'll return to in greater depth later on. However, actual research is not what my doppelganger was up to when she floated her pulpy theories about Snowden and ISIS and Ebola. Nor is it what she was doing when she imagined plots in the appearance of oddly shaped clouds (which she has intimated are part of a secret NASA program to spray the skies with "aluminum on a global level," potentially causing epidemics of dementia). Nor is it what she was doing when she shared some truly remarkable thoughts on Twitter about 5G cellular networks, including this one: "It was amazing to go to Belfast, which does not yet have 5G, and feel the earth, sky, air, human experience, feel the way it did in the 1970s. Calm, still, peaceful, restful, natural." The observation sparked a transnational pile-on of the kind of howling mockery for which the platform is infamous, most of it pointing out that (1) Belfast had launched 5G by the time she visited and (2) in the 1970s Northern Ireland was in the grips of a horrific, bloody armed conflict that took thousands of lives.

It may seem hard to believe that all of this comes from the same author who wrote *The Beauty Myth* as a Rhodes Scholar at Oxford. "What little girls learn is not the desire for the other, but the desire to be desired," she wrote back then. "Girls learn to watch their sex along with the boys; that takes up the space that should be devoted to finding out about what they are wanting, and reading and writing about it, seeking it and getting it. Sex is held hostage by beauty and its ransom terms are engraved in girls' minds early and deeply with instruments more beautiful than those which advertisers or pornographers know how to use: literature, poetry, painting, and film."

There were major statistical errors in that book, a foreshadowing of what was to come, but there was also patient archival work. Wolf's online writing today is so frenetic and fantastical that it can be startling to read her early words and remember that this is a person who clearly loved language, thought deeply about the inner lives of girls and women, and had a vision for their liberation.

At the dawn of the 1990s, Germaine Greer declared *The Beauty Myth* "the most important feminist publication since *The Female Eunuch*"

(Greer's own bestseller, published in 1970). Some of this was timing. After the lost decade of the 1980s—when feminism was suddenly too earthy and earnest to make it in prime time—the corporate media were ready to declare a third wave of the women's movement, and *The Beauty Myth* lifted up Wolf as its telegenic face. She was hardly the first feminist writer to expose the impossible beauty standards imposed on women, but she had a unique angle. The core of Wolf's argument was that during the 1980s, just as the second-wave feminist movement had succeeded in winning greater equality for women in postsecondary education and the workplace, the pressure on women to meet impossible standards of thinness and beauty had increased sharply, putting them at a competitive disadvantage with men in their fields. This was no coincidence, she argued. "The ruling elite" knew, Wolf wrote, that they held jobs that would be at risk if women were free to rise unencumbered, something that "must be thwarted, or the traditional power elite will be at a disadvantage." The "myth" of beauty was invented, she speculated, to drain women's power and focus—to keep them busy with mascara and starvation diets instead of free to climb the professional ladder and outcompete their male rivals. In essence, she posed the heightened beauty standards of the 1980s as a backlash to the feminism of the 1970s.

Yet the feminism Wolf proposed in response was not a throwback to the radical demands of the 1960s and '70s, a time when feminism had been linked with anti-imperialism, anti-racism, and socialism and activists had built their own collectives, movement publications, and insurgent political candidacies that set out to challenge and transform dominant power systems from the outside. On the contrary, just as Bill Clinton and Tony Blair moved their respective parties away from policies that championed universal public services and redistribution of wealth toward a pro-market, pro-militarism "Third Way," Wolf's version of third-wave feminism charted a path to the center, one that had little to offer working-class women but promised the world to white, middle-class, highly educated women like her. Two decades before Sheryl Sandberg's *Lean In*, Wolf published her second book, *Fire with Fire*, which called on feminism to drop the dogma and embrace the "will to power."

She took her own advice. Rather than building power inside the women's movement, as her feminist foremothers had done, Wolf launched herself like a missile into the heart of the liberal establishment in both New York City and Washington, D.C. She married a journalist who became a speechwriter for Bill Clinton and a *New York Times* editor; she consulted with the political operative Dick Morris, who played a key role in Clinton's lurch to the right; and she helped start an institute on women's leadership. It appeared that Wolf did not want to tear down elite power structures—she wanted to enter them.

The press could not get enough of Wolf, who, in her first decade in the public eye, looked very much like Valerie Bertinelli in my favorite childhood sitcom, *One Day at a Time*. Not only was she poised and beautiful as she shredded the beauty industry, but she also wrote graphically and boldly about sex and young women's right to pleasure.

Many excellent feminist theorists who came up before and after Wolf made powerful connections between intimate experiences—including rape, abortion, domestic violence, race-based sexual fetishism, illness, and gender dysmorphia—and the broad social structures that produced those experiences. The 1980s had been full of such books, many by Black feminists: *Ain't I a Woman*, by bell hooks; *Women, Race & Class*, by Angela Davis; and *Sister Outsider*, by Audre Lorde, among others. *The Vagina Monologues*, the breakthrough feminist play by Eve Ensler (now named V), was first staged four years after *The Beauty Myth* was published. These works contained personal revelations that helped weave together mass movements for collective justice in which the personal became political. What set Wolf's writing apart from these kinds of movement intellectuals was an apparent paucity of curiosity about the lives of women who were not her, and whose lives were markedly different from her own. This came up in her first book, which somehow managed to be a study of the impact of white, European beauty ideals without engaging with the particular and acute impacts of those ideals on Black, Asian, and other nonwhite women (let alone queer and transgender women).

While there were always skeptics—her rival Camille Paglia dismissed Wolf as a "*Seventeen* magazine level of thinker"—critiques of her work rarely reached beyond women's studies departments. And by the end of the decade, Wolf was considered such an authority on all things womanly that during the 2000 presidential election, Al Gore, the Democratic Party nominee, hired her to coach him on how to appeal to female voters. Her widely reported advice was that Gore had to get out from under Bill Clinton's shadow and transform himself from a "beta male" to an "alpha male"—in part by wearing earth-toned suits to warm up his robotic affect. Wolf denied providing fashion advice, but the reports still sparked a torrent of mockery, including from Maureen Dowd in *The New York Times*, who wrote that "Ms. Wolf is the moral equivalent of an Armani T-shirt, because Mr. Gore has obscenely overpaid for something basic."

In the new millennium, something changed in Wolf. Maybe it was Gore's electoral loss (or George W. Bush's electoral theft), and the way some of the post-vote recriminations focused on her controversial campaign role. Perhaps it was something more personal—an unraveling marriage with two young kids (she has made reference to "a year of chaos, right after I turned forty"). Whatever the cause, Wolf's soaring profile dropped significantly in the early and mid-2000s. In 2005, she published a small book called *The Treehouse: Eccentric Wisdom from My Father on How to Live, Love, and See*. In this daughter-father version of *Tuesdays with Morrie*, Wolf depicts herself as a prodigal daughter returning, after decades of rebellion, to the wise, paternal fold. Her father, Leonard Wolf, teaches her how to build an elaborate treehouse for her daughter—and how to live a good life.

During her time as a feminist intellectual, Wolf writes, she had valued hard facts and material change. This went against what her father, a poet and literature scholar with a specialty in gothic and horror, had taught her to value: "My father had raised me to honor the power of the imagination above all." Leonard, she writes, understood that "heart" mattered "over facts, numbers, and laws." At the time, this was taken by most reviewers as benign if twee advice about creativity—in retrospect, given the creative way in which Wolf would go on to play with facts, numbers, and laws related to Covid-19, it feels more like gloomy foreshadowing worthy of one of Leonard Wolf's favorite books of gothic fiction.

More than this, what got my attention in *The Treehouse* was one of Leonard's key life lessons—his directive to "Destroy the box." According to Wolf, her father said, "Before you can even think about finding your true voice, you have to reject boxes . . . Smash them apart." She stressed this point: "Look at what box you may be in and be willing to destroy it."

Up until that time, Wolf, by her own admission, had been squarely in the feminist box. But two years later, she smashed it, coming out with the patriotically paranoiac *End of America* in 2007. There was nothing in it about women's issues, and she appeared to have turned on the elite institutions that she had once worked so hard to access. She now had a new focus: the ways authoritarianism descends on once free societies, and the dangers of covert government actions.

Looking back, this is really when the problems started for me; the point when Wolf stopped seeming quite as much like her—the Naomi who wrote books about the battles waged over women's bodies—and started sounding, well, more like me—the Naomi who writes about corporate exploitation of states of shock. Am I saying that this confusion was intentional on Wolf's part? Not at all. Just deeply unfortunate.

And it wasn't just that one book. I had started writing about the Green New Deal in 2018. She did, too, shortly after, only with her special conspiracy twists. I began publishing about the dangers of geoengineering as a response to the climate crisis, with a particular focus on how high-altitude simulations of volcanoes that were intended to partially dim the sun risked interfering with rainfall in the Southern Hemisphere. She was busily speculating on social media about chemical cloudseeding and covert mass poisonings. I based my writing on dozens of peer-reviewed papers and managed to get access to two closed-door geoengineering conferences, where I interviewed several of the key scientists involved in lab-based research on sending particles into the upper atmosphere to control the sun's radiation. She started taking photographs of random clouds in upstate New York and London, prompting the environmental magazine *Grist* to declare, in 2018, that "Wolf is a cloud truther."

I always know when she has been busy—because my online mentions fill up instantly. With denunciations and excommunication ("I can't believe I used to respect Naomi Klein. WTF has happened to her??"). And with glib expressions of sympathy ("The real victim in all this here is Naomi Klein" and "Thoughts and prayers to Naomi Klein").

How much does this identity merger happen? Enough that there is a viral poem, first posted in October 2019, that invariably shows up in these moments, and that been shared many thousands of times:

> If the Naomi be Klein
> you're doing just fine
> If the Naomi be Wolf
> Oh, buddy. Ooooof.

As in any doppelganger story, the confusion flows both ways. Wolf maintains a large and seemingly loyal following across several platforms, and occasionally I have noticed her correcting people, telling them that she is flattered, but no, she did not write *The Shock Doctrine*.

For most of the first decade of the confusion, my public strategy was studious denial. I would complain privately to friends and to Avi, sure, but publicly I was mostly silent. Even when, in 2019, Wolf started tagging me daily in her tweets about the Green New Deal, clearly trying to draw me into a debate about her baseless theory that the whole thing was a sort of green shock doctrine—a nefarious plan by bankers and venture capitalists to grab power under cover of the climate emergency—I did not engage with her. I did not try to address the confusion. I did not join those mocking her.

I thought about it, but it never seemed wise. There is a certain inherent humiliation in getting repeatedly confused with someone else, confirming, as it does, one's own interchangeability and/or forgettableness. That's the trouble with doppelgangers: anything you might do to dispel the confusion just draws attention to it, and runs the risk of further cementing the unwanted association in people's minds.

In this way, confrontations with our doppelgangers inevitably raise existentially destabilizing questions. Am I who I think I am, or am I who others perceive me to be? And if enough others start seeing someone else as me, who am I, then? Doppelgangers are not the only way we can lose control over ourselves, of course. The carefully constructed self can be undone in any number of ways and in an instant—by a disabling accident, by a psychotic break, or, these days, by a hacked account or a deep fake. This is the perennial appeal of doppelgangers in novels and films: the idea that two strangers can be indistinguishable from each other taps into the precariousness at the core of identity—the painful truth that, no matter how deliberately we tend to our personal lives and public personas, the person we think we are is fundamentally vulnerable to forces outside of our control.

François Brunelle, a Montreal artist who has been photographing hundreds of pairs of doppelgangers over decades for a project called *I'm Not a Look-Alike!*, put it like this: "Someone, out in this world, is looking at himself in the mirror and seeing more or less the same thing that I am seeing in my own mirror. Which brings us down to the question: Who am I exactly? Am I what I see in my reflection or something else that cannot be defined and is invisible to the eyes, even my own?"

In the dozens of books that have been written about people who encounter their doubles, doppelgangers consistently signal that the protagonist's life is about to be upended, with the double turning their friends and colleagues against them, destroying their career, or framing them for crimes, and—very often—having sex with their spouse or lover. A standard trope in the genre is a nagging uncertainty about whether the double is real at all. Is this actually an identical stranger, or are they a long-lost twin? Worse, is the double a figment of the protagonist's imagination—an expression of an unhinged subconscious?

In Edgar Allan Poe's short story "William Wilson," for instance, the reader begins by believing the "detestable coincidence" that there is another person with the same name, birthday, and general appearance as the pompous narrator. Suspicions quickly emerge, though, that the coincidences are a little too perfect. By the end, it is clear that the double, who could not speak "above a very low whisper," never existed outside the narrator's paranoid, self-loathing subconscious and that, by killing his "arch-enemy and evil genius," William Wilson had killed himself. The same fate befalls the protagonist of Oscar Wilde's novel *The Picture of Dorian Gray*, which tells the story of a vain and lustful man who, after having his portrait painted, makes a demonic deal to stay young and beautiful forever. As Gray holds on to his youth, the face in the painting grows older and uglier, a kind of virtual doppelganger. When Gray tries to destroy his gruesome double, he is the one who ends up shriveled and lifeless on the ground.

The whole mess puts me in mind of my dog, Smoke, who, every evening at sundown, sees her reflection in the glass of our front door and begins to bark ferociously. She is convinced, evidently, that an adorable white cockapoo doppelganger (dogpelganger?) is bound and determined to gain access to her home, eat her food, and steal the affections of her humans.

"That's you," I tell Smoke in my most reassuring voice, but she always forgets. And this is the catch-22 of confronting your doppelganger: bark all you want, but you inevitably end up confronting yourself.

Not Me

There was another reason I didn't bother much with correcting the record for the first few years of my doppelganger trouble: with the exception of the Manhattan bathroom incident, getting confused with Naomi Wolf appeared to be a social media thing. My friends and colleagues knew who I was, and when I interacted with people I didn't know in the physical world, her name did not come up; neither were we entangled in articles or book reviews. I therefore filed away Naomi confusion in the category of "things that happen on the internet that are not quite real" (back when we were silly enough to do that about all kinds of things). I told myself that I was not being confused with Wolf, but that our digital avatars were getting mistakenly swapped—the thumbnail-sized photos of us, and the tiny boxes that prescribed the parameters of our speech on those platforms, just as they flattened and blurred so much else.

Back then, I saw the problem as more structural than personal. A handful of young men had gotten unfathomably rich designing tech platforms that, in the name of "connection," not only allowed us to eavesdrop on conversations between strangers but also actively encouraged us to seek out those exchanges that mentioned us by name (a.k.a. our "mentions"). In a way, it was perfect that the first time I heard my name confused with Wolf's was in an eavesdropped conversation taking place in a public restroom. When I joined Twitter and clicked on the little bell icon signifying my "mentions," that was my initial thought: I was reading the graffiti written about me on an infinitely scrolling restroom wall.

As a frequently graffitied-about girl in high school, this felt both familiar and deeply harrowing. I instantly knew that Twitter was going to be bad for me—and yet, like so many of us, I could not stop looking. So perhaps if there is a message I should have taken from the destabilizing appearance of my doppelganger, this is it: Once and for all, stop eavesdropping on strangers talking about you in this crowded and filthy global toilet known as social media.

I might have heeded the message, too. If Covid hadn't intervened.

2

ENTER COVID, THE THREAT MULTIPLIER

"Can I just read you this one tweet?" I say, wandering into the kitchen balancing my laptop in one hand.

"Fine," Avi replies, lips tightening. He has decided to run for a seat in Canada's Parliament and is juggling all kinds of high-stakes decisions: he needs to hire a campaign manager, draft a platform, raise a hundred thousand dollars.

"She just wrote, 'vaccinated people's urine/feces' needs to be separated 'from general sewage supplies/waterways' until its impact on unvaccinated people's drinking water is established. Can you believe that? She thinks vaccinated people are biohazards! She wants to build a parallel sewage system!"

"Where are you going with this?" Avi asks, not particularly patiently.

Where indeed?

In the years before Covid, floating conspiracy claims seemed to be a kind of hobby for Wolf. She hopped from one theory to another—Ebola, Snowden, 5G, ISIS—but never stayed with any one subject for long, certainly not long enough to actually prove anything. She was just "raising flags" and "asking questions," and then she invariably moved on. This is classic "conspiracy without the theory," as described by Russell Muirhead and Nancy L. Rosenblum in their 2020 book, *A Lot of People Are Saying*, part of the growing body of literature attempting to make sense of the surge in belief in a wide range of off-the-wall, unproven claims.

But as I watched Wolf's output in the Covid-19 era, I quickly realized that something was different. She was no longer hopping from subject to subject asking questions. She seemed to have only one subject: the virus—its origins, the shutdowns, the tests, the mask mandates, the vaccines, the vaccine mandates, the vaccine verification apps. None of it was as it seemed. To hear her tell it, we were not hit with a novel and highly contagious zoonotic virus that demanded hard trade-offs from all of us, a virus our political class and health bureaucracies—hollowed out by fifty years of neoliberal clawbacks—repeatedly fumbled or failed to control, while drug companies maximized their profits by protecting patents that should never have been in place. Instead, she said, we were part of an experiment, a plot, a coup, an act of war designed to turn us into technoslaves and convince us to voluntarily relinquish our freedoms, while wiping out large swaths of humanity in the process. It's "a genocide," Wolf has claimed again and again, while drawing on a rolling array of parallels with Nazi Germany, apartheid South Africa, the Jim Crow South, and modern-day China.

Within a year of the pandemic being declared, Wolf had become a key node in the networks blasting out this kind of terrifying misinformation, nearly doubling her following on Twitter from the year before to reach 138,000. On at least seven tech platforms that I could count, she portrayed virtually every measure health officials had taken to control the virus as part of these plots, ones with the nefarious goals of grabbing our DNA, sickening us, sterilizing us, killing our babies, tracking our every move, turning children into affectless drones, overthrowing the U.S. Constitution, eroding the power of the West. She speculated that the virus might be a biological weapon—and so, too, might the vaccines, possibly being used to assassinate politicians ("local leaders are dying too," she has written. "[It's] Why I fear this is an attack. The dosages differ"). She likened Anthony Fauci, then director of the U.S. National Institute of Allergy and Infectious Diseases, to Satan and called attempts to counter vaccine misinformation "demonic."

A "transnational group of bad actors—including the WEF, The WHO, the Bill and Melinda Gates Foundation, tech companies and the CCP—used the pandemic to crush humanity and in particular to destroy the West," she wrote. "How better to cripple the world's other superpower than by destroying our American front lines and our American next generation, with tainted, murderous vaccines, flowed easily enough into the West via (not even that many) shell companies and cutouts? How easy to do the same to Western Europe, to Canada and Australia, as a whole?"

Early on, it was clear that Wolf's emergence as a relentless source of Covid-related misinformation was yielding real-world results. Through her website, DailyClout, as well as new alliances with an array of Republican state lawmakers, Wolf claimed partial credit for successfully pushing legislation barring mask mandates and vaccine passports in dozens of Republican states.

My doppelganger is prone to exaggerating her own influence—in reality, she is but one voice in a global cacophony that speaks many languages, reaches tens of millions of people, and stretches across every platform and media tool. That said, within this global network, a few individuals—because of their high profile pre-Covid, their social media skills, and their relentless hustle—have played an outsize role. And while they started with Covid, they are rapidly moving to all kinds of other plots supposedly designed to usher in tyranny.

Wolf is one of those individuals, particularly when it comes to medical misinformation targeting the group who first lifted her to international fame: women. In one of her widely circulated Covid-related tweets, shared with her fast-growing audience, she wrote that "hundreds of women . . . say they are having bleeding/clotting after vaccination or that they bleed oddly being AROUND vaccinated women."

The viral myth linking vaccines to infertility proved particularly damaging in the online world of women's wellness, where one influencer, proclaiming herself "passionate about womb health," cautioned her followers against getting too close to anyone who had had "the jab."

At least one private school in Florida moved to ban *vaccinated* teachers from its classrooms, in the name of protecting students from vaccine "shedding." An NPR investigation, done with the help of specialized data analysts, found that a great deal of these false beliefs could be traced to "a very highly followed influencer in what we call the pseudo-medical community": Naomi Wolf.

Or, for those reading a little too fast: Naomi Klein.

This flurry of activity by Other Naomi during the Covid era meant that the stakes of getting confused with her had become significantly higher than they were in that restroom in Manhattan. Her earlier forays into unfounded conspiracies were frequently offensive and no doubt hurtful to those who she hinted were spies or crisis actors. But they never put large numbers of people into active danger.

With Covid, that changed. And when it came to the notorious "vaccine shedding" fiction, it was easy to see why she was getting so much traction. The claim that vaccinated people could somehow infect unvaccinated people with dangerous particles started circulating at a crucial moment in the pandemic when many were deciding whether or not they were going to trust the shots. For some healthy people who were convinced that the virus posed little threat to them, but who worried about possible adverse effects from vaccination, the manufactured shedding threat provided a handy way to turn the tables.

Take the case of a prominent fitness trainer and anti-vax influencer in Toronto who calls herself "Glowing Mama." The trainer became obsessed with the vaccine shedding theory, claiming she was "bleeding between [her] period" because people around her had been vaccinated. In a video that went viral for all the wrong reasons, Glowing Mama brought herself to tears as she raged about how her daughter's grandparents, who had been vaccinated, wanted to hold their granddaughter, clearly indifferent to the risks they posed to both the child and to her. "They are sterilizing an entire generation of people," she said between sobs. She could not believe the selfishness of these older people, who had "one foot in the grave"—selfish for getting vaccinated and still expecting to have a loving relationship with their granddaughter.

The video was bananas—there is no link between vaccination and infertility, vaccines don't "shed" through hugs, and there are many resources easily available to prove both points. But in this display, the appeal of the shedding theory, which my doppelganger had done so much to spread, is laid bare as the ultimate tool of projection and absolution. Wolf and her fellow travelers had taken the argument for vaccines—which is that we belong to communities of enmeshed bodies, so what we do and don't do to our bodies affects the health of other bodies, especially vulnerable bodies—and flipped it on its head. In their telling, it was actually vaccinated people who were the selfish ones sacrificing the vulnerable, and who were the spreaders and shedders.

All of this, it seemed to me, considerably upped the ante on my getting confused with her. So did the frequency of identity-confusion events. No longer was it a periodic annoyance every few months. In that first Covid year, it was a daily avalanche. And that's how I justified, a few months into this mess, starting to fight back. I briefly added "Not that Naomi" to my social media bio and, in February 2021, when she was making a Fox News tour warning that governments imposing Covid measures were "autocratic tyrants," I tweeted: "This is your periodic reminder to keep your Naomis straight." When her Twitter account was suspended, seemingly permanently, I went with "Still here, sadly." These two sentences were "liked," last I checked, twenty thousand times.

That's because, amid the extreme isolation and anxiety of early pandemic life, Naomi confusion became one of Left Twitter's favorite jokes. The internet hive mind not only enjoyed laughing about what outrageous thing Other Naomi had said now but equally delighted in the prospect that I would get at least some of the credit/blame ("Thoughts and prayers to Naomi Klein"). We were a pastime for profoundly bored people addicted to dopamine hits from our machines. It was giving people not pleasure exactly, but something synthetically adjacent to it—a fake communal experience in those lonely and anxious times.

And look, it *was* confusing, and also, in a gallows way, funny, even to me. Again and again, she was saying things that sounded a little like the argument I made in *The Shock Doctrine* but refracted through a funhouse mirror of plots and conspiracies based almost exclusively on a series of hunches. She continually called Covid's severity into question, describing it as "a much-hyped medical crisis," even when it had already killed hundreds of thousands in the United States alone. She told Tucker Carlson that the Biden administration was, under the "guise" of a medical emergency, using "emergency orders" to "strip us of our rights—rights to property, rights to assembly, rights to worship, all the rights the Constitution guarantees."

Watching this, I felt like she had taken my ideas, fed them into a bonkers blender, and then shared the thought-puree with Carlson, who nodded vehemently. All the while, Wolf's followers hounded me about why I had sold out to the "globalists" and was duping the public into believing that masks, vaccines, and restrictions on indoor gatherings were legitimate public health measures—as opposed to a pretext for a worldwide shock doctrine, of the kind I had warned about in my books. "I think she's been got at!" someone whose handle is "RickyBaby321" said of me, telling Wolf, "I have relegated Naomi Klein to the position of being: 'The Other Naomi'!" It's a vertiginous thing to be harangued on social media about your alleged misunderstanding of your own ideas—while being told that another Naomi is a better version of you than you are.

The dark doppelganger comedy *Dual*, starring Karen Gillan, captures some of the absurdity of my Naomi trouble. Diagnosed with a fatal disease and given a negligible chance of survival, Sarah, Gillan's character, opts to clone herself to save her loved ones the trouble of grieving. But her clone is competitive and begins to replace her in all of her closest relationships. When it turns out that Sarah was misdiagnosed and isn't dying at all, the only solution is a stylized duel to the death between the doubles. "We can't have two of you walking around. That would be ridiculous," Sarah is told. Indeed it would be. Ridiculous and serious. Seriously ridiculous. Which is why, like Sarah, I started dueling with my dual, too, if only by wading into the digital fray with my terse little "Keep your Naomis straight" posts.

Like so many of us during Covid, I was online much more than usual, because, well, where else was I going to be? Previously, I had kept my social media use under pretty tight control. But in the isolation of Covid, and my isolated life on the rock, that all fell away. Social media was one thing I didn't have to give up in the name of that damn virus, so, I reasoned, why should I?

The more time I spent scrolling through my mentions, the more real they started to feel. Covid had canceled so many of the things that had, for years, told me who I was in the world. A planned book tour. A series of lectures. Places where people would come up to me and share what my work meant to them and where I would learn new things from them. I still spoke at all kinds of what we came to call "virtual events"—get-out-the-vote rallies and book festivals and press conferences—but it was all from the exact same chair, in the exact same room, on the exact same rock, with my energy and hopes poured into the exact same dead void of the computer camera's green light. After each event, I would check Twitter to get any kind of confirmation that I had actually reached other humans. And often I would find only her: her outrageous theories, the confusion, the backlash, the wry jokes.

The world was disappearing, and so was I.

It makes sense that the confusion got so much worse during the pandemic, a time when so many of us were represented to the world beyond our homes by avatars offering ever more approximated versions of our physical selves. About a year into Zoom living, a friend told me about the platform's "touch up my appearance" tool. Now I deliberately blur my face for public events, just a bit; I have discovered that I like being blurry. "An uncanny effect often arises when the boundary between fantasy and reality is blurred," Freud wrote, "when we are faced with the reality of something that we have until now considered imaginary." After two years of pandemic living, I looked less like the me I was before all this, and less still like the photos of me online, especially the most circulated publicity shot, which was taken in 2014 in my publisher's office with a makeup artist and professional lighting. The relationship between that glossy Naomi and the Naomi that is me writing these words, in leggings and tank top, my hair in a chaotic high ponytail to capture my self-cut bangs, feels as approximate as the relationship between my own publicity photo and Naomi Wolf's.

It was amid all this severing and blurring, all these performed selves and distorted selves and digitized selves, that the barriers between me and her got blurred as well. My public self had shrunk down to that thumbnail-sized photo and Twitter's 280-character limit, and now, thanks to her, I didn't even have that. I felt like shrunken Alice telling the Caterpillar, "I'm not myself, you see . . . being so many different sizes in a day is very confusing."

So, no, if I am honest with myself, I did not join the Twitter pile-ons simply because what Wolf was saying about Covid was so very important to dispel—I also did it because *I* was feeling less important, like I was disappearing. Isn't that why so many of us typed so furiously during those lonely days?

It's in the Code

Gordon Pennycook, a behavioral scientist at the University of Regina, explains that as the virus spread, conspiracy peddlers found a ready audience with a public that was in a state of generalized fear of getting seriously ill and possibly dying, and simultaneously had very real worries about what public health measures like stay-at-home orders, school closures, and masking would mean for their livelihoods and loved ones. "Those fears distract people from judging the accuracy of the content they may read online," he told *The New York Times*, adding, "As a rule, people don't want to spread false content. But at a time like this, when people are worried about the virus, headlines like 'Vitamin C Cures Covid' or 'It's All a Hoax' tend to travel widely."

Wolf was guilty of this kind of trigger-happy posting. So, too, were many of her followers, who jumped to share her claims. But here's where things get messier: a great many of the people who leapt to attack Wolf for spreading misinformation were also barely reading what they were posting. And I should know, because, in their haste to be seen and to get engagement, they ended up posting about me. Even when Wolf's correct name appeared in boldface in an article's headline.

This raised something even more troubling. For a long time, people had clearly been confusing me and Wolf, getting our names mixed up, as happens to all of us sometimes. But as Covid wore on, and all of this not-really-reading took on an ever more breathless quality, it became clear that we were being not confused but *conflated*, treated as one interchangeable Naomi.

This is the most destabilizing part of the Naomi-Naomi conversations I stumbled across online. More than once, someone typed: "OMG. I just now realized they are not the same person." Or: "TIR [today I realized] that Naomi Wolf is not Naomi Klein and honestly things make a bit more sense now." Someone else claimed *The Shock Doctrine* was "One of the most informative books written" and that, in it, I lay out "the 10 steps that lead to a fascist government"—which I have never done but Wolf has.

I resisted the truth about this conflation for a long time. Beyond what I consider to be our different approaches to facts and research, there are plenty of other differences between the two of us. She grew up in the United States, I in Canada. She is a liberal who reverentially references the founding fathers, fetishizes a highly individualistic version of "liberty," and wrote an entire book addressed to a "young patriot." I am a third-generation leftist who believes freedom is won collectively and gets itchy around flags. She went to private universities in the United States and the United Kingdom; I dropped out of a public one in Canada. Her eyes are blue; mine are brown.

I have come to accept, however, that while these distinctions matter to me, and no doubt to her, most people couldn't care less. And why should they? We are both Naomis with a skepticism of elite power. We even have some of the same targets. I, for instance, was furious when Bill Gates sided with the drug companies as they defended their patents on lifesaving Covid vaccines, using the World Trade Organization's insidious intellectual property agreement as a weapon, despite the fact that vaccine development was lavishly subsidized with public money, and that this lobbying helped keep the shots out of the arms of millions of the poorest people on the planet. Naomi Wolf was furious that people were being pushed to get vaccinated at all and boosted conspiracies about Bill Gates using vaccines to track people and to usher in a sinister world order.

Those are substantive differences, reflecting the different belief systems of two separate people. But I have come to accept that, for plenty of folks glancing at social media during the boring bits of Netflix shows, we're just a blur of opinionated Naomis saying stuff about states of emergencies and Bill Gates.

On a particularly bleak day, someone tweeted that I had been losing my mind for years and that I now equated having to get a Covid vaccine with Jews in Nazi Germany having to wear yellow stars. He linked, of course, to a statement by Naomi Wolf saying that very thing. The yellow-star analogy really pisses me off, so after composing and deleting a series of profanity-laced responses, I settled on one that was chilly and restrained: "You sure about that?" The mixed-up poster took another look, quickly deleted what he had written, and apologized: "Oh Jesus, it's Wolfe [*sic*] . . . damn twitter autocomplete. Sorry about that."

Autocomplete?!?

I felt blood rush to my face. In that moment, nine months into living on the rock at the end of the road, thirteen months of remote teaching and indoor masking, an eternity since seeing my closest friends, it suddenly hit me: the confusion was now so frequent that Twitter's algorithm was prompting it, helpfully filling in the mistake for its users, to save them precious time. This is how machine learning works—the algorithm imitates, learning from patterns. So, if my name is repeatedly mixed up with Wolf's, even in jokes, then my name would start being suggested instead of hers, leading to even more mix-ups. Which also meant that anything I did to correct the record—or state my own position on what had become her pet topics—would just train the algorithm to confuse us even more.

This is what happens when we allow so many of our previously private actions to be enclosed by corporate tech platforms whose founders said they were about connecting us but were always about extracting from us. The process of enclosure, of carrying out our activities within these private platforms, changes us, including how we relate to one another and the underlying purpose of those relations. This goes back to early forms of enclosure, beginning in the Middle Ages. When common lands in England were transformed into privately held commodities surrounded by hedges and fences, the land became something else: its role was no longer to benefit the community—with shared access to communal grazing, food, and firewood—but to increase crop yields and therefore profits for individual landowners. Once physically and legally enclosed, the soil began to be treated as a machine, whose role was to be as productive as possible.

So, too, with our online activities, where our relationships and conversations are our modern-day yields, designed to harvest ever more data. As with corn and soy grown in great monocrops, quality and individuality are sacrificed in favor of standardization and homogenization, even when homogenization takes the form of individuals all competing to stand out as quirky and utterly unique.

This is why *The Matrix* and its sequels have proved such enduring metaphorical landscapes for understanding the digital age: it's not just the red pills and blue pills. In *The Matrix*, humans, living their lives in synthetic pods, are mere food for machines. Many of us suspect that we, too, have become machine food. And, in a way, we have. As Richard Seymour writes in his blistering 2019 dissection of social media, *The Twittering Machine*, we think we are interacting—writing and singing and dancing and talking—with one another, "our friends, professional colleagues, celebrities, politicians, royals, terrorists, porn actors—anyone we like. We are not interacting with them, however, but with the machine. We write to it, and it passes on the message for us, after keeping a record of the data."

Zadie Smith saw all this coming more than a decade ago. Writing about the rise of Facebook, and by extension all the other social media platforms, she observed, "When a human being becomes a set of data on a website like Facebook, he or she is reduced. Everything shrinks. Individual character. Friendships. Language. Sensibility. In a way it's a transcendent experience: we lose our bodies, our messy feelings, our desires, our fears." But we aren't transcending to something higher, just less ourselves. And a flattened, reduced version of ourselves is easier to confuse with a flattened, reduced version of someone else.

None of these are problems I can solve, no matter how many times I post snarky, haughty, or restrained corrections. At least I cannot solve them on my own. And so, one year into the pandemic, I began to feel oddly speechless, unable to say much of anything at all. A newspaper editor asked me to write about Bill Gates's new book on climate change, which was topping bestseller lists and which cautioned against responses to the climate crisis that I consider critical, like regulating polluters and returning energy grids to public ownership to speed the transition to renewables. I made some notes about Gates's interference on Covid-19 health policy, how he had shown his bias toward protecting corporate profits over human safety, and that we shouldn't let him to do the same to our climate responses. But then I remembered that anything I wrote about Gates would likely fuel my Other Naomi problem. In the speed glossing of the internet age, wouldn't it all blend and blur together, sound like one big conspiracy? Wouldn't it further confuse the algorithms that now shape our lives, leading to more people getting my name as autofill when they are actually looking for her? Would Twitter start suppressing my content? Was it doing so already? I stalled out midway through the piece.

As I went speechless, Wolf kept talking. And typing. Taking up enough space for both of us and a few more Naomis to spare.

In the books and films about doppelgangers that had come to fill my evenings, I was struck by how reliably this phenomenon occurred: eventually, the double replaces the original, through sheer energy and tenacity, while the original fades away or worse. Dostoyevsky's novel *The Double* ends with Golyadkin, the tormented protagonist, being taken away to an asylum, driven mad by his imposter's duplicity.

Was this my fate? To be carted away? Did I need to start screaming more in order not to be deprived of my own identity? Probably. To prove to others—and to myself—that I do indeed exist, I needed to give the machine fresh content: new takes, new rage, new intimacy. Yet I found myself utterly unable to deliver, unable to do the basic identity maintenance I had done for my entire adult life and that the attention economy demands. Having developed the out-of-body habit of watching my doppelganger blow back on me, it was as if all I could do was watch: me, her, the confusion. A spectator to my own life. Which meant, according to my mentions (now almost all about her), that I was fading away.

In the 2013 film adaptation of *The Double*, Jesse Eisenberg gives a memorable performance as Simon, the unremarkable bureaucrat whose identity is stolen and life destroyed by an unscrupulous and flamboyant look-alike, also played by Eisenberg. Near the end of the film, his face bloodied by battle, Simon looks into the camera and says: "I'd like to think I'm pretty unique."

We'd all like to think that, wouldn't we? The trouble is, there are just so damn many of us out there trying to be unique at the same time, using the same preprogrammed tools, writing in the same fonts, answering the same prompts. No wonder Eisenberg saying those words has become a viral meme, circulating on the same platforms where we are all competing for uniqueness, authenticity, and, for some, proof that in these unreal times we're still really us.

Book of Naomi

It occurred to me, one night while doomscrolling, that all of my doppelganger trouble could have been avoided if I had made good on my teenage threat to legally change my first name. In Montreal's Jewish community, where I grew up, almost everyone pronounced it "Nye-oh-me," with a flat "eye" on the first syllable that sounded whiny and dreary to my ears. No matter how many times I introduced myself as "Nay-oh-me," it came back with the "Nyeeee-oh-me" drone.

"You gave me a name with a built-in whine," I whined to my mother when I was in tenth grade.

We were in the yard in early spring, the winter's dog shit having recently melted into a foul dead-grass soup. Mom-Mom, my mother's mother, was dozing in a lawn chair. By then she was in the haze of advanced Alzheimer's, another way we humans lose control over our carefully tended selves.

"As soon as I turn eighteen, it's gone," I threatened.

"You are named after Nathan," Mom replied patiently. Mom-Mom, hearing the name of her long-dead husband, stirred slightly. Nate, the maternal grandfather I never met, had died of a sudden heart attack a year before my birth.

I persisted. "Yes, but why not 'Natalie'? That has the same first three letters as 'Nathan.' 'Naomi' only has two. Or why not 'Natalia'? That's even better. Or 'Natasha.' Or 'Nadia.' I'm changing it to 'Nadia.'"

Unbeknownst to her, I had already been trying "Nadia" out on college guys in bars, thanks to Quebec's famously lax attitude toward underage drinking. With its sexy Eastern European vibe, "Nadia" felt like a name out of one of Milan Kundera's steamy novels, my teenage favorite. Also, it was the 1980s and Nadia Comăneci was the reigning gymnastics queen, she of the tiny svelte body, perfect 10 scores at the Moscow Olympics, and rumors of an imminent defection from the Soviet bloc. But "Natalie" was fine, too. It struck me as a perky, whine-free name—the kind of standard-issue handle that could be found on necklaces hanging off carousels in roadside souvenir shops, next to the saltwater taffy. "Naomi," no matter how many times I twirled those squeaky displays, was never, ever there.

But "Natalie" wasn't Jewish enough for my mother, who grew up in a Kosher home in Philadelphia and went to seminary in the distant hope, despite her disqualifying gender, of becoming a rabbi. And yet somehow, in the late 1960s, she found herself pregnant and married into a family of communists who staunchly agreed with Karl Marx that religion was the opiate of the masses, distracting the working classes and numbing them to the injustices of life under capitalism. When my physician father deserted the U.S. Army Medical Corps because he refused to have anything to do with what he saw as an illegal and immoral war in Vietnam, my parents ended up in Montreal. It was there that my mother reached for a name for me that was Old Testament enough to bind us both to our ancient tribe.

In Hebrew, "Naomi" means "pleasant," or "pleasing," and is sometimes translated as "sweet." When I asked her recently, my mom remembered its meaning as "comforting"—though I can find no evidence for this. Perhaps that's her memory because comfort was what she was looking for when she carried a daughter while grieving a father on that frozen, French-speaking island.

My name appears in the Old Testament's book of Ruth, which tells of an Israelite mother, Naomi, whose husband and two sons die, leaving her with only her sons' widows as kin. Ruth, the more devoted daughter-in-law, stays with her, and they travel together to Naomi's hometown of Bethlehem. When the townspeople greet their old friend by her given name, she tells them that it does not fit: she has lost too much and is no longer pleasant, pleasing, or sweet. They should instead call her Mara, which means "bitter": "Don't call me Naomi . . . Call me Mara, because the Almighty has made my life very bitter."

In the third grade, I had a best friend named Mara who lived three blocks over and, unlike me, had the patience of a saint and was able to make her Halloween candy stash last for the entire year. Cheeks bulging with stale jawbreakers, we would recite this line to each other, feeling that it sanctified our bond as two Jewish girls in a WASP neighborhood. "Don't caw me Naomi, caw me Mara."

As my Other Naomi problem dragged on (and on), that line would occasionally find its way into my head once again. "Don't call me pleasant," I would think to myself, scrolling through the furious denunciations and sarcastic memes. "Call me bitter."

Except, as this period of double vision continued, mirroring the intellectual and ideological mayhem of the Covid era, I found that my bitterness was steadily fading, giving way to more complex, and unexpected, emotions. Being chronically confused with another person may be humiliating, but that's not all it is. It is also an oddly intimate experience. The boundaries between you and alter-you begin to wear down, becoming thin, even diaphanous. Their problems are your problems, their shame your shame. A doppelganger is your trail, your shadow, a bit like in the biblical story from which we derive our name, in which Ruth proclaims to Naomi: "Where you go, I will go, and where you stay I will stay." Perhaps this is why I became, increasingly, not bitter or angry about the confusion, but intensely interested.

Interested, as the world grew ever weirder, in what this all meant. And in why she was doing what she was doing—and in what she was going to do next.

3

MY FAILED BRAND, OR CALL ME BY HER NAME

There are simpler words to describe what I have been dancing around, and I should probably address them directly before going any further. Dan Hon, a prominent digital strategy consultant, tweeted that he had been utterly confused by Wolf's actions because he had been attributing them to me the whole time. The problem, as he saw it, was obvious: "Naomi Klein should sue for trademark dilution and brand harm." In short, according to Hon, my brand was in crisis.

I looked for a current definition of "brand dilution" on a popular marketing website and found that there are three main causes for this kind of damage:

1. "Stretching Capacity Too Thin" (like a restaurant franchising so quickly it loses control over quality).
2. "Introducing Unrelated Services or Products" (like that time Colgate got into frozen dinners, only to discover people didn't want their beef lasagna from the same people who make their toothpaste).
3. "Losing Control of the Brand" (like, oh, I don't know, having the words and actions of a serially deplatformed conspiracy monger attributed to you amid a deadly pandemic).

At the time Hon offered his free advice, brand dilution was making headlines because Nike had announced it was suing Lil Nas X and the art collective MSCHF for that very violation. Without the sports giant's approval, the marketing-savvy artists had taken 666 pairs of Nike Air Max 97 running shoes, inserted drops of human blood into their soles, renamed the sneakers "Satan Shoes," and sold them for $1,018 a pair. It was all part of the promotional rollout for Lil Nas's blockbuster single "Montero (Call Me by Your Name)," whose video featured the singer giving a lap dance to the devil. Nike claimed that Satan Shoes were "likely to cause confusion and dilution" for its brand, since consumers would assume the altered sneakers had something to do with the company. The lawsuit played directly into Lil Nas's hands by generating a boatload of free publicity, and Nike quickly settled. (As I type this, I am realizing that this is a terrible analogy for my situation: it casts me as a giant litigious multinational and Other Naomi as Lil Nas X, who is a genius.)

Still, Hon was right. My doppelganger trouble was definitive proof that I had flunked at one of the most valued activities of contemporary capitalism: developing, maintaining, and defending my personal brand. As any marketing expert will tell you, a brand is a promise—of consistency and dependability. And my promise had clearly been both diluted and degraded. How else could so many confuse me with a person who can't seem to tell the difference between temporary public health measures and a coup d'état?

If my brand had indeed been diluted, it stood to reason that I should immediately endeavor to become a better, more distinctive brand, while aggressively defending its edges against all would-be infringers. There was, however, one glaring problem with this plan. I have a deeply conflicted relationship with this whole idea of humans behaving like corporate brands. My first book, *No Logo*, was a treatise against the rise of lifestyle branding, including the idea that individual people should shape and market themselves as commodities. Me treating Wolf like a branding problem would be about as off-brand as I could get.

In the late 1990s, as I was researching and writing *No Logo*, the first murmuring could be heard that personal branding was something to which all of us, even noncelebrities, should aspire. In the book, I explored this new and controversial idea: that the insecurity we all felt about the rapid disappearance of stable jobs could be solved if everyone made like Michael Jordan and Oprah and branded up. The management guru Tom Peters laid out the new rules in a 1997 cover story in *Fast Company* titled "The Brand Called You":

> Regardless of age, regardless of position, regardless of the business we happen to be in, all of us need to understand the importance of branding. We are CEOs of our own companies: Me Inc. To be in business today, our most important job is to be head marketer for the brand called You . . . The good news—and it is largely good news—is that everyone has a chance to stand out . . . Start by identifying the qualities or characteristics that make you distinctive from your competitors—or your colleagues. What have you done lately—this week—to make yourself stand out?

Interestingly, Peters was roundly mocked for this at the time; the magazine even published a mea culpa, disavowing the article and its dystopic vision of a world in which office mates compete with one another over brand-name recognition. Would it not be insufferable? The end of collegiality? There was also a more practical problem: it was one thing for world-famous celebrities and entrepreneurs like Jordan and Oprah and Richard Branson to position themselves as their own brands—and quite another for a university student or a middle manager or a laid-off factory worker to do it. Peters had written that individuals now had the same need for visibility as major corporations, which are able to purchase "a full flight of TV and print ads designed to get billions of 'impressions' . . . If you're brand You, you've got the same need for visibility—but no budget to buy it."

Well, exactly: normal humans don't have ad budgets, which is why the whole concept seemed absurd to our 1990s brains. This was, remember, well before Facebook, let alone TikTok or Substack. Even reality television wasn't yet up and running to pick wannabe celebrities out of obscurity. In short, the idea of personal branding began as a ruse—a transparent sop being pitched in lieu of actual jobs or a stable income by companies and their management consultants, drunk on the cost savings and stock-price inflation born of sweeping downsizing and outsourcing.

When I published *No Logo*, these were some of the truths my twenty-nine-year-old self imagined to be carrying out into the world, like a tray of challenging but original appetizers at a garden party. Fresh from my return from Nike's Asian sweatshops, I would tell the truth about branding's false promises and seamy underside.

Instead, in interview after interview, I got the same question: "Aren't *you* a brand?"

Anti-Brand Branding Trouble

Back in the early days of my writing career, when journalists accused me of being a brand, I insisted that this was not the case. I would say, dripping with disdain, "I'm an author. Not a brand. The product isn't me. I am trying to communicate *ideas*. The ideas are in the book. Read the book." I pointed out that I had no side products, no brand extensions, no T-shirts or tote bags, nothing for sale other than a book. There had been authors who sold lots of books before—why weren't they accused of being brands?

The fact is, though, that I was kind of full of it. I had been very deliberate about how *No Logo* was designed and positioned. Having spent years studying effective corporate branding, I wanted my first book to be fluent in the same language. I somehow convinced one of the top graphic designers in the world, Bruce Mau, to do the design, well before I even had a publisher. The cover was sleek and all black—shocking at the time—and the title was itself an instantly iconic red, white, and black logo. I made sure that my publishers didn't try to capitalize on it by selling *No Logo* merch, but I did pay out of pocket for free *No Logo* seam rippers to hand out at the launch so that readers could remove their own logos. (I still use mine, mainly to protect my son's neck from scratchy tags.)

The British cultural theorist Stuart Hall had described the left during the era of Margaret Thatcher as "historically anachronistic"; the U.S. political theorist Wendy Brown, writing a decade later, saw a left "caught in a structure of melancholic attachment to a certain strain of its own dead past, whose spirit is ghostly, whose structure of desire is backward looking and punishing." As the child of 1960s radicals, I had grown up in that ghostly culture; I didn't want my work to join the dusty books of the left. I wanted to dress *No Logo* up in capitalism's own shiny clothing.

All of this attention to packaging and style was, I told myself, a wink—better yet, a hack of the world of corporate branding. It also worked: *No Logo* sold over a million copies, beyond anything I could have imagined. And as I toured continuously for two years, I kept playing with the idea of being an anti-brand brand. I had a look that was simple but consistent: black trousers, T-shirt, denim jacket—mainly to make packing easier. I ginned up a No Logo logo and taped it to my water bottle. During speeches I would swig from it and joke dryly, "I just don't understand why all these journalists keep saying I'm a brand."

There was a disingenuousness to this theater; I see that clearly now. I wanted it both ways: to be the No Logo girl (the face of an emerging anticapitalist movement) and to deny that I cared a bit about building a brand. To be the only clean one in a dirty business. And isn't that what so many of us want as we try to win the game of personal branding—or at least not to get slain by it? We carefully cultivate online personas—doubles of our "real" selves—that have just the right balance of sincerity and world-weariness. We hone ironic, detached voices that aren't too promotional but do the work of promoting nonetheless. We go on social media to juice our numbers, while complaining about how much we hate the "hell sites."

It's a precarious line to walk, as I discovered early on, when my No Logo anti-brand shtick quickly slipped well beyond my control. As the long 1990s were starting their slow winddown, and an anti-corporate ethos was beginning to take root, I had to concede that my book had become a kind of signifier—an object or an accessory to be carried around and not read. Marketing students bought it in droves, some to signal that they were closet revolutionaries, all to get ideas for future campaigns.

One of my publishers had tried to persuade me to trademark the title, if only to prevent others from profiting from it. I self-righteously refused: what a mockery that would make of everything I had written about the walling-off of culture behind aggressive copyright laws. Sure enough, within a year someone else had filed for the trademark and was using a knockoff No Logo logo to sell golf shirts in Florida. A boutique food company in Italy started making No Logo olive oil and other sundries. A No Logo craft beer showed up in the United Kingdom. A slightly seedy No Logo restaurant in Geneva, Switzerland, opened up (I had a coffee there and introduced myself to the owner, who looked panicked and ran into the kitchen).

By then, when journalists asked me if I had become a brand, it was no longer credible to feign innocence. I was clearer, however, about why being a brand sat so uneasily with me. Good brands are immune to fundamental transformation. Conceding to having become one at age thirty would have meant foreclosing on what I saw as my prerogative to change, evolve, and hopefully improve. It would have locked me into performing this particular version of me, indefinitely.

Part of it was a certain amount of youthful idealism. The dictates of good branding struck me as antithetical to the dictates of being a good journalist, let alone a trusted political analyst. Those roles rest on a tacit commitment to following one's research wherever it leads, even if that turns out to be a very different place from what was originally expected. Trusted analysts have to be willing to be changed by what they discover. For a trusted brand, the duty is the opposite: to keep embodying your brand identity—your "promise"—no matter what the world throws at you. Good branding is an exercise in discipline and repetition. It means knowing exactly where you are headed all the time—which is essentially in concentric circles.

No Logo turned me into a brand; it was too late to change that. But I figured that I still had one good option left, and that was to become a poorly managed brand, one that broke the rules against dilution and overextension. (This, I suppose, is my version of Leonard Wolf's dictate "Destroy the box.") In practice, that meant letting the knockoffs reign free and swearing off the thing that had made me briefly famous—writing and talking about branding and marketing. I declined various offers to play the role of the celebrity anti-brand activist in ad campaigns, including a weird one from the designer Helmut Lang. At one point *Vogue* asked me to accompany a feature writer on an upscale shopping trip where I would be encouraged to criticize all the beautiful clothes for their labor and environmental crimes. Their proposed headline was "Shopping with the Enemy."

"Is the enemy me, or you?" I asked.

There was a pause.

"You."

I declined that, too.

Instead of performing these various versions of No Logo me, I began work on my next book, which took five years to complete and came out seven years after *No Logo*—an eternity in market terms. It was also on a totally different topic—how neoliberal economic hegemony had been birthed by the systematic exploitation of large-scale shocks. *The Shock Doctrine* contained not a word about marketing. It was a book of history and political economy that I knew was going to lose many of the people who had carried *No Logo* around as a lifestyle accessory. My next book, different again, was about climate change.

I was following a clear thread as I moved from one subject area to the next—each book was about the ravages of expanding market logics and corporate power, with the blast zone growing ever larger. From a movement-building perspective, that trajectory made sense: movements that want to grow have to reach across silos and beyond the already converted. But from a branding perspective (or even, for that matter, from a bookstore categorization perspective), my books were all over the map, shifting from marketing to militarism to environmentalism. I had achieved my goal of killing my own brand, or so I told myself.

Looking back at the crossroads where I faced a clear choice between following the dictates of being a curious writer and being a well-managed brand, I realize that the choice was largely made for me. If I had said yes to the *Vogue* shopping trips (and the corporate speeches, and the ad campaigns), the movement I was a part of would have torn me to shreds.

And rightly so. This was a good decade before personal branding had been normalized—we still called people who tried to cash in on mass movements careerists and sellouts. Which made those marketing decisions pretty easy: I didn't want to lose all my friends.

What I couldn't see at the time was that *No Logo* came out on the cusp of a new world. I wrote it on a chunky, rectangular Macintosh Plus computer that accessed the internet via a dial-up modem connected to my landline. By the time the book came out, in January 2000, I had a high-speed connection and could watch my book sales click up live on Amazon, which we were all sure would destroy the publishing industry but which I nonetheless checked obsessively, an early taste of the addictive power of social media's credit systems of likes, views, and follows.

It also became clear that a great many of us were dead wrong about the impossibility of everyday people being brands. Ten years after Peters's discredited "Brand Called You" article, the iPhone launched, and soon enough, Facebook, Twitter, and YouTube were at our fingertips. Suddenly, everyone on those free platforms had the tools to fashion a personal brand—quirky, glam, edgy, nerdy, revolutionary—and project it well beyond their own circles, all for the low, low cost of consumer tech and some well-chosen accessories. The age of the influencer was upon us.

Toronto, the city where I was living then, seemed particularly good at producing this new breed of online celebrity. In our sprawling suburbs, talented teens and young adults, many from immigrant families, set up cameras in their bedrooms and wrote, goofed, sang, sewed, painted nails, and gamed their way past the cultural gatekeepers who a few years earlier would almost certainly have stood in their way. Some, like the Toronto comedian Lilly Singh, made it all the way from YouTube to global stardom. Others burned bright and then seemed to disappear, unable to cope with the algorithms' ever-changing demands for fresh content or the abuse that came with such intense and continuous personal exposure. One thing was clear, however: noncelebrities (or not-yet-celebrities) without an advertising budget, and often without family connections, could indeed apply the principles of corporate branding to their intimate selves, and more than a few of them would win the personal branding lottery.

Digital Doubles

For several years, I have been teaching a university course called The Corporate Self, in which my students and I explore, among other things, the history and impacts of personal branding. In one class exercise, I ask the students, most of whom are in their early twenties, to locate their earliest memory of when the concept of being a brand was introduced to them. Many report that it started in middle school, when they were pushed to do certain extracurricular activities because it would "look good" to some amorphous audience down the road. Others recall stern parental lectures about the perils of incautious social media posts: everything you put online now, they were told, will be read by college admission officers and future employers, so be careful to curate and package yourself through their imagined eyes. Alice Marwick, in her book *Status Update*, refers to this as "The (Safe for Work) Self"—and some students have been trained to cultivate such a self well before they have any clue about what kind of work they want to be "safe" for.

Without fail, students describe the crafting of their college admission essays as the decisive moment when their private sense of self was subsumed by the imperative to create a consumable, public-facing identity. They faced essay prompts like "Some students have a background, identity, interest, or talent that is so meaningful they believe their application would be incomplete without it. If this sounds like you, then please share your story" or "The lessons we take from obstacles we encounter can be fundamental to later success. Recount a time when you faced a challenge, setback, or failure. How did it affect you, and what did you learn from the experience?"

The prompts may sound benign, but many students reported that through these high-stakes writing exercises, they learned to tell stories about their young lives that had less to do with truths as they knew them than with meeting the imagined needs and requirements of an audience of strangers for certain kinds of identities. There were many nods when one student described the process as "packaging up your trauma into a consumable commodity." It's not that the traumas they wrote about were fake; it's that the process required them to label difficult experiences in specifically marketable ways, and to turn them into something fixed, salable, and potentially profitable (since universities are themselves branded as the requisite first step to any lucrative career). A partitioning was occurring between these young people and this thing they were supposed to become to succeed.

Self-branding is yet another form of doubling, an internal sort of doppelganging.

Of course, for these students, the doubling required of self-branding did not stop once they got into university. One, an exile from the business school, shared that one of his first assignments had been to develop a thirty-second elevator pitch for himself. As he distilled himself down to his most marketable qualities, he told his classmates, "I felt my soul leave my body." They all seemed to know how he felt—these were the early days of pandemic Zoom classes, and they filled their little boxes with heart emojis.

The invocation of souls is interesting, a reminder that this is not the first generation to shape itself for an omniscient eye. What is an all-seeing God, capable of knowing our thoughts and intentions, if not the most effective surveillance tool ever invented? The genius of this form of religion is the way it seduces believers into performing purity in life in order to reap rewards after death. And unlike today's surveillance state—which knows only what we type, say, and do—monotheistic gods claim to know our intentions as well.

The Austrian psychoanalyst Otto Rank, who collaborated closely and later broke with Freud, saw the soul—the self believed to live beyond the body after death—as the original doppelganger, the most intimate of doubles. The choice to believe in a soul, he wrote, was "a wish defense against a dreaded eternal destruction." Freud concurred, writing, "The double was originally an insurance against the extinction of the self... 'an energetic denial of the power of death', and it seems likely that the 'immortal' soul was the first double of the body."

As with the doubles we perform in the digital ether, there is a menacing side to all this, because, as Freud notes, it's a reminder that we will not always be alive. The soul, in this way, "becomes the uncanny harbinger of death." Depending on the cosmology, a poorly lived life can land your spirit double in burning hell for all eternity or can assure its reincarnation as a cockroach. Because the stakes of this form of doubling are so high, it is often, according to Freud and Rank, accompanied by the creation of another kind of double—an evil twin, or abject self—onto which all of our sins and wrongdoings are projected. These doubles, who take on our sins so that we can stay pure, are the stuff of monsters in doppelganger books and films: they are the projected selves that get stabbed by the protagonists, who mistakenly kill themselves in the process. These doubles are the unwanted selves that we made some kind of deal with the devil to be free of, now seeking their revenge.

A poorly managed brand is distinctly less consequential than a poorly managed soul—but, on the other hand, the consequences occur in this realm, not the next. In our class discussions, we try to tease out precisely how the logic of personal branding shapes the emergence of this thing we call the self. What does it mean for young people to grow up knowing that every casual photo, video, and observation posted online could, when they are years older, be the thing that keeps them from getting a job, or getting into a school, or getting approved for an apartment? And, conversely, what does it mean when those same posts—trying on a cute outfit, dancing alone in their rooms—could also be the ticket to influencer fame and riches? Given the huge stakes, what do they do, and what don't they dare even try? And what happens to their abject selves while they are busily performing their perfected selves? What evil twins get created in this partitioning?

My students may not have real live doubles making chaos for them, as I appear to have with Other Naomi. But they have nonetheless grown up with an acute consciousness of having an externalized double—a digital double, an idealized identity that is partitioned from their "real" selves and that serves as a role they must perform for the benefit of others if they are to succeed. At the same time, they must project the unwanted and dangerous parts of themselves onto others (the unenlightened, the problematic, the deplorable, the "not me" that sharpens the borders of the "me"). This triad—of partitioning, performing, and projecting—is fast becoming a universal form of doppelganging, generating a figure who is not exactly us, but whom others nonetheless perceive as us. At best, a digital doppelganger can deliver everything our culture trains us to want: fame, adulation, riches. But it's a precarious kind of wish fulfillment, one that can be blown up with a single bad take or post.

All of this is on top of the omnipresent and very real possibility of having your email or social media accounts hacked, and discovering to your horror that someone who, for all intents and purposes, seems to be you is inundating your friends and colleagues with nefarious content. Which is why part of me can't help feeling for my doppelganger when she complains, of all things, "There is a fake 'Naomirwolf' on Telegram, and that fake entity has 38,000 followers, all of whom probably believe that they are following me"! Not only does this fake account have, according to Wolf, "unspeakable prose style," but it spreads all kinds of wacky conspiracy theories, like the QAnon favorite that claims that John F. Kennedy Jr., who died in a plane crash in 1999, is actually still alive. Wolf has a conspiracy about this conspiracy, claiming that the "fake me" account is clearly an "attack" designed to discredit her fearless investigations and make her "look like a lunatic." It is, she writes, an intolerable situation, "like having a tacky, blowsy, overdressed, grammatically-intolerable doppelganger." Ahem.

Fear of our digital doubles taking over our lives and fooling those around us is a theme also found in Netflix's underappreciated 2018 movie *Cam*, directed by Isa Mazzei. It tells the story of an online sex worker who gets locked out of her cam girl account and finds herself facing the ultimate horror in the age of the monetized self: watching someone who looks exactly like her steal her fans, followers, income, life—and, as in so many doppelganger tales, doing a better job of being her than she ever did.

This fantasy is fast becoming a reality. In late 2022, social media was inundated with iridescent, smoothed-out, slimmed-down versions of friends, family members, and online acquaintances who had succumbed to the "magic avatar" craze. They had uploaded ten photos of themselves to the app Lensa, and, in return for supplying this precious data, had received these avatar versions of themselves: sleeker, CGI-like (and, often, whiter and more overtly sexualized than the photos the simulations were based upon). While feeling pangs of desire to build my own faker, prettier version of me, I also found myself wondering about unintended consequences. For those who had engaged in this supposedly fun exercise in doubling, would looking in a normal mirror or at a non-altered photograph now feel like a kind of betrayal? Would their artificial self destroy the self-esteem of their real self? Many also pointed out how this could go wrong in more nefarious ways: someone other than you could pretend to be you, upload your photos, including ones you would never choose to share, and create their own personal doppelganger to exploit, sexually or otherwise.

Doppelganger stories often feature reflections or projections that break away from their original and take on a dangerous life of their own. In Hans Christian Andersen's 1847 fairy tale "The Shadow," a man's shadow becomes animate, displacing and then replacing him. In the 1913 silent horror film *The Student of Prague*, a poor student sells his own reflection to climb social classes, only to have that reflection destroy him. This is a warning that recurs often in doppelganger books and films: be careful about falling in love with your projection; it could well overtake you.

Interestingly, one person who is rather cavalier about the possibility of our digital doubles usurping us is Stephen K. Bannon, Trump's former campaign manager and chief strategist, now a full-time propagandist for authoritarian and neofascist movements from Italy to Brazil. In the 2000s, way before his Trump days, he worked at a company called Affinity Media (previously Internet Gaming Entertainment) in Hong Kong and got a crash course in multiplayer gaming. He told the documentarian Errol Morris that he was struck by the realization that, for the players, these games felt more real than real life. And the digital doubles they had created online—their avatars—seemed more real than their real, embodied selves. By way of example, he talked about a notional "Dave in Accounting" who leads a dreary, unremarkable life but turns into "Ajax," a gun-toting evil-slayer, when he is at home with his gaming console. "Now who's more real," Bannon asked—Dave or Ajax? You might say Dave, but Bannon saw it differently.

"People take on these digital selves that are a more perfected version of themselves and where they can control things in a digital way that they can't control in the analogue world," he said of the gamers. So, he explained, Dave should back down and let Ajax take over. "I want Dave in Accounting to be Ajax *in his life*," Bannon told *The Atlantic*'s Jennifer Senior. She observed, rightly, "That's precisely what happened on January 6. The angry, howling hordes arrived as real-life avatars, cosplaying the role of rebels in face paint and fur. They stormed the Capitol while an enemy army tried to beat them away . . . They skipped a day of work. And then they expressed outrage—and utter incredulity—when they got carted away. The fantasy and the reality had become one and the same."

Notably, Bannon appears to have no desire to make Dave's life better, to help him lead a life from which he would not need to escape. Rather, his goal seems to be to turn reality into a game played with live ammunition.

If Mark Zuckerberg's plans for the "Metaverse" proceed as he hopes, with all of us represented by personalized animated avatars to our banks and our friends, this is only going to get more confusing. It already is. In March 2022, South Korea elected Yoon Suk-yeol as its new president. The conservative politician campaigned, in part, by seeding the internet with a deepfake version of himself, known as AI Yoon. This version, created by his younger campaign team, was funnier and more charming than the real Yoon. *The Wall Street Journal* reported that for some voters the fake politician—whose fakeness was not hidden—felt more authentic and appealing than the real one: "Lee Seong-yoon, a 23-year-old college student, first thought AI Yoon was real after viewing a video online. Watching Mr. Yoon talk at debates or on the campaign trail can be dull, he said. But he now finds himself consuming AI Yoon videos in his spare time, finding the digital version of the candidate more likable and relatable, in part because he speaks like someone his own age. He said he is voting for Mr. Yoon." Yoon's digital doppelganger was created by a Korean company called DeepBrain AI Inc.; John Son, one of its executives, remarked that their work is "a bit creepy, but the best way to explain it is we clone the person."

After the aging members of ABBA allowed themselves to be similarly cloned, and those CGI clones began performing sold-out "live" shows in 2022, it's hard to imagine a future in which this kind of live-action fakery isn't a pillar of mass culture. "These digital doppelgangers look almost indistinguishable from real people from every angle," a review of the ABBA show in *Variety* observed, "with each tuft of hair and outlandish '70s costume rendered in occasionally terrifying detail. They can dance, they can jive, they can even make bad jokes about pausing for costume changes—and the crowd are having the time of their lives, teetering on the brink of delirium throughout."

Then there is the growing field of "grief tech," aiming "to take the sting out of death," as a *Financial Times* headline recently put it. The article explained, "Companies such as HereAfter AI are building 'legacy avatars' of living people that can be called upon after their deaths to console the bereaved." Is there something you always wanted to say to a parent but never had the chance or the courage? Tell their afterlife avatar.

The students I teach are troubled by where all of this doubling is leading. Nonetheless, almost all feel duty bound to participate in creating their own digital doubles on social media (as do I). One student shared that she had gotten off Instagram because the pressures to perform an idealized version of herself, and the inundations of images of others doing the same, were ravaging her mental health. But then came the 2020 Black Lives Matter uprisings. "My friends all told me I had to get back on Instagram and post pro-BLM," she said, "or everyone would think I was racist"—this despite the fact that she had been participating in all the protests in her area, albeit in a quiet, behind-the-scenes way. She logged back on and posted, but reluctantly; she knew there was something wrong with a culture that valued public performances of a virtuous self over more tangible solidarities and relationship building.

These views are born of my students' own experiences and enhanced by our readings, particularly Simone Browne's landmark 2015 book, *Dark Matters: On the Surveillance of Blackness*. Browne, a professor of African and African Diaspora Studies at the University of Texas at Austin, traces the origins of modern-day branding to the literal branding of African people in the transatlantic slave trade. "This is a difficult archive to write about," Browne observes, "where iron instruments fashioned into rather simple printed type became tools of torture. It is also a painful archive to imagine, where runaway notices speak of bodies scarred by slavery and of those that got away."

Provocatively, Browne calls this brutal branding "a biometric technology." Today, biometric identification—the recruitment of a permanent part of the body to measure and track—evokes sleek machines with blue or green light scanning faces, irises, or finger pads. Browne makes the case that physical branding played the same function for enslavers, allowing them to track racialized bodies via a permanent, unchangeable marker: "Branding in the transatlantic slave trade . . . was a measure of slavery's making, marking, and marketing of the black subject as commodity." The permanence of the brand was its power—it was designed to follow the enslaved person for the rest of their life, insurance against the irrepressible will to be free. This bloody and barbaric process, Browne argues, was a defining act by which slavers attempted to transform African people into what the great anti-colonial theorist Frantz Fanon called "an object among other objects."

Given these roots, the casualness with which our culture has come to discuss the idea that humans should strive to be brands is itself a kind of violent erasure. Branding today, many believe, is an act of empowerment, with the individual now fully in charge of their own commodification, and reaping a significant portion of the profits. For Browne, however, the commodification of the self, particularly of Black selves, cannot and should not be separated from the brutality of its past, despite the enormous changes in context, agency, and profit flows.

Branding is a process that requires what the author and psychotherapist Nancy Colier describes as an imperative to "relate to our self in the third person." A commodified self may be rich, but commodification still requires a partitioning, an internal doubling that is inherently alienating. There is you, and then there is Brand You. As much as we might like to believe that these selves can be kept separate, brands are hungry, demanding things, and one self necessarily impacts the other. If countless numbers of us are doubled, all partitioning and performing ourselves, it becomes harder for anyone to know what is real and what and who can be trusted. Which of our opinions are genuine, and which are for show? Which friendships are rooted in love, and which are co-branding collabs? What collaborations don't happen that should because individuals' brands are pitted against one another? What doesn't ever get said, or shared, because it's off-brand?

Many of the students I teach intend to work in media, where the fastest-growing business models, and the most seemingly reliable ones, involve media-makers having direct sales relationships with their readers, listeners, and viewers, whether via YouTube, Patreon, Substack, or some other platform. They have no choice but to join this hustle—but they also have concerns: in a sales relationship, the customer is always right, and the customer, as a rule, wants more of what they just received. You can tweak a brand, spin it off, and refresh it—but change its fundamentals and you have yourself a dilution crisis and many indignant customers. In the absence of a stable salary (since those have largely evaporated), that displeasure can translate into a direct drop in personal income.

In his essay "Self-Reliance," Ralph Waldo Emerson famously wrote, "A foolish consistency is the hobgoblin of little minds"; in the same passage, he worried that individuals were getting stuck in "a reverence for our past act or word because the eyes of others have no other data for computing our orbit than our past acts, and we are loath to disappoint them." Data. Computing. That was written in 1841, but it sounds very much like the cri de coeur of many a modern YouTuber or Twitch streamer, stuck churning out near-identical videos almost daily, lest fickle subscribers abandon them for one of the legions of new copycat influencers whom the algorithm recommends in the column next to or underneath their own videos.

When Lilly Singh announced that she was taking a hiatus from

YouTube in 2018, she explained that the platform "is a machine, and it makes creators believe that we have to pump out content consistently even at the cost of our life." A machine, in other words, that turns people into machines. And Singh is far from the only one to have publicly shared her private distress: there is a crowded subgenre of videos featuring famous influencers having these kinds of breakdowns.

The undergraduates I teach howl with laughter when we watch these confessionals. As empathetic as they are with one another, they have little but cynicism when it comes to the professed pain of wealthy influencers, even (especially?) when the influencers are roughly the same age as themselves. They place videos with titles like "Burnt Out at 19" in the same category as apology videos, wherein a YouTube or Instagram star overperforms contrition after getting caught crossing a line, like being photographed eating fish when they built their brand on sharing vegan recipes.

I gently push back on this: Why should surpassing a certain follower count preclude the possibility of feeling real pain? Why treat every emotion expressed online as a hollow performance? Alas, they invariably gang up on me, patiently explaining that in today's self-branding game, influencers are in an authenticity arms race, competing over who can be rawer and more revelatory. They also point out that the breakdown videos that I find so moving rarely forecast a decision on the influencer's part to abandon the hustle and grind of personal branding. Rather, they usually signal a brief hiatus, after which comes some kind of spectacular relaunch—a new venture on a more traditional media platform or a new product line.

I understand their cynicism, but I'm too old and soft to share it. It seems to me that both things can be true: these young influencers can be in real emotional distress over the pressure to produce mediated widgets and the cruelty they continually face from those they have invited into their lives, *and* they can simultaneously be figuring out how to monetize that pain. Because that is what they have been told they must do if they are to avoid becoming attention-economy roadkill. And, like so much else, it's a vicious cycle. If you successfully thing-ify yourself, then other people will begin to believe you are a thing and will throw all kinds of hard objects at you, sure that you will not bleed. And then you have to conjure up even more revealing forms of self-exposure—up to and including having a full-blown nervous breakdown in your bedroom with the webcam rolling. *Don't come for me*, these influencers seem to be pleading to their fans-turned-foes, *I'm wounded—can't you see that I'm bleeding here?* Forgetting that the pack loves blood and there is nothing bloodier than performative trauma.

Pulped Nonfiction

If personal branding has become a cultural imperative, what happens when our brands falter, fail, or fuck up irredeemably? What becomes of the person beneath the brand? What sort of mania ensues? ("Come for the nectar of approval," Richard Seymour writes in *The Twittering Machine*, "stay for the frisson of virtual death.") This raises an important plot point in the life of my doppelganger, one that I suspect may have a great deal to do with the choices she has made in the Covid era and beyond. Because that virtual death Seymour writes about? It happened to her. Boy did it happen to her.

In May 2019, less than a year before pandemic lockdowns began, Wolf went on BBC Radio 3 to promote *Outrages: Sex, Censorship, and the Criminalization of Love*, a book about the persecution of gay love in Victorian Britain that drew on research she'd done at Oxford University for a late-in-life PhD and was in many ways a throwback to her earlier work about sexuality and gender. What ensued was an event that I can barely think about without experiencing vicarious heart palpitations.

Wolf shared what she apparently considered to be the most explosive finding of her research: that well into the nineteenth century there were "several dozen executions" of men convicted of sodomy. She based this on finding the term "death recorded" in court documents. The BBC interviewer, Matthew Sweet, informed Wolf, live on the air, that she had misunderstood the term, which actually meant the exact opposite of what she had claimed: that these men had been found guilty and then released. It also turned out that several of the charges she referenced were not for consensual gay sex, but rather for child abuse, and that by conflating the two, she had perpetuated a dangerous fallacy linking gay men with pedophilia. With such basic errors exposed at the heart of her thesis, Wolf was dropped by her U.S. publisher and the book was pulped. Very rarely does a reputation collapse as publicly or as seemingly decisively as hers did in that excruciating moment. When the audio began circulating on Twitter, it was as if the entire platform had thought of the same cruel joke at once: Naomi Wolf had just had her own "death recorded."

University courses, seeking to instill in students a healthy fear of sloppy research, started using excerpts of *Outrages* as a cautionary tale. Publications where she once appeared regularly, like *The Guardian*, stopped publishing her, seemingly for good. Wolf, unsurprisingly, saw a plot. In January 2020, she told an interviewer that the "viral attack" she faced after her foundational errors in *Outrages* were exposed was part of a shadowy effort to destroy her reputation and take her "off the chessboard." All of this came at what was surely a tough time for Wolf—just a few months before the BBC interview, she had lost her father, the man she treated with such reverence in *The Treehouse*. This confluence of events means that she went into the destabilizing period of the pandemic in an already highly destabilized state, with little left to lose—and, as I would soon learn, with a great deal to gain.

Singular Personality Disorder

At one point in class, a student expressed the belief that if every human is supposed to define and defend themselves as a fixed, rigid brand, then humanity itself was "being made less human"—less capable of changing and evolving, even in the face of pressing ecological and political crises. This cut to the heart of the matter for me, identifying a problem I could not yet articulate when I was first writing about branding all those years ago. In *The Origins of Totalitarianism*, Hannah Arendt described the process of thinking as a form of doubling, because it is a "dialogue between me and myself." When each of us thinks and deliberates, we are in dialogue with the "two-in-one" that is our self, a self that, unlike a brand, is not a fixed, singular identity, or else what would there be to think about—or with? Dr. Richard Schwartz, who developed the therapy mode of Internal Family Systems, suggests there are actually more than two parts in our selves: every self is made up of a multiplicity, or mosaic, of often contradictory voices, hopes, and urges. In extreme cases, when those parts become disassociated from one another, this becomes a pathology—what used to be called multiple personality disorder. Most of the time, however, the capacity to have an internal dialogue (or round-table discussion) with the various parts of ourselves is healthy and human. Moreover, for Arendt, it is when everyday people *lose* their capacity for internal dialogue and deliberation, and find themselves only able to regurgitate slogans and contradictory platitudes, that great evil occurs. So, too, when people lose the ability to imagine the perspectives of others, or as she put it in her essay "Truth and Politics," "making present to my mind the standpoints of those who are absent." In that state of literal thoughtlessness (i.e., an absence of thoughts of one's own), totalitarianism takes hold. Put differently, we should not fear having voices in our heads—we should fear their absence.

This points to what may well prove to be the deepest danger of our era of branded humans. Brands are not built to contain our multitudes; they demand fixedness, stasis, one singular self per person. Human statues. The form of doubling that branding demands of us is antithetical to the healthy form of doubling (or tripling, or quadrupling) that is thinking and adapting to changing circumstances. That would be a problem at any time in history, but in a moment like ours, with so many collective crises demanding our deliberation, debate, and elasticity, the stakes feel civilizational.

It has often struck me, as I have contemplated my own branding crisis at a time when I felt I should be more properly focused on the climate crisis, that I am hardly the only one who has turned away from large fears in favor of more manageable obsessions. In fact, it makes a certain kind of sick sense that our era of peak personal branding has coincided so precisely with an unprecedented crisis point for our shared home. The vast, complex planetary crisis requires coordinated, collective effort on an international scale. That may be theoretically possible, but it sure is daunting. Far easier to master our self, the Brand Called You—to polish it, burnish it, get the angle and affect just right, wage war against all competitors and interlopers, project the worst onto them. Because unlike so much else upon which we might like to have some sort of impact, the canvas of the self is compact and near enough that it feels like we might actually pull off some measure of control. Even though, as I have discovered, this, too, is a grand illusion.

And so the question remains: What *aren't* we building when we are building our brands?

4

MEETING MYSELF IN THE WOODS

One of the most celebrated depictions of doppelgangers in Western art is a lush Pre-Raphaelite painting by Dante Gabriel Rossetti. It depicts a couple in medieval dress in a dark forest who come across another couple who are their mirror image. It is not a happy encounter. The man who sees his double draws his sword in anger, while his female companion faints, overcome by the uncanny sight. The piece is titled *How They Met Themselves.*

When I first came across it, I realized that this is what it means to embark on a doppelganger journey—when I set off, I too had my figurative sword drawn, ready to do battle and be the last Naomi standing. Now, in these shadow-laden woods, I find myself confronting not her but myself, and the uncomfortable truth that I still care, far too much, about the image I am projecting into the world; that if I am serious about rejecting personal branding, I still have a good deal of work to do.

small names, Big Ideas

One person who thought a great deal about how to navigate the tension between outsize, individual selves and the demands of collective work was the late author and theorist bell hooks. "People with healthy self-esteem do not need to create pretend identities," she wrote. In my course The Corporate Self, we look at the various ways hooks worked to subvert and undercut personal branding and celebrity activism, well before these concepts hit the mainstream. Her given name was Gloria Jean Watkins and she wrote under bell hooks, her great-grandmother's name, in part to honor her, and in part to put some distance between her everyday identity and her author identity. "I'm walking around in the dailiness of my life as just the ordinary Gloria Jean," she told *The New York Times* in 2015. She also, famously, always wrote her pen name in lowercase letters—not to make herself small, she explained, but as a reminder to keep the focus on the "substance of books, not who I am."

This might seem surprising at a time when the highest praise is to be declared an icon. But she did not want the name bell hooks—the persona or the idea in people's heads—to upstage bell hooks's ideas, and she understood that there is an unavoidable tension between the baggage a name can come to carry—its relative bigness in the world—and the ability of one's words to reach people and be adopted as their own. A gulf can open up between author and reader, and hooks was making an attempt to close it. Of course, inevitably, the hooks name became its own kind of market signal, as everything in our capitalist culture does. But this did not seem to be her intent: on the contrary, hooks cared enough about her work, her ideas, not to want to weigh them down with a heavy name.

She wrote similarly about the identity labels so many of us have come to heap on ourselves. As a political theorist, hooks believed fiercely in the power of naming systems—her recurring phrase, in defining what we are up against, was "white supremacist capitalist patriarchy." But she was far more ambivalent about the impulse to attach identity signifiers to our beings, to brand ourselves as a *this*, or a *that*. In her landmark 1984 book, *Feminist Theory: From Margin to Center*, hooks cautioned readers to "avoid using the phrase 'I am a feminist'" and opt instead for "I advocate feminism," explaining that unlike the "I am" label, which triggers the listener's prior beliefs about what and who is a feminist, the latter is far more likely to begin a conversation about what concrete changes feminism is trying to achieve and "does not engage us in the either/or dualistic thinking that is the central ideological component of all systems of domination in Western society."

Revisiting hooks's text in the context of my own dualistic duel was clarifying, and more than a little shaming. So much of intellectual and activist life today is about credit claiming. I do it; I've done it repeatedly in these pages. I wrote that. I said that. That's my phrase. My buzzword. My hashtag. I was horrified the first time I noticed a colleague self-cite, embedding quotes from his earlier work in a column—"as I wrote here [link] and here [link]." Why was he quoting himself? Quoting is what we do to bring in the voices of others, to expand the frame, not to narrow it further. Now self-citing happens all the time: "As I wrote here" . . . "See my earlier tweet" . . . "Just bumping this up." We have to do it, or so many of us believe—we are caught in a roaring river of voices that seems to wash away all that came before. If we don't remind people of what we have said and done, surely we will soon be floating downstream to the sea with all the other cultural detritus.

In 2014, well acquainted with our amnesiac habits, hooks launched the bell hooks Institute in Berea, Kentucky, a space devoted to her work, artifacts, and ideas. She explained that her sister had died recently, and it had her thinking about her own legacy and "what happens if we don't take care of ourselves, if we don't value ourselves rightly." She worried that she would suffer the fate of so many Black writers, their contributions lost to history. She had hoped, she quipped in a 2015 talk, that there might be "somebody else out there who cares enough about bell hooks to be working on preserving her artifacts, but no one came to the fore." So she did the work of building the institute, not to serve as a shrine to her ego, but rather to keep the ideas alive. Because her ideas—about love as a driving force for politics, about breaking down interlocking systems of domination—matter. And bell hooks matters—not the brand, but the human being who did all that work, writing more than thirty books in her sixty-nine years, changing countless people's lives for the better. That was worth preserving and defending against the forgetful river.

Brands may be vain and damaging things, but ideas are not. Ideas are tools of transformation, personal and collective. So it concerns me when

Wolf's exaggerations, speculations, and baseless claims get conflated with the shock doctrine—not because it's a brand in need of protection, but because it's a framework that has given people some language to guard against profiteering and attacks on democracy during confusing periods of emergency. When that concept is mangled by association with unhinged conspiracy theories about global cabals, it becomes harder for it to serve that purpose. It all gets mixed up, rendered absurd ("too ridiculous to take seriously and too serious to be ridiculous").

Wolf has similarly twisted the feminist movement's core tenet that all people have the right to choose whom they have sex with and whether to carry a child. Now she was distorting that principle to cast Covid tests and vaccine mandates as violations of "bodily integrity" akin to those endured by women who underwent forced vaginal exams, claiming that all are examples of "the state penetrating their body against their will." Clearly, that kind of language fills a cultural need, one bound up in the social currency of victimization, a theme I'll return to later. But the point here is that abusing such terms is dangerous: it drains them of their intended meaning, their legibility, and their power.

Most gravely, Wolf and her fellow travelers have spent years mangling the meaning of the fight against authoritarianism, fascism, and genocide—nothing less than humanity's worst crimes. And they have done it at a time when we are in dire need of a robust anti-fascist alliance, in large part thanks to their own relentless inflammation and misinformation and the resentments they have sown. Brand dilution and brand harm are trivial matters—but these crimes and the ability to name them matter a great deal.

What do we do when important ideas and concepts are being distorted in this way, when absurdity seems to take over, making serious discussion impossible? What do we do when we seem to be surrounded by warped doubles and imposters? I was searching for answers to that question late one night, when, working my way through the doppelganger cinematic canon, I landed on Charlie Chaplin's daring satire about the rise of Hitler, *The Great Dictator.* At the end of the film, the persecuted Jewish barber (played by Chaplin) disguises himself as the Hitler-esque dictator (also played by Chaplin), sneaks behind enemy lines, and delivers to the fascist masses one of the greatest anti-fascist speeches of all time.

Though originally released in 1940, Chaplin's message felt as relevant as ever: When faced with a double threatening to engulf you and your world (or an army of them), distance offers no protection. Far better to radically upend the table and become, in some sense, their impersonator, their shadow.

That, at least, is how I rationalized listening to so much Steve Bannon.

PART TWO

Mirror World

(Projection)

"But what of it? Do you suppose it is beyond us to produce a dual system of astronomy . . . Have you forgotten doublethink?"

—O'Brien, in George Orwell's *1984*

5

THEY KNOW ABOUT CELL PHONES

In an effort to impose some kind of order on my doppelganger's behavior during the first two years of the Covid-19 pandemic, I have found it useful to divide the period into two phases: Before Bannon and After Bannon.

Before Bannon was a troubled, chaotic time for Other Naomi. She was tweeting and livestreaming with a worrying relentlessness, but her grievances were scattershot and diffuse. She shared her belief that children had lost the reflex to smile due to enforced mask-wearing, based on no evidence except her own observations of random children who might have been having rough days. She claimed to have overheard two Apple employees in a Manhattan restaurant discussing "vaccines w nanopatticles [*sic*] that let you travel back in time" (apparently mistaking a conversation about Apple Watch's Time Travel feature for a secret meeting about an actual time machine). And let's not forget the extraordinary ones about quarantining the feces of vaccinated people. Or the tear she went on about vaccine "shedding" and infertility.

It must have been a miserable time. She was repeatedly suspended and locked out of her social media accounts for violating rules against medical misinformation. She was getting bombarded with abuse and mockery online (as I knew better than anyone but her). By her own telling on Twitter, friends were sending her one-word texts saying simply: "Stop." Meanwhile, a series of "What Happened to Naomi Wolf?" articles appeared in publications that once regarded her seriously, often taking a new critical look at her past work: "The Madness of Naomi Wolf," *The New Republic*; "Naomi Wolf's Slide from Feminist, Democratic Party Icon to the 'Conspiracist Whirlpool,'" *Business Insider*; "A Modern Feminist Classic Changed My Life. Was It Actually Garbage?," *Slate*. Yet she kept going, spraying the internet with a steady aerosol of her bizarre theories.

A particularly dismal moment came when she fell for an online prank and shared a photo of a "doctor" who seemed to be questioning the vaccination drive. Only it turned out that the doctor she quoted was not a doctor, but rather a well-known male porn star dressed in scrubs with a stethoscope around his neck. The tweet revealing the prank (pulled off by *The Intercept*'s Ken Klippenstein) was "liked" seventy-one thousand times.

Wolf's fortunes changed markedly in March 2021, one year after the global pandemic was first declared. This is the start of the After Bannon era. In this period, Wolf both shifted and honed her Covid message, zeroing in on a set of fears related to the prospect of so-called vaccine passports. The idea of using vaccine-verification passports for international travel had been floated months earlier in a slick video produced by the World Economic Forum as part of its "Great Reset" campaign. Israel was already using digital vaccine apps to control access to indoor venues, and the British government had begun to float the idea as well. Wolf predicted that North America would be next (a safe bet), and she claimed that the world was therefore approaching a "cliff" for human liberty from which there would be no returning, a message she shared on multiple right-wing news outlets, including the then top-rated cable news show in the United States, Fox's (now canceled) *Tucker Carlson Tonight*, with its daily average of three million viewers. The Fox News host—known for fawning over authoritarians like Hungary's Viktor Orbán and for fanning the flames of anti-immigrant violence by parroting the so-called Great Replacement theory—fell hard for Wolf and her attention-grabbing message. It was a message best summed up in the headline she selected for one of her most successful self-produced videos, viewed more than 180,000 times on YouTube alone: "Watch Dr Naomi Wolf Discuss 'Why Vaccine Passports Equal Slavery Forever.'"

My doppelganger has rarely shied away from extreme rhetoric—she has predicted domestic coups and accused the United States of tipping into "fascism" continuously since 2007 and said that "Obama has done things like Hitler did." This kind of intemperance presents a challenge, I have noticed, when Wolf is trying to raise a new alarm: How to find words powerful enough to convince people that, this time, it's the Big One? Look, I get it: I've published well over two thousand pages about the climate crisis and am forever trying to find new ways to express the fact that we are unraveling the fabric that sustains human and other-than-human life—the difference being that it's true.

On vaccine passports, Wolf found new weapons of escalation. The passports are "a tyrannical totalitarian platform" and "the most dangerous tool humanity has faced in its lifetime," she claimed, and "the people who have this data are going to run the world."

In the "slavery forever" video, as well as on Carlson's show and on Steve Hilton's Fox News show (*The Next Revolution*)—all recorded within days of one another—Wolf laid out her case. She declared that vaccine verification apps, which some governments unwisely referred to as "passports," were not what they seemed. In what she described as her "most serious warning" to date, Wolf said the apps were actually a backdoor attempt to usher in a "CCP-style social credit score system"—a reference to China's all-pervasive surveillance net that allows Beijing to rank citizens for their perceived virtue and obedience, a chilling hierarchy that can determine everything from access to schools to eligibility for loans, and is one piece of a broader surveillance dragnet that pinpoints the location of dissidents for arrest and ruthlessly censors speech that casts the ruling party in a critical light. The vaccine app was like all that, Wolf said, a system that "enslaves a billion people."

She explained that the vaccination-status QR codes that would be scanned to gain access to restaurants, theaters, and the like would not merely give health authorities data on a person's presence in these indoor venues. They would also allow a "tyrannical" state to know who you were gathering with and what you were talking about—not only in those restaurants where the code had been scanned but also, she claimed, inexplicably, in your own living room: "If you're talking about staging a protest or writing an op ed or mobilizing support for a representative to pass a bill to roll back this system, the platform will know." In Israel, she said, the passports had already produced a "two-tiered society," with "second-rate citizens." Notably, this was not a reference to Palestinians, who have long lived as actual second-class citizens, but to Israeli Jews who decided not to get vaccinated. Once similar apps came to the United States, she warned, if you do not get vaccinated or are otherwise "a dissident," you will "be in a second-class category for the rest of your life. Your family will be too."

Wolf had previously cast the vaccines themselves as grave health threats, and would do so again, suggesting, without evidence, that the shots were a deliberately deployed Chinese "bioweapon" against the West. In these Fox News dispatches, however, she seemed to be saying that the Covid vaccine itself was beside the point. She told Hilton:

> It's not about the vaccine, it's not about the virus, it's about your data . . . What people have to understand is that any other functionality can be loaded onto that platform with no problem at all. And what that means is, it can be merged with your PayPal account, with your digital currency, Microsoft is already talking about merging it with payment plans, your networks can be sucked up, it geolocates you everywhere you go. Your credit history can be included, all of your medical history can be included.

She claimed, in the "slavery forever" video, that "machine reading assesses what you've been saying on social media. So if you've been too conservative or too liberal . . . machine reading will let PayPal know, PayPal will switch off or dial up your interest on a credit card." The app, she went on, will even be tracking your search histories. And if you do something wrong, it "has the power to turn off your life."

Just in case viewers weren't frightened enough, she latched onto a detail about IBM providing data support in New York State to go all the way there. "IBM has a horrible history with Nazi Germany," Wolf told Hilton. "Its subsidiary created a kind of precursor of this with punch cards that allowed the Nazis to keep lists of—again a two-tiered society—Aryan and Jews, in such a way that they could round up Jews, round up dissidents, round up opposition leaders, very, very quickly. It's catastrophic, it cannot be allowed to continue." But how, you might well ask, could this gruesome dystopia be ushered in via one vaccination app? Easy, Wolf explained. All it took was "a tweak of the back end."

To be clear, once again: this is not true. Scanning a QR code to get into a restaurant or a stadium does not also allow the government to listen to the conversations you have at that restaurant, as Wolf claimed. When it is not being scanned (which is most of the time), a QR code also does not have the power to "geolocate you"; neither can it find you in your home. It does not know your search history, is not linked to PayPal, and cannot turn your life on and off. It is not a social credit system, and it has nothing to do with what IBM did in Nazi Germany. It's just a yes/no on vaccine status, and no "tweak of the back end" changes these facts. Wary of being overly trusting, I confirmed this with the Electronic Frontier Foundation, the leading organization defending digital privacy and civil liberties online. Alexis Hancock, director of engineering and vaccine passport expert at EFF, explained in an email that "the technology itself does not send some signal to the government of your location" and that the claim the app is listening "is really outlandish."

There have been a couple of instances in Western Australia in which police accessed data from vaccine app scans as part of investigations into violent crimes. The government quickly introduced legislation to bar this kind of use, making it clear that the app was not a crime-solving tool. But here is what got my attention about this steep drop-off in Wolf's Covid roller-coaster ride: what she was describing on Fox was actually not a vaccine passport at all. Rather, she was describing what it increasingly feels like to be at the mercy of omnipresent technologies that are governed according to opaque algorithms and whose often-arbitrary, hugely consequential decisions are outside the reach of existing laws. Seen in that context, it shouldn't be a surprise that her state of alarm resonated with people who came across her videos. Her facts were largely fantastical, but Wolf was nonetheless providing people with something they clearly wanted and needed: a focal point for their fear and outrage over digital surveillance.

The Roads Not Taken

We can have legitimate debates about the decisions of governments to put so much of the burden of controlling a surging virus on vaccines and smartphone apps—as opposed to, say, maintaining indoor masking requirements and making greater investments in public health-care systems, including hiring many more nurses and giving them pay raises, to prevent hospitals from being overrun. Not to mention providing a steady supply of free at-home rapid tests, proper protective gear at work, and, critically, adequate sick leave for all workers so that no one feels obliged to show up to work in an infectious state. In the early phase of the pandemic, there could also have been major investments in contact tracing at the community level, which would have had the added benefit of creating jobs in neglected areas. And there could have been far more robust efforts to install high-quality air filters in public spaces, including schools, while hiring more teachers and teacher's aides so class sizes could be smaller—all measures proven to reduce the virus's spread, with plenty of knock-on benefits to students and educators. These are just a few of the ways that frayed social services and safety nets could have been expanded and reinforced in order to allow us all to live less stressed, happier, and fuller lives with the virus in our midst.

In April 2022, Beatrice Adler-Bolton, a disability justice advocate, laid out what such an alternative approach might have looked like in the United States:

> We cannot rely on pharmaceutical technology alone. We also have to use all of the social, economic, and political technologies at our disposal—just as much tools as vaccines and antivirals—like social distancing, masking, paid leave, eviction prevention, community harm reduction,

> upgraded ventilation, infrastructure investments, Medicare for All, debt cancellation, decarceration and so much more. These are just some of the potential social and fiscal tools that we could use to help people not just survive the pandemic but thrive *in spite of it.*

Unfortunately, there was never a truly mass organizing strategy to push for that kind of ambitious agenda, so governments rarely felt obliged to consider it seriously, opting instead for the easier (and big-donor-friendly) route of looking to vaccines and verification apps to carry almost the entire load of virus control in North America and Europe. Like so much else in our culture, from abusive labor practices to climate breakdown, the burden of pandemic response was shifted from the collective to the individual, all in the name of getting back to business as usual: "Did you get your jab?" "Show us the proof." Less frequently did we ask employers if they had provided safe workplaces, or if governments had guaranteed safe learning environments or transportation systems.

By far the most significant measure governments of wealthy nations could have taken to stop the spread of new variants would have been to make vaccines free and available to the entire global population at the same time as they were rolled out domestically; the suspension of pharmaceutical company patents would have been more than justified, since public money so heavily subsidized the development and rollout of the vaccines. And the cost would have been relatively low: the chief economist at the Organisation for Economic Co-operation and Development estimated that the entire world could have been vaccinated for $50 billion, just a little more than Elon Musk paid to turn Twitter into his personal plaything. But doing so would have required a waiver of intellectual property protections at the World Trade Organization, which would have facilitated lifting the patents that have allowed a handful of pharmaceutical companies to treat the vaccines as permission to print money. And so Pfizer alone earned $37 billion from the Covid vaccine in 2021. At the end of that year, while countries like mine were already rolling out third doses, just 7.5 percent of Africans had received one shot.

Patrick Wilcken, Amnesty International's head of business and human rights, described the hoarding and profiteering as "a failure of catastrophic proportions," adding, "The apparently unquenchable thirst for profits of big pharmaceutical companies, like Pfizer, is fueling an unprecedented human rights crisis. If left unchecked, the rights of billions of people around the world to life and to health will continue to be in jeopardy."

And because viruses mutate and hop over borders, it was also extraordinarily unwise. As the World Health Organization's vaccine director, Kate O'Brien, correctly predicted of vaccine nationalism, "It's not going to work. It's not going to work from an epidemiologic perspective and it's not going to work from a transmission perspective unless we actually have vaccine going to all countries." (As doppelgangers teach us, walling off that which is inherently connected rarely ends well.)

There were also social costs inside wealthy countries to placing so much of the virus-control strategy on vaccinations and verification apps. Whenever access to spaces and services requires a smartphone and QR codes, it further marginalizes those who are unhoused and otherwise vulnerable and are less likely to have access to those tools—"the viral underclass," as the author Steven W. Thrasher has described the already marginalized groups who are treated as disposable during times of pandemic.

These are difficult and important debates to have, alongside an honest reckoning with the brutal histories that underlie mistrust toward government-mandated health programs among many Black, Indigenous, Puerto Rican, and disabled people. These are just some of the communities that have been the targets of forced sterilization programs and covert medical experimentation over the past century. Among the most notorious was the Tuskegee experiment of the 1930s, in which hundreds of Black men in Alabama were given placebos instead of the best treatments for syphilis, with many dying as a result. Like other real conspiracies, the cruel and unethical experiment was covered up for decades, and those who attempted to raise the alarm were dismissed.

Reckonings with these histories are long overdue; in their absence, public health bureaucracies found that their efforts to battle Covid in marginalized communities were frequently met with skepticism. These dynamics also made some of these communities easy prey for peddlers of misinformation like my doppelganger, with her inflammatory claims on Fox that vaccine apps were tantamount to IBM's collaboration with the Nazi death machine.

Tapping Into Our Tech Fears

There was something else that was new about my doppelganger in this period. As Wolf zeroed in on vaccine apps as the focal point for her dire warnings, she also adopted a new way of referring to herself and her expertise, one clearly intended to bestow authority in this particular debate. For three decades, Naomi Wolf identified herself as an author and a former political consultant. She still does. But when she started going on Carlson's show and others of its ilk, she began prefacing her remarks about the vaccine apps with something I hadn't heard before: "Speaking as a tech CEO" and "I'm the CEO of a tech company."

I am? I mean: She is?

This surprising assertion turned out to be a reference to DailyClout, a then obscure, low-traffic website that hosted her blogs and videos and also made the eyebrow-raising claim of being a technological breakthrough because it allowed easy access to pieces of draft legislation by putting them online (never mind that U.S. bills are already public and online elsewhere, via free sites like GovTrack.us). Before she started making the rounds on Fox, the site—which claimed to turn everyday people into lobbyists—reportedly averaged just a few thousand visits a month, with one month seeing a mere thirteen visitors.

I started noticing other shifts in this new, Fox-ready, tech-CEO incarnation of my doppelganger. Since *The End of America*, Wolf has leaned heavily on U.S. patriotism as a reason to resist restrictions on civil liberties. ("The founders did not create liberty for America, but America for liberty," was typical fare.) These vaccine passport dispatches, however, took a far more nationalistic and pro-capitalist tone than anything I had seen from her previously. She painted a world in which Covid health measures are the front lines in a civilizational war between East and

West. Again and again, she invoked the Chinese Communist Party (CCP)—in her fifteen-minute "slavery forever" video, she referenced "the CCP" five times, the same number of times as she said "the West."

"This is literally the end of human liberty in the West if this plan unfolds as planned," she told Steve Hilton in March 2021. If the passports become a reality, she said in her own video, "there won't be capitalism." Already, she said, the tech companies (with their deplatforming of misinformation) and the government (with its various Covid mandates) were engaging in "CCP-type conditioning . . . conditioning us not to be members of the West." All the Covid responses, were, at bottom, about "weakening the West, weakening our society, weakening our children." It was, she said, "un-American."

Luckily, Wolf had a plan for fighting back. She explained that her website was being turned into a clearinghouse for "model legislation" that activists could use at the state level to block future public health measures and defend what she termed the "Five Freedoms." She defined these as the right to be free of: mask mandates, vaccine passports, school closures, emergency declarations, and restrictions on commerce and religious gatherings. In short, "freedom" meant denying governments all of the most robust tools they had used to control the virus, while calling for nothing to replace them. But since she had been playing down the severity of the pandemic for months, why would governments need those tools?

I admit that when Wolf first started talking about vaccine passports as mass surveillance networks, I really didn't understand the effect it was having. I was focused on the many wrong facts she was sharing, as well as the true fact that her newfound celebrity on Fox was blowing up my own social media.

What many of us who were cringe-following Wolf at the time missed was the extent to which her new messaging had struck a chord—not only with Fox's audience but also with a sizable cohort of people who identify as leftists or progressives and were terrified of the *Black Mirror* surveillance world she was describing. Her "slavery forever" video was personally forwarded to me by several sources. One was a known conspiracy theorist who urged me to "study" it and said we had to fight the new threat "with every last ounce of our strength." One asked if I had advice for deprogramming a loved one, a Black Lives Matter–supporting alternative health practitioner who had taken Wolf's words as gospel and was in a QAnon-like spiral about this being the last frontier in the fight for "freedom versus slavery."

I went back and looked at the nearly one thousand comments under Wolf's "slavery forever" YouTube post, bracing for the usual misogynist bile for which the platform is notorious. Jarringly, the comments were nearly universally glowing, expressing adoration for this "warrior" and her "courage" to speak the truth. Many quoted scripture and declared the vaccines, as well as the passports, "the mark of the beast."

My spirits perked up briefly when a tech executive interrupted the lovefest to explain that "the vaccine passport is NOT 'the same platform' as Chinese 'social credit'" and neither was it "handed down from a centralized authoritarian super-government." My spirits promptly crashed when he added: "It is obvious to me that Klein—who I had respected til now—is towing some kind of Western-Centric line here." (Wolf's new fans took care of him: "Go to China and stay. We don't want communists like you here. Some day it actually might be dangerous for you. Just sayin.")

Not only did Wolf appear on Fox seven times in less than two months, but she went on a tour, speaking at the "FreedomFest" at Mount Rushmore and testifying, at the invitation of various Republican lawmakers, at multiple statehouses against mask and vaccine mandates. In the Maine House of Representatives, her host was disciplined by legislative leaders for allowing Wolf into the then closed statehouse and barred from bringing future guests. Eight days later, she traveled to Michigan, which was then one of the leading states in new coronavirus cases, to testify before the state's House Oversight Committee that vaccine passports were akin to the early treatment of Jews by the Nazis.

One person who took immediate notice of the resonance of Wolf's new message was Steve Bannon. Within a week, he began having "Dr. Wolf" as a regular guest on his wildly popular and influential podcast, *War Room*, which he had been developing through various iterations since losing his post as Donald Trump's chief strategist in 2017—while also, as he boasted to *The New York Times*, building "the infrastructure, globally, for the global populist movement." Bannon could not get enough of Wolf: he sometimes hosted her several times in a single week, always lavishly plugged her website and its "Five Freedoms" legislation mill, which was suddenly anything but obscure. I checked the traffic: in April 2021, the month she started appearing regularly on Bannon's podcast, DailyClout broke 100,000 unique visits—up from a mere 851 one year earlier. "We want everyone in the posse to go and support Dr. Wolf," Bannon said in a typically effusive endorsement. Accused by *The Atlantic* of misleading his viewers by repeatedly referring to Wolf as "Doctor" when discussing medical research, Bannon replied that her doctorate in philosophy was "good enough" for him.

In retrospect, it shouldn't be all that surprising that Wolf's vaccine passport messaging struck such a chord. When she focused in on tech and surveillance, she began tapping into deep and latent cultural fears about the many ways that previously private parts of our lives have become profit centers for all-seeing Silicon Valley giants. It was as if she had taken everybody's cumulative tech terrors—about being tracked by our cell phones, monitored by our search engines, eavesdropped on by our smart speakers, spied on by our doorbells—bundled them all together, and projected them onto these relatively anodyne vaccine apps, which, to hear Wolf tell it, took every creepy surveillance abuse perpetrated by Big Government and Big Tech and programmed them into one QR code, on "the back end."

The words she was saying were essentially fantasy. But emotionally, to the many people now listening to her, they clearly *felt* true. And the reason they felt true is that we are indeed living through a revolution in surveillance tech, and state and corporate actors have indeed seized outrageous powers to monitor us, often in collaboration and coordination with one another. Moreover, as a culture, we have barely begun to reckon with the transformational nature of this shift.

"Wait until they hear about cell phones." That is the recurring liberal sneer directed at people like Wolf, who have been spinning theories about vaccines and vaccine passports secretly tracking our every move. I laughed the first few times I came across the joke, feeling just as superior as it was meant to make me feel. But now, after months of following the emergence of a new and powerful political constellation in which Wolf's star shines brightly, I am no longer laughing. It is a serious mistake to underestimate her, or the movements she now helps to lead. Because here is a non-snide version of the "Wait until they hear about cell phones" quip: They know all about cell phones. They just don't know what to *do* about cell phones (or smart speakers or search histories or shadow banning or email and social media metadata . . .). And neither, it seems, does anyone else, including those in power, who are patently unwilling to rein in what the Harvard professor Shoshana Zuboff has called "surveillance capitalism." And Wolf, with her "Five Freedoms" campaign and her calls for anti-vax civil disobedience, is giving her followers something to do. She is telling them that it's not too late to get their privacy, and their freedoms, back.

Of course this is an appealing message. The past two decades have been a nonstop drip of shocking revelations about the myriad ways in which the record of our daily and intimate lives has somehow become the property of others. First came the Patriot Act and the post-9/11 spawning of a global surveillance industry. Then the AT&T whistleblower came forward to tell us of secret rooms where data about global internet traffic was being forwarded to the National Security Agency. Then came Edward Snowden's harrowing leaks and the confirmation of this massive data dragnet, followed by the Cambridge Analytica scandal and the revelation that Facebook was selling users' data to third parties for political manipulation. Then came Pegasus, the self-cloaking Israeli-designed spyware that was being used by governments around the world to gain full access to the phones of their opponents and critics.

On and on. Drip. Drip. Drip. "Alexa Has Been Eavesdropping on You This Whole Time," read a 2019 headline in *The Washington Post.* "Your Apps Know Where You Were Last Night, and They're Not Keeping It Secret," went one in *The New York Times* in 2018. "You're Not Paranoid: Your Phone Really Is Listening In," said *USA Today.* Drip. Drip. Drip. We heard about the "nanny cams" taken over by hackers and turned into surveillance devices; the Ring doorbell footage handed over to police; Uber's "God View" software, allegedly used by employees to spy on passengers as well as ex-girlfriends; the billions of personal photos scraped by facial recognition companies to train their software; the period-tracking apps that could be used to prosecute people who choose to end their pregnancies in any of the states that have rushed to criminalization.

Everyone who is online today knows at least some of this. Knows that where we go, who we love, what we believe, and how our bodies behave is out there in the ether, beyond our control. And yet the response to this extraordinary reality has so far been strangely muted, with much of it sublimated into ironic humor, like "Wait until they hear about cell phones."

Digital Golems

In my Corporate Self course, we explore this surveillance architecture as the shadowy back end of personal branding and identity performance culture. The more we accept the premise that we must be online for everything—liking, loathing, sharing—and the more we accept the tacit contract of trading privacy in exchange for app-enabled convenience, the more data points tech companies are able to hoover up about us. And with that data, they create our real digital doppelgangers—not the aspirational avatars many of us consciously create with those carefully curated and filtered photos and those posts with the perfectly calibrated tone, but the doubles that countless machines create with the data trails we leave behind every time we click, or view, or fail to disable location tracking, or ask a "smart" device for anything at all. Every data point scraped from our online life makes our double more vivid, more complex, more able to nudge our behavior in the real world.

This machine-made doppelganger—or perhaps we should call it a digital golem since it is cobbled together from bits of inanimate data—is not made by us. It is made by exterior perceptions, interpretations, and predictions about us. In this way, it has a great deal in common with a human doppelganger: a person whom the world confuses with you but who is not actually you and yet can impact your life in profound ways.

And now that the machines have devoured so much of us, gorged on so many of our ways and our quirks, they can make rather credible replicas of us near instantly. My friends who are visual artists and songwriters are terrified about what their futures hold when artificial intelligence programs can be instructed to make art "in the style of" them—and then churn out passable replicas within moments. Nick Cave, when confronted with a ChatGPT-generated version of a Nick Cave song, described the phenomenon as "replication as travesty . . . a grotesque mockery of what it is to be human."

There is something uniquely humiliating about confronting a bad replica of one's self—and something utterly harrowing about confronting a good one. Both carry the unmistakable shudder of the doppelganger. A shudder that turns into a quake when we realize that it is not just individuals who are being artificially copied, however poorly, but the entirety of human existence. Artificial intelligence is, after all, a mirroring and mimicry machine: we feed in the cumulative words, ideas, and images that our species has managed to amass (and digitize) over its history and these programs mirror back to us something that feels uncannily lifelike. A golem world.

"I'd rather see an ad for cute shoes that I am going to like than see ads for a bunch of ugly stuff I don't want," one student said in an early class. In our discussions, we came to call this the "cute shoes problem" because it encapsulates one of the main reasons why surveillance capitalism and the AI revolution were able to sneak up on us with so little debate. Many of us do appreciate a certain level of automated customization, especially algorithms that suggest music, books, and people who might interest us. And at first, the stakes seemed low: Is it really a big deal if we see ads and suggestions based on our interests and tastes? Or if chatbots help clear our email backlogs?

Yet now we find ourselves neck-deep in a system where, as with my own real-life doppelganger, the stakes are distinctly higher. Personal data, extracted without full knowledge or understanding, is sold to third parties and can influence everything from what loans we are eligible for to what job postings we see—to whether our jobs are replaced by deep learning bots that have gotten shockingly good at impersonating us. And those helpful recommendations and eerie impersonations come from the same algorithms that have led countless people down perilous information tunnels that end in comparing a vaccine app to the Holocaust and may yet end up somewhere far more dangerous. So it turns out that none of it was ever benign—not even the cute shoes.

Listening to undergrads struggle with the implications of their unshakable data trails always makes me feel intensely nostalgic about my pre–cell phone years as a teen and young adult. Looking back, I realize that my friends and I moved through the world like phantoms—our dramas, sex lives, protests, musical tastes, adventures, and fashion choices left virtually no trace behind. They trained no algorithm, were stored in no cloud, and left no history in any cache—save for the occasional cache of bent photos, water-stained journals and letters, or fading graffiti on a bathroom wall. It was unthinkable that anyone but us (and maybe our nosy parents) would have had the slightest interest in the trivia of our young lives. The world was indifferent to us, and we had no idea how lucky we were.

The Faustian bargain of the digital age—free or cheap digital conveniences in exchange for our data—was only ever explained to us after it was already a done deal. And it represents an enormous and radical shift not only in how we live but also, far more importantly, in *what our lives are for.* We are all mine sites now, data mine sites, and despite the intimacy and import of what is being mined, the mining process remains utterly obscure and the mine operators wholly unaccountable.

Remembering this helps me to understand Other Naomi, and the sudden power she has found in terrifying large numbers of people with claims of "tyrannical" vaccine passports with a "CCP-style social credit score system." She is tapping into these barely submerged fears, which are rooted not in fantasy, but reality. Vaccine passports aren't a social credit system, but social media itself kind of is. Those QR codes on our phones aren't putting our lives under constant surveillance, but as all those clever jokes suggest, our phones themselves and many other smart devices are, or at least could.

It is, moreover, extremely dangerous and troubling that corporate platforms can arbitrarily delete users and cut them off from the web of connections they built with their own words, images, and labor over years. When Wolf says that "they start purging your enemies, then they purge you," she's not wrong. Before Elon Musk bought Twitter, progressives in North America had been pretty complacent about this threat because it had mostly been their political adversaries getting booted off platforms. But well before Musk started suspending the accounts of Twitter users who displeased him, the same kinds of power abuses had deplatformed Palestinian human rights activists at the behest of the Israeli government, and advocates for the rights of farmers and religious minorities at the behest of India's Hindu-supremacist government. Yet in North America, raising the alarm about the fact that we have outsourced the management of our critical informational pathways to algorithms run by for-profit companies, working hand in glove with governments, somehow became the terrain of the Bannonite political right, which points to a dangerous ceding of ideological territory.

Establishing a democratic, noncorporate media—through public broadcasting and community access to the airwaves—was once a core progressive demand. Though there are civil liberties groups that still stand up against corporate censorship, as well as civil rights groups that fight for net neutrality, progressives today have not, for the most part, made fighting for a democratic and accountable information sphere a cornerstone of their political agenda. On the contrary, many happily cheered corporate deplatformings—until the same dynamics came for them.

The spread of lies and conspiracies online is now so rampant that it threatens public health and, quite possibly, the survival of representative democracy. The solution to this informational crisis, however, is not to look to tech oligarchs to disappear people we don't like; it's to get serious about demanding an information commons that can be counted upon as a basic civic right. The tech writer and theorist Ben Tarnoff, in his book *Internet for the People*, argues that this is an achievable goal but it must begin with a process of "deprivatization"—putting the tools that have become our public square into the public's hands, under democratic control. "To build a better internet, we need to change how it is owned and organized," Tarnoff writes, adding, "What is at stake is nothing less than the possibility of democracy—a possibility that an internet organized by the profit motive precludes."

It's a reminder that just because something is currently enclosed in a certain kind of financial arrangement does not mean it must forever stay enclosed. History is filled with successful struggles against earlier forms of enclosure—colonial powers were ejected from their onetime colonies; foreign-owned mines and oil fields have been nationalized and put under public control; Indigenous peoples have won legal victories reclaiming sovereign control over their ancestral territories. Unjust ownership structures have been changed before and they can be changed again.

It bears remembering that many of the technologies that form the building blocks of modern tech giants were first developed in the public sector, with public dollars, whether by government agencies or public research universities. These technologies range from the internet itself to GPS and location tracking. In essence, Big Tech has appropriated commonly held tools for private gain, while adopting the discourse of the commons to describe their gated platforms. For instance, when Musk bought Twitter, he described it as "the digital town square where matters vital to the future of humanity are debated."

He was right about that—why then should it be held hostage to the capricious whims of one man? Like decolonial movements of the last century up until the modern day, we could fight to claim back the vital common assets we have lost. Tarnoff's recommendations are less a prescriptive checklist of to-dos than an urgent call for experimentation. There is no silver bullet for deprivatizing the information sphere, but, he argues, the internet can be taken back piece by piece, including through internet service providers owned by communities rather than conglomerates. Tarnoff cautions, however, that this is not something the political class, enmeshed and entwined with Silicon Valley at every level, is going to do on its own: "From the edges to the core, from the neighborhoods to the backbones, making a democratic internet must be the work of a movement."

The trouble, once again, is that the kind of mass movement Tarnoff is describing does not yet exist. And it is inside this vacuum that my doppelganger is currently wreaking havoc. Because Wolf, with her *Black Mirror*–inspired stories about vaccine apps that can "turn off your life," not only validates those latent tech fears but also, along with her new partner Steve Bannon, has something progressives lack: a plan for what to do about it, or at least a facsimile of one. The plan is to push "Five Freedoms" and "no mask" laws wherever you live. The plan is to barge into your local school board meeting, accuse its members of being Nazis, and get elected to take their place. The plan is to stick it to Big Tech by subscribing to new right-wing platforms and "stay ahead of the censors," as Bannon's tagline declares. The plan is to get you to send them money, to join their wars.

The result is a troubling dynamic—one that sits at the heart of our doppelganger culture. Rather than being defined by consistently applied principles—about the right to a democratically controlled public square, say, and to trustworthy information and privacy—we have two warring political camps defining themselves in opposition to whatever the other is saying and doing at any given time. No, these camps are not morally equivalent, but the more people like Wolf and Bannon focus on very real fears of Big Tech—its power to unilaterally remove speech, to abscond with our data, to make digital doubles of us—the more liberals seem to shrug and sneer and treat the whole package of worries like crazy-people stuff. Once an issue is touched by "them," it seems to become oddly untouchable by almost everyone else. And what mainstream liberals ignore and neglect, this emerging alliance lavishes with attention.

All of this helps me to understand my doppelganger—but not in a way I find at all reassuring. Because it means she represents a larger and more dangerous form of mirroring—a mimicking of beliefs and concerns that feeds off progressive failures and silences. And watching Bannon's glee in absorbing Wolf's vaccine passport fantasies into the terrorizing and galvanizing story he tells his listeners daily, I started to wonder what other unaddressed fears and outrages were being exploited in her new home—the place I have come to call the Mirror World.

6

DIAGONAL LINES

"Really?" Avi asks.

It's eleven o'clock on a warm night in early June, and he has walked in on me doing yoga before bed, a nightly practice to help with back pain. When he arrives, I am in Pigeon Pose, breathing into a deep and challenging hip release. And, yes, okay, I am also listening to Steve Bannon's *War Room*. Life has been hectic lately, with the end of the school year and Avi's campaign for federal office heating up, so when else am I supposed to catch up on Other Naomi's flurry of appearances?

My obsession has become a growing gulf between Avi and me. And not just between us—it is intensifying my already deep isolation, cutting me off further from other friends and family. No one I know listens to *War Room*, and I feel increasingly that it is impossible to understand the new shape of politics without listening to it. Still, it has gone pretty far: for days, I have been unable to get the show's rabidly anti-communist theme song out of my head ("Spread the word all through Hong Kong / We will fight till they're all gone / We rejoice when there's no more / Let's take down the CCP").

I pledge then and there to give it a rest, to put this least charming of pandemic hobbies aside. It seems like the right time to reassess anyway. Twitter has just suspended Wolf's account, seemingly permanently. I'm not comfortable with this heavy-handed corporate censorship, but I tell myself that Wolf losing her main public communication tool surely means that she won't be able to get herself (and me) into nearly so much trouble.

"I'll block Twitter," I tell Avi. I promise to spend the summer not only helping more with the campaign but also focusing on our son (still deep in his shark phase) and the rest of our woefully neglected family.

A few weeks later, one year into living on the rock and traveling exactly nowhere, we go east. My father-in-law, Stephen, has had a recurrence of cancer, and this time it is inoperable. He has requested a month with his three children and his four grandkids, and despite his discomfort, he wants to go to his favorite place: Prince Edward Island, a picture-perfect bar of red sand carpeted with potato farms and dotted with lighthouses on the edge of eastern Canada.

This will be good, I tell myself, unpacking shorts and T-shirts into dresser drawers at a crisp, newly built rental house. I resolve to spend my time coming back into my lost self. I will cook healthy and delicious meals. I will meaningfully engage with all members of my family, device-free. Most of all: I will not expend any more of my limited time on earth on Other Naomi. There will be no more books or films about doppelgangers, no more podcasts related to Covid conspiracies, no more Bannon, and definitely no Twitter. I pin a message to my profile declaring that I will be back in September. Insurance against a relapse.

When the island's mandated quarantine is over, and we are free to go outside and gather, the whole extended family is swept up in a wave of happy reconnecting and group logistics. My nephews are new and fascinating people, and my ears have completely lost the knack of sorting through the cross talk of eleven opinionated people sharing a meal. It's delightfully all-consuming, and I suddenly realize that I haven't thought about her in over two weeks. Progress!

Well, barely thought about her. I did have one tangentially related conversation with Michele, my spectacular mother-in-law, about the book of Ruth, which I struck up one bright morning over coffee. Michele has done historical research on Judaism's overlooked female figures, and I was hoping to go a little deeper on the origin story of my/our name.

"It's all about loyalty," Michele says of the biblical story. Ruth's loyalty to Naomi after the deaths of their respective husbands makes her, in the words of Bethlehem's village women, "better . . . than seven sons."

This is a nice message, we agree, even a proto-feminist message, about women's bonds beyond bloodlines. Sort of like the bond between us, which predates my relationship with Avi. In light of the caricatured figure of the hectoring mother-in-law in popular culture, the biblical Naomi is a pretty progressive figure, a good person to be named after.

I have a few minor follow-up questions though. Once in Bethlehem, Naomi, now poor and desperate, does instruct her daughter-in-law to put on perfume; sneak onto the barley threshing floor, where an old, well-off relative, Boaz, is sleeping; and "uncover his feet and lie down." The goal is for this to result in a hookup that will set Ruth and Naomi up for life. After some haggling, it ends in marriage, eventually leading, three generations on, to the birth of King David.

"Naomi does sort of pimp Ruth out to Boaz," I gently point out. "Is that really a nice person to be named after?" Michele pauses. She is eighty-two and sharp as hell. We agree that it's probably best not to impose our values on biblical stories and return to our coffees in someone else's sun-drenched kitchen. (If I did want to impose my values, I might say that Old Testament Naomi was a bit of a hustler, doing what it took to get by in a broken system, protecting her people's future at all costs.)

That was pretty much it for Wolf-adjacent content, and it wasn't even really about Wolf. I preferred to think of it as an impromptu feminist Bible study. Michele did ask what had brought on this curiosity, at which point it would have been rude not to tell her a little bit about my Wolf research. Also, I thought she might have some intel: Michele wrote a popular newspaper column for decades, and I had a vague memory that she met Wolf in the 1990s.

"What was she like, back in the day?" I asked, trying to sound nonchalant.

"Well, I didn't think much of that *Beauty Myth* book; there wasn't much new there. But we were all glad that this pretty young woman was choosing to identify as a feminist."

That made a lot of sense. The 1980s had been a grim slog for second-wave feminists. It must have been a balm to have Wolf come along at the dawn of a new decade and wear the badge as if it were a chic bolero jacket, as was the style back then.

And that was that. Seriously. The whole discussion. It was fleeting, and certainly not a full-blown relapse into my doppelganger's world. That didn't come for at least another week.

Here is how it happened, and I'm not going to sugarcoat it. I was in significant back pain and, because we were on a small island with some of the lowest Covid rates outside New Zealand, I decided I would take my chances and seek professional help.

The appointment was a forty-five-minute drive away, and I set off midmorning, under clear skies on a virtually empty two-lane road banked by sand dunes, red cliffs, and crashing Atlantic waves. As I drove, I realized I was something I had barely been in sixteen months: alone. Alone and surrounded by natural beauty. Elation flooded my body, down to the tips of my fingers clasping the steering wheel.

In that perfect moment, I could have listened to anything. I could have rolled down the windows and filled my ears with the surf and the gulls. I could have blasted Joni Mitchell's "Blue," which I had recently rediscovered thanks to Brandi Carlile's cover. But I didn't do any of that. Instead, I touched the purple podcast app, pulled up Steve Bannon's *War Room*, and read the capsule summary of the most recent episode. It was a speech by Donald Trump, recorded live, in which he announced that he was suing the Big Tech companies for deplatforming him, followed by reaction from . . .

What? Why her?

I scrolled down and saw that I had missed several other recent appearances by my doppelganger while abiding by my no-Wolf diet. I gulped them all, one after another. And that's how I ended up on the side of the road, with my hazards on, late for a much-needed treatment, on my first vacation in two years, scribbling in a tiny red notebook as I tried to transcribe the words coming through my phone's speaker: "black shirts and brown shirts," "Fauci demonic," "petrifying," "your body belongs to the state," "like China's one-child policy and forced sterilization," "geotracking," "evil x2."

This was a full-blown relapse.

In my meager defense, Wolf's elevated status on Bannon's podcast marked a major development in the life of my doppelganger. It's one thing to be invited onto a flagship show of the Trumpian right to freestyle about vaccine passports or to trash Joe Biden—any semi-prominent self-described Democrat would be welcome to pull that stunt. It's quite another to be the person whom Steve Bannon goes to for exclusive reaction to one of the first post–White House speeches by Donald Trump—a man whom the vast majority of Bannon's listeners are utterly convinced is the rightful president of the United States (and whom Wolf had referred to, in her earlier life, as "a horrible human being, an awful person"). It's not just that it sells books and subscriptions to her website. It signals real power—the ability to reach and potentially influence the behavior of millions of people.

A few weeks earlier, when Wolf was kicked off Twitter, many on the platform rejoiced as if she had just been deleted from planet Earth. People dug up screenshots of her most outrageous posts and made little videos of them, set to Celine Dion music, thanking her for the memories. Someone tweeted "Ding dong the witch is dead"—and that was precisely the vibe, at least among progressives. I admit that I felt a combination of relief and emptiness at her ejection. She had caused me so much misery—could her wild ride really be over? Could it possibly be that simple?

What I realized on the side of that road was that it most definitely is not that simple. Bannon used to keep a ticker at the top of his website that claimed to track how many times his show had been downloaded. At around that time, the number was nearing 100 million—that on top of the millions of live feeds he claimed on multiple video and television platforms. Those figures shouldn't be taken at face value, coming as they do from the architect of Trump's shiny tower of "alternative facts." Still, there is no question that Bannon's *War Room* is just that: a nerve center for the far-right presidency in waiting, whether headed by Trump or someone even more dangerous.

"Action! Action! Action!"

That is *War Room*'s mantra. Bannon repeats it often. It appears on a plaque behind his head when he broadcasts. He sends it with the pieces of content he pushes out on Gettr ("the Twitter killer") and in his newsletter (*Daily Command Brief*).

He means it. Unlike Fox News, which, despite its obvious bias, still has the trappings of cable news, *War Room* has built an explicitly activist media platform—or, more precisely, a militarist one. Rather than television's airbrushed talking heads, Bannon cultivates a feeling that his audience is part of a rolling meeting between a commander and his busy field generals, each one reporting back from their various fronts: the Big Steal strategy (challenging the results of the 2020 election); the precinct strategy (putting ideological foot soldiers in place at the local level to prevent the next election from being "stolen"); the school board strategy (challenging "woke" curricula as well as masks and vaccine policies); the "command by negation" strategy (pressuring Republican representatives to deny Biden every possible legislative victory).

The hosts and guests may be talking to one another in that particular moment, but talking is not the point of the show—the point is doing. "Stick around after, I want to talk to you more about this off air," Bannon will often say at the end of a segment, and the audience gets the thrill of feeling that they are eavesdropping on history in the making. Key to the show's appeal is its lack of slickness, underlined by Bannon's trademark personal dishevelment: dark, rumpled doubled-up button-down shirts; chaotic waves of gray hair, rivaling Wolf's for volume; and blotchy face, pointedly shunning the fakery of television makeup. This is a show with no spectators, only proud members of the "War Room posse" or, when Bannon is particularly keyed up, the soldiers in his "cavalry."

If Naomi Wolf was Bannon's go-to guest not just to rail against vaccine mandates but now to live-spin Trump's speeches, that meant she had crossed an entirely new threshold, becoming a full-blown player in this world. Shortly after, Wolf would go so far as to join Trump's class-action lawsuit against Twitter as a co-plaintiff, challenging her own ouster from the platform (though she still claimed to "profoundly" disagree with Trump "ideologically"). It was there, on the side of that road, that I became convinced that whatever was happening with her wasn't just relevant to me because of my admittedly niche doppelganger problem—it was far more serious than that. If someone like her could be shifting alliances so radically, it seemed worth trying to figure out what was driving that transformation—especially because, by then, it was also clear that quite a few prominent liberals and leftists were making a similar "post-left" lurch to the hard right.

Even after following Wolf's antics for years, or rather, after having them follow me, I was taken aback by the decisiveness of this boundary crossing. How did she—a Jewish feminist who wrote a book warning how easily fascism can throttle open societies—rationalize this alliance with Trump and Bannon? How, for that matter, did Bannon—a proud anti-abortion Catholic who was once charged with domestic assault and whose ex-wife told a court that he didn't want their daughters "going to school with Jews"—rationalize teaming up with Wolf? (Bannon pleaded not guilty to the domestic assault charges, which were dismissed after his wife did not show up in court, and he denies the remark about Jews.)

Despite these contradictions, Wolf was not merely a regular guest on Bannon's *War Room*; she was fast becoming one of its most recognizable characters. At the peak of their collaboration, Wolf would appear on *War Room* nearly every single weekday for two weeks. They even partnered up on co-branded "DailyClout *War Room* Pfizer investigations" into various vaccine rabbit holes and packaged them into an e-book. Clearly, neither was letting past principles stand in the way of this union.

What I was trying to figure out was this: What does this unlikeliest of buddy movies say about the ways that Covid has redrawn political maps in country after country, blurring left-right lines and provoking previously apolitical cohorts to take to the streets? What did it have to do with the "freedom fighters" blocking ambulances outside hospitals that required their staff to get vaccinated? Or refusing to believe the results of any elections that didn't go their way? Or denying evidence of Russian war crimes? Or, or, or . . .

A Global Diagonal Meridian

The reshaping of politics that is one of Covid's primary legacies is far bigger than Wolf and Bannon, of course. The hallucinatory period when the pandemic melded with economic upheavals and climate disasters accelerated all manner of strange-bedfellow coalitions, manifesting in large protests first against lockdowns and then against any sensible health measure that would have helped make the lockdowns unnecessary. These new alliances eventually kicked off the self-described Freedom Convoy that shut down Ottawa, the capital city in my own country, for three weeks, and then spread to the United States and Europe, branching out from Covid-related grievances to a more general, amorphous cry for "freedom."

These formations bring together many disparate political and cultural strains: the traditional right; the QAnon conspiratorial hard right; alternative health subcultures usually associated with the green left; a smattering of neo-Nazis; parents (mainly white mothers) angry about a range of things happening and not happening in schools (masks, jabs, all-gender bathrooms, anti-racist books); small-business owners enraged by the often-devastating impacts of Covid controls on their bottom lines, which gave way to rage at everything from inflation to induction stove tops. Significant disagreement exists inside these new convergences—Wolf, for instance, is neither a QAnon cultist nor a neo-Nazi. Yet galvanized by large-platform misinformers like her and Bannon, most seem to agree that the pandemic is a plot by Davos elites to push a reengineered society under the banner of the "Great Reset."

If the claims are coming from the far right, the covert plan is for a green/socialist/Venezuelan/Soros/forced-vaccine dictatorship, while the New Agers warn of a Big Pharma/GMO/biometric-implant/5G/robot-dog/forced-vaccine dictatorship. With the exception of the Covid-related refresh, the conspiracies that are part of this political convergence are not new—most have been around for decades, and some are ancient blood libels. What's new is the force of the magnetic pull with which they are finding one another, self-assembling into what the *Vice* reporter Anna Merlan has termed a "conspiracy singularity."

In Germany, the movement often describes its politics as *Querdenken* (which means lateral, diagonal, or outside-the-box thinking) and it has forged worrying alliances between New Age health obsessives, who are opposed to putting anything impure into their carefully tended bodies, and several neofascist parties, which took up the anti-vaccination battle cry as part of a Covid-era resistance to "hygiene dictatorship." (This was meant to trigger memories of Nazi-era "race hygiene," as if the Nazi atrocity of treating human beings as germs and treating germs as germs was in any way the same thing.) Inspired by the term *Querdenken*, but taking it beyond Germany, William Callison and Quinn Slobodian, both scholars of European politics, describe these emergent political alliances as "diagonalism." They explain: "Born in part from transformations in technology and communication, diagonalists tend to contest conventional monikers of left and right (while generally arcing toward far-right beliefs), to express ambivalence if not cynicism toward parliamentary politics, and to blend convictions about holism and even spirituality with a dogged discourse of individual liberties. At the extreme end, diagonal movements share a conviction that all power is conspiracy."

Despite claims of post-partisanship, it is right-wing, often far-right, political parties around the world that have managed to absorb the unruly passions and energy of diagonalism, folding its Covid-era grievances into preexisting projects opposing "wokeness" and drumming up fears of migrant "invasions." Still, it is important for these movements to present themselves (and to believe themselves to be) ruptures with politics-as-usual; to claim to be something new, beyond traditional left-right poles.

That's why having a few prominent self-identified progressives and/or liberals involved is so critical. Importantly, the role of these progressives is not to renounce the goals of social justice and embrace a hard-right worldview (the journey made by well-known ex-Trotskyists like Irving Kristol in the mid-twentieth century). On the contrary, they must continue to identify as proud members of the left, or devoted liberals, while claiming that it is the movements and tendencies of which they were once part that have betrayed their own ideals, leaving these uniquely courageous individuals politically homeless and in search of new alliances. These exiles from progressivism package themselves not as defectors, but as loyalists—it's their former comrades and colleagues, they claim, who are the imposters, the fakes.

Among several such figures, my doppelganger has become particularly practiced at this maneuver. For instance, when Wolf first started appearing on right-wing media outlets in 2021, her posture was reticent, anything but defiant. She talked about having voted for Biden, stressed that she used to write for *The New York Times* and *The Guardian* and appear on MSNBC, described herself as a liberal "media darling." But now, she said, right-wing shows like Carlson's and Bannon's were the only ones courageous enough to give her a platform.

For their part, every time a fiery right-wing host had Wolf on as a guest, they would indulge in a protracted, ornate windup listing all of her liberal credentials, and professing shock that they could possibly find themselves on the same side. "I never thought I would be talking to you except in a debate format," Tucker Carlson said the first time he had Wolf on. Then, referring to a tweet in which Wolf said she regretted voting for Joe Biden, he added, "I was struck by the bravery it must have taken you to write it—I'm sure you lost friends over it, and for doing this [show]." Wolf smiled wistfully and nodded, accepting the hero's welcome.

When she appeared on the podcast hosted by one of Britain's most vocal climate change deniers and far-right provocateurs, James Delingpole, he began by saying, "This is so unlikely . . . five years ago, the idea that you and I would be breaking bread . . . I sort of bracketed you with the other Naomi—you know, Naomi Klein, Naomi Wolf, what's the difference?" (Insert silent scream from me.) He went on: "And now, here we are. I mean, I think we are allies in a much, much bigger war. And you've been fighting a really good fight, so congratulations." Once again, she drank it in, playing her demure part on these awkward political first dates.

As time went on, and Wolf became more of a fixture, she seemed to relish her new role, eagerly playing the part of the coastal liberal elite that right-wing populists love to hate, even dropping French words into her Steve Bannon appearances. During a segment on France's lockdown rule, she asked, "Whatever happened to '*Liberté, égalité, fraternité*'?"—as if most of his listeners weren't the very same people who changed the name of "French fries" to "freedom fries" after France refused to join George W. Bush's 2003 invasion of Iraq. And the first time she went on his show, she told Bannon, "I spent years thinking you were the devil, no disrespect. Now I'm so happy to have you in the trenches along with other people across the political spectrum fighting for freedom . . . We have to drop those labels immediately in order to come together to fight for our constitution and our freedoms."

That is the key message we are meant to take away from diagonalist politics: the very fact that these unlikely alliances are even occurring, that the people involved are willing to unite in common purpose despite their past differences, is meant to serve as proof that their cause is both urgent and necessary. How else could Wolf rationalize teaming up with Bannon who, along with Trump, normalized a political discourse that dehumanized migrants as monstrous others—rapists, gang members, and disease carriers? This is also why Wolf leans so heavily and continuously on extreme historical analogies—comparing Covid health measures with Nazi rule, with apartheid, with slavery. This kind of rhetorical escalation is required to rationalize her new alliances. If you are fighting "slavery forever" or a modern-day Hitler, everything—including the companion you find yourself in bed with—is a minor detail. It's similar, in many ways, to how evangelical Christians were coaxed by their leaders to set aside the fact that Trump's behavior—the philandering, the alleged sexual assaults, the lying, the cruelty—violated their professed values. To get over all that, they had to cast him, in all seriousness, as the Lord's messy messenger, put on earth to fight God's own doppelganger: the devil. With stakes as high as eternal salvation, what's a little pussy grabbing?

But in the Bannon-Wolf alliance, what is that greater cause, exactly? What is each one getting out of the other?

Klondike Covid

People ask me variations on this question often: What drove her over the edge? What made her lose it so thoroughly? They want a diagnosis, but I, unlike her, am uncomfortable playing doctor. I could offer a kind of equation for leftists and liberals crossing over to the authoritarian right that goes something like: Narcissism(Grandiosity) + Social media addiction + Midlife crisis ÷ Public shaming = Right-wing meltdown. And there would be some truth to that bit of math.

The more I learn about her recent activities, however, the less I am able to accept the premise of these questions. They imply that when she went over the edge, she crashed to the ground. A more accurate description is that Wolf marched over the edge and was promptly caught in the arms of millions of people who accept every one of her extraodinary theories without question, and who appear to adore her. So, while she clearly has lost what I may define as "it," she has found a great deal more—she has found a whole new world.

Feminists of my mother's generation find Wolf's willingness to align herself with the people waging war on women's freedom mystifying. And on one level it is. As recently as 2019, Wolf described her ill-fated book *Outrages* as "a cautionary tale about what happens when the secular state gets the power to enter your bedroom." Now she is in league with the people who stacked the U.S. Supreme Court with wannabe theocrats whose actions are forcing preteens to carry babies against their will. Yet on another level, her actions are a perfect distillation of the values of the attention economy, which have trained so many of us to measure our worth using crude, volume-based matrixes. How many followers? How many likes? Retweets? Shares? Views? Did it trend? These do not measure whether something is right or wrong, good or bad, but simply how much volume, how much traffic, it generates in the ether. And if volume is the name of the game, these crossover stars who find new levels of celebrity on the right aren't lost—they are found.

"Some writers take to drink, others take to audiences," Gore Vidal said back in 1981. Wolf took to audiences, in a way that would have been unimaginable to Vidal, whose heyday predated social media. Wolf grasped the magnitude of the shift to the attention economy earlier than most authors of her generation. She joined Facebook in 2008 and fully embraced its self-publishing potentials, sending long, unedited, frequently fact-free theories into the world and then, when the technology became available, live videos.

Wolf may be a poor researcher, but she is good at the internet. She packages her ideas in listicles for the clickbait age: "Fascist America, in 10 Easy Steps." (Beware Step #10.) "Liberate Our Five Freedoms." Her website, DailyClout, demonstrates Wolf's success in mastering the art of internet monetization: not only collecting attention but turning that attention into money. She takes advertising; sells swag festooned with a stylized wolf logo ("The power is in the pack"); and charges $3.99 a month for a "premium" membership and $9.99 a month for a "pro" one. She also collects donations, despite this being a business, not a charity, and never mind that one of the original points of the site—providing access to draft bills and resolutions—is selling something that is already free and readily available. It's a little like setting up a private toll booth outside a public library, a bold grift.

Seen in this context, the name Wolf chose for her site is telling. Because what Wolf turned into over the past decade is something very specific to our time: a clout chaser. Clout is the values-free currency of the always-online age—both a substitute for hard cash as well as a conduit to it. Clout is a calculus not of what you do, but of how much bulk youness there is in the world. You get clout by playing the victim. You get clout by victimizing others. This is something that is understood by the left and the right. If influence sways, clout squats, taking up space for its own sake.

So if there is a pattern to the many, many conspiracies Wolf has floated in recent years, it is simply this: they were about subjects that were dominating the news and generating heat at the time. Of course none of us who offers analysis on current events as part of our profession is immune to the hot-take hustle. But from Assange to Ebola to ISIS, what Wolf did went well beyond that: by claiming to possess some secret piece of knowledge that she alone had uncovered, and by claiming she was being terribly persecuted by daring to share it, she was able to insert herself in the middle of countless trending cultural conversations. Where there was heat, there was her.

And nothing had ever been nearly so hot, so potentially clout-rich as Covid-19. We all know why. It was global. It was synchronous. We were digitally connected, talking about the same thing for weeks, months, years, and on the same global platforms. As Steven W. Thrasher writes in *The Viral Underclass*, Covid-19 marked "the first viral pandemic also to be experienced via viral stories on social media," creating "a kind of squared virality."

This squared virality meant that if you put out the right kind of pandemic-themed content—flagged with the right mix-and-match of keywords ("Great Reset," "WEF," "Bill Gates," "Fascism," "Fauci," "Pfizer") and headlined with tabloid-style teasers ("The Leaders Colluding to Make Us Powerless," "What They Don't Want You to Know About," "Bill Gates Said WHAT?!?")—you could catch a digital magic-carpet ride that would make all previous experiences of virality seem leaden in comparison. The players know the game: for instance, the viral video *Plandemic* got the Covid conspiracy ball rolling in the early lockdown days, collecting eight million views in its first week. Its director, Mikki Willis, told the *Los Angeles Times*, "We knew the branding was conspiratorial and shocking. Unfortunately, in this age, you kind of have to be that to get people's attention."

Disaster Doppelgangers

This is a twist on the disaster capitalism I have tracked in the midst of earlier shocks. In the past, I have reported on the private companies that descend to profit off desperate needs and fears in the aftermath of hurricanes and wars, selling men with guns and reconstruction services at a high premium. That is old-school disaster capitalism picking our pockets; this is disaster capitalism mining our attention, at a time when attention is arguably our culture's most valuable commodity. Conspiracies have always swirled in times of crisis—but never before have they been a booming industry in their own right. Covid was a "capitalizable conspiracy," as William Callison and Quinn Slobodian put it.

So, in addition to the usual attempts to smuggle in policies that benefit corporate elites at the expense of broader publics, and to directly profiteer off the need for medical equipment and treatments (both phenomena we most certainly have seen during the pandemic), we have also been confronted with a small army of diagonalists peddling over-the-top conspiracy theories about how the whole disaster was manufactured by a shady cabal so that it can bring in their New World Order/eugenicist agenda. I have come to think of this army, which relies so heavily on conjecture and clickbait exaggeration, as disaster doppelgangers, since their highly profitable performances serve to distract from the very real scandals that are right before our eyes and urgently need our attention.

The economic incentives for this kind of online content go a long way toward explaining the breed of public figure who seems to have turned into a different kind of person during that first Covid year—more manic; angrier; more willing to burn bridges, to make outlandish claims, and to share unreliable and poorly sourced information if it was likely to be carried by a strong current in the digital ocean. I could make a list, but I'm sure you are making your own in your head right now: "I used to really trust [X]. What has happened to them? It's as if they had an alter ego and they have succumbed to it completely."

Addiction is likely the most relevant lens for understanding these jarring personality transformations. In Robert Louis Stevenson's classic of doppelganger literature, *The Strange Case of Dr. Jekyll and Mr. Hyde*, Dr. Henry Jekyll turns back and forth into the murderous Edward Hyde when he drinks a mysterious serum; but over time, the serum stops working and the original Dr. Jekyll gets lost completely. When I look at the behavior over the past few years of several people I once knew and whose company and work I once enjoyed, it's obvious that they are swilling a dopamine-releasing serum that has turned them, perhaps permanently, into digital-age versions of Mr. Hyde. I feel certain that my doppelganger is familiar with this particular cautionary tale because of yet another uncanny detail I came across on this journey: in 1995, her father, Leonard Wolf, published *The Essential Dr. Jekyll & Mr. Hyde: The Definitive Annotated Edition of Robert Louis Stevenson's Classic Novel*, which billed itself as "the most comprehensive edition" of "Robert Louis Stevenson's classic tale of duality," containing "everything you ever wanted to know about literature's most famous split personality."

Yet even if Wolf had reason to be wary of the dangers of getting hooked on digital dopamine, few had more to gain from the highs it offered in the pandemic period than her—because few had experienced a clout-crash like the one she had after that unbearable BBC interview in 2019. If you want an origin story, an event when Wolf's future flip to the pseudo-populist right was locked in, it was probably that moment, live on the BBC, getting caught—and then getting shamed, getting mocked, and getting pulped. Rosie Boycott, a British feminist who knew Wolf from her *Beauty Myth* days, observed that after the *Outrages* debacle, there would be no return to the liberal intelligentsia, so "she had to find a new world to fit into where facts don't matter and that's the world she has gone to. Of course, she would become a superstar within it."

The Opposite of Canceled

This is the irony of liberal Twitter celebrating Wolf's seeming disappearance (at least until Musk welcomed her back). Since most liberals and leftists don't watch or listen to Bannon, or the other shows where she has become a regular, they thought she had evaporated as a cause for concern.

"RIP."

"Death recorded."

This is a bit like kids who think the world disappears when they close their eyes. Because Wolf is very far from banished from the public sphere: thanks to Bannon and Carlson, she has a brighter spotlight and a larger platform now than at any other point since her glory days in the 1990s.

Yet the widespread belief in her irrelevance got me wondering if this thing so often referred to as cancel culture is partly a result of the way these platforms have programmed us with their tools. It's been years since I blocked anyone on Twitter, but I mute pretty freely—as soon as I see a bad-faith attack, or notice someone whose posts are reliably putting me in a foul mood, I click "mute." It's satisfying and feels a little like self-determination on platforms where everything else is determined by others. But I am also unsettled by the ease with which we can turn off other humans. I fear that there is something habit-forming about making other people disappear with a keystroke. (Just as there is surely something habit-forming in the sadistic pleasure that comes from being part of a pack that drives someone off a platform for good.)

Once we have personally made people disappear—poof! problem gone!—it may be easier to accept that the tech companies can do the same and eject people with an automated message. It may even be easier to do the same in our real-world relationships, which clearly happened to Other Naomi. Wolf has published thousands of words detailing the family members, neighbors, and friends who effectively deleted her over her Covid antics, including a best friend who "left the country without having said goodbye" and "the friend whose daughter had a baby, and who would not let me indoors to see the child" and "the friend who said he did not sit indoors with unvaccinated people."

When people are ejected in these ways from our social networks—whether online or in our daily lives—they can genuinely seem to have disappeared, to have been muted for real. But that is very far from the truth. When someone is pushed out of progressive conversations or communities because they said or did something hurtful or ignorant, or questioned an identity orthodoxy, or got too successful too fast and was deemed due for a takedown, their absence is frequently met with celebration, as Wolf's exile from Twitter was. But these people don't disappear just because we can no longer see them. They go somewhere else. And many of them go to the Mirror World: a world uncannily like our own, but quite obviously warped.

Kicked off Twitter? Sign up for the copycat site Gettr, the right-wing Twitter rival started by the former Trump aide Jason Miller: "Unlike the Silicon Valley oligarchs, Gettr will NEVER sell your data." (Wolf has nearly 200,000 followers there, more than on Twitter before she got booted.)

Censored by YouTube? Get an account on Rumble.

Shadow banned on Instagram? Try Parler. "Speak freely," the company urges, on "the premier social media app guided by the First Amendment."

Did GoFundMe refuse to distribute the money you raised to support your favorite Freedom Convoy, claiming the funds would be used to support violence and harassment? Don't worry, GiveSendGo, "The #1 Free Christian Fundraising Site," will distribute the cash, along with a prayer, no questions asked.

Bannon is even selling his own currency, starting with the "FJB coin"; the initials stand, of course, for "Fuck Joe Biden." Because, he says, you can't trust the U.S. currency anymore, the Democrats have devalued it, and it's "crushing you every day—that's why you have to have alternatives."

Almost everyone I talk to these days seems to be losing people to the Mirror World. People who were familiar but have somehow become alien, leaving us with that unsettled, uncanny feeling.

"I can't talk to my sister anymore." "My mother has gone down the rabbit hole." "I am trying to figure out how to get my grandmother off Facebook." "He used to be my hero. Now every conversation ends in a screaming match."

What happened to them?

When looking at the Mirror World, it can seem obvious that millions of people have given themselves over to fantasy, to make-believe, to play-acting. The trickier thing, the uncanny thing, really, is that's what they see when they look at us. They say we live in a "clown world," are stuck in "the matrix" of "groupthink," are suffering from a form of collective hysteria called "mass formation psychosis" (a made-up term). The point is that on either side of the reflective glass, we are not having disagreements about differing interpretations of reality—we are having disagreements about who is in reality and who is in a simulation. Curtis Yarvin, a house intellectual of the Bannon-esque right, says, "My job . . . is to wake people up from the Truman Show." Naomi Wolf says that kids who wear masks in school turn into spooky, ghostlike creatures "becalmed . . . like Stepford kids."

This Stepford theme is one she returns to often. In July 2022, Wolf went on a right-wing podcast carried by something called *Today's News Talk* and shared what she described as her "latest thinking." She had noticed that when she went into New York City, where the vast majority of the population has been vaccinated, the people felt . . . different. In fact, it was as if they were not people at all.

"You can't pick up human energy in the same way, like the energy field is just almost not there, it's like people are holograms . . . It's like a city of ghosts now, you're there, you see them, but you can't *feel* them." And she had noticed something even more bizarre: "People [who are vaccinated] have no scent anymore. You can't smell them. I'm not saying like, they don't smell bad or they don't smell—like I'm not talking about deodorant. I'm saying they don't smell like there's a human being in the room, and they don't *feel* like there's a human being in the room."

This, she explained to the host, was all due to the "lipid nanoparticles" in the mRNA vaccines, since they "go into the brain, they go into the heart, and they kind of gum it up." Perhaps even the "wavelength which is love" was experiencing this "gumming up . . . dialing down its ability to transmit."

She concluded, "That's how these lipid nanoparticles work."

That is not how lipid nanoparticles work. It is not how vaccines work. It is not how anything works. Also, and I can't quite believe I am typing these words, *vaccinated people still smell like humans*. Perhaps Wolf had Covid herself and her own sense of smell was compromised, as has been the case for many long Covid sufferers. And yet the host confessed that she also had noticed that vaccinated people seemed like ghosts. She was so glad that Wolf had the courage to put it into words!

This, obviously, is gonzo stuff, the kind of thing that makes me feel smug and superior, like those cell phone jokes. But here, once again, is the trouble: many of Wolf's words, however untethered from reality, tap into something true. Because there is a lifelessness and anomie to modern cities, and it did deepen during the pandemic—there is a way in which many of us feel we are indeed becoming less alive, less present, lonelier. It's not the vaccine that has done this; it's the stress and the speed and the screens and the anxieties that are all by-products of capitalism in its necro-techno phase. But if one side is calling this fine and normal and the other is calling it "inhuman," it should not be surprising that the latter holds some powerful allure.

In my doppelganger studies, I have learned that there is a real medical syndrome called Capgras delusion. Those who suffer from it become convinced that people in their lives—spouses, children, friends—have been replaced by replicas or doppelgangers. According to the film historian Paul Meehan, the discovery of the syndrome likely inspired sci-fi classics like *Invasion of the Body Snatchers* and *The Stepford Wives*. But what is it called when a society divides into two warring factions, both of which are convinced that the other has been replaced by doppelgangers? Is there a syndrome for that? Is there a solution?

To return to the original question: What is Wolf getting out of her alliance with Bannon and from her new life in the Mirror World? Everything. She is getting everything she once had and lost—attention, respect, money, power. Just through a warped mirror. In Milton's *Paradise Lost*, Lucifer, a fallen angel, thought it "better to reign in Hell, than serve in Heaven." My doppelganger may well still think Bannon is the devil, but perhaps she thinks it's better to serve by his side than to keep getting mocked in a place that sells itself as heavenly but that we all know is plenty hellish in its own right.

What about Bannon? What is he getting out of diagonal alliances with people like Wolf? What does she have that he needs? What, moreover, was he getting out of Covid and all the conspiracies swirling around it, sinister stories that now frame his entire show (which used to be called *War Room* but since 2020 has been branded *War Room: Pandemic*). Bannon isn't in it for clout, which he has plenty of, at least not for its own sake. He has an endgame, and what was becoming clear to me was that, within it, my doppelganger had an absolutely critical role to play.

7

MAGA'S PLUS-ONE

When I was a kid, I learned more than I probably should have about the nitty-gritty of giving birth. My father, Michael Klein, was a family doctor and pediatrician, and, in addition to delivering hundreds of babies, he worked as a research scientist at McGill University, where he ran large randomized control trials across Montreal's hospitals. The studies measured the impact of various kinds of interventions on health outcomes for mothers and babies—inductions, epidurals, forceps, episiotomies, cesareans. When data came in that was particularly striking, he could not keep the results to himself, which meant that I knew about postnatal incontinence and vaginal tearing before I hit puberty—and very much wished that I did not.

There were other distressing details as well. He and his colleagues trained medical residents, and one evening in the late 1970s, when I was about eight years old, he came home bubbling with excitement about an innovation they had installed in a couple of the examination rooms: one-way glass. Before, he explained, he and the other doctors had needed to hover over the residents' shoulders to make sure they were providing patients with the right kind of care, which tended to make everyone self-conscious, resident and patient alike. Now the patients, including pregnant women, could have one-on-one consultations with the resident.

But there would be something in the room that looked like a mirror, as well as a microphone. My father, or one of the other staff doctors, would sit in a small room next door watching it all through one-way glass, ready to intervene if necessary.

"But what about the patients? Do they know you are there?"

My father assured me that they did. Well, sort of.

"We explain to all our patients that they are in a teaching hospital and may be observed. And if they ever want more privacy, they can request it."

I was not reassured, not one bit. All I could think of was those poor women with their big bellies in their flimsy robes, watched like rats in a cage. To this day, I can't go to a doctor's office without scanning for fake mirrors and wondering who is lurking on the other side.

Lately, I also think about that one-way glass when I am listening to or watching Steve Bannon.

"Listening to Steve Bannon? Why would you do that?!?"

That is the response I get most frequently when I mention something I've heard or seen on his show. "How can you stand to hear his voice? See his face?"

Because, like the doctors watching patients in those exam rooms, he can see us.

One-Way Glass

Bannon is hardly ignored in the liberal media. He gets lots of attention, but mainly the reporting has focused on the various ways he is using his large media platform to intervene in the U.S. electoral process. Since Bannon is one of the primary pushers of the Big Lie that Trump won the 2020 election and was betrayed by Republican representatives and operatives who refused to overturn Biden's victory, many of his listeners have been organizing to make sure that, next time, they will have thousands of foot soldiers in place, at the precinct level, who will refuse to certify another election win by the Democrats. And, of course, we've heard a lot about Bannon's decision to defy a subpoena from the House probe into the storming of the U.S. Capitol on January 6, 2021, for which he could well face jail time.

All of that is important. But interfering in elections is only a fraction of what Bannon is up to. Just as important are the ways he is trying to actually win elections. The precinct strategy is the backup plan in case the winning strategy fails. But the winning strategy is designed to succeed, at least enough to put an election within the margin that the precinct strategy can, with any kind of plausibility, steal.

When I started to listen to Bannon's show, I would tune in to Wolf's interviews and skip everything before and after. But then I would hear Bannon hype upcoming segments, and I started to hang in and listen to those as well, out of curiosity. The next thing I knew I was just listening to the show, whether she was on or not, curious to know how it would cover major events.

The more I listened to him, the more I began to feel that Bannon's deepest skill is in constructing and expanding the various reflective surfaces in the Mirror World. And not just the dodgy coins but, much more dangerously, the mirror arguments and mirror political agenda carefully designed to repel arguments deployed by his adversaries. Some of this is standard political fare: Democrats talk about the Big Lie (the idea that Trump won the election); Bannon talks about the Big Steal (the idea that Biden stole it). Democrats talk about how Trump fomented the January 6 insurrection; Bannon says Democrats enabled rioters to burn down cities during the 2020 racial justice uprisings. Democrats are scandalized that Trump wouldn't recognize the legitimate election results; Bannon is scandalized that Democrats never recognized Trump as a legitimate president. In the Mirror World, there is a copycat story and answer for everything, often with very similar key words.

This builds on Trump's signature counterpunch move, honed on the campaign trail. Whatever he was accused of, he punched back with a claim that his opponent was guilty of the same thing—corruption, lying, foreign collusion—only worse. Bannon's fingerprints were all over that strategy, most infamously after Trump was caught on tape bragging about sexual assault. Hours before he was set to debate Hillary Clinton, Trump held a press conference with a lineup of women who had accused

Bill Clinton of a range of sexual crimes. Bannon, then Trump's campaign manager, could be seen smirking on the sidelines, as if thoroughly enjoying the show. Mirroring, deflection, and projection all work well, especially when you've got a point.

Vladimir Putin, too, is a master at mirroring, and has been since the early days of his career in politics. Throughout Russia's illegal invasion and occupation of Ukraine, Putin would accuse the Ukrainian government of the precise crimes he was busily committing, or considering committing, himself. When, in October 2022, Russia accused Ukraine of being about to set off a dirty bomb in its own territory and then pin the blame on Russia, Ned Price, a State Department spokesman, said it was part of a pattern of "mirror imaging," adding, "The Russians have accused the Ukrainians, the Russians have accused other countries, of what it itself was planning." And yet, if Putin was able to sell these upside-down claims to many, it's partly because the U.S. government consistently does this kind of mirror imaging itself, feigning outrage over Russian interference in U.S. elections with no concern for the irony that its intelligence operatives have meddled in elections and helped overthrow democratically elected governments the world over since the 1950s, from Iran to Chile to Honduras—and let's not forget the gloves-off U.S. interference in post-Soviet Russia to back Boris Yeltsin, who passed the baton on to none other than Putin.

Bannon has other, more unsettling mirror tricks. These relate to the way he latched onto legitimate fears of surveillance and Big Tech, and the way those surveillance fears were going largely unaddressed in liberal circles. That is far from the only liberal failing on which he has pounced.

Reverse Marionettes

Like most of us, I don't know where the Covid-19 virus originated—whether a wet market in Wuhan, or the Wuhan Institute of Virology's Biosafety Level 4 lab, or somewhere else entirely. But I do realize, in retrospect, that I was too quick to take the official story—that it came from a wet market where wild animals were sold—at face value. If I'm honest,

I accepted it because it served my own motivated reasoning and reinforced my worldview: the pandemic was a little less frightening to me if it was yet another example of humans overstressing nature and getting bitten on the ass for it. Then, as time went on, and the "lab leak theory" became a key talking point from people like Wolf and Bannon in the Mirror World, where it was mixed with baseless claims about bioweapons, along with plenty of anti-Asian racism, there seemed to be further reason not to take another look at the facts. Even though more and more facts and documents were piling up that supported a serious consideration of the lab leak hypothesis, most liberals and leftists didn't bother looking for months because we didn't want to be like *them*, in the same way that I didn't want to be like *her*. In an odd way, their over-the-top conspiracies fed our overcredulity; their "question everything" led to many of us not questioning enough.

Similarly, questions about the safety of brand-new vaccines for people who are pregnant or considering getting pregnant could have been treated far more respectfully than they were. Rather than commentators summarily shutting down questions as frivolous or nutty, there should have been ample room in public debates and reliable media for concerns about how the vaccines would impact reproductive health. These should have called on medical experts in fertility and pregnancy to explain the vaccine research methods, along with the special vulnerabilities to Covid during pregnancy, when immune systems are particularly weak. Because it's perfectly reasonable to worry about a vaccine for a novel virus when you are pregnant or thinking of becoming pregnant—I worried about eating soft cheese when I was pregnant. Moreover, plenty of people, pregnant and not, have good reasons not to trust both Big Pharma and Big Government, let alone the two acting in coordination. In an era when whole cities like Flint, Michigan, have had their water poisoned; when gas companies tell you that fracking is safe, never mind the earthquakes and flammable tap water; when Monsanto lobbies ceaselessly against attempts to ban its herbicide Roundup despite it having been credibly linked with cancer; and when Big Pharma peddled the drugs that set off the opioid crisis, it is entirely rational to be skeptical toward monopolistic power. Johnson & Johnson, one of the major vaccine makers, not only is caught up in the opioid lawsuits but also has been ordered to pay out billions in legal settlements in recent years over alleged harm caused by several of its prescription medications and even its ubiquitous talcum powder (found to have contained asbestos). Against this backdrop, and given the lack of debate and allowable questioning of the vaccines in many progressive spaces, it's no surprise that so many went off to "do their own research"—finding my doppelganger, and many more like her, waiting with their wild claims about vaccine shedding and mass infertility.

It wasn't only the fertility concerns that were dismissed. There has been a persistent reticence at most serious news outlets to provide anything more than sporadic coverage of adverse reactions to Covid vaccines, whether rare cases of heart inflammation among teenage boys and young men after receiving the original mRNA shots, a phenomenon being monitored by the U.S. Centers for Disease Control, or a possible small uptick in strokes among seniors who received the bivalent Covid-19 vaccine made by Pfizer and BioNTech, a concern flagged by the CDC in early 2023. There are risks to every vaccine (and indeed any medical procedure or medication) and these reports of harmful reactions, even if confirmed, in no way negate the value or importance of getting vaccinated: Covid itself still represented a far more significant health risk for the population at large.

This could have been easily explained by medical experts skilled in helping the public weigh the pros and cons of health decisions. Many media outlets, however, seemed gripped by the fear that anything more than a passing report on possible risks would damage vaccine uptake and provide fodder for the conspiracy crowd. Except the opposite turned out to be true: without easy access to reliable, in-depth information about vaccine risks, rumors about friends of friends falling ill or dropping dead after getting "the jab" coursed through the digital grapevine. A door was left wide open for my doppelganger and other attention-economy hustlers to position themselves as fearless medical investigators, combing through raw vaccine trial data and supposedly suppressed CDC reports that people without medical degrees generally lack the expertise to interpret. Of course that didn't stop them from cherry-picking every self-reported claim or actual negative reaction to support their incessant cries that a vaccine "genocide" was underway and being covered up by the Big Pharma–funded lackeys in the lamestream media.

This is, once again, transparent projection: in April 2022, researchers estimated that a quarter of the one million Americans deaths from Covid-19 "could have been prevented with primary series vaccination." A quarter of a million people dead who could have been saved had they gotten the shots. The responsibility for that catastrophic loss rests, in significant part, with the people who have spread dangerous lies about vaccines that, while not risk-free, are remarkably safe and effective at reducing Covid's severity. Still, we should probably acknowledge that the decision at many media outlets to downplay or outright ignore rare adverse vaccine reactions may have helped drive people to shoddier sources. When editors and journalists steer clear of important topics for fear that their audiences can't cope with complex truths, it doesn't throttle conspiracies—it fuels them.

The debates about the trade-offs of closing schools for in-person learning suffered under similar polarized logics. There is no doubt that there have been points when schools and businesses needed to be shut down—but where were the debates about why shopping malls and casinos were allowed to stay open in many of those same periods? After the initial, unavoidably chaotic lockdown period in the spring of 2020, we should have paid more attention to the toll of online learning: the terrible equity impacts on lower-income families who didn't have the tech; the way it left out many students with developmental disabilities who needed in-person supports; the way it made it impossible for single parents to work outside the home and often inside it, with devastating effects for mothers in particular; the mental health impacts that social isolation was having on countless young people.

The solution was not to fling open school doors where the virus was still surging and before vaccines had been rolled out. But where were the more spacious discussions about how to reimagine public schools so that they could be safer despite the virus—with smaller classrooms, more teachers and teacher's aides, better ventilation, and more outdoor learning? We knew early on that teens and young adults were facing a mental health crisis amid the lockdowns—so why didn't we invest in outdoor conservation and recreation programs that could have pried them away from their screens, put them in communities of other young people, generated meaningful work for our ailing planet, and lifted their spirits all at the same time?

Stuck in the binary of lock down versus open up, we failed to consider so many options during the first years that we lived with the virus, and there were so many debates we didn't have. Faced with the torrent of lies coming from the conspiratorial right, many liberals and progressives opted to simply defend status quo measures, despite the fact that we could, and should, have demanded far more.

It is as if when something becomes an issue in the Mirror World, it automatically ceases to matter everywhere else. This has happened on so many issues that I sometimes feel as if we are tethered to each other as reverse marionettes: their arm goes up, ours goes down. We kick, they hug.

There are also uncomfortable ways we have begun to imitate each other. We who complied with the public health measures judged those who did not for their refusal to put the well-being of the immunocompromised ahead of their own convenience, and for their indifference to the huge sacrifices made by health-care workers as unvaccinated people filled up the Covid wards. How could they be so heartless? So willing to rank human life as more or less worthy of protection and care? And yet when unvaccinated people became ill with Covid, many of the people who claimed to have been appalled by their callousness talked about how maybe they didn't deserve health care, or told bad jokes (which were not always jokes) about how perhaps Covid would rid the world of stupid people, or went as far as French president Emmanuel Macron, who said that unvaccinated people were not full citizens. We defined ourselves against each other and yet were somehow becoming ever more alike, willing to declare each other non-people.

How did we cede so much territory? Become so reactive?

After months of listening to Bannon, I can say this with great certainty: While most of us who oppose his political project choose not to see him, he is watching us closely. The issues we are abandoning, the debates we aren't having, the people we are insulting and discarding. He is watching all of it, and he is stitching together a political agenda out of it, a warped mirror agenda that he is convinced is the ticket to the next wave of electoral victories—it's an agenda too few on our side of the glass have tried to comprehend. Bannon calls it "MAGA Plus"—a supersizing, as he sees it, of Trump's original "Make America Great Again" coalition, and it's rapidly being picked up and adopted outside the United States as well.

Steve Bannon, regardless of whatever else he may be, is first and foremost a strategist. And he has a knack for identifying issues that are the natural territory of his opponents but that they have neglected or betrayed, leaving themselves vulnerable to having parts of their base wooed away. This is what he helped Trump do in 2016. He knew that a large sector of unionized blue-collar workers felt betrayed by corporate Democrats who had signed trade deals that accelerated factory closures in the 1990s, and that their anger deepened when the party bailed out banks instead of workers and homeowners after the 2008 crash. He paid close attention to the ways Occupy Wall Street was dismissed and then crushed, and to how Bernie Sanders, whose left-populist 2016 presidential campaign grew out of that movement, faced all kinds of dirty tricks from the Democratic Party establishment as it closed ranks around Hillary Clinton. Bannon saw an opportunity to peel away a portion of the male unionized workforce that had always voted for Democrats—most of it white, but not all of it. Bannon crafted a campaign message out of the betrayals of his rivals: Trump would be a new kind of Republican, one who would stand up to Wall Street, shred corporate trade deals, close the border to supposedly job-stealing immigrants, and end foreign wars—moreover, unlike Republicans before, he pledged to protect social programs like Medicare and Social Security. This was the original MAGA promise.

Of course, it was a bait and switch—Trump filled his administration with former Wall Street executives, made mostly minor changes to trade policy, escalated tensions abroad, and lavished the rich with tax cuts. Of his populist campaign rhetoric, all that really survived was the race baiting—against immigrants, Muslims, Black Lives Matter protesters, and anything having to do with China. It was enough to hold on to his base, but not enough to win reelection, certainly not after his murderous mismanagement of Covid-19.

At the time my doppelganger started appearing on *War Room*, less than three months into the Biden presidency, Bannon was getting serious about sculpting his new MAGA Plus coalition. It was in this context that he recognized Wolf's "slavery forever" message about vaccine passports as a potentially potent crossover issue. Other Naomi's surveillance warnings, regardless of how divorced they were from the reality of the apps, were generating deep passion among a sizable number of people who were concerned about privacy and surveillance but were being dismissed by establishment liberals in politics and media. That's Bannon's kind of issue: ripe for the picking.

He quickly folded the vaccine apps into a basket of issues he calls "Big Tech Warfare," a category that includes not only familiar complaints about social media companies suspending the accounts of high-profile conservatives but also more obscure and even esoteric concerns. For instance, Bannon has a dedicated "transhumanism" correspondent whose sole role appears to be to scare listeners with accounts of the many ways that technology companies dream of an "upgraded" humanity aided by implants, robotics, and gene splicing. Once again, Bannon has identified a neglected issue with cross-partisan appeal: many leftists are concerned about the dehumanizing impacts of tech on workers treated as extensions of machines (I know I am), not to mention the dystopian possibilities of a future in which the rich can buy genetic upgrades for themselves and their kids. Many conservatives, meanwhile, oppose this kind of techno fetishism for different reasons; they see it as an affront to God's plan.

Bannon recognized similar neglect happening with regard to Big Pharma. Drug company price gouging and profiteering have traditionally been the purview of the left; they're the kind of thing Bernie Sanders rails against. But aside from some grumbling, there was weak resistance among progressives to the way vaccine manufacturers were profiteering from the pandemic, and so Bannon became the one taking on Big Pharma's greed—but, once again, via unfounded conspiracy theories rather than the real scandals.

Bannon sometimes plays audio montages of MSNBC and CNN

shows being "brought to you by Pfizer"—the clear implication being that they cannot be trusted because they are in the pay of these companies. It's rule "by the wealthy, for the wealthy—against you," he says. "Until you wake up." When he does this, it strikes me that he sounds like Noam Chomsky. Or Chris Smalls, the Amazon Labor Union leader known for his EAT THE RICH jacket. Or, for that matter, me. But, as always in the Mirror World, nothing is as it seems.

There are many rising stars on the right who follow a similar playbook. Flush with dollars from tech oligarchs like Peter Thiel, and endorsed by Trump, they promise a mix-and-match of bringing back factory jobs that pay family-supporting wages, building the border wall, fighting the toxic drug supply, liberating speech from Big Tech, and banning "woke" curricula. Among those building careers around versions of this platform in the United States are JD Vance in Ohio, Josh Hawley in Missouri, and Kari Lake, who narrowly lost her bid to become governor of Arizona (and claimed, of course, that the election was stolen). Very similar versions of electoral diagonalism have taken root in countries around the world, from Sweden to Brazil.

I'm not surprised that these messages are resonating. For years I was part of internationalist left movements that protested outside meetings of the World Trade Organization, the World Economic Forum in Davos, G8 summits, and the International Monetary Fund for their roles in undermining democracies and advancing the interests of transnational capital; in the United States, we called out both major parties for being beholden to corporate donors and serving the rich rather than the people who voted them into office. This was the energy behind Occupy Wall Street, and then behind Bernie, and that coursed through various battles against new oil and gas projects. But our movement never won power.

And now our critiques of oligarchic rule are being fully absorbed by the hard right and turned into dark doppelgangers of themselves. The structural critiques of capitalism are gone, and in their place are discombobulated conspiracies that somehow frame deregulated capitalism as communism in disguise. This trend is perfectly distilled by Giorgia Meloni, who became Italy's first female prime minister in October 2022 and is leader of the Fratelli d'Italia (Brothers of Italy), which has deep fascist roots in the country. An early partner in Steve Bannon's international populist project, Meloni threads her speeches with pop-culture references and rails against a system that reduces everyone to consumers. She also declared, in a supposed rebuke to "woke" ideology, that "I am a woman, I am a mother, I am Italian, I am Christian."

Watching her meteoric rise, I was reminded of how different Italy was in the summer of 2001, when the alter-globalization movement reached its highest point, drawing hundreds of thousands of people to the streets of Genoa during a G8 summit to protest corporate attacks on democracy and culture, and the effects of rampant consumerism. That movement came from the left—young Italians, alongside farmers and trade unionists, defended labor rights as well as migrant rights, while taking pride in their country's distinct culture. But in a pattern that repeated itself in many countries, left-wing parties lost their confidence after the September 11 attacks and attendant security crackdowns, and the legacy of that surrender is obvious: today it is Meloni denouncing a system in which everyone is reduced to being "perfect consumer slaves"—only instead of offering an analysis of capital, a system that must enclose all aspects of life inside the market in order to mine them as new profit centers, she blames trans people, immigrants, secularists, internationalism, and the left for a hollowness at the core of modernity. And while she rails against the "big financial speculators," she has no policies to rein them in, only attacks on Italy's meager unemployment protections.

Bannon isn't offering his listeners any real alternative to the corporate predation he rails against, either—he's just fleecing them in more small-time ways, telling them to buy precious metals and FJB coins and disaster-ready meals, as well as towels from his main sponsor, MyPillow. ("The *War Room* is a cash machine because it costs nothing to produce," he told *The Atlantic*.) He adopts many of the arguments of what was once a robust anti-war left to oppose ballooning U.S. military spending in Ukraine, accusing the "cartel" ruling Washington of being in the pocket of "the military-industrial complex"—and then does everything he can to aim that same sprawling complex directly at China, a surefire recipe for World War III. Still, you can't blame a strategist for being strategic. And it's highly strategic to pick up the resonant issues that your opponents have carelessly left unattended.

To return to an earlier theme, corporate branding offers some useful tools for understanding the dynamic. Under trademark law, a brand that is not actively being used can be deemed dormant and thus fair game for another party to usurp. I started to feel that what had been happening to me, with Other Naomi, has happened to the left much more broadly—with Bannon and Vance and Meloni and others. Issues that we had once championed had gone dormant in a great many spaces. And now they were being usurped, taken over by their twisted doubles in the Mirror World. If the arrival of one's doppelganger is a message that something needs attending to, it feels like this flashing message is something to which a great many of us need to attend.

A Theater of Inclusion

As Bannon gazes through the one-way glass, he is not only learning what issues his opponents are neglecting and ignoring, and finding fertile new territories to claim as his own, or at least pretend to. He is also taking note of more subtle failings—the way issues are discussed, the way disagreements are negotiated, the way people are treated by their friends and comrades. Through the one-way glass, he is studying all our hypocrisies and inconsistencies so that he can make a show of doing the exact opposite.

Speaking of the movements I know something about, I can say this: On the democratic socialist left, we favor social policies that are inclusive and caring—universal public health care, well-funded public schools, decarceration, and rights for migrants. But left movements often *behave* in ways that are neither inclusive nor caring. And in contrast to Bannon's courting of disaffected Democrats, we also don't put enough thought into how to build alliances with people who aren't already in our movements. Sure, we pay lip service to reaching out, but in practice most of us (even many who claim to be staunchly anti-police) spend a lot of time policing our movements' borders, turning on people who see themselves as on our side, making our ranks smaller, not larger.

And there is something else that I have noticed while listening to Bannon—he sticks, fairly judiciously, to the issues where there is the most common ground: hating Biden, rejecting vaccines, bashing Big Tech, fearmongering about migrants, casting doubt on election results. He skates lightly over more traditionally conservative issues that he may care about but that are likely to alienate some of his newfound friends, including abortion and gun rights. He doesn't ignore them, but they don't take up nearly as much airtime as one might expect.

This, once again, is the opposite of what happens on large parts of the left. When we have differences, we tend to focus on them obsessively, finding as many opportunities as possible to break apart. Important disagreements need to be hashed out, and many conflicts that arise in progressive spaces are over behaviors that, when unchallenged, make those spaces unwelcoming or dangerous for the people they target. But it's not a great secret that plenty of people routinely go too far, turning minor language infractions into major crimes, while adopting a discourse that is so complex and jargon-laden that people outside university settings often find it off-putting—or straight-up absurd. ("Speak in the vernacular," the radical historian Mike Davis once pleaded with young organizers. "The moral urgency of change acquires its greatest grandeur when expressed in shared language.")

Moreover, when entire categories of people are reduced to their race and gender, and labeled "privileged," there is little room to confront the myriad ways that working-class white men and women are abused under our predatory capitalist order, with left-wing movements losing many opportunities for alliances that would make us stronger and more powerful. All of this is highly unstrategic, because whichever groups and individuals we kick to the curb, the Mirror World is there, waiting to catch them, praise their courage, and offer a sympathetic ear.

Bannon's signature move is to reach out to anyone who has recently been exiled by the left or pilloried by *The New York Times* and offer them a platform. For instance, after one such takedown, he handed an entire episode over to Robert F. Kennedy Jr. to spread his anti-vaccination gospel. Bannon was solicitous to the point of mawkish, praising the Kennedy family's long history of public service and devotion to the poor. This, of course, was a preview for RFK's presidential primary run. Bannon was also making an unsubtle point. He was saying that, unlike those liberals, who regard the people who listen to *War Room* as "deplorables" and as subhumans, he can have polite—even generous—conversations across partisan divides, and his posse will never cancel him for it.

Bannon, who has done as much as anyone in contemporary times to unleash the floodgates of xenophobic hate in the United States, has even begun to adopt the language of "othering" to describe how liberals treat his listeners. This is key, he says, to why he has been forced to build the Mirror World, with its mirror social media and mirror currency and mirror book publishing. Because his people were being "othered." But no more. "Never again will they be able to other you, disappear you . . . That's what the Chinese Communist Party did, that's what the Bolsheviks did, that's what the Nazis did," Bannon told his listeners right before Christmas 2021 (he was trying to sell them FJB coins). And he added, "Nobody in this audience will ever do that to anyone. You wouldn't think of it. You would say 'that's not fair.'"

This is Bannon's tone much of the time: warm, welcoming, protective of his "community," constantly praising listeners for their kindness, intelligence, and courage. All of it is designed as a rebuke to the harshness, snobbishness, sectarianism, and identity absolutism on parts of the highly educated left. Of course, Bannon has another mode—the one in which he bares his teeth and threatens to put "heads on pikes." But that mode is reserved exclusively for his enemies.

As part of building MAGA Plus, Bannon has made clear efforts to tone down the overt racism of his show. Opposition to what he calls "border warfare" is still a pillar of the project, but alongside it is a great deal of talk about what he now calls "inclusive nationalism." Bannon claims (and polling supports this claim) that growing numbers of Black and Latino people, particularly men, are open to voting Republican, in part over frustrations with how Covid measures affected their jobs and small businesses, and also over discomfort with their kids coming home with unfamiliar ideas about the mutability of gender.

Similar attempts at diversifying the hard-right base can be seen in Australia and France. These movements are still built around hate and division—on scapegoating migrants; on pathologizing trans youth; on bashing teachers trying to support these students or tell a truer story of their nations' past; and on scaremongering about communists and Islamists. "Inclusive nationalism" just means that they have found some new blocs of voters who are also looking for scapegoats, and not all of them are white, or male.

The endgame is not hidden. Bannon tells his posse that they are going to "run this country for one hundred years, [for] every ethnicity, every color, every race, every religion—that's an inclusive nationalism." Though it didn't pan out in the 2022 midterms, it's possible this approach will be enough to cobble together another presidential victory—but, if not, there are backup plans in the works. According to the results of a Public Religion Research Institute poll released in November 2021, among Republicans who say they believe that the 2020 election was stolen from Trump, almost four in ten say that "true American patriots might have to resort to violence in order to save our country."

Sandwiched between segments alleging that the 2020 election was stolen, Bannon personally pitches an at-home target-practice system, which uses lasers instead of live ammunition in your automatic rifle and helps build "muscle memory" for the real thing.

Step 3. Develop a thug caste

When leaders who seek what I call a "fascist shift" want to close down an open society, they send paramilitary groups of scary young men out to terrorize citizens. The Blackshirts roamed the Italian countryside beating up communists; the Brownshirts staged violent rallies throughout Germany. This paramilitary force is especially important in a democracy: you need citizens to fear thug violence and so you need thugs who are free from prosecution . . . Say there are protests, or a threat, on the day of an election; history would not rule out the presence of a private security firm at a polling station "to restore public order."

The person who wrote that (back in 2007) is Naomi Wolf, now found regularly on the *War Room*, hosted by a man trying to make sure that, next election day, the thugs will be at every polling station.

Rebrand Complete

In the early months, when I would hear Wolf on *War Room: Pandemic* describing some straightforward plan to encourage vaccination as one step away from concentration camps, I sometimes thought I could detect a suppressed giggle in Bannon's voice, as if he was thinking, *I cannot believe this feminist chick actually went further than I ever would. Do go on . . .* He keeps his composure, however. Just as he knew in 2016 that Trump could not win without pissed-off, mostly white union guys, he is sure now that pissed-off, mostly white suburban moms—nerves frayed from those years of yo-yo remote schooling and closed gyms; still revved up about vaccine mandates and getting shadow banned on Instagram; genuinely worried about the well-being of their kids and their small businesses; done being dismissed and mocked as "Karens" by mean liberals—are the path to the next right-wing resurgence. Last time, Bannon railed against Wall Street and the globalists who had fleeced the Everyman; now he rails against that plus Big Pharma, Big Tech, and "woke capitalism," all of which are tormenting the Every*mom* by poisoning the minds and bodies of her kids.

That is the essence of MAGA Plus: it's the old red-baseball-hat brigade, *plus* my doppelganger and all that she has come to represent. It is no exaggeration to say that Bannon has cast Wolf as a kind of mom in chief for the voting bloc he is hoping to secure: a former high-profile Democrat, a onetime-famous feminist who now wants to speak to the manager on all of their behalf.

"All these moms who are listening to Naomi Wolf," Bannon says on his show, crediting her as a key leader of the people he now calls "Warrior Moms" or the "Army of Moms," and she accepts the crown. Over the months, Wolf and Bannon's relationship has grown progressively warmer as their political projects have converged, nagging ironies be damned. She warns Bannon gravely of the fictional threat that the state could soon wrench children away from their unvaccinated parents, apparently undisturbed that he faithfully served a president who forcibly separated more than five thousand children and babies from their families as they sought entry to the United States. Bannon, in turn, flatters her lavishly, declaring every fractionally understood piece of information flotsam that she brings onto his show "a huge story" and urging her to write it up, "in your brilliant way." In May 2021, he said she was on his "shortlist for woman of the year."

Before Bannon, Wolf stood alone. Now she has her very own "Wolf Pack." Bannon, commander in chief of the *War Room*, understands this primal need for belonging, purpose, and connection on a cellular level. He understands it in his listeners—the constantly praised and engaged "*War Room* posse"—and he understands it in Wolf. At one point, the two even had co-branded T-shirts made up to sell to the thousands of volunteers they claimed to have recruited to help wade through vaccine trial data, sort of like a deranged baseball team. VACCINE INVESTIGATION TEAM they say at the top; WAR ROOM POSSE MEMBER on the bottom. In between is a picture of a busted vaccine syringe with particles flying everywhere. Yours for just $29.99.

As Wolf finds her people, she changes, becoming ever more what they seem to want her to be. She posted a video of herself doing weapons training on a country road, coached by her new husband, a former soldier turned private investigator/bodyguard named Brian O'Shea, who founded a private security company and does not seem to like being referred to as a "mercenary."

She is a quick study and has learned the rules of her new culture. Where, in the past, she put out plaintive videos about the unfairness of having her accounts suspended, she now wears deplatforming as a badge of honor, exploiting it as a fundraising pitch. "We really need you," she tells Bannon, "because since we've been reporting on this, we've been deplatformed again! . . . We got bumped off of YouTube so come please to DailyClout.io." When her Twitter account was reactivated by Musk's conspiracy-friendly regime, her first salvo back was: "Greetings. Signed, Deplatformed seven times and still right." She knows that in the Mirror

World, only "sheeple" get to speak unhindered, while prophets must battle to be heard.

She is still a pro-choice feminist, she says. But when the Supreme Court rolled back *Roe v. Wade*, she shrugged it off, saying the decision "does something that's needed, I think, which is, it turns the decision back to the states." These days, she reserves her feminist outrage for male conspiracy theorists who she is convinced are not crediting her for coming up with the conspiracies first. Like the time she went off on *Infowars*, the show produced by the industrial-scale liar Alex Jones: "Gosh darn I am TIRED of breaking stories by dint of very hard work and finding the connections, and then having (usually male) OTHER commentators claim credit for the information . . . Please STOP, @infowars."

The depths of Wolf's realignment became clear to me after the Trump-backed Republican Glenn Youngkin won the election to be governor of Virginia, in large part because he rode a wave of parental anger. Bannon saw it as a bellwether for the power of MAGA Plus. A decisive issue was Youngkin's opposition to schools adopting anti-racist curricula, but his opposition to mask and vaccine mandates helped him out, too, as did his politicization of new transgender-inclusive policies in schools. In short, the Warrior Moms won, and Bannon was elated about this supposedly populist victory, never mind that Youngkin had just stepped down after twenty-five years leading the Carlyle Group, a notoriously secretive investment firm with ties to a cast of former presidents, prime ministers, and dynastic families—a "globalist" outfit if ever there was one. The day after the election, Bannon spent the show checking in with his Army of Moms, including my doppelganger.

Wolf had, up until this point, claimed to still be a Democrat, or at least independent, so I didn't expect her to openly celebrate Youngkin's victory. Boy was I wrong. She declared it "an historic day for the issues I care about . . . especially women's rights and the voices of women." As recently as 2020, Wolf had strongly pushed back against the attacks on trans rights by some feminists of her generation, hinting they had become tools of the right. Now she was making common cause with the very women who linked all-gender bathrooms with sexual assault. The results of this "huge victory" showed, she said, the "gigantic plutonium weapon" represented by "suburban women who will do anything for their children"—parents who had become aware that "there are dark forces arrayed at their kids . . . all kinds of weird abuse of children going on."

That day on the *War Room*, she said women deserved the credit—but Bannon should also take a bow. "You did so much," Wolf gushed, "more than most men I've been advocating to for twenty-five years to showcase the voices of moms as leaders . . . nobody has sufficiently understood until now."

In fact, fascist and neofascist movements from Mussolini to Pinochet have recognized the powerful role played by women, particularly when cast in their supposedly "natural" role as mothers and protectors of nationalist traditions and healthy bloodlines (e.g., Giorgia Meloni). Hitler rewarded women deemed of good Aryan stock who agreed to quit the workforce and become baby-making machines. Wolf, with her "10 Easy Steps" she claims every autocratic leader follows, appeared to have missed this historical detail.

By the 2022 midterm elections, Wolf would join Bannon in full-blown election denialism, refusing to accept the legitimacy of the results in New York State. A few months after that, she issued "a full-throated apology" to "Conservatives, Republicans, MAGA" for having believed media accounts of the violent January 6 assault on the Capitol. After watching Tucker Carlson air a laughably whitewashed version of those events, in which he portrayed rioters as curious sightseers, she realized "I was duped" by "full-spectrum propaganda." She even decided to reassess her low opinion of Donald Trump, writing, "I have been lied to about him so much for so long, I can't tell."

This is a head-spinning political transformation by any measure. But witnessing this about-face in someone whose face is perennially confused with my own sends a particular kind of chill; once again Freud's description of the uncanny comes to mind: "that species of the frightening that goes back to what was once well known and had long been familiar."

The horror of the society that flips fascist from within—without the aid of a foreign invasion—lies precisely in this unsettling feeling of familiarity. When that ferocious force is conjured up to wage war on a portion of the domestic population, there are no outsiders to blame. It's the nice, normal people down the street who turn out to be capable of monstrosity—monstrousness is revealed as the evil twin of nice, the doppelganger of normal.

In trying to understand this terrifying duality, artists have frequently turned to the figure of the doppelganger to put material weight to their dread. Indeed, many doppelganger books and films are about the latent potential for fascism within our societies, even within ourselves. In films like Denis Villeneuve's *Enemy*, about a professor who teaches university students about the perils of fascism, only to find himself ensnared in a duplicitous web with his amoral double (or is it his twin? or his alter ego?), the allegories are often subtle and veiled. Time feels too short to even bother veiling mine.

Machine Men and Machine Hearts

The most celebrated film in the doppelganger/fascism genre is one I have already mentioned: *The Great Dictator*. Part of Charlie Chaplin's genius as a director was casting himself in both lead roles. He played the kindly, persecuted Jewish barber and the vain, ridiculous, and murderous dictator—and then he had the former impersonate the latter. By doubling himself, and blurring the boundaries between the two characters of victim and victimizer, he implicitly asked the question "What does it take to turn into our evil twins?" This may have been particularly troubling for Chaplin because of some uncanny similarities between the filmmaker and Hitler—not just their matching miniature mustaches, or even that they were born within four days of each other in 1889, but also that they were both concerned, albeit in very different ways, with the plight of the ordinary, forgotten man. A 1939 editorial in the magazine *The Spectator* remarked of Chaplin and Hitler, "Each is a distorting mirror, the one for good, the other for untold evil."

So what determines which version wins out? Chaplin seemed to believe that individuals are faced with a choice between these forces, one they must make at pivotal moments in history. That was the message of the film's famous final speech, which Chaplin, as the Jewish barber disguised as the evil dictator, delivers to the assembled troops in full fascist regalia:

> Soldiers! Don't give yourselves to brutes—men who despise you—enslave you—who regiment your lives—tell you what to do—what to think and what to feel! . . . Don't give yourselves to these unnatural men—machine men with machine minds and machine hearts! You are not machines! You are not cattle! You are men! . . . Soldiers, don't fight for slavery! Fight for liberty!

The Great Dictator came out before the full horrors of the Holocaust were known. That final speech was directed to Chaplin's home audience, in the United States, where domestic fascism was spreading and many were still reluctant to enter the war against Hitler. So here's what unsettles me most: today, the person with the biggest platform speaking for the forgotten Everyman and the Everymom, while shouting about "machine men with machine minds and machine hearts," is Stephen K. Bannon, with Giorgia Meloni and my doppelganger at his side, all urging their various audiences to resist the "slavery" of being a mere consumer for Big Tech.

In Chaplin's film, when the dictator's soldiers hear the Jewish barber's rousing speech, they immediately snap out of their fascist spell and cheer for "reason" and "democracy." In the Mirror World, something altogether different is underway.

8

RIDICULOUSLY SERIOUS, SERIOUSLY SPEECHLESS

Before we go any further, I feel the need to confess that Other Naomi is not the first Naomi to cause some confusion in my life. It happened before, many times, with another Naomi altogether. Before this all took such a political turn, my working theory was that this name of ours was just uncommon enough that the first Naomi a person became aware of tended to imprint herself in their mind as a kind of universal Naomi. Any other Naomi this person subsequently encountered inevitably got muddled with that original. I realize this sounds far-fetched, but I don't know how else to explain the fact that, for the first decade of my public life as a writer, television hosts would say, "Coming up next, a conversation with Naomi Campbell."

It didn't happen every time. But it happened frequently enough that it felt necessary to develop a self-deprecating schtick, which consisted of me apologizing for disappointing viewers who were expecting a luminous supermodel to prowl into the studio and ended up with a five-foot-six anti-capitalist author instead. On at least one occasion, this unlikely signal crossing worked to my tangible advantage. In 2004, while reporting on the U.S. invasion of Iraq, I received a cache of leaked Carlyle Group documents that seemed to show that the former secretary of state James Baker III was attempting to use his position as President George

W. Bush's envoy on Iraq's debt to pressure the government of Kuwait into making deals with the Carlyle Group, where he was senior counselor and an equity partner with an estimated $180 million stake. Before publishing my article, I needed verification that the documents I had were real—which wasn't coming from the Carlyle Group so could come only from the prime minister of Kuwait. Having no contacts in Kuwait, I placed a cold call to the PM's office, left a message with a receptionist, and fully expected to hear nothing back. To my surprise, I got a call at an ungodly hour from Ahmed al-Fahad, the prime minister's undersecretary. I lunged for a notepad and quickly got the verification I needed to publish.

Before signing off, al-Fahad made a confession. "Do you know that the only reason I returned your call was because I thought it was Naomi Campbell?"

I played this story for laughs, mainly to fellow journalists, for a good long time. Some were baffled that the appointed head of a corrupt oil emirate would have expected a call from Campbell in the first place. I had no inside knowledge, but it's slightly less weird when you consider that Campbell testified as a witness at the international war crimes trial of the former Liberian president Charles Taylor, over allegations that the notorious butcher had gifted Campbell a pouch of blood diamonds after they met at a dinner party hosted by Nelson Mandela. From which we can only conclude that once you reach a certain level of fame, wealth, and/or power, everyone takes one another's calls. (It's this intuitive awareness that elites occupy an interconnected world of their own, one where the laws governing the rest of us are shrugged off, that is the wellspring of today's conspiracy singularity.)

The slippery quality of my name is rarely as helpful as it was on the Baker story—but it's frequently entertaining. In the wilds of the internet, for instance, there is video of a panel discussion that was held in Croatia at a particularly tumultuous juncture in Europe's post-2008 financial crisis. The conversation featured Alexis Tsipras, then on the cusp of being elected prime minister of Greece, and the Slovenian philosopher and provocateur Slavoj Žižek. Raging against the brutal austerity that Greeks were facing at the time, Tsipras declared, "They tried to implement this doctrine of shock, as Naomi Campbell said." Žižek, sitting angled toward him on stage, nodded gravely. A slight look of panic crossed the moderator's face.

A Surly Ghost Enters the Scene

I had intended, when I started this project, to pepper my prose with many weighty and serious literary references to add depth to wacky anecdotes like these. I planned to draw more heavily on Freud's theory of the uncanny, as it relates to doubles and the repressed id. I would contrast it with Carl Jung's theories of synchronicity and the shadow self. I would apply these notions of the repressed unconscious to works about doubles by Poe, Saramago, and Dostoyevsky, and to Charles Dickens's *A Tale of Two Cities*. I would delve into real-world examples of writers being tormented by their doubles. Like Graham Greene, who, in his 1980 essay collection, *Ways of Escape*, described how his doppelganger passed himself off as Greene for decades, using his likeness to gain entrance to glamorous festivals, seduce beautiful women, and defraud all manner of people.

But here is the trouble: while these readings did provide glimmers of insight here and there, there is really only one author in this entire upside-down chapter of my life who seemed to genuinely understand the specific texture of my pain, with its peculiar combination of absurdity and gravity. I could find only one writer who had seriously considered what it might feel like to be double-yoked to a clown, a joke, who is nonetheless quite possibly contributing to a wave of needless human suffering and death—and also might, very occasionally, have a point. Only one writer who had thought about what it would do to a writer to find themselves in competition for their own identity with someone who has become not just a writer but a very active and dangerous doer.

That writer is Philip Roth.

As with my earlier brand-defense conundrum, this was awkward for me for highly personal reasons. The main one being that my last encounter with Roth on the page was when I, at age twenty, whipped a copy of *The Counterlife* across my University of Toronto dorm room, vowing to never read another book by Philip Roth ever again. I was done learning, in intricate detail, about the complex life of his male characters, their intimate psychological dramas, and their big global ideas, only to have the female characters bounce across the page like scantily clad nurses in a Benny Hill sketch.

I had furtively read *Portnoy's Complaint*, *The Professor of Desire*, and *Goodbye, Columbus* as a preteen, books that felt less like fiction than fraught visits with the New Jersey wing of my own family. Which was very nearly true: my father was raised in the same working-class Newark neighborhood and went to the same school as Roth, Weequahic High, just a couple of grades behind. I remember thinking, as the book hit the wall, that I was done with all of it. That the human experience is vast and rich, and I already knew just about all I needed to know about the mommy issues of middle-aged Jewish men from the tri-state area. It was time to clear some mental space for some new ethnic archetypes with some less familiar neuroses.

I stuck by that pledge for thirty years. So I was annoyed when my research into literary doppelgangers kept leading me, like a persistent dog scratching at my door, to *Operation Shylock*, a doppelganger novel that many considered Roth's masterwork. My annoyance was compounded by the fact that, just as I grudgingly ordered the novel and was waiting for it to make its way to our rock, Roth, who died in 2018, was suddenly all over the news like a surly ghost.

His authorized biography was out, all nine hundred pages of it, which prompted a spate of stories about the extraordinary and often cruel lengths to which the late author had gone to protect his literary and interpersonal legacy. He had ended a contract with at least one biographer, supposedly put draconian controls on his archive, and finally entrusted his story to the writer Blake Bailey, perhaps because Bailey seemed like the kind of man's man who wouldn't judge Roth for his less-than-ideal treatment of women, on and off the page. Roth seemed to have judged correctly. Most of the reviews were glowing, filled with praise for the greatness of both men. Laura Marsh, writing in *The New Republic*, observed archly, "In Bailey, Roth found a biographer who is exceptionally attuned to his grievances and rarely challenges his moral accounting."

Then, mere weeks after the splashy reception, it all came crashing down. Sexual assault allegations surfaced about Bailey, and the U.S. publisher made the shocking announcement that it was taking *Philip Roth: The Biography* out of print. New articles poured forth trashing both Bailey and Roth, the usual suspects brayed that it was yet another case of "cancel culture," and I watched the whole mess in a state of escalating anxiety. It seemed to me that Roth had done just about everything a writer can possibly do to control and protect the meaning of his name in the world—spending a lifetime telling and retelling versions of his own life in novel after novel, going to war with his ex-wife over her temerity to tell her version of the story (Claire Bloom's *Leaving a Doll's House*), then using the last of his life force to ensure that his official biography locked in his legacy where he believed it belonged. And then, just like that, it all disappeared in a cloud of scandal and heavy-handed corporate ass-covering. If Roth, a titan of U.S. letters, had failed so spectacularly to protect his name, despite these herculean efforts, what hope did minor-league me have of getting my Other Naomi situation under control?

Then the book arrived. Not the biography (though that is back in print), but *Operation Shylock*, first published in 1993. The critics were right: it is by far Roth's most sophisticated work, not to mention the most gripping doppelganger book I had encountered in my now in-depth study of the genre. And twenty-year-old me was also right: the only sustained female character is Jinx, a bouncy blond nurse in cahoots with Roth's doppelganger. Fifty-year-old me found this far sadder for Roth than bruising to me, however, and I was able to focus my attention on the rest of the book.

Roth always favored protagonists who were thinly disguised doubles of himself: masturbating Alexander Portnoy, philandering Nathan Zuckerman, a tortured writer named Philip in his 1990 novel *Deception*. But this went further. *Shylock* is written in the voice of a writer named Philip Roth, who has authored the exact same books and led the same life as the actual Philip Roth. We'll call him "Real Roth." He begins the novel already destabilized, having recently emerged from a mental-health breakdown initiated by the sleeping pill Halcion. It had been so severe that, in a psychotic state, he had asked his wife, "Where's Philip?"—an early and harrowing reminder that a person's self can slip away from them without anybody else's help. While recovering from this trauma, Real Roth discovers that there is a man who calls himself Philip Roth, dresses like Philip Roth, and looks very much like Philip Roth and is getting into all kinds of trouble far away in Jerusalem. We'll call this character "Fake Roth."

Fake Roth has been holding public talks and giving media interviews about his view that the creation of the state of Israel was a grave mistake. It is so surrounded by enemies, Fake Roth believes, that it will surely end in another Jewish Holocaust. So Fake Roth has started a movement called "Diasporism" to encourage Israeli Jews to make a reverse-exodus from Israel to the same Eastern European lands they had departed decades earlier, fleeing bloody pogroms and concentration camps. To that end, Fake Roth has even met with European heads of state, all the while passing for the actual Roth. The little problem of persistent anti-Semitism in these Eastern European countries could be solved, Fake Roth insists, with an aggressive rollout of "Anti-Semites Anonymous," a hate-detox program he originally designed for his own hot, anti-Semitic girlfriend, Jinx.

Real Roth is convinced that this is all extremely dangerous, which leaves him with no choice but to pull a Charlie Chaplin and impersonate his impersonator when he travels to Jerusalem. Hijinks, as well as sex with Jinx, ensue.

The reason I began defacing the book—with underlines and asterisks and exclamation marks—the moment it arrived is that *Operation Shylock* explores, with frankly uncanny precision, many of the bizarre mental and political traps I had been experiencing ever since my own doppelganger problems escalated. The cringe of confronting a parody-worthy version of one's self. The catch-22 of defending one's personal brand. The fascistic shadow selves doppelgangers can reveal inside ourselves. The way whole societies can have sinister doppelgangers. The novel contained all of that, and more.

In *Operation Shylock*, Roth mines the tension between the profound human desire for uniqueness and the equally powerful craving to see one's self reflected in another person's being. The latter of those drives is an aspect of doppelganger mystery that I have neglected so far. So it is certainly worth recalling that millions of people voluntarily upload their photographs to doppelganger-finder services like Twin Strangers, dearly hoping that the websites' facial recognition software will locate their match somewhere in the world. Countless best friends spend hours "twinning" with one other: meticulously synchronizing their outfits and styles so that they appear as doubles. Evidently, a great many of us want nothing more than to find another person who knows precisely what it is like to live inside our bodies and minds—and that desire coexists with the drive to be unmistakably different. The 2023 remake of *Dead Ringers*, starring Rachel Weisz as twin-sister obstetricians, mines, in the words of one reviewer, "the contradictory drives toward individuation and the need for others, repulsion and love." It is this ambivalence that gives doppelgangers their emotional charge.

In *Shylock*, Roth assigns these contradictory feelings to the two different Roths. Real Roth is horrified by his unruly doppelganger and sets out to angrily confront him over his subterfuge and identity theft. He expects his double to panic or cower when caught by the man he has been impersonating. Instead, when the two men come face-to-face in a Jerusalem hotel lobby, Fake Roth flings his arms around Real Roth, embracing him like a brother, and sheds messy tears of intimate familiarity. "'I'm looking at myself,' he said, ecstatically, 'except it's *you*.'"

Real Roth is destabilized yet again. He had planned for a showdown over who was the rightful owner of their face and name and finds himself being adored instead. He is not able to muster the rage he had prescripted, but neither can he share Fake Roth's familial delight in looking into a living mirror. After all, he has a name to protect. "Your name! Your name! Do you ever, ever, ever think of anything *other* than your fucking name!" Jinx demands. And I could only cry-laugh at a scene in which Fake Roth concedes that the author Roth could well have a trademark case against him, if he chose to pursue it. He even points him to a helpful precedent: a successful (and real) suit lodged by the talk-show host Johnny Carson against Here's Johnny Portable Toilets.

There is the paradox of literary brand protection exactly. Do nothing, and you lose all control. Try for control, and you concede to being a two-bit shill: some hawk books, some hawk toilets, it's all the same hustle. Real Roth does not sue, opting instead for a wild journey impersonating his impersonator through the West Bank and beyond.

Dumbpelgangers

This all felt extremely familiar. But not as familiar as Roth's sense that his imposter had taken his lifetime of words and ideas and turned them into a parody of themselves.

"Philip, I feel that I'm reading to you out of a story you wrote." So says the fictionalized novelist Aharon Appelfeld to the fictionalized Philip Roth about an article describing how Fake Roth had gone to Poland to meet with the country's president, Lech Wałęsa, and convince him to welcome Israeli Jews back to their original European homelands and admit that the Zionist experiment had failed. This is key to the novel's vertigo: Fake Roth's opposition to Israel as a Jewish state—his concerns about what it was doing to Jewish morality and safety, as well as his belief that the diaspora was the best place for Jewish culture and ideas to thrive—did not come from nowhere. They came from Philip Roth—not the character, but the man.

Roth had been attacked as a "self-hating Jew" since he was in his twenties. His New Jersey characters were too crass, too flawed, and Roth was accused by no less an authority than the Rabbinical Council of America of putting his people at risk by making them look bad. Roth doubled down, expanding his critical gaze from Newark to Israel and, as in *The Counterlife*, to the violent radicalization that was fueling the expansion of Jewish outposts in the Occupied Territories, with émigrés from New York and New Jersey among Israel's most zealous settlers. This was another kind of exploration of doppelgangers: Roth presented the gun-toting, muscle-bound Israeli "New Jew" as a kind of collective doubling of the Old Jew, the artists and intellectuals, like Roth himself, whom many Israelis branded as soft and useless from inside their tough nationalist project. Or perhaps the New Jew was a Maccabean mirror of the chauvinist nationalists in Poland, Ukraine, and Germany who had used Jews as their scapegoats for so long. This skepticism toward Zionism, along with his defense of diaspora as an exciting and wholly legitimate place to be a Jew, is a big part of what I always appreciated about Roth, despite the long parade of Jinxes.

In *Operation Shylock*, Fake Roth appropriates all of Roth's real social and political critiques and takes them to fanatical and cartoonish extremes, all while performing an over-the-top amalgam of the psychosexual neuroses that Roth had implanted in so many of his previous protagonists/literary doppelgangers, from Portnoy to Zuckerman. It's "all of them in one, broken free of print and mockingly reconstituted as a single satirical facsimile of me," Roth wails of his imposter.

This is a bit how I have felt getting confused with Wolf as she declares every major shock and lesser crisis—whether Covid-19 or a baby formula shortage—to be a plot against America, to use another Rothism. I am trapped in the *zozobra* push and pull that Roth summarizes so perfectly: "It's too ridiculous to take seriously and too serious to be ridiculous."

I know that the diagonalist alliance Wolf has built with Bannon, as it translates into political power at the state level and beyond, will continue to affect countless lives, and dramatically for the worse. Yet despite this obvious gravity, the sheer ridiculousness of Wolf's antics—the time-travel tweets, the VACCINE INVESTIGATION TEAM T-shirts, the promiscuous and continuous Holocaust analogies—make it almost impossible to fully take her seriously. Or, put another way, Wolf may be a joke, but she's not a funny one. And yet, if I'm honest, my doppelganger has me on the edge between laughter and tears almost all the time!

In *Operation Shylock*, Real Roth attempts to exercise some kind of control over his "preposterous proxy" by refusing to call him by their shared name and instead renaming him Moishe Pipik—*pipik* being the catchall diminutive given to naughty kids and schlemiel-like characters in his childhood home; the name literally means "Moses Bellybutton" (fitting for all this navel-gazing). The renaming delivers short-term relief, but ultimately it backfires: Fake Roth is still ensnared in what Roth terms "pipikism," or bellybuttonism, "the antitragic force that inconsequencializes everything—farcicalizes everything, trivializes everything, superficializes everything."

Is it possible to escape a tractor beam like pipikism? Once an idea has been pipiked, can it ever be serious again? This, in some sense, is the trouble with all the monstrous clowns that have reshaped modern politics in recent years: Trump in the United States, Boris Johnson in the United Kingdom, Rodrigo Duterte in the Philippines. And then there is Putin casting himself as a global truth-teller about the crimes of Western colonialism and an upholder of the anti-imperialist, anti-fascist traditions—Putin as Pipik. These figures spread pipikism everywhere they go. And it doesn't just farcicalize what they say; it farcicalizes what many of us are willing and able to say afterward.

For instance, when Bannon states that his armed and authoritarian posse is being "othered" by leftists and liberals, he is appropriating an important term that analysts of authoritarianism have used to describe how fascists cast their targets as less than human, making them easier to discard and even exterminate. But he is doing more than that, too. He is also making a mockery of the whole concept of othering, which in turn makes it harder to use the term to name what Bannon does as a matter of course—to migrants, to Black voters, to trans and nonbinary youth. Similarly, when Trump, after the 2016 election, accused half the press corps of being "fake news," he was beginning a process that would lead his supporters to doubt everything they read and watched in the mainstream press. But he was also doing something else. He was appropriating a term that had been used by communications scholars to describe a very real phenomenon: manufactured propaganda that is designed to seem like real news but is entirely made-up. Fake articles like that had been a boon to Trump, including one particularly viral one that falsely reported that the pope had endorsed him. But now, thanks to his appropriation of the term "fake news," we were all robbed of a useful phrase to describe the phenomenon.

Or consider Tucker Carlson taking a break from riling up white nationalism to claim that his competitors on MSNBC, by saying the words "white people," were practicing "open race hate" and had become the equivalent of Hutu radio broadcasters in Rwanda who stoked the fires of anti-Tutsi hatred before the 1994 genocide. "This is Hutu radio," he stressed, while claiming that a segment on racism in pro football was "genocidal talk," adding, "Not an overstatement. That's exactly what it is."

When the figure of the buffoon becomes central to public life, the problem is not only that they say foolish things but also that everything they touch becomes foolish, including—especially—the powerful language we need to talk about them and what they are doing. I think of these figures as "dumbpelgangers," and they pipik so many terms and concepts that they risk leaving us all speechless.

In 2014, *The New Statesman* ran an early "What Happened to Naomi Wolf?" piece that offered a tongue-in-cheek explanation, one inspired by Wolf's many pulpy conspiracies: "Some time in the last five years, the real Wolf was discreetly 'neutralised' and replaced with an actor, who has worked tirelessly since then to make left-wing politics in general and feminism in particular look like a shower of clown shoes who will believe pretty much anything as long as it starts from the premise 'America is bad.'"

How comforting it would be if Wolf were a fake we could unmask—and not a symptom of a mass unraveling of meaning afflicting, well, everything. Yet reading Roth wrestle down the forces of trivialization in *Shylock*, I began to think about the ways that I have been letting the forces of pipikism change me. Ever since I started noticing the fact-free, clout-chasing remixes of *The Shock Doctrine* circulating in the Mirror World, I had been unsure of how to respond. Did I bring this on myself? In my writings on shock exploitation, I thought I had been careful to stress that the catalyzing crises were not being manufactured as part of a grand backroom plot to exploit them. Rather, they were (and still are) exploited opportunistically, as a strategic means of circumventing political opposition to unpopular policies. But should I have done more? Were the ways that I have asked people to be suspicious of power during moments of shock feeding into this mushrooming of conspiracies? Was all my doppelganger trouble trying to tell me this? Or—and this possibility worried me more—was the trouble that I, and many others on the left, had been too timid and obedient during the Covid era? Had we gone along too readily with pandemic measures that offloaded so much onto individuals? And had we failed to forcefully take on the corporate greed that has run rampant in this period?

The Screen New Deal

Politicians and corporate leaders have repeatedly used shock doctrine strategies during the Covid years. The British government crafted a "high-priority lane" to produce masks and other pandemic protective gear that looked very much like a chance to line the pockets of friends and donors (yielding, in some cases, unusable equipment). When the chronically under-resourced National Health Service (NHS) became overwhelmed by Covid and other health crises at the end of 2022, the Tory government smuggled in various forms of private care as supposed solutions—with fears that a fuller auctioning off of Britain's cherished NHS could be in store. There have been similar attempts at backdoor health care privatization in several Canadian provinces, once again using pandemic-overwhelm as the excuse. And in the name of preventing further "learning loss," the right-wing government in Ontario tried to strip public-sector education workers of their legal right to strike—one of countless attacks on public schools that took place under cover of crisis. In India, meanwhile, the government launched a series of historic attacks on economic protections for the country's farmers during the pandemic, which it eventually had to withdraw after waves of protests. Several governments, including those of Serbia and Greece, used the crisis to bolster security powers and crack down on opponents. China's extreme "zero Covid" policies represented a severe attack on labor rights, with workers unable to leave their factories for weeks.

I kept a thick file, and, in the early months, I often wrote and spoke about these forms of pandemic opportunism and profiteering. In May 2020, I published a long, reported piece in *The Intercept* and *The Guardian* about how large tech companies like Google and Amazon were taking advantage of lockdowns to push a wish list of "no touch" technologies, rapidly rebranding them as "Covid-safe." As one particularly egregious example, I quoted Anuja Sonalker, CEO of Steer Tech, a Maryland-based company selling self-parking technology. "There has been a distinct warming up to human-less, contactless technology," she said, adding, rather chillingly, "Humans are biohazards, machines are not."

This was during that first devastating wave—before we could get good masks, let alone vaccines, back when staying away from one another was pretty much the only tool we had to stop the spread of a virus we barely understood. But the former Google CEO Eric Schmidt and other tech billionaires seized on those stopgap emergency measures to push for more permanent changes that would represent huge profit-making opportunities for their sector—everything from moving large parts of education permanently online to creating so-called smart cities, which would radically increase the surveillance of daily life. The future they were seeing in the crisis was one in which not only our homes are never again exclusively personal spaces but also, via high-speed digital connectivity, our schools, our doctor's offices, our gyms, and, if determined by the state, our jails. It was a grim, AI-enabled vision of a touchless society that would employ far fewer teachers, doctors, and drivers. It would accept no cash, and have skeletal mass transit and far less live art.

All of these trends were underway pre-pandemic. But during those early months of lockdown, they underwent a warp-speed acceleration. None of what I wrote in my reporting was speculative—it was based on public statements from tech companies as well as documents released under the U.S. Freedom of Information Act. Something resembling a coherent pandemic shock doctrine was beginning to emerge, which I playfully called the "Screen New Deal."

A few months after that piece came out, I started to see examples of these same trends being cast in far more conspiratorial ways: maybe the tech companies had planned the whole thing. Maybe it was the World Economic Forum and its plan for the Great Reset; maybe the whole pandemic wasn't real and the death toll numbers were an elaborate hoax. Maybe, as my doppelganger seemed to suggest, it was all a ploy to get us to accept a CCP-style social credit police state.

I began to doubt myself. Should I not have reported how tech companies were exploiting the crisis? Could I have done more in all of my shock-related writings to stress that real emergencies do exist and do require emergency measures? The truth is that I backed off—not completely, but too much. When Wolf started doing the rounds on Fox in her new role as "CEO of a tech company," sounding, however unintentionally, like my preposterous proxy, I just couldn't figure out how to keep talking about how the large tech firms were exploiting the crisis without it being sucked into the whirring conspiracy mill. I couldn't see how a serious discussion of actual disaster capitalism could avoid getting blended with truly dangerous anti-vaccination fantasies and outright coronavirus denialism. Pipikism had thwarted me.

The Green New Reset?

More disturbingly, the forces of farcicalization in the Mirror World also seemed to be undercutting nascent and fragile attempts to actually address many of the real crises we face, from climate breakdown to mass incarceration to the ruinously exploitative working conditions that the pandemic laid bare. It seems so distant now, but there were a few months in 2020—a good half a year—when there had been a widespread belief that the pandemic might be a catalyst for a great many of the structural changes our societies had been collectively procrastinating and avoiding. Many of us even let ourselves dream that the emptiness of our highways, the rest the skies were receiving from planes, and all of the talk about missing nothing more than one another would actually lead to a meaningful change in how we decided to live when the pandemic finally eased. These were the weeks when so many of us shared and quoted and posted Arundhati Roy's essay "The Pandemic Is a Portal," imagining that a global calamity might take us somewhere not just different but better.

Those untamed hopes only deepened when, that first spring and summer, the carless streets filled with protesters demanding an end to police killings of Black people, alongside a radical reimagining of public priorities and spending. This was the period when activist groups and progressive policy shops collaborated on platforms calling for a "People's

Recovery" from Covid—plans that married the vision for a green world with a vision for a racially just and equal one.

And yet, just a few months later, much of the sense of possibility that characterized those early months of pandemic protest had evaporated. We passed through the portal to a changed world, but not in the ways so many of us had hoped. The reasons were many: the U.S. presidential elections sucking up so much political energy; the push to get back to normal picking up velocity; the grind of maintaining focus while we were still so physically isolated; the fact that many movements were riven with internal strife, much of it relating to tensions over whether they were building brands around key figures or building bases of participants and members.

But there was something else getting in the way: the very idea of treating the pandemic as a portal to something new—something better, greener, and fairer—was being systematically pipiked in the Mirror World by people like my doppelganger. It was getting all mixed up and conflated with the conspiracy talk about how "globalist elites" at the World Economic Forum were trying to harness the recovery for their Great Reset. By early 2021, any discussion about how our societies could and should change in response to the reality of overlapping and intersecting crises was immediately shouted down by the diagonalists as being part and parcel of a conspiracy hatched on a Swiss mountaintop by Bill Gates. Suddenly "climate lockdowns" started trending—an entirely made-up threat, with strong links to the Heartland Institute, the foremost climate-change-denial think tank, which made the absurd claim that once the globalists were done locking you in your house to fight Covid, they were going to lock you in your house to lower greenhouse gas emissions. And some, like the onetime-respected *60 Minutes* journalist and now full-time conspiracy monger Lara Logan, claimed that they were "the ones who want us eating insects, cockroaches, and that they dine on the blood of children"—a point of view that got her banned from the right-wing channel Newsmax but is nonetheless shared by countless QAnon believers around the world.

The effect of this constantly expanding sphere of pipikism is that it's not just more difficult to talk about real examples of disaster profiteering or the need for a Green New Deal. Gradually, it has come to feel as if every idea of any import, every word that might express the magnitude of our moment, has been boobytrapped before it can even be uttered.

I remember the moment when it hit me how dangerous this pipiking had become. I was writing an article about how hard-right local politicians in Northern California had ordered police to evict survivors of the state's deadliest wildfire from the tents where some were living in public parks. I typed a sentence about it being an ominous portent of an "ecofascist future," in which ecological fears are harnessed to rationalize violent security crackdowns against those deemed lesser humans, often immigrants and the poor. Ecofascism is a real threat, and it is becoming more explicit on parts of the right. But I deleted the term in favor of "eco-authoritarianism"—a bit weaker. But throwing the term "fascism" around is what Other Naomi does, and hadn't she helped make the very word absurd? Then I realized what I had done: "ecofascism" is the accurate term to describe the threat. And how convenient it is for coalescing fascist forces if the term has been so abused and pipiked that anti-fascists are loath to use it to accurately describe events in the real world.

At around that time, my friend Alex called from Australia and we caught up over video. "Is it true that Covid lockdowns are turning Australia into a fascist state?" I asked. "Because that's what Naomi Wolf just told Steve Bannon. I can't seem to find reliable reports."

Alex, one of my few friends unfazed by my listening habits, shrugged and replied, "The police are bad. But it's weird: I used to know who the fascists were and who the anti-fascists were. There would be street fights. It was clear which side was which. But now the fascists have totally taken our language. I feel speechless."

Hearing her use the word "speechless" made me feel oddly better. I had been thinking that my speechlessness was the result of my own highly specific Naomi-Naomi problem. But it turned out that, in this time of great loneliness, a lot of us were watching the world go by with our mouths hanging open.

The problem of speechlessness goes deeper than the continuous abuse that important words are taking in the Mirror World. I think it may also have to do with a creeping uncertainty about the role words play, their basic utility. Words are still useful for practical purposes, like arranging after-school pickups and making grocery lists and writing catchy songs—but for changing the world? My friend Bill McKibben often talks about why he took the leap from writing articles and books to starting the climate change organization 350.org (where we were both board members for a decade). Bill says that when he was young and naïve and writing *The End of Nature*, the first book about climate change for a general readership, he "thought books changed the world." Then, after a couple of decades of watching policy makers ignore his books and the library of others, not to mention the careful work of thousands upon thousands of increasingly panicked climate scientists, he came to the conclusion that, while words help, it's "movements of people who change the world." But here's the question that has been eating away at me: What if our books, and our movements as they are currently constructed (often in ways that resemble corporate brands), are only changing words? What if words—written on the page or shouted in protest—change only what people and institutions say, and not what they do?

"I AM THE YOU THAT IS NOT WORDS," Fake Roth announces to Real Roth, touching on the central question of many doppelganger stories: Who is real and what is real? Is the real one whoever claimed the identity first? Or is the real one whoever does the most with it? In Dostoyevsky's *The Double*, Fake Golyadkin is so active and gregarious that he easily upstages and replaces the original. In *Operation Shylock*, Real Roth is a full-time pretender, a writer of stories not a doer of deeds. Fake Roth is an activist and a would-be maker of history. He chides Real Roth for frittering away the cultural power he amassed through literary fame by merely writing more neurotic novels, spilling more words—as opposed to concretely acting to help the Jewish people who are the subjects of his novels.

For Fake Roth, the answer of what makes a person real is obvious: the faker is the one hiding behind representation, the real one acts "beyond words." This speaks to the quicksand underpinning our age: the confusion between saying/clicking/posting and doing. The tension between the virtual nature of lives led in the blue glow of screens and the reality of the embodied labor (digging, harvesting, soldering, sewing, scrubbing, boxing, hauling, delivering) and material inputs (oil, gas, coal, copper, lithium, cobalt, sand, trees) that makes it all possible.

That is the real source of my speechlessness in this unreal period: a feeling of near violent rupture between the world of words and the world beyond them. In recent years, left social movements have won huge victories in transforming the way we talk about all kinds of issues—billionaires and oligarchic rule, climate breakdown, white supremacy, prison abolition, gender identity, Palestinian rights, sexual violence—and I have to believe that those changes represent real victories, that they matter. And yet, on almost every front, tangible ground is being lost. Changing the discourse did not prevent the world's ten richest men from doubling their collective fortunes from $700 billion to $1.5 trillion in the first two years of the pandemic; it did not stop police forces from increasing their budgets while teachers have to pay for basic supplies out of pocket; it did not prevent fossil fuel companies from collecting more billions in subsidies and new permits; it did not prevent the Israeli police forces from attacking the funeral of the revered Palestinian American journalist Shireen Abu Akleh after a bullet that was almost certainly fired by an Israeli soldier took her life.

"We did change the discourse . . . ," a friend remarked to me the other day, and then the thought trailed off. We did. But we appear to have done it at the precise moment when words and ideas underwent a radical currency devaluation, a crash connected, in ways we have barely begun to understand, to the torrent of words in which we are swimming on those screens. A torrent that assiduously amplifies the most operatic forms of virtue performance and the most cynical forms of pipiking. Angela Davis, in the spring of 2022, put the tension of the historic post–George Floyd protests like this: "In many ways, nothing has really changed at all, but at the same time, everything has changed."

Beyond Blah, Blah, Blah

These are difficult themes to write and talk about, because all we have are those very same cheapened words. Which is why I greatly appreciated

Greta Thunberg's various interventions during the 2021 climate summit in Glasgow, which essentially consisted of making fun of people saying things about climate change while doing very little about climate change. The shaming took the form of her repeating, many times, the words "Blah, blah, blah."

It is worth recalling that Thunberg's first protest was her refusal, as a young girl, to speak. She learned about the ecological crisis, she saw how little was being done about it, and she stopped speaking to anyone beyond her family. She started speaking when things started changing—at first small things, like members of her family committing to becoming vegetarian, and then larger things, like millions of people joining climate strikes around the world.

Then she spoke a lot, to all kinds of audiences, and you could tell by the care she put into those speeches that a part of her believed they might yield action. What was interesting about the version of Greta that showed up in Glasgow is that she had clearly lost that earlier faith—lost faith in the spectacle of herself giving speeches to shame leaders for doing nothing. So she started making speeches that were less about climate change and more about the absurdity of the whole charade. "Build back better. Blah, blah, blah. Green economy. Blah, blah, blah. Net zero by 2050. Blah, blah, blah," she said in the run-up to the summit. "This is all we hear from our so-called leaders. Words, words that sound great but so far has led to no action. Our hopes and dreams drown in their empty words and promises." Asked by the BBC two days later what she thought of the final agreement to come out of Glasgow, Greta replied, "They even succeeded in watering down the blah, blah, blah, which is quite an achievement."

This is far more scathing than what Greta used to do at such esteemed gatherings. She used to scold. She used to plead. She used to cry. And though she was harsh to the leaders listening to her, her words still implied a kind of faith in them. But it would seem that Greta no longer believes in that theory of change. She has come to the place at which so many of us have arrived: the realization that no one is coming to save us but us, and whatever action we can leverage through our cooperation, organization, and solidarities.

There is a power in naming this, rather than just filling up airtime. Because if you find yourself saying, as some activists more diplomatic than Greta did, that a climate summit is a "good start" and that the summit is officially called Conference of the Parties 26—because it had literally happened every year since 1995 at that point (save Covid-wracked 2020)—then it might be time to admit that words are no longer doing what we expect them to do.

I have been writing about how Bannon and Wolf are pipiking words, making a mockery of concepts that matter, and that is deeply disorienting. But so, too, is what more centrist leaders have been doing for much longer: using words as intended, yet with no intention of acting on them. And one form of denialism feeds the other: the outright denialism in the Mirror World is made thinkable by the baseline war on words and meaning in more liberal parts of our culture.

"At some point you'd have to live as if the truth was true," The Weather Station's Tamara Lindeman sings in her climate ballad "Loss." At some point—but apparently not yet.

For my entire adult life I have been writing about the severing of signs from meaning. I had no idea, though, how far it would go. When I filled pages of *No Logo* with close textual readings of early lifestyle-branding campaigns that appropriated revolutionary iconography to sell sneakers and laptops and checking accounts—Martin Luther King Jr.'s and Gandhi's dead faces showing up on Apple billboards, the anthems of the anti–Vietnam War movement selling Nikes—I thought I understood why this was dangerous. On the one hand, transformational movements and ideas were being severed from their contexts, being made less powerful, less real, in the process. On the other hand, powerful revolutionary iconography was being used to actively hide and distract from the all-too-real shadow worlds that created the products being advertised—the homesick and chronically harassed teenage girls in Indonesia and China making the sneakers and electronics; the pollutants and toxins seeping out of the global supply chain at every stage; the jobs that were turning into slippery contracts while we were told to buck up and be our own brands. It was a co-optation, a cover-up, and a con all at once.

But there was a bigger picture that I didn't quite see, and that was the all-out war on meaning that this new stage of progressive-cloaked capitalism represented. In the end, what mattered most about those campaigns was the boldness with which they were broadcasting that, from here on out, nothing means anything anymore: if MLK and Gandhi and Bob Dylan can all be conscripted as neoliberal shills, then absolutely anything and anyone can be severed from their contexts and made to mean their precise opposite. The story beneath the story was the normalization of the disassociation between words from reality, which could only usher in the era of irony and flat detachment, because those seemed like the only self-respecting postures to adopt in a world in which everyone was lying all the time. And from there we were all primed to dive headlong into the sea of social media non sequiturs, the scroll that scrambles the narrative structures of argument and story in favor of a never-ending thought confetti of "this" and "this" and "this" and "look over there."

If nothing means anything and nothing follows from anything else, then, as Hannah Arendt warned, everything is possible. Reality is putty to be shaped and molded at will. That impulse looks pretty wild in the Mirror World, with influencers like my doppelganger claiming daily that they alone can "connect the dots" between the plot points of a world gone mad: Epstein, Gates, Davos, Fauci, CCP. But it's pretty wild on this side of the glass, too, with teenagers desperately telling world leaders that the planet is on fire, and those leaders responding by taking selfies with the feisty teens, fist-bumping them for Twitter, or, in the case of Canadian prime minister Justin Trudeau in 2019, joining the massive climate strike that was staged to protest the policies of the government that he himself leads, as if Trudeau had genuinely forgotten that he had the power to do more than march.

I appreciated Greta's "Blah, blah, blah" speeches because they precisely captured the pervasive feeling of speechlessness, far better than my own impotent and sullen silences in this period. Greta had found a way not only of critiquing language but also of protecting language: she was mocking their words, and what happens to her words in their ears, but she was also saving her words for spaces where they still might matter, where they still can be married with principles and actions, where people are not merely performing for cameras. Soon, she would be detained by police while joining other activists who were attempting to block the expansion of a coal mine in western Germany.

Though I hesitate to suggest it, this is a place where we could stand to learn a little from Steve Bannon. From his bloody-minded approach to strategy and building winning coalitions despite differences. From his transformation of listeners and watchers into highly organized doers. From his focus on "Action! Action! Action!"

It's likely too late to get back everything that has been lost to the forces of pipikism—but there is one thing that we must never surrender, and that is the language of anti-fascism. The true meanings of "genocide" and "apartheid" and "Holocaust," and the supremacist mindset that makes them all possible. Those words we need, as sharp as possible, to name and combat what is rapidly taking shape in the Mirror World—which is an entire cosmology built around claims of superior bodies, superior immune systems, and superior babies, bankrolled by supplement sales, bitcoin, and prenatal yoga.

It all would be so ridiculous—if it weren't so serious.

9

THE FAR RIGHT MEETS THE FAR-OUT

When the election date was set and the sign wars began, our son, T., cheered every time we passed an orange placard with his dad's name on it. I mentioned to Avi and his team that the research I was doing on the Mirror World could have some relevance to their campaign, but this was the summer of 2021 and they brushed it off as a U.S. breed of batshit.

I wasn't so sure. Through one of the conspiracy-themed podcasts I listen to, I had recently learned that a woman living not far from us named Romana Didulo had declared herself "Queen of Canada, Head of State and Commander in Chief" and was busily issuing decrees that ordered businesses to cease checking for proof of vaccination or face the death penalty (which Canada does not have). That was odd enough. Even more bizarre was that she seemed to have thousands of loyal subjects, some of whom had been delivering her "cease and desist" orders by hand, informing businesses, schools, and even police that they were "complicit in Crimes against Humanity and will be prosecuted by We The People" via military tribunals. I had also started to notice a small cluster of protesters who gathered periodically at the busiest intersection in the town down the road. They held signs familiar to me from following the adventures of Other Naomi: I DO NOT CONSENT, PLANDEMIC, and FEAR IS THE VIRUS. Still, back then, barely a year into the pandemic, the only person I knew who agreed with me that Canada was headed straight for the Mirror World mayhem raging south of the border was my fitness instructor; she had been getting inundated with threats ever since she started requiring vaccination to enter her studio.

I understood why the campaign was skeptical: Canadian smugness is a powerful drug. Here in British Columbia, Canada's westernmost province, the government had delegated almost all of its crucial Covid communications to Dr. Bonnie Henry, a supremely sensible-seeming public health officer who was a kind of anti-Trump. In a soothing voice just above a whisper, she told us daily about the latest data and entreated us, "Be kind, be calm, be safe." Infection levels stayed low during that first year, and for a time "Dr. Bonnie" fever ran so high that artists painted murals of her blond-bob-framed face and John Fluevog designed a pair of patent leather Mary Janes in her honor.

Covid denialism and Great Reset hysteria were circulating in Canada, but it still seemed to be cordoned off on the political right. Many voters were leaving the staid Conservative Party and flocking to the fringe and fiercely anti-immigrant People's Party, which had lifted its election talking points straight from the Mirror World. "Say No to Vaccine Passports!" a pamphlet stuffed into my mailbox declared. Stand strong against "the tyrannical dictates of the establishment." Avi thought this wasn't likely to be much of a factor among the progressive voters he hoped to reach. He was running with the NDP, Canada's onetime proudly socialist New Democratic Party, which his grandfather and father had help found, and which, in line with global trends, had long been more left-ish than actually left. This election, the party was promising to strengthen the social programs that had gotten the country through the first waves of Covid comparatively well. Avi was betting that many Canadians would be ready to embrace an even more activist form of government to meet the climate and housing emergencies. And so, tapping into the high hopes many of us still had back then, the slogan he landed on was "The pandemic recovery must be a Green New Deal for all!"

I tried to warn him, I really did. I told him that denialism was slicing a diagonal line across borders, in ways that were hard to predict through the old left-right axis. I warned him that in the community where we live, where energy healer and life coach are career paths at least as popular as nurse and teacher, and where free births and full-moon forest raves are very much a thing, there were going to be voters—his potential voters—who had followed people like my doppelganger into the Mirror World. I urged him to read up on vaccine passports, familiarize himself with the Great Reset, develop careful and thoughtful positions on all of it.

He didn't have time. He was too busy drafting policy positions on real crises: water shortages because of chronic drought, skyrocketing rents and high housing costs, inadequate public transit, the logging of our last old-growth forests. Sweet man: he still thought reality was on the ballot.

Then we started knocking on doors.

Political canvassing is never particularly comfortable, but doing it seventeen months into a surreal global event that had sowed fear of other people's exhalations was its own special kind of eerie. To some of the people answering their doors or peering through curtains, it was clear that strangers on their steps was a jarring apparition.

After about an hour, my canvassing partner Tak and I had rung a bunch of bells and logged only one positive interaction on our clipboard. Mostly, people didn't answer their doors at all, even though we could sometimes hear them screaming at one another inside. Then we got to a house with a solar array on the roof and an electric car charging in the driveway.

"Our people," Tak declared confidently.

It was about three in the afternoon, and the fortysomething woman who opened the white front door was vaguely disheveled.

"Sorry, I'm not dressed yet," she said, clearly embarrassed and gesturing toward bear-festooned pajama bottoms.

"Oh my god, I'm the last to judge," I replied, hoping the huge smile my mask was covering would show up as warm eye-crinkles. "I can't believe I'm not in my pajamas right now! My son hasn't worn actual clothes in over a year!"

We laughed. Her black labradoodle charged out of the house, barking and circling.

"Don't mind him. He's not used to people anymore. Like me."

We laughed some more. I told her about my desocialized and dim cockapoo, the one at war with her dogpelganger; charmed the labradoodle; and complimented her on her solar panels. We were off to a good start.

"We're here to find out what issues are on your mind ahead of the federal election," I explained. "We're with the NDP—"

The mood changed sharply. She took a step back inside and fixed me with what I have come to think of as Internet Eyes.

"I voted for the NDP my whole life. My parents voted for you. My grandparents voted for you. But I have to tell you that I am so disappointed with your leader and the way he sold out to the globalists."

The globalists? My hair follicles tingled, sensing code for "Jews." Still, I was there to get votes, not make friends. I tried extending what, in canvassing trainings, is called "a bridge."

"I'm a writer. Actually, I wrote a book about corporate globalization back in the day. And the NDP has always stood up to big business and bad trade deals. They want a wealth tax—"

"Nah. I've had it," she said, calling back her dog and retreating farther. "I'm going with the People's Party this time."

And with that, she and the black labradoodle disappeared behind a firmly closed white door.

Tak and I walked away in a daze.

"I've worked a few campaigns," he said slowly. "But that's the first voter I ever met who flipped NDP to People's Party."

She certainly had boarded an express train: Canada has two establishment parties—the Liberals and the Conservatives—that hug the political center and traditionally lob power back and forth between them. This voter had gone from the NDP on the left to the People's Party on the far right without so much as a pit stop with either of those parties in the middle. I understood being frustrated with the NDP; I was, too. From climate action to soaring inequality, they had failed to offer a true left alternative in recent years. That's why Avi was running: to push them to live up to their original ideals. But using frustration over compromised leftism to leap straight to the far right? What the hell was happening?

We knocked on a few more doors, received our warmest reception from Punjabi Canadians who appreciated the NDP's support for farmers in India who were in the middle of a mass uprising, and Tak and I started to feel a little less like we'd tumbled down a Reddit-thread rabbit hole.

With our clipboard now full of voter data, and the names of a couple of possible "super-volunteers," we headed for the scheduled debrief at the home of a party stalwart. Avi, who had been knocking on doors a few blocks over, showed up moments later. He seemed shaken and was sputtering something about how he could "smell the sandalwood." Once he had de-masked and drunk some water, he told us the whole story. He had gone to a home where the front door was ajar, and the scent of said incense wafted to the curb. The windowsills were lined with bronze statues; he recognized Buddha and Ganesh. Like us with the solar panels, he figured the Green New Deal shouldn't be too hard a sell at a home like this. Like us, he was sorely mistaken.

A white woman with ropey muscles came out to the porch dressed in yoga gear and ready for a fight. Putting her hand over her mouth in lieu of a mask, she had exactly one question for him: "What is your position on vaccine passports?"

Avi replied that the party was in favor of checking vaccination status for indoor activities, which made good epidemiological sense at that stage of the pandemic, and asked what her position was.

That's when she started to talk about her "bodily autonomy" and "sovereign citizenship" and how she had "a strong immune system."

"That's great," Avi said, extending his version of the bridge. "It's great that you are healthy. The concern, I guess, is that not everyone has a strong immune system. Some people have compromised systems, and health problems that make the virus more likely to make them seriously ill, or even die."

Her response, in this hippy-dippy West Coast community, was: "I think those people *should* die."

And with that, she disappeared into a cloud of sandalwood.

After these harrowing encounters, we both started to see evidence of diagonalism's spread all around us. On community noticeboards. At local council meetings. And that little cluster of demonstrators in town? It was growing fast. A couple of weeks into the campaign, I drove past the sleepy hospital where T. was born and saw a crowd of three hundred people outside—the biggest protest I could remember in this rural community. Definitely more than came out against the invasion of Iraq, and probably for the 2019 climate strikes.

Demonstrators interfered with patients needing urgent care and hurled abuse at nurses—all part of a coordinated "World Wide Walkout" day against vaccine mandates that my doppelganger had been hyping on her new Gettr account. At one point, the crowd sang a mostly mumbled rendition of the Women's Warrior Song, a sacred anthem for many Indigenous communities in this region, including the shíshálh Nation, whose band council office was directly across the street. The council put out an immediate statement condemning the appropriation as an insult to their culture. Meanwhile, on the other side of the country, Trudeau canceled a scheduled rally because anti-vaxxers were threatening violence, hurling expletives, and calling for new Nuremberg Trials.

"So, what would you say about vaccine passports?" Avi asked me that night, trying to sound casual.

"I'd first validate their fears about data. Tell them that your top priority is safeguarding their privacy and keeping their personal information out of the hands of private tech companies. Pivot the conversation to the need to regulate those companies, break them up, treat them as public utilities, guarantee everyone's right to be part of a digital town square. Show them that there is a way to stick it to Big Tech without putting their life and other people's lives in danger."

He was listening.

"Same with Big Pharma. Remember, people have good reason to loathe these companies. Pivot to common ground: why lifesaving treatments and medicines shouldn't be run for profit in the first place. Shift to the need to expand public health care to include prescription drugs. Talk about how we can create good jobs in public health and preventive medicine."

He knew all these arguments inside out, had been making them for years. It was just a recasting, a way to take some territory back from the Mirror World. I thought this strategy had a decent chance of working with some voters, ones who had only glanced into the looking glass here and there. But for those people who had stepped all the way through, I didn't hold out much hope that Avi, charming as he is, was going to bring them back.

In the coming weeks, some took the opportunity to try to convince him he had it all wrong, writing letters that, quite cleverly, used my work against him:

> I have been doing much research on what it is we are dealing with and was hoping Naomi was going to be writing a follow up to "Shock Doctrine" with what is happening in our world right now with losing our freedoms, being discriminated against if we do not wish to take an experimental "shot" . . . This "plandemic" has cost our world dearly and I want to see justice served and those held accountable for their part in it all, namely Anthony Fauci, Bill Gates, Big Pharma, The Media.

Most had no desire for even that level of dialogue.

Even after months mired in the Mirror World, I was shocked by some of the things that Avi and I were seeing and hearing from our neighbors. At the start of the pandemic, there had been various loud voices calling for the sick and elderly to be sacrificed in the name of keeping the economy going. But those had been smarmy Republicans; cruel, but on brand. What I did not expect was to find lifelong voters for the NDP—the party pivotal in securing Canada's system of universal public health care—shrugging off mass death. Nor did I expect someone from whom I might have taken a Vinyasa class to actively advocate a die-off of the physically weak ("I think those people *should* die"). Or for a People's Party sign to appear right next to the one for Bliss or Bust Deep Meditation and Deep Tissue Massage. Or to hear longtime environmentalists say, in private conversations, that the right to be unvaccinated was their single issue in this election, a principled stand, as they saw it, against Big Pharma. (Later we would discover that the man who violently attacked Nancy Pelosi's eighty-two-year-old husband, Paul, in their San Francisco home grew up just up the road from here.)

Whatever I once thought the line was between "them" and "us," it was no longer holding. Clearly, a poison had been released in the culture, and it was not only coursing among right-wingers with the help of a few liberal crossover stars. This was something else: a poisonous compound enmeshed with powerful notions of natural living, bodily strength, fitness, purity, and divinity—alongside their opposites: unnaturalness, bodily weakness, slothfulness, contamination, and damnation.

Fitness and alternative health subcultures have long mixed with fascist and supremacist movements. In the United States, early fitness and bodybuilding enthusiasts were also enthusiastic about eugenics, and the prospect of breeding for what they saw as a superior human form. Nazi propaganda was crowded with images of young men hiking, and Hitler was convinced that "natural" food was central to the success of the Reich (though his vegetarianism appears to have been somewhat exaggerated). The Nazi Party was riven with health fads and extreme occult beliefs, which were all marshaled in the project of building an Aryan super race of godlike men. Put another way, the entire mission of building a supposedly golden race had an occult quality, which is why it merged so easily with New Age health fads and various naturalist fetishes.

After the horrors of the Second World War, the fascist/fitness/New Age alliance broke apart. When the New Age experienced its next big wave of popularity, in the 1960s, it was firmly associated with hippies, environmentalism, and the Beatles studying transcendental meditation. Now, however, it seemed as if the movement's older, supremacist roots were reasserting themselves.

The people Avi and I were meeting at the extreme end of this spectrum didn't seem to deny Covid outright. Rather, they cast the virus as a kind of cleansing, or "culling of the herd," with some mixing in ecofascist beliefs and imagining the pandemic as a means by which the natural world would be rehabilitated from human stresses. This line of thought was rampant in the early days of lockdowns, when THE EARTH IS HEALING and WE ARE THE VIRUS memes overran the internet, along with videos (plenty of them faked) of wild animals taking back our ghostly cities and towns. But now the embrace of a certain amount of human death was becoming more overt, and explicitly linked to opposing the vaccines. At around this time, Rob Schmitt, a former Fox News host who moved over to Newsmax, mused on air, "I feel like a vaccination in a weird way is just generally kind of going against nature. Like, I mean, if there is some disease out there—

maybe there's just an ebb and flow to life where something's supposed to wipe out a certain amount of people, and that's just kind of the way evolution goes. Vaccines kind of stand in the way of that."

These are ideas with blood-soaked histories in the Americas, reaching back to the stories European conquerors and colonists told about how the infectious diseases that ravaged Indigenous populations—already weakened after settlers stole their lands and decimated their food sources—were actually God's handiwork, a divine sign that these continents were meant for white Christians. "A wonderful plague" is how King James of England described pandemics in the 1620 Charter of New England. "Almighty God, in his great goodness and bounty towards us," had sent it "among the savages." In 1634, John Winthrop, the first governor of the Massachusetts Bay Colony, described the diseases that tore through the native Algonquian-speaking peoples in similar terms: "But for the natives in these parts, God hath so pursued them, as for 300 miles space the greatest part of them are swept away by smallpox which still continues among them: So as God hath thereby cleared our title to this place." In 1707, the former Carolina governor John Archdale also cast mass death as heaven-sent, writing of "the Indians" that it "pleased Almighty God to send unusual Sicknesses amongst them, as the Smallpox, etc., to lessen their Numbers; so that the English, in Comparison to the Spaniard, have but little Indian Blood to answer for." This was not true—there was plenty of blood to answer for, and disease was only one of many killers in these waves of genocide. But the idea that pandemics are carrying out the work of a greater power—whether that power is imagined as God or as nature—is integral to the origin myth of the modern world.

That ecofascist thought would surge in our particular historical moment is, sadly, predictable. We live in a time when having two jobs is no guarantee of affording a home and many of our governments consider bulldozing homeless encampments to be a viable policy solution. Meanwhile, every day brings us closer to a future of climate breakdown that, if it is not slowed and reversed, will surely lead to the culling of large parts of our and other species, hitting the most vulnerable first and worst. The process is already well underway. Being alive in a knife-edge moment like this, being forced to be complicit in it, while our so-called leaders fail so miserably to act, unavoidably generates all kinds of morbid symptoms. Inevitably, people reach for narratives to make sense of this reality.

Among such narratives is the one that the climate justice movement has been telling for years—the same one Avi was running on: people of good conscience, across all the lines meant to divide us, can band together, build power, and transform our societies into something fairer and greener, just in the nick of time. But that story is getting harder to believe with each day that goes by. So, another narrative, this one spreading much faster, goes like this: I'll be okay, I'm prepared, with my canned goods and solar panels and relative place of privilege on this planet—it's other people who will suffer. The trouble with that narrative, though, is that it requires finding ways to live with and rationalize the mass suffering of others. And that's where the stories and logics that cast other people's deaths as an unavoidable form of natural selection, perhaps even a blessing, come into play.

Like the fascist/New Age alliance, all of this is playing out on a kind of historical loop. Whenever one group has chosen to allow terrible violence to be inflicted on another group, there have been stories and logics that provided the permission for the beneficiaries of the violence either to actively (even gleefully) participate or to actively look away. Stories that said things like this: The people being sacrificed/enslaved/imprisoned/colonized/left to die so that others can live comfortably are not the same level of human. They are other/substandard/lesser/darker/more animal/diseased/criminal/lazy/uncivilized. These logics have been resurgent on the right for years now, evident in the presence of protofascist and authoritarian leaders in Brazil, India, Hungary, the Philippines, Russia, and Turkey, among others. But what we were seeing on the campaign trail was that these logics were spreading, diagonally, from authoritarian conservatives through to parts of the green and New Age left, following well-worn neural pathways with long and sinister histories.

The thread that connects them is simple and stark. It's a comfort with culling.

The Who's Who of Woo

When we were still living in New Jersey, which at the time trailed only New York as the state with the highest number of Covid deaths, the early anti-lockdown defiance came mainly from two groups. The first were the extremely religious: evangelical Christians, many of whom packed megachurches despite the lockdowns, and our Orthodox Jewish neighbors, who came into conflict with local authorities for continuing to congregate for large funerals and other services despite the health orders. That was to be expected: many ultra-religious people believe that their faith acts as a kind of force field against harm, or that sickness is a small price to pay for performing their religious obligations. Within that logic, failing to follow God's directives for communal prayer posed a greater risk than braving the aerosol particulates of their fellow believers at church or synagogue. One night, while bingeing cable news during those early weeks of lockdown, I caught a report about thousands of people crowding into an illegal, mostly unmasked service at a megachurch. Asked if she was worried about catching Covid, one worshipper beamed: "No way! I'm bathed in the blood of the Lord!"

The second group that insistently defied health orders in those same weeks was a little less expected. It was gym rats, some of whom organized demonstrations less than two months into the pandemic. They did sit-ups and push-ups in the streets, while demanding the right to lift weights indoors. The owner of Atilis Gym in Bellmawr, New Jersey, broke the law and opened his business—an act of defiance that turned the tattooed and bearded ex-felon into an unlikely hero on Fox News. (He would go on to run an unsuccessful bid to be a congressional candidate in the Republican primaries.)

At first, I couldn't figure out the connection between these two groups and the two very different activities they represented—what was the shared bond between extreme faith and extreme fitness, between worshipping the Lord and worshipping the body? It grew clearer when I started spending time in the Mirror World, particularly in those corners where New Age wellness influencers were sharing Covid conspiracies.

This was an evolution of the mindset that was first described in a 2011 academic paper as "conspirituality," a term that has since been popularized through the book and podcast of the same name (the one I listen to far too much). Like the subset of the ultra-religious who were unconcerned about contracting Covid, this subset of the ultra-fit also believed they had special protections from the virus: that their temples—which were their own detoxed and buffed bodies—would keep them safe. Wellness and fitness was their force field, or so they seemed to think.

This helps make some sense of the outsize role among the diagonalists of a group I will broadly describe as body people. We are all body people, of course, living inside bodies as we do, trying to enjoy them and keep them from harm. But here I am talking about people who are in the business of bodies. Not doctors (though there are a few of those sprinkled in) and certainly not epidemiologists with actual expertise in infectious disease. Rather, these are people who, like gym owners and advanced yoginis, can make a claim to special knowledge about what is right for other people's bodies: trainers, yoga teachers, CrossFit instructors, masseuses, mixed martial artists, chiropractors, lactation consultants, doulas, nutritionists, herbalists, menopause coaches, and certified juice therapists.

Plenty of people in these fields are highly trained and extremely knowledgeable about human physiology and have taken Covid seriously; many owners of gyms and yoga studios have gone to great (and costly) lengths to keep their clients safe. The fact remains, however, that some of the most prominent figures in this lucrative sector have gone full-blown Covid-QAnon. When the Center for Countering Digital Hate issued its list of what it termed "the Disinformation Dozen," a group of twelve individuals that its research found were collectively responsible for originating roughly 65 percent of the junk claims circulating about Covid and vaccines, the list wasn't populated with well-known right-wing media stars, as one might expect. Instead, it had a chiropractor and three different osteopaths, including one in Florida with a booming supplement business; a couple that sells essential oils to cure cancer and DVD sets on "taking back" your health; the editor of *Health Nut News*, who posts anti-Semitic memes about how the Rothschilds and "the Global elite are running the show. . . . #NewWorldOrder #TruthTeller"; and the guru behind the newsletter *GreenMedInfo*, who posts memes about how Bill Gates is using the vaccine to depopulate the earth in between advice about healing yourself with superfoods.

There were also a few women on the list who, like Wolf—with her books extolling natural beauty, natural childbirth, and life-altering orgasms—had built personal brands around being experts on women's bodies in particular. Christiane Northrup, a lapsed ob-gyn who wrote the Oprah-friendly, bestselling *Women's Bodies, Women's Wisdom*, made the Disinformation Dozen list after she began peppering her advice on nontoxic cleaning products and "vibrant health" with QAnon-tinged Covid denialism. So did Kelly Brogan, a "holistic psychiatrist" and bestselling author as likely to post a video of herself pole dancing as she is to tell you to "thank your body" for fighting off Covid without the help of vaccines or masks (which she urged her followers to take off in an act of liberation similar to second-wave bra burning).

It was, in short, a who's who of woo—alternative health, women's wellness, and spirit-infused diet and fitness. All were now hopelessly entangled with the surging far right and had become card-carrying citizens of the Mirror World.

Many have claimed that we are simply seeing the horseshoe theory in action: the idea that the right and the left each bend at their farthest reaches until they almost touch. But that is to confuse the far left—which is where the socialists and revolutionaries reside—with the far-out, which is where the wellness and New Age spiritualists hang out. Moreover, the members of these subcultures who made the Disinformation Dozen list had all figured out how to monetize the far-out—they have some of the largest online platforms and the strongest personal brands, which they use to sell high-priced retreats and seminars and memberships and newsletters and tinctures. These are big-name influencers with countless smaller-time followers.

Once this is understood, the new alliances start to make more sense. Small businesses and freelancers who work with or on bodies were among the hardest hit by pandemic lockdowns. Some of the reasons for that made epidemiological sense: therapeutic work didn't allow for social distancing, and exercise studios necessarily involve heavy breathing in enclosed spaces. But there were also ways that this sector got a particularly raw deal. Early Covid relief programs were heavily biased toward larger workplaces with many staff employees; small owner-operated fitness studios where most workers are on contract often fell through the cracks of government aid, even as they were still on the hook for massive urban rents.

Many gym owners took on large personal debts to keep operating under stringent new rules, only for the rules to continually change in often arbitrary ways as the pandemic wore on. Where I live in Canada, for instance, gyms were shut down in response to the 2022 Omicron surge, but, as many fitness enthusiasts pointed out (with more than a little judgment) fast-food restaurants and strip clubs seemed to be just fine. Meanwhile, small fitness studios seemed to face many more restrictions than giant sports stadiums and ski resorts, which could afford to pay lobbyists to protect their interests.

The net effect was an economic slaughter. Close to ten thousand U.S. health clubs were forced to shut down for good by early 2022, according to data compiled by the International Health, Racquet & Sportsclub Association. Justin Grover, co-owner of a gym in Kamloops, British Columbia, summed up the sense of outrage that was pervasive in the sector: "You can go eat deep-fried pickles and get sloshed in a pub on cheap draft and that's essential, but the person who has been 20 years in AA and uses a fitness facility to keep their head straight, they're not recognizing that."

Such grievances set the stage for many wellness workers to see sinister elite plots in everything having to do with the virus. But does getting hit particularly hard by lockdowns explain the virulence of conspiracies in the wellness world? Why didn't community theater owners go off the deep end? What was it about the quest for optimal fitness and "vibrant health," as Northrup calls it, that turned so nasty?

Body Doubles

In *The Beauty Myth*, Wolf argued that the elevated beauty expectations imposed on women in the 1980s were patriarchy's tax on feminism's successes. Now, on top of all the demands of work, and a second shift of housework and childcare, there was also a "Third Shift [added] to their leisure time. Superwoman . . . had to add serious 'beauty' labor to her *professional* agenda."

Three decades after Wolf made this argument, another feminist writer, one more attuned to political economy, looked at the same spike in interest in fitness and beauty in the 1980s and saw something else. In *Natural Causes: An Epidemic of Wellness, the Certainty of Dying, and Killing Ourselves to Live Longer,* Barbara Ehrenreich, who died in September 2022, tracked the ways that the quest for health and wellness became obsessive pursuits in the Reagan and Thatcher era and has only grown in influence since. She argued that this turn was a reaction not to feminism's successes, but rather to the failures of revolutionary movements, when the high hopes of the 1960s and '70s slammed into the brick wall of '80s neoliberalism.

With dreams of justice dashed, along with collective visions for a good life, it was everyone for themselves—a world of atomized individuals climbing over one another to get an edge in newly deregulated, precarious job markets. It was in this context, she argued, that so many turned their attention toward perfecting the body, with treadmills replacing protest marches and free weights replacing free love. The pressures were far greater for women at the start, but soon enough even heterosexual cis men would face their own unattainable fitness and beauty standards and myths. For Ehrenreich, this was all "part of a larger withdrawal into individual concerns after the briefly thrilling communal uplift some had experienced in the 1960s . . . If you could not change the world or even chart your own career, you could still control your own body—what goes into it and how muscular energy is expended." It was in this context that Jerry Rubin, onetime yippie provocateur and Chicago Seven defendant, became, in the 1980s, a proud yuppie and fitness evangelist.

Explaining her own longtime, often conflicted relationship with the gym, Ehrenreich wrote: "I may not be able to do much about grievous injustice in the world, at least not by myself or in very short order, but I can decide to increase the weight on the leg press machine by twenty pounds and achieve that within a few weeks." I've never been a gym rat, but I can relate. There have been long periods when yoga felt like the only thing bringing me any sense of control. I couldn't stop the U.S. invasion of Iraq—though millions of us tried like hell—but I could coax my body into Crow Pose and, on a very good day, do a handstand. Years later, when I got a cancer diagnosis, my practice grew more obsessive: pushing myself to new levels of strength and flexibility felt like the one area where my body would obey me. As the climate crisis accelerates, with the land heaving beneath us and burning around us, I expect that many of us will continue to find comfort in whatever small bodily obeyances we can muster. There is solace to be found there.

Yet I also know, from personal experience as a teenage bulimic and *Jane Fonda's Workout* addict, that this quest, in its extreme and unhealthy forms, is itself a kind of doubling. For the person dedicating themselves to transformation through diet and fitness, there is you as you are now, and—ever present—there is you as you imagine you could be, with enough self-denial and self-discipline, enough hunger and enough reps. A better, different you, always just out of reach. Ehrenreich wrote evocatively of the strange silence of gyms, a place where people gather together in close quarters but barely speak to one another except to negotiate access to machines. This, she observed, is because the primary relationship at play is not between separate people working out, but between the person working out and themselves as they wish to be, their body double.

In *Her Body and Other Parties*, Carmen Maria Machado explores the relationship between the thin self and the fat self as a form of inner doppelganger. In the story "Eight Bites," Machado's narrator despises her body as it is—its heaviness, softness, and sagginess: "I was tired of flat, unforgiving dressing room lights; I was tired of looking into the mirror and grabbing the things that I hated and lifting them, clawing deep, and then letting them drop and everything aching." So she undergoes bariatric surgery and shrinks down to a more socially acceptable size. But the narrator is haunted by what she first thinks is a ghost and then discovers is something much creepier: the fat she shed as a result of the surgery, one hundred pounds of it, which has taken a featureless human form in her home. It is a fat golem, the self she could not bring herself to love and so chose to cut away. "I kneel down next to it," the narrator says. "It is a body with nothing it needs: no stomach or bones or mouth. Just soft indents. I crouch down and stroke its shoulder, or what I think is its shoulder. It turns and looks at me. It has no eyes, but still, it looks at me. *She* looks at me. She is awful but honest. She is grotesque but she is real." The narrator then beats her double with terrible violence.

The hatred and rage at the imperfect, unfit self can be the flip side of the quest for a perfected, controlled body, achieved through the right combination of workouts, diets, surgeries, and assorted wellness interventions. And it can grow more intense as we engage in another kind of body doubling: aging, that process of witnessing the changing of our face and form via such ravages as pregnancy, sleepless parenting, stress, pollution, and just being alive for enough revolutions around the sun. "Old age isn't a battle; old age is a massacre," Philip Roth, my problematic king of doppelgangers, observed.

The longer we stick around, the more unfamiliar we can become to ourselves, each distorted version of our younger "prime" selves a little less recognizable than the last. Cling too hard to your youthful double and risk becoming a surgerized, injected parody. Or worse. That, after all, is the unmissable warning carried by *The Picture of Dorian Gray*: if you seek eternal youth, and deny your aging double its reality, you'll both end up dead.

The desire for perfect wellness and perennial glowing youth is certainly what is driving a great many people to influencers like Christiane Northrup, the Martha Stewart of the conspiritualist world, who promises unending vitality if you buy her books, menopause supplements, eye serum, and vaginal moisturizer, all for sale on her website. There are other forces propelling many into these circles, including the limits and missteps of conventional medicine. Specialist doctors and pharmaceutical companies frequently fail people with complex diseases and disorders. And as I learned early on from those inappropriate dinner-table conversations about my father's research, reproductive health is woefully understudied, and women's legitimate complaints are too often discounted, dismissed, or disbelieved as hypochondria. Childbirth can be a terribly disempowering experience, and all of these failures and abandonments by conventional medicine are vastly more severe for

Black and Indigenous women, who are consistently treated as unreliable narrators of their own bodies. According to the U.S. Centers for Disease Control, "Black women are three times more likely to die from a pregnancy-related cause than white women," while a 2021 study found that infant mortality rates were more than twice as high for babies born to Black women than to white women.

All of this and more have pushed millions of people to try to heal, cure, and control themselves through an ever-expanding array of self-help directives and wellness concoctions, plenty of which have real benefits. This is the trouble with the Mirror World: there is always some truth mixed in with the lies; always some devastating collective failure it has identified and is opportunistically exploiting.

The Bad Births to Covid Conspiracy Pipeline

Take Glowing Mama, the Toronto-based influencer who was upset about the prospect of her daughter having imaginary vaccine particles shed on her by her loving grandparents. Before Covid, Glowing Mama was focused on coaching women to get fit before, during, and after pregnancy. ("Let me show you how simple it can be to optimize your health and fitness, and feel your best, in the midst of this crazy #momlife.") During Covid, she pivoted to leading a movement of maskless moms as they occupied shopping malls calling for an end to health mandates.

The journey, jarring as it may seem, had a certain logic to it. Trying to figure out how to be maximally healthy while carrying and then nursing a child can be a profoundly radicalizing experience. Many people who have never paid attention to environmental toxins get a crash course in the fact that a great many things they might put in, on, or near their bodies contain chemicals that could, in sufficient quantities, pose health risks to a developing fetus or child. There is also every chance that, while exploring what kind of birth they want, this future parent will get bombarded with other people's horror stories—about impatient doctors who pushed drugs to induce birth and set off a cascade of further interventions that ended in an emergency cesarean section that led to ongoing health challenges. They might even have skimmed a hand-me-down copy of my doppelganger's 2001 book, *Misconceptions: Truth, Lies, and the Unexpected on the Journey to Motherhood*, which explores her own such experience and the feelings of anger and disempowerment it instilled in her.

Because Western medicine is often dismissive of these concerns, many people who become pregnant seek out alternative sources of information and alternative supports—places where they are told that the medical profession is built to make them feel helpless, dependent, and weak. That they are capable of finding their intuitive power, innate strength, and maybe even, according to a 2008 documentary featuring Christiane Northrup, have a "birth-gasm." Much of this can be positive and healthy: it's a wonderful thing to have choices in what birth can be. But this is where the white, wealthy, libertarian streak in the wellness industry can become lethal. Because while it is true that many doctors give up on vaginal births too soon, or rely too much on surgical interventions, or express alarm over low-risk home births, it is also true that complications from pregnancy and childbirth remain major causes of death around the world. Even in a country as wealthy as the United States, a great many women and gender-marginalized people need more (and more sensitive) health care, not less.

Dr. Michelle Cohen, a family physician and assistant professor in the Department of Family Medicine at Queen's University, has tracked the often insidious role of pseudoscientific women's wellness influencers in the Covid era. While recognizing the real failures of her profession, she argues that these influencers are exploiting "medicine's sexism to create a new and gendered market for snake oil"—instead of trying to fix the system, they profit from its abandonments. "The wellness industry isn't pushing for more and better science into women's health—it wants instead to create a secondary pathway for women's issues outside of the mainstream. The subtler risk is that wellness will continue to evolve along a gendered path, disproportionately exposing women to the harms of quackery."

This is a marked shift from the early days of the feminist health movement in the 1970s, which was, in its low-key way, anti-capitalist, focused on efforts like boycotting Nestlé because the company marketed powdered infant formula to poor mothers in the Global South. Feminist health, back then, was a movement fighting for changes at the collective and institutional level—like birthing centers inside hospitals, and certification of midwives and doulas, and access to safe abortions, and building research institutions focused on long-ignored aspects of women's health. It was also about the right to go on paid parental leave and the right to breastfeed without being criminalized. Having grown up inside this movement, thanks to my father's research and my mother's advocacy, I can attest that nothing about it was glamorous. Midwives and doulas got paid (not very much); family doctors got paid more, but still far less than obstetricians; copies of *Our Bodies, Ourselves* helped fund the Boston Women's Health Book Collective, but nobody was getting rich.

There is, moreover, still huge value in what is broadly termed "wellness." Many of us lead dangerously sedentary lives; our work demands it. Chances are that moving our bodies in whatever free time we have will make us healthier and feel better. Food prepared with fresh ingredients is more nourishing than fast food picked up on the fly. None of it will prevent death, or deliver eternal youth, but it's good to be active and strong; good to eat nutrient-rich foods; good to expand the horizons of health beyond Big Pharma's fixes. Everyone should have access to those kinds of options wherever they live, along with the time and resources to take advantage of them, which is far from the case today.

Throughout the pandemic, there have been doctors and alternative health practitioners who have made these kinds of arguments not as an alternative to vaccines, masks, and prescription medications, but as important complements to them. Dr. Rupa Marya, for instance, has been highly critical of Covid conspiracy theorists, calling anti-science attitudes "a leading cause of death in the U.S." But she also sees plenty that needs fixing in the medical status quo, which is why, along with Raj Patel, she coauthored *Inflamed: Deep Medicine and the Anatomy of Justice*. She and Patel acknowledge that the wellness gurus are absolutely right when they say we live in a culture that makes people sick as a matter of course—but rather than presenting individual peak wellness as the high-priced solution, they advocate for "deep medicine": structural changes that would detoxify our world and make healthy choices accessible to all.

Many more people who are knowledgeable about alternative health and preventive medicine could, like Marya and Patel, have used their expertise to advocate for collective and structural responses to our collective health crises during the pandemic. That is what happened during the Great Depression in the United States, when New Deal programs created millions of jobs building public swimming pools as well as hundreds of state and national parks. The guiding philosophy of these ambitious public works projects was that exercise and access to nature were rights that should not be reserved for the rich. Similar programs could be launched today, with an emphasis on the Black and Brown neighborhoods that never received their share of New Deal infrastructure, or that lost it afterward when whites revolted against integration. Rather than attack nurses and teachers, experts in wellness could have joined with them and fought for kids to have more outdoor education and access to nature, and for their parents to have shorter workweeks with better pay and union protections—all of which make it easier to lead an active life, and to choose and prepare healthier food.

None of this, however, is the kind of influence most high-profile wellness influencers have chosen to wield. Instead, it's more promises about the perfect life that awaits if we attain our perfected body double. *Our Bodies, Ourselves*, the health bible my mother regularly consulted, has been supplanted with an all-pervasive ethos of "my body, my worth"—the corollary of which seems to be "your body, your problem."

The look and the formula of the sector are familiar by now. Overwhelmingly white, conventionally beautiful hyperfit women photographed and filmed against blasted-out white backdrops. Faces cartoon-smooth thanks to photo filters and injectable fillers. Snug tank tops with empowering slogans, paired with patterned leggings. And then there are wavy-haired momfluencers turning child-rearing into a series of airy tableaux of sponsored organic content. These influencers gaze at us through the camera's lens with so much heart-bursting love that it's easy to forget that what they are actually looking at is their own faces on their phones—their digital doubles—as they coach us all to reach for our own best selves, our body doubles, in the never-ending house of mirrors.

Like so much else online, glowing influencer culture, for a time, didn't seem all that dangerous. Yes, Instagram and TikTok could be brutal on self-esteem, and, sure, a good bit of quackery and dodgy diuretic teas was being peddled. But there were also healthy recipes, and free exercise tips, and some genuinely helpful information.

Then came Covid—and this booming, unregulated industry of self-styled health experts collided with a global health crisis that scared the hell out of pretty much everyone, including the professionally well. After all, their yoga studios, CrossFit boxes, and massage clinics were, for the first time, locked tight, and their incomes and futures were suddenly highly uncertain. As Ehrenreich taught us, we turn toward the body when life feels out of control. It was in this period that so many of those fit and beautiful influencers stopped merely cooing soothingly and offering encouraging words to motivate our home workouts and green juicing and started whispering to us alarmingly, about dark forces coming to poison us, and eventually, to gag, jab, and dominate us. It was then that the diagonal lines started to race toward one another.

United by Hustle

Steve Bannon clearly is nobody's idea of a health nut; Donald Trump is defiantly devoted to fast food; and a favorite Fox News pastime is railing against liberals who try to tell real Americans to eat their vegetables (Michelle Obama's White House garden was a favorite target). Nonetheless, common ground has been located—and lots of it.

What unites the far right and the far-out is the hustle on the one hand, and a faith in hyper-individualism on the other. In the alternative-health world, everyone is selling something: classes, retreats, sound baths, essential oils, anti-metal-toxin sprays, Himalayan salt rock lamps, coffee enemas. Supplements alone were worth an estimated $155 billion worldwide in 2022. It's much the same on Bannon's *War Room* or Alex Jones's *Infowars*, with their manly supplements, survivalist supplies, Freedom Fests, precious metal offers, colloidal silver toothpaste, and weapons training—and let us not forget Tucker Carlson's 2022 documentary in which he recommended that men regularly tan their testicles with a special infrared light in order to increase testosterone levels in preparation for the "hard times" ahead.

The voices of these two kinds of pitches are distinct—one intimate, the other gruff and bullying. (Jones, as his legal woes have worsened, has resorted to pushing his branded products by screaming at his audience, "If you don't support us, you're helping the enemy.") But the underlying message is quite similar: society is crashing, and you as an individual (not a member of a society) need to prepare and toughen up, whether by optimizing your body, stocking your disaster bunker, or both. In many ways, the most successful influencers in the wellness and fitness worlds—the people who make fortunes from selling idealized versions of themselves and the idea that you, too, can attain nirvana through a project of perpetual self-improvement—are a perfect fit with far-right economic libertarians and anarcho-capitalists, who also fetishize the individual as the only relevant social actor. In neither worldview is there any mention of collective solutions or structural changes that would make a healthy life possible for all.

Do the far right and the far-out actually believe the same things about vaccines? Carlson claims not to have been vaccinated against Covid-19 and Bannon strongly hints the same, but there is no way to know for sure. What we do know is that they saw enormous political advantage in sabotaging what could have been a hugely successful and popular government program: the dissemination of free, lifesaving vaccines in the middle of a pandemic.

Some of this clearly had to do with the fact that the program was rolled out after Trump lost the 2020 election and while the Democrats still controlled all three branches of government. A smooth process that achieved high levels of vaccination would have saved many lives, but it also would been a significant win for Democrats. Instead, thanks to the spread of nonstop medical misinformation, states like Wyoming and Mississippi struggled to get half their eligible people fully vaccinated.

There may have been deeper ideological reasons for opposing the vaccines as well. If the U.S. efforts to control Covid through free vaccination and wage-replacement programs had been more successful, that would have demonstrated that the federal government, when it sets its mind to something, can still provide timely, universal, and humane care to the entire population. But that raises some questions: If they can do it for Covid-19, why stop there? Why not launch similarly ambitious public programs to tackle other human emergencies? Could the government tackle hunger, soaring housing costs, and the need for universal health care? A successful Covid response would have set a precedent for a modern, activist government—a precedent many on the right consider dangerous. So it's worth considering the possibility that Covid public health measures may have been in the crosshairs for people like Bannon and Carlson for a deceptively simple reason: because they were public.

The wellness gurus and hucksters who populate the Disinformation Dozen (and those who aspire to such influence) also see themselves as being at war with official health authorities, though for more mercenary reasons. "Health is NOT THE GOAL of the medical establishment. Sign up for my newsletter and learn the True Causes of Health!" Christiane Northrup announces at the top of her website, next to lots of pictures of her strangely ageless face. Or, to quote a much-circulated meme: "I didn't get my flu shot! Because I'm smart enough to realize that the medical industry prefers a chronically-ill population over a healthy one." (There is some truth to the second claim, but it has nothing to do with whether or not to get a free flu shot.)

These statements sum up a pervasive logic in the more entrepreneurial parts of the wellness sector: doctors and drug companies want you to be sick so they can sell you Band-Aids, while fitness and wellness professionals want you to be well—but first you have to buy whatever they are selling instead. The larger and more profitable the wellness industry grows, the fiercer this competitive perspective becomes, to the point where even going to the doctor or getting a prescription filled can seem like a failure of wellness—clear evidence that you did not juice or train hard enough. Lining up with all of those regular (i.e., toxic, unfit) people to get injected with something that requires no special knowledge or virtue to access and, most suspicious of all in a market system, doesn't cost any money, can be enough to cause a full-blown identity crisis.

When Covid hit, competition among many prominent people who specialize in wellness and those they dismissed as specializing in sickness (i.e., doctors and scientists) reached new levels, and for a simple reason. For months, conventional medicine had nothing for us. This was the period when, if you thought you might have Covid, the reigning advice offered by doctors was far from reassuring: "Try not to give it to anyone else"; "Stay home unless you can barely breathe"; "If you can't breathe, call an ambulance and try your luck with the local hospital, from which there is a solid chance you will never reemerge."

This was not a conspiracy, and most of it wasn't even really a failure. Yes, our health-care systems could have been better prepared with larger stockpiles of masks, more ventilators, more beds, and more nurses. But that wouldn't have changed the underlying problem, which was that it takes time to understand a novel virus. Time to do research before serious scientists will make claims about the best course of action.

It was inside that vacuum that so many wellness hustlers saw a first-mover advantage. Sure, they didn't understand the virus either, but for plenty in this unregulated sector, that had never stopped them from making inflated claims about what a particular herb or diet will do before. And so, unlike the epidemiologists who were busy trying to understand SARS-CoV-2, many wellness gurus wasted no time pitching all manner of supplements, tinctures, and miracle cures that all claimed to do what the doctors could not: protect us. It was a bonanza—until, of course, the vaccines showed up and threatened to spoil all the fun.

Is it any wonder wellness went to war?

The Black Plague

So far, I have presented the diagonalist alliance as one of convenience. Both the propagandists of the far right and the influencers of the far-out had their own good reasons to poison the well for the vaccine rollout. The former feared the precedent of a functional, caring state (and a political win for their rivals); the latter feared losing explosive growth in their sector. But I've come to believe that the bond is deeper and more troubling—that in these worlds reaching toward each other, there are also increasingly explicit shared beliefs, ones having to do with whose lives count most and whose deaths might be "nature" doing its work.

There are deep and healthy pleasures to be found in exercise, as there are in other aspects of wellness. For many of the evangelists in these worlds, however, both fitness and diet are intensely value-laden endeavors. Achieving goals means setting rigorous targets and displaying relentless discipline to meet them (a.k.a. "putting in the work"). That's how you reach your idealized body double. Which is all fine if it stays there. But the trouble is, it often doesn't. As Carmen Maria Machado draws out in her doppelganger short story, once the slim, perfected body has been achieved, the less controlled body that once was can persist as an ever-present shadow self—and this discarded double is deeply loathed. In "Eight Bites," the narrator's daughter is hurt and angry about her mother's surgery and subsequent transformation because she perceives it as an attack. "Do you hate my body, Mom?" she asks, voice full of pain. "You hated yours, clearly, but mine looks just like yours used to, so—" And that is the trouble with this more private kind of doppelganger: when body mania sets in, the fit self may well not be satisfied with crushing its own unfit self; it may look for other targets, its self-hatred seeping out and projecting itself onto other people's less fit, less conventionally able bodies.

These kinds of moralistic physical judgments deepened during the pandemic, especially when it became clear that obesity, diabetes, and some forms of addiction increased the risks posed by Covid-19, alongside other factors, including age. Much of the pressure to wear a mask and get vaccinated, meanwhile, was framed as a duty to care for those with greater vulnerabilities. It was then that wellness culture, and its barely submerged hostility toward less conventionally perfect bodies and less "clean" lifestyles, began to bare its teeth.

There are too many foul examples to cite, but one exchange sums it up for me, coming from our old friend Glowing Mama, who in her many videos about Covid conspiracies on Instagram, often admits to being lightheaded. "Sorry guys, I'm on day three of a fast," she will say. Certainly, the hunger lends an edge to the videos. At one point in year two of the pandemic, she filmed herself in a rage over the suggestion that by refusing to mask or be vaccinated, she and her daughter might pose a health threat to others. The idea that her healthy body could be anything but a source of radiant positivity was clearly inconceivable, and her response to her imagined critics was this: "Go fucking eat a carrot and jump on a treadmill." This remark was then cheered on by another trainer, who remarked, "I'm realizing it doesn't matter to me if someone who is metabolically unsound heals themselves or improves their condition at all . . . Just realize and acknowledge that their health is their responsibility and my health is mine . . . period!" Then she went back to posting about paleo-friendly muffins (#CleanEating).

It's clear from these comments that, at least for these trainers, if you aren't as peak fit as they are, you don't have a right to have opinions on any aspect of health—and you definitely don't have a right to ask anything health-related of them. The core Covid-era public health message—that we all needed to undergo some individual inconveniences for the sake of our collective health—enjoyed majority support. Yet it simply could not be reconciled with the wellness industry's own overarching message: that individuals must take charge over their own bodies as their primary sites of influence, control, and competitive edge. And that those who don't exercise that control deserve what they get. Neoliberalism of the body, in distilled form.

One month into the pandemic, we still knew very little about the virus. But we did know this: it was more of a threat to Black people than to white people. Writing in *The New Yorker* in April 2020, the Princeton historian Keeanga-Yamahtta Taylor called Covid-19 "the Black Plague," noting, "Thousands of white Americans have also died from the virus, but the pace at which African-Americans are dying has transformed this public health crisis into an object lesson in racial and class inequality." That is not the lesson that many conspiratualist health influencers took away, however. On the contrary, the lesson they seem to have extracted from the race and class disparities of Covid's early death toll was "This virus is going to kill people who do not look like me." (While that was true at first, it changed as the pandemic wore on, in large part thanks to misinformation about vaccines and mask wearing.)

This willingness to write off huge swaths of humanity that are cast as lesser within supremacist narratives is the strongest glue that binds together the pastel-hued, self-loving world of women's wellness with the fire-breathing, immigrant-bashing world of the Bannon right. I doubt that the thin white fitness trainers who lobbed insults about how people who wanted them to get vaxxed should "eat a carrot and jump on a treadmill" were thinking about the fact that those who would pay the highest price for Covid's unchecked circulation were, at that time, disproportionately poor, Black, and Brown. It remains the case, however, that these realities neatly lined up with the white supremacist goals of the far-right members of the diagonalist alliance. The people put most at risk were part of the same groups Bannon casts as invaders in his "Border Warfare" segments and from the same neighborhoods Trump cast as war zones in his "American Carnage" inauguration speech (reportedly written by Bannon, with help from other aides).

There are other points of connection as well. As the transnational extreme right—from Giorgia Meloni to Jair Bolsonaro—landed on anti-trans fearmongering as a powerful adhesive to bind together its Frankenstein of "inclusive nationalism," many of the same people in the wellness world who railed against the unnaturalness of Covid vaccines have begun to speak more openly about the supposed naturalness of the gender binary, and of traditional family roles. Far from the unlikely bedfellows they first seemed to be, large parts of the modern wellness industry are proving to be all too compatible with far-right notions of natural hierarchies, genetic superiority, and disposable people.

Yellow Stars and Wild Projection

Wolf was one of the earliest in the anti-vax scene to liken mask and vaccine mandates to the yellow stars that Jewish people were forced to wear throughout Nazi-occupied Europe. It is one of many direct analogies with the Nazi Holocaust favored by the movement: Justin Trudeau and Emmanuel Macron are routinely depicted as Hitler, Anthony Fauci as Josef Mengele, quarantine hotels as concentration camps, and the list goes on. So popular are these specious comparisons that a hat store in Nashville, Tennessee, began selling yellow Star of David–shaped patches with NOT VACCINATED embroidered on them ("they turned out great! $5ea . . . we'll be offering trucker caps soon," the store owner boasted on Instagram). But I have yet to come across anyone who dwells on the Nazi analogies quite as enthusiastically as my doppelganger.

In addition to the direct Nazi comparisons, she has repeatedly claimed that we have endured a "biofascist" coup. Why? Because vaccine mandates are supposedly based on the fascist notion that certain bodies (vaccinated ones) are superior to other bodies (unvaccinated ones). As is so often the case with Wolf, the layers of projection at work are revealing. First, the Nazis relaxed vaccination programs in Germany and actively opposed them in the lands they annexed precisely because they favored the die-off of non-Aryan populations. ("The Slavs are to work for us. Insofar as we don't need them, they may die. Therefore compulsory vaccination and German health services are superfluous," wrote Martin Bormann, Hitler's chief of staff and the head of the Nazi Party, in 1942.) More to the point, vaccination programs that ask strong, healthy people to accept small inconveniences to protect themselves—as well as people who are sicker, older, and more medically vulnerable—are the precise opposite of biofascism. On the contrary, they are acts of what we might call biojustice.

When we get vaccinated against diseases that pose a greater threat to other members of our communities than they do to us, we are saying that all people, no matter their bodily impairments or challenges, are of fundamentally equal value and have a right to equally access the public sphere and a good life. This is the principle at the heart of the disability justice movement, which, after decades of struggle, is thankfully encoded in some (though not enough) of the laws in most constitutional democracies. This struggle is the reason buildings have ramps and elevators, and the reason public schools are required to have accommodations for kids whose brains and bodies are atypical. But these victories are under constant assault because the idea that we should think and function as communities of enmeshed bodies with different needs and vulnerabilities flies in the face of a core message of neoliberal capitalism: that you are on your own and deserve your lot in life, for better or worse. And, relatedly, it also flies in the face of a core message of neoliberal wellness culture: that your body is your primary site of control and advantage in this cruel and polluted world. So get to work optimizing it!

The disability justice advocate and author Beatrice Adler-Bolton refers to the mindset that has animated so much Covid denialism as "deaths pulled from the future"—which she defines as the judgment-laden posture that frames "deaths from Covid-19 as somehow preordained" because the people doing most of the dying were probably going to die prematurely anyway. Covid just moved up the timeline a few years, so what's the big deal? And that's at the moderate end of the spectrum—at the extreme, sandalwood-scented end, those deaths pulled from the future are actually welcomed. Like the yoga woman said, "I think those people *should* die."

At the risk of causing more confusion by sounding like my doppelganger, this is fascist thought. More specifically, it is genocidal thought. It recalls the ways in which colonial massacres were rationalized because, within the ranking of human life created by pseudoscientific racists, Indigenous peoples, such as the original residents of Tasmania, were cast as "living fossils." Lord Salisbury, the UK prime minister, explained in an 1898 address that "you may roughly divide the nations of the world as the living and the dying." Indigenous peoples were, in this telling, the pre-dead, with extermination merely serving to accelerate the inevitable timeline.

These are the histories currently being conjured up in mainstream wellness culture, which has adopted Silicon Valley's notion of self-optimization, itself a by-product of the personal-branding culture that torments so many young people today. Every step counted. Every sleep measured. Every meal "clean." And it is this context that has prepared the ground for a redux of the 1930s fascist/New Age alliance. The very idea that humans can and should be "optimized" lends itself to a fascistic worldview—because if your food is extra-clean, it can easily mean other people's food is extra-dirty. If you are safe because your immune system is strong, it can flip to mean others are unsafe because they are weak. If you are optimized, others are, by definition, suboptimal. Defective. Next door to disposable. This is also the context in which some prominent anti-vaxxers have taken to calling themselves "purebloods," since their blood is supposedly untainted by the jabs, never mind the term's chilling supremacist overtones.

Which brings us to the Mirror World's most pipiked projection of all. From the very first ripples of Covid conspiracy theories to the tidal waves of lies that would go on to inundate us, one claim has recurred with more frequency than any other: that the plan behind all of this was to cull large parts of humanity. First, it was that the virus was a bioweapon designed by the Chinese to cull us; then it was Bill Gates, supposedly a closet eugenicist, who cooked up the virus to push the vaccine, which was the real mechanism to cull us. But who is actually engaging in behaviors that have contributed to a culling, to mass and unnecessary human sacrifice? It is the diagonalists themselves—by systematically refusing the simple and safe measures that were our best chance of preventing a highly infectious disease from culling the more vulnerable members of our communities: the already sick, the disabled, the immunocompromised, the elderly. Culling the herd of its weaker members to strengthen the genetic stock is the central goal of eugenics. And to a large extent, it has happened. Of the first 800,000 people who died of Covid-19 in the United States, three-quarters were over the age of sixty-five. And, according to an analysis conducted by the Poor People's Campaign, people living in poor U.S. counties died at almost twice the rate as those living in wealthy ones; during the outbreak of the Delta variant, people in the poorest counties of the country died at *five times the rate* as those who lived in the wealthiest areas. These numbers tell a story of Covid as class war.

So that's it, then, right? The blame for this monstrous human sacrifice rests with those lost to the Mirror World. The rest of us can feel good about what we did when we were tested by this terrible virus. We wore our masks and got the jabs and tried to flatten curve after curve.

The more difficult truth, though, is that this is a doppelganger story, and doppelganger stories are never only about *them*; they are always also about *us*. The literature is unequivocal. Jean Paul, the German writer credited with coining the term *Doppelgänger* in his three-volume 1796–97 novel *Siebenkäs*, defined it as meaning "*Leute, die sich selber sehen*" (people who see themselves).

So have I? Have I stared myself squarely in the eyes and unflinchingly taken in all of my own many flaws, failings, and leaden shoes? In peering closely at Other Naomi and her new allies, what am I still refusing to see about me and mine? About the people I think of when I say "us" and "we"?

What *would* we see if we, like the couple in that Pre-Raphaelite painting, met ourselves in the woods? I fear that many of us would also faint from fright. Because in mapping the contours of the Mirror World, I can't avoid seeing that the mindset that is the poison at the heart of this strange and tragic chapter reaches well beyond the diagonalist axis. On this side of the glass, how much did we do to push our governments to keep mask mandates in place to protect the immunocompromised? Or to make clean, filtered indoor air a right in every workplace? Or to share the vaccines beyond our borders? In North America and Europe, our governments wanted us to get our second and third shots. What if we had refused until everyone in the world had their first ones? What bodies did we tacitly sacrifice by going with the flow? And how much did those of us who were lucky enough to work from home do to make sure that the workers we celebrated as "essential" were actually paid and protected as if they *were* essential? Did we fight for their right to organize, or did we keep ordering from Amazon simply because it was convenient? The truth is that most of us could have done much more.

And this, I think, is part of the challenge of pulling people back from the Mirror World: What is the alternative that is being offered on this side of the glass? Do we have a plan for a world without sacrificial people? And does that plan feel credible, rooted in action—or does it seem like more blah, blah, blah? Put another way, how do we convince people being seduced by fantasy that it is still possible to exert power to change reality in big and important ways? When Avi and Tak and I went knocking on doors to meet our pandemic-addled neighbors, that is what we were asking them to do with us—believe that we can make the battle against climate pollution and systemic poverty an overarching societal mission. We met some people who were more than ready to take that leap of faith with us—hungry for it, in fact, as if they had just been waiting for an invitation. But we also met people who might once have been open to that kind of collective mission but were now lost to new and more ominous narrative frequencies.

And I couldn't shake the feeling that unless something big shifted, this was only the beginning of a mass migration of minds.

The election results bore out what we saw at the door: Trudeau, who had called a snap election because he was certain he could parlay Canada's fight against Covid into a parliamentary majority, ended up exactly where he started: still the prime minister, but with a parliamentary minority. Avi managed to double the number of NDP votes in his district, but the Trudeau Liberals still held the seat (not a surprise). Meanwhile, the far-right People's Party tripled its vote nationally. It could have been worse, but it wasn't good.

One year later, the diagonal lines met again, reaching further this time—and closer to home. In October 2022, Vancouver had municipal elections and the city council, long in the hands of green-tinged, centrist progressives, suddenly flipped right, and with a nasty edge. Vancouver is the third most expensive city in North America, ahead of San Francisco and Los Angeles, and is also at the epicenter of the poisoned drug crisis. Rather than proposing solutions to the housing and drug emergencies, the winning slate of candidates riled up fear of the city's unhoused and mentally ill, while promising to hire a hundred more police officers.

Many commentators speculated that the deciding factor in tipping the election may have been a huge influx of money from the third-richest man in the city: Chip Wilson, the founder of the yoga apparel giant Lululemon. In 2013, Wilson had earned the wrath of many of his customers when he responded to complaints about the quality of the company's leggings by saying, "They don't work for some women's bodies . . . It's really about the rubbing through the thighs." He stepped back from leading the company soon after, but he is still a major shareholder. For a while he busied himself sharing bizarre views on his own blog, including a deleted post titled "Are Erections Important?" in which he claimed that "the continuation of the human race" was under threat because women were insufficiently "feminine," thereby threatening men's arousal.

More recently, Wilson has been using his vast wealth to fund right-wing politicians and sensational media operations, including in the run-up to those elections in Vancouver. As friends and colleagues reeled from the upset at the polls, Garth Mullins, host of the podcast *Crackdown*, observed, "The election was about fear of crime, ginned up by dark yoga money."

A hundred new cops underwritten by a yoga-pants empire founded by a fatphobic billionaire worried about the future of masculinity? The Mirror World was definitely spreading, and it would only become more bizarre. December 2022 brought news of a foiled plot to overthrow the German government in a violent coup and reinstate the monarchy, a plan cooked up by a diagonalist coalition of heavily armed far-right extremists and conspiratorial fantasists who, like followers of Canada's QAnon Queen, had convinced themselves that Germany's current government was itself an illegitimate fantasy. The next month featured a failed insurrection in Brazil, with followers of defeated far-right president Jair Bolsonaro calling for a military coup as they stormed the houses of government. For weeks, Bannon and the *War Room* posse had been amplifying false claims that the Brazilian election had been rigged and that Lula was staging a Marxist takeover of the continent at the behest of the CCP.

As the strong men and well women have grown ever more entangled, and ever more ambitious in their goals, I have felt a mounting foreboding about what their cookie-cutter version of perfection will mean to the countless people who fall outside their embrace. I have also felt a more personal sense of menace. Because in this obsession with pure children and perfected bodies, I hear an unmistakable, if implicit, attack on my own child.

10

AUTISM AND THE ANTI-VAX PREQUEL

Because time marches on, even when you have fallen down a rabbit hole, T. turned ten recently; by the time these words enter the world, he will be eleven. From the start, I made a conscious decision in my work neither to describe raising a neurodivergent kid in any detail nor to discuss the merits of the labels that a doctor, who spent two hours with him, chose for him when he was four. A bit like a personal brand, defining T. in those ways would fix him at a single point in time and through the eyes of others. The decision about when (and if) to share his private world are T.'s to make. So I have included a few lighthearted anecdotes about his love of predators, and a preternaturally wise observation here and there, but I selected these because they could be true of most any child.

What I will do, because it has become sadly relevant, is write about my own experiences in a very specific subculture: the autism parent community.

There was a time when I was desperate to find these parents—to talk to someone, anyone, who might know what my family was going through. T. was born where we now live in British Columbia, but when he was a few months old, we moved to Toronto to be close to Avi's family and big-city services. Except it turned out that for kids like T., those services were extremely scarce. The doctor who diagnosed him warned us that the wait list to access government-covered therapy could be years long. He also said that early intervention was "critical." Kindergarten at our local public school nearly broke us: thirty kids in the class, five of them with developmental challenges; one teacher; and one amazing teaching assistant. The teacher went on health leave and never returned; the assistant became so stressed by the impossibility of her job that she transferred to another district. "I could have changed those five kids' lives," she told me later. "But not five plus the other twenty-five." There was one "autism team" serving hundreds of schools; they made it to T.'s class ten days before the end of the school year.

I needed to meet other parents who had somehow made these broken systems work for their kids. I imagined support groups, maybe with alcohol, where we would laugh and commiserate, while sharing tips on how to shake resources out of cash-strapped school boards. I did find a few fellow travelers in this new and unfamiliar world, and a couple of them helped a good deal. But as I went deeper, I also found something else: an industry of strange magical cures—under-the-table children's vitamin injections; extreme eliminationist diets; immersive around-the-clock therapy; sound waves and subliminal messages that promised to reprogram brains and reminded me of the research I did into the CIA's MKUltra experiments on psychiatric patients. Online, I found people who identified as Autism Warrior Parents because they were at "war" with the autism in their child; some coached one another on horrific "treatments," including getting their kids to drink chlorine dioxide, a bleach commonly used in pulp and paper mills. Several people told me that when they got the diagnosis, they quit their jobs and became their child's full-time therapists in applied behavior analysis, a system of rewards and punishments with a sinister history that once included electroshock and is still often administered in cruel ways designed to "extinguish" all signs of autistic difference in young children. "Aggressive early intervention is everything," one of these parents told me. "If you don't catch it early, it's too late."

Not long after the diagnosis, I was at the YMCA where I used to do ninety-minute yoga classes and now found myself standing on the edge of a cavernous gym watching T. drag around large foam blocks. I struck up a conversation with a defense lawyer I knew from a different stage of life. He had dark circles under his eyes and told me that his toddler had been diagnosed with autism. The child had been fine, he said, but after they got vaccinated, they changed, withdrew, regressed. It was definitely the vaccine, he told me. He recommended that I do my own research and then we could talk. Over the next few years, this man became one of the anti-vax movement's most prominent attorneys (and would go on, in the Covid era, to help lead the campaign against supposedly tyrannical health mandates).

None of this was what I wanted when I started reaching out to parents of autistic children. I wasn't looking for someone to blame or to sue. I was just looking for company in navigating a world that wasn't built for kids like ours, or even just a lead on a music therapist or a dentist who understood sensory processing challenges. I accepted a chair at Rutgers University in 2018 in part as a Hail Mary. Rutgers is known for its research into neurodiversity, and New Jersey is renowned for having some of the best accommodations for children like T. in its public schools. As a Canadian used to feeling some pride in our public health and education systems, it was a surprise to learn that the Americans with Disabilities Act and the Individuals with Disabilities Education Act were significantly tougher tools than anything we had north of the border, and that parents in New Jersey had been using the hell out of them to push the local schools to provide meaningful access for their kids.

When we arrived the summer before T. started first grade, the difference was startling: our new public school had a nurse, a psychologist, a speech therapist, and an occupational therapist, shared with only two other schools. When they descended on T. like a disability Ocean's Eleven, I wept with relief. After two straight days of testing, they presented us with a detailed educational plan that involved putting T. in a class with just five students, all on the autism spectrum, supported by three teachers. Outside of school hours, we explored a dazzling array of extracurricular activities geared toward neurodiverse kids—music lessons, adapted plays, and Buddy Ball, a sweet weekly sports program that paired neurotypical teens with kids on the spectrum, one-to-one. This truly seemed like a new world.

One thing that wasn't different, however, was the search for cures. Within five minutes of arriving at Buddy Ball, I met a father who pressed a glossy brochure into my hand about the supposed link between vaccines and autism. He laid out his evidence, which amounted to a control group of two. His older child, he explained, was born abroad and was not vaccinated. That child is neurotypical. His youngest was born in the United States, was vaccinated, and is autistic. "So," he declared, "it's obvious it's the vaccines!"

Such is the power of what doctors refer to as the "vaccine-autism myth"—the viral narrative that insists that childhood immunizations for measles, mumps, and rubella, which children start getting after their first birthday, is the cause of autism. It's a narrative that would, in many ways, lay the foundation for what would become the anti–Covid vaccine movement. The earlier claims rely on an entirely discredited paper suggesting that the measles, mumps, and rubella (MMR) vaccine may be associated with autism (and bowel disease), published in the prestigious British scientific journal *The Lancet* in 1998. Twelve years later, it was retracted by its publisher, who described the claims as "proven to be false." Ten of the paper's thirteen original coauthors had issued a note of retraction years earlier, in 2004, based on faulty "interpretation" of the study's data. The main author, the gastroenterologist Andrew Wakefield, was banned from practicing medicine in Britain in light of undisclosed conflicts of interest and what Britain's General Medical Council described as his "callous disregard" for the children in his study.

Yet almost a quarter century after Wakefield's paper first appeared, and with no further evidence supporting the claim, the myth is more prevalent than ever. It continues to be spread by a global network of Facebook groups, YouTube channels, and slickly produced documentaries that do a fair job, for those untrained in reading scientific papers, of impersonating investigative journalism. The network has its own medical pseudo-experts, celebrities, influencers, and lawyers, most prominently Robert F. Kennedy Jr. Their debunked claims have contributed to a resurgence of diseases including measles, which in 2000 was declared eliminated in the United States but has since returned with a vengeance. In 2019, the World Health Organization reported a global measles surge, "reaching [the] highest number of reported cases in 23 years" and taking 207,500 lives—a 50 percent increase in deaths in just three years.

The blame for the spike in misinformation falsely claiming that vaccines cause autism is usually linked with the rise of social media, and the fact that junk vaccine science circulated there unchecked for years. Telling parents that children are being permanently disabled by routine vaccinations is certainly a sensational message, one seemingly made for the attention economy. But as with misinformation related to Covid, social media only intensified tendencies that were already present. In my conversations with autism parents who have gone the vaccine-blaming route, I am always struck by their sense that they have been cheated or wronged; that someone or something robbed them of what they were sure were their rightful, neurotypical kids and substituted them with ones who were different and defective; that their families had somehow been invaded.

My doppelganger is now thoroughly entangled in the autism misinformation movement: she platforms its key figures, and they excitedly platform her; she proudly posts photographs of herself with RFK Jr. and tells him, regarding his rabidly anti-vax Children's Health Defense that, "I respect all the research your organization does. It seems incredibly well-sourced to me." Their two publishers have even partnered to offer their latest pandemic-themed books as a box set. ("This Christmas, give the gift of truth!") She has also shared ignorant slurs describing the culture under Covid as "Asperger's-like" and said that schools, by trying to prevent the virus's spread, are promoting "a kind of Asperger's quality in otherwise normal children."

The Child as Double

This part of our doppelganger story has little to do with Wolf, however. It has to do with a more pervasive kind of doppelganging—the doubling that can occur between parents and their children. Procreation has long been viewed, particularly by those who come from wealth, as a form of temporal doubling, with the child sometimes given the same name as the father or mother, extending the parent's legacy and fortune into the future (e.g., RFK Jr.). In our time of personal branding and optimized selves, you don't need inherited wealth or a title to do something similar. You can simply treat your child as a spin-off or brand extension—you and your little mini-me can dress up in matching outfits for Instagram or share adorable dances on TikTok.

Glowing Mama does this with her very cute daughter—posting sweet videos of their living room dance parties. And she also posts distinctly less sweet videos. "Don't you tell me that our healthy children are putting *you* at risk," she rages into the camera while her daughter naps in the back seat of her car. "You take care of your lifestyle, okay? Stop shoving garbage in your mouth, sitting on your ass, consuming the fucking media . . . And then tell me that my beautiful, vibrant child is a threat to your unhealthy, stupid, unmotivated ass. Fuck you. Fuck you, okay?"

This, I think, is a corollary of all the shame and pathologizing of kids who are different in our culture—an outsize pride taken in kids who seem to check all the boxes, meet all the social standards, are perfect little children. Children in need of protecting, keeping pure from all transgressors. So many of the battles waged in the Mirror World—the "anti-woke" laws, the "don't say gay" bills, the blanket bans on gender-affirming medical care, the school board wars over vaccines and masks—come down to the same question: What are children for? Are they their own people, and our job, as parents, is to support and protect them as they find their paths? Or are they our appendages, our extensions, our spin-offs, our doubles, to shape and mold and ultimately benefit from? So many of these parents seem convinced that they have a right to exert absolute control over their children without any interference or input: control over their bodies (by casting masks and vaccines as a kind of child rape or poisoning); control over their minds (by casting anti-racist education as the injection of foreign ideas into the minds of their offspring); control over their gender and sexuality (by casting any attempt to discuss the range of possible gender expressions and sexual orientations as "grooming").

This same inability to see children as autonomous beings is part of the reason why, for so long, disabled children were hidden away in cruel institutions. If a double that reflects well on them is what many parents are after, then disability arrives as an unwelcome interruption to those best-laid plans. Or, in today's language, if your kid is your brand extension, then having a child who challenges social standards of normalcy might mean that your whole personal brand is in crisis.

This is not a partisan issue. There are conservatives who are stronger advocates for kids with disabilities than some liberals. And I don't know anyone who is outside the reach of these pressures. Our culture lavishly credits parents for their children's successes and judges them harshly for their children's challenges; I am certainly not immune. What has helped me, strangely, is the ambivalence I had toward motherhood for much of my life. I never was one of those people with a fixed image in my head of who I would be as a parent and who my children would be to me; it just wasn't a feature of my fantasy life. That probably made me a less instinctual parent, but it also may have made me more genuinely curious to meet whoever showed up. I say this because I have noticed, in my conversations with parents of autistic children, that they often undergo an intense grieving period as they mourn the fantasies that had taken deep root in their hearts. So sad are they about the child-double who wasn't that they can't really see the singular child who is. It's not unlike what some parents of trans kids go through: they often need a little time to grieve the daughter or son they thought they had before they can fully accept their child's gender identity.

Sometimes this is just a short, painful phase on the parent's part, whether they are grieving the gender-conforming child or the neurotypical one (or, as is the case not infrequently, both). Kids, to our good fortune, tend to be pretty understanding about these difficult parental phases. The trouble is, as I have learned in the autism parent scene, there are plenty of mothers and fathers who can't seem to get past the shattering of their fantasies, and these are the ones who get stuck searching for cures, conspiracies, and extreme therapies that seek to "extinguish" behaviors rather than understand and support them.

In 2018, *The Washington Post* published a piece adapted from Whitney Ellenby's autism mom memoir, *Autism Uncensored: Pulling Back the Curtain*. In the excerpt, Ellenby describes, in wrenching detail, the way she forced her autistic five-year-old to see *Sesame Street Live!* in a loud and cavernous auditorium, despite "his intense fear of indoor spaces." Her son kicks and wails, but she forcibly restrains his limbs and wrestles with him on the ground, eventually overpowering this five-year-old "thoroughbred of resistance." Once inside, the boy, whom she names but I will not, settles into a placid state and watches the show. Ellenby is triumphant, declaring his phobia overcome and framing her actions as tough love.

That is not how many autistic people read the piece. Aaden Friday, who is autistic and nonbinary, wrote in response:

> Many, many autistic children grow up in environments rife with physical confrontations like the one that occurred in Ellenby's article, or in homes that reject basic, peer-reviewed medical science, or with parents who demonstrate a complete and utter disregard for their autistic children's autonomy—and all of it is framed as love.
>
> But it is not love; it is abuse . . . We are survivors who don't want autistic children of any age to be abused. Listen to us. Believe us. Your child does not need to be cured, they need to be respected, listened to, and above all, loved—truly loved.

The most telling line in Ellenby's piece may be one in which she describes her son, having lost the pitched battle, sitting quietly in the auditorium. In these "precious moments," she writes, he "is indistinguishable from his peers." It is a direct echo of a notorious claim made by the psychologist credited with inventing applied behavior analysis (ABA), Ole Ivar Lovaas: in a 1987 article, he wrote that nearly half the children treated with his version of ABA became, according to their teachers, "indistinguishable from their normal friends."

This is a terribly painful message to send to young people whose minds are different: that their very existence is a problem for others to solve, a disorder to cure, or at least to hide. Having a child who does not fit conventional definitions of normalcy, who is distinguishable from their peers, can be an extraordinary gift. And it is also hard—for parents, for teachers, and most of all for the child navigating a world of whirring machines and buzzing lights and *Sesame Steet Live!*, none of which were built with their minds in mind. For some parents, this experience of not fitting, of being extremely and glaringly distinguishable, and not in ways that bestow status, clearly triggers deep fears about falling behind in the perfectibility race in this world of so many little mirrors.

And so another race begins: for those magic-bullet cures, extinguishment therapies, and, often, someone to blame.

Despite billions spent on autism research, we do not know why some brains are wired differently. We do have some answers, however, to the question of why there has been a dramatic increase in diagnosed cases of autism over the last two to three decades, to the point that the Autism and Developmental Disabilities Monitoring Network, a program funded by the U.S. Centers for Disease Control, reports that 1 in every 44 eight-year-olds was diagnosed with autism in 2018, up from 1 in 150 in 2000. One answer is that the clinical definition of autism expanded significantly in the 1990s to include many neuroatypical people who would have previously been excluded. This, in turn, led to many more people deciding to get tested, which contributed to a spike in diagnoses and greater understanding of the different ways autism presents. More recently, doctors have gotten better at recognizing autism in girls, who tend to mask it better, and, to a lesser extent, in Black, Indigenous, and Latino boys, who still are too likely to be disciplined and/or written off as "troublemakers," rather than be supported and accommodated for their neurodiversity. There may also be another important factor in the rising numbers. Parents like me are having kids later. Multiple peer-reviewed studies show that children born to older parents are more likely to be diagnosed with autism.

The persistent appeal of the vaccine-autism myth, no matter how many times and in how many ways it has been debunked, is that it gives parents who see difference as tragedy something external to blame. *It's not the genetic lottery. It's not parental age. It's the jab,* they tell themselves, egos safely protected. Similarly, for new parents who are following willowy momfluencers to help them figure out how to perfect and optimize a new and daunting chapter in their lives, not getting their kids vaccinated is a way to feel in control of something that is, in fact, not in any of our control. Much like the promise of wellness itself.

It's no surprise, then, that the people who have done the most to keep the vaccine-autism myth alive are not defrocked doctors, but celebrities who moonlight as wellness influencers and momfluencers. These are people (mostly women) who cannot seem to believe that anything less than conventionally perfect showed up in their rigorously optimized lives, who cling to the fantasy that their children will mirror everything they most value about themselves. The model turned wellness influencer Elle Macpherson (product line: WelleCo) was reportedly in a romantic relationship with Andrew Wakefield and helped promote his anti-vax propaganda film. And Byron Bay, a luxe New Age beach town known as Australia's "influencer capital," is also known, not coincidentally, as the country's "anti-vax capital": in 2021, just 66.8 percent of one-year-olds in Byron had been fully immunized, compared with the state average of 94.8 percent, contributing to a return of diseases like diphtheria.

But the person who has done more than any other to popularize the myth is the model/actor/TV host Jenny McCarthy, who, in her many high-profile interviews on the topic, repeatedly characterized her son's autism as a cataclysm that invaded an otherwise perfect life. When a doctor gave her the diagnosis, McCarthy reports, "I died in that moment." She has continued to spread misinformation for well over a decade, telling PBS's *Frontline* in 2015, "If you ask 99.9 percent of parents who have children with autism if we'd rather have the measles versus autism, we'd sign up for the measles."

The argument is now a ubiquitous one from the Covid era: I would rather have a virus that, despite its potential lethality to many, I have determined is nothing more than a bad cold for me and my healthy family. There is a reason that the measles and Covid arguments sound so similar: one was the prototype for the other. Long before Warrior Moms were going on Bannon's show to rail against Covid vaccines and critical race theory, McCarthy was out there on all the big shows, hawking her book *Mother Warriors: A Nation of Parents Healing Autism Against All Odds.*

Eric Garcia, author of *We're Not Broken: Changing the Autism*

Conversation, recognized these connections early. He explains that "the world we live in has been shaped by years of autism fearmongering," adding that "many of the people who now question everything from the efficacy of Covid-19 [vaccines] to the integrity of U.S. elections cut their teeth promoting conspiracy theories and outright falsehoods about autism."

This is a key feature of the topography in the map of right now. Terror of having an autistic child, and of disability more generally, is part of what led us here. To quote the late free-market economist Milton Friedman, an old nemesis from my *Shock Doctrine* days, "the ideas" were "lying around," ready for the right shock—so, too, were the digital informational pathways to carry those ideas far and wide. It was all at the ready: the skilled communicators; the gauzy appeals to the "natural"; the dodgy techniques to inflate self-reported, unverified claims of injuries and deaths from vaccines; the conspiracies about Big Pharma and Big Government colluding to wage war on otherwise healthy bodies; the quack cures involving bleach. (Donald Trump had long flirted with the vaccine-autism myth, well before he began advocating Covid quackery.)

The reason *Plandemic*, the pseudoscientific documentary that did untold early damage, was able to be churned out so quickly is precisely because it was a remix of the anti-vax movement's preexisting claims. Many of the members of the Covid "Disinformation Dozen," meanwhile, had their anti-vax arguments ready and waiting because they had been making them for years about altogether other vaccines, and they knew exactly how to deploy them, often to convince desperate and scared parents that they would do better to buy whatever high-priced supplement/seminar/health regime they were selling. (The grift goes back to the original paper by Wakefield: when he published it, he did not disclose that his research had received partial funding from a grant secured by Richard Barr, a lawyer who represented people alleging harms from the MMR vaccine, or that Wakefield himself had applied for a patent for a different vaccine and thus stood to potentially profit from the discrediting of the MMR vaccine.)

In this convergence of worlds, we can see more than a shared infrastructure of misinformation: there is also a shared worldview, a shared mindset, a shared way of seeing people as either normal or deviant, pure or tainted, successes or failures. And even, as in all doppelganger stories, real or impostors.

"Boom—the soul's gone from his eyes." That's how Jenny McCarthy described the effect of a vaccine on her autistic son. She wasn't the first person to speak about a disabled child that way.

"Take Yours and Bring Me Mine!"

The person responsible for expanding the definition of autism, leading to a huge uptick in diagnoses, was the English child psychiatrist Lorna Wing. When she began her work in this area in the late 1950s, autism was considered such a rare, extreme, and debilitating condition that only two to four in ten thousand children received the diagnosis. The syndrome was first diagnosed in 1943 by the psychiatrist Leo Kanner and, according to his definition, autistic children, though "unquestionably endowed with good cognitive potentialities," lived in their own worlds, engaged in repetitive motions, became obsessed with objects, often had limited speech, and struggled to perform the basics of self-care.

Wing knew that this definition was so narrow that it excluded many children who were neuroatypical and needed supports. So she developed the idea that autism was not a fixed set of symptoms, but a spectrum, presenting in a range of different ways depending on the individual, and could include people who are very verbal and physically capable. Her research eventually led to autism being diagnosed as a "spectrum disorder." To bolster her argument for a more expansive definition, she called attention to then-obscure writings by an Austrian pediatrician named Hans Asperger, who had done research into autism at the same time as Kanner, but in Vienna, including in the period when Austria was under Nazi control. In the 1990s, thanks in large part to Wing's work, "Asperger's syndrome" entered the American Psychiatric Association's *Diagnostic and Statistical Manual of Mental Disorders* as a particular form of "high-functioning" autism, a distinction that would, later, be called into question.

In addition to her clinical work, Wing, whose daughter was autistic, had a side interest in the way autistic people were portrayed in folktales, religion, and literature, long before there were medical terms of any kind to describe them. She traced the earliest portrayals of autistic people to Irish and Celtic legends and "the myth of changeling children, left in place of real human babies who had been stolen by fairies."

Interestingly, changelings are also early portrayals of doppelgangers. The legend goes like this: Fairies would snatch healthy human babies and young children from their beds and secret them away to the fairy realm. In their place would be the magical changelings, who were identical doubles of the kidnapped children, only with physical deformities or behavioral "trickster" challenges, like having a withdrawn, otherworldly affect. To Wing and her coauthor, the autism advocate David Potter, it was clear that these legends of fairy doppelgangers were ways of making sense of disability. "In some versions of these [changeling] myths," they write, "the description of the beautiful but strange and remote changeling sounds very like a child with autism." There are versions of the changeling mythology in many cultures: German, Egyptian, Scandinavian, and English, among others.

In some of these stories, families raise the changeling as their own out of fear of punishment from the fairy world. In others, the recommended response is to torment the doppelganger, at times to death, in an effort to entice the fairy parents to reclaim their kin and return the supposedly stolen human child. In a 1968 paper, Carl Haffter, a Swiss psychiatrist and professor at the University of Basel, goes into detail about the kinds of torment that the legends describe to drive away the double:

> [The changeling] must be beaten nine times with birch rods until it bled while the parents called out: "Take yours and bring me mine!" One should hold it over boiling water and threaten to plunge it in. The oven should be heated with nine different kinds of wood and the child placed on the shovel as if it was intended to thrust it into the fire . . . It should be fed on leather and red-hot iron, it should be given poison to drink.

If the torments were successful, the stories went, the changeling would be driven out of the house, scurry up the chimney, and disappear back to the fairy realm. In some tales the "real" child would be returned; in others it was enough resolution to be rid of the double.

At the time of their telling, these stories were not viewed as fiction; most, including gruesome ones by the Brothers Grimm, purported to be true. Some parents, moreover, clearly understood them as how-to manuals for dealing with disabled or otherwise divergent children. D. L. Ashliman, a leading scholar of folk legends who has studied the origins and legacy of changeling mythology, writes that they were often based on actual events—sadistic ways that families, under the guidance of other community members, actually treated children with disabilities. "There is ample evidence," he notes, "that these legendary accounts do not misrepresent or exaggerate the actual abuse of suspected changelings."

Ashliman continues, "Stories with these fantasy endings provided hope, wish fulfillment, and escape to an era that was plagued with birth defects and debilitating infant diseases." Reading these accounts, I couldn't help thinking of my encounters with vaccine-scapegoating parents by the soccer field or at the Y. The stories they told me to explain their child's sudden strangeness conform almost precisely to that of the changeling: my child was perfect, normal, until an event (the vaccine) happened, and that event turned them into something else—a distorted, doppelganger version of themselves. To quote McCarthy again: "Boom—the soul's gone from his eyes."

Steve Silberman, in his 2015 book *Neurotribes: The Legacy of Autism and the Future of Neurodiversity*, writes that ever since autism diagnoses started increasing, "stories began to circulate on the Internet about babies that seemed to be developing normally until they received a routine immunization . . . Parents referred to their sons and daughters as having been kidnapped, as if a thief—dressed in a pediatrician's white coat—had stolen them away in the night."

Some ways that parents have responded to these supposed child-swaps also have eerie echoes of the changeling legends. No, today's Autism Warrior Parents are not scalding their kids in boiling water, but too many of them continue to put their kids through various forms of abuse in the name of a cure. And these parents are certainly howling, metaphorically if not literally, the ancient changeling incantation: "Take yours and bring me mine!"

This is the chilling consequence of so many parents, coached by con artists of various stripes, deciding that their child's disability is not actually a part of them, but rather some outside malevolent force that invaded them. If disability is an invader, an outsider, a soul-stealer, then, as with a changeling, almost any cruelty can be justified as parents attempt to exorcise the invader and bring back the normal, perfect life they had pictured for themselves. Like the barely suppressed rage at people who are fat and less workout-obsessed in parts of the wellness world, this, too, is a deeply dangerous mindset, playing out inside the family, inflicted on the bodies and minds of vulnerable children. And it is bound up in another kind of doppelganger turn, this one afflicting whole societies, whose entire mood and personality can seem to flip under certain extreme circumstances. Places like Vienna.

Palaces for Children

In the early years of Nazi rule, a group of doctors in Austria became intensely interested in studying children who did not conform to the homogenous and supremacist version of the Aryan collective, the *Volk*, that was at the center of the supremacist project. There was a painful irony in this fact because, just a few years earlier, some of these same doctors had been part of a progressive flowering of child development in what was known as Red Vienna.

At the end of the First World War, Vienna was in desperate straits: hundreds of thousands of impoverished refugees, many of them Jews, crowded into unsanitary housing where infectious diseases were rampant; children, orphaned by war, roamed the streets, while disabled veterans, maimed on the battlefield, faced bleak futures. It was in this context that the Social Democratic Workers' Party of Austria was voted into power in 1919 and, until the fascists secured control in 1934, turned the city into a laboratory for socialist and humanist policies, a haven for secularists and Jewish intellectuals inside a country dominated by conservative Catholic politicians. Red Vienna introduced radically new and inclusive ways of living, putting up blocks of elegant public housing filled with natural light and airy courtyards. Some 200,000 working-class people were housed in this effort—11 percent of Vienna's population at the time—and it is still studied today as a beacon of progressive social housing policy.

Tamara Kamatovic, a Vienna-based scholar of this period, writes, "The Viennese socialists were among the first in Europe to create universal welfare programs designed to alleviate childhood poverty and redress inequality in a systematic way." Many of the new apartment buildings had basic services built into them, including maternal health centers, Kamatovic explains, so that "women could get information about infant disease and nutrition from health professionals close to where they lived—[which] represented bold efforts to integrate public health services into the everyday lives of workers."

At the core of this democratic socialist experiment was the radical new idea that children were not mere appendages of their parents, nor were their futures predestined by their class, nor should the goal of education be an indoctrination in obedience or the preparation of poor children for lives of servitude. Based on breakthroughs in the understanding of children's complex inner lives (this was Freud's hometown), Viennese policy makers adopted the belief that children had rights of their own and that the role of education was to unlock their full potential. As the socialist education theorist Otto Felix Kanitz wrote in 1925, "No longer subjugated, no longer robbed of the joys of childhood, no longer threatened by the lie of being objects of charity, these children can grow into proud, free, complete, and creative individuals."

In Red Vienna, that started at birth, when poor mothers were sent packages of diapers and clothing so that they would not have to resort to wrapping their newborns in newsprint. "No Viennese child should be born on newspaper," the campaign declared. Armies of "care workers" were hired in health, education, and social services; glorious parks, working-class summer camps, and public swimming pools were constructed; and a wave of kindergartens and after-school programs were established. Schools incorporated experimental new forms of outdoor and art education, much to the mockery of conservatives, who claimed the children would never learn to read and write.

They were wrong. Children in Red Vienna flourished, and this child-centered society was, in many ways, a European prototype of the New Deal, though with a more explicitly egalitarian goal. Many of the social welfare programs were overseen by the doctor turned socialist politician Julius Tandler, who understood that these kinds of early-life investments were a way of avoiding criminalization later. He memorably declared, "He who builds children palaces tears down prison walls."

It wasn't paradise. These were years when eugenicist thought was surging on both sides of the Atlantic, embraced by progressives and conservatives alike. In the United States, programs that forcibly sterilized the so-called feebleminded and others deemed a threat to the gene pool were already in place in several states. Some of Red Vienna's socialist leaders, including the revered Tandler, saw little place for severely disabled and mentally disturbed people and spoke favorably of U.S. sterilization programs, though they never put their own version in place.

Instead, Vienna's doctors, psychiatrists, and social workers, as they attempted to enact the city's child-centered vision, took an activist and interventionist approach with developmentally challenged children. Many were placed in various kinds of rehabilitative institutions and foster homes, of varying quality. As the historian Edith Sheffer writes in *Asperger's Children: The Origins of Autism in Nazi Vienna*, it was a time of experimentation: "Vienna had become a crucible of ideas, where an abundance of educators, pediatricians, psychiatrists, and psychoanalysts brought different theories to bear in schools, courts, clinics and a burgeoning welfare system."

The flagship child welfare institution was the therapeutic education clinic at the University of Vienna's Children's Hospital, called Heilpädagogik. This was where children who previously might have been warehoused in jail-like institutions, or met the lash of discipline to extinguish divergent behaviors, were referred for assessment, education, and treatment. There they encountered therapeutic approaches that were shockingly progressive for their time: a mix of music, art, nature, exercise, speech therapy, and games, along with the traditional school curricula. As Silberman documents in *Neurotribes*, when psychiatrists came from the United States to visit the clinic, they were stunned by the absence of the regimented testing and discipline that were the norm back home. Many young people in the clinic displayed characteristics the doctors described as "autistic"—from the Greek *autos*, meaning "self," in the sense of being inwardly focused—and struggled with social norms. For years, however, the Vienna clinic rejected the idea of placing diagnostic labels on these children, or even classifying them as "abnormal." The educators observed that many of the traits causing social difficulties had been present throughout history, expressing themselves through archetypes like the hyperfocused artist or the absent-minded professor, and so did not need to be treated as diseases. Instead, in keeping with Red Vienna's ethos of child-centered policy, the educators simply saw these behaviors as different ways of being human and developed tailored supports for the children in their care. But it wouldn't last.

Hans Asperger Finds His Shadow Side

By the early 1930s, with the Social Democratic Workers' Party having held power in Vienna for over a decade, fascist forces were gaining ground in the Austrian countryside. In 1933, those forces eventually seized power and quickly moved to ban rival political parties as well as trade unions. Many fought back to defend the gains of Red Vienna, but after a brief civil war, the Austrofascists took the city. By May 1934, the entire country was under the control of the Fatherland Front and, four years later, Austria was annexed to Nazi Germany. Red Vienna's era of progressive experimentation was definitively over. Socialist leaders, many of them Jewish, fled into exile. Some who stayed, including the utopian theorist of liberated childhood Otto Felix Kanitz, would eventually be murdered in Nazi death camps.

Under Nazi rule, there was a new view of the child: not as a complex individual with rights, but as the key to building a master race—a project that required encouraging the procreation of desirable Aryan babies and preventing the births, or ending the lives, of those babies and children who they deemed a threat to collective purity.

In Vienna, the Nazis did not exactly abolish all the socialist child- and family-focused programs and policies—rather, they flipped them, turning them into their sinister doppelgangers. Programs that had universally supported mothers and children, including many Jewish refugees, were repurposed to provide support and care to Aryan mothers and children exclusively—part of the central Nazi mission of building a master race. Kamatovic explains that "'family welfare' under the Nazis was reformulated into a system of racialized welfare." Red Vienna's programs designed to better understand and support children with social and developmental challenges were instead turned into diagnosis machines, places where doctors sorted out those who were considered useful to the Nazi project from those who were, in the party's parlance, "unworthy of life."

Well before they began killing Jews on an industrial scale in the death camps, the Nazis practiced and refined their methods on the disabled in asylums. In a euthanasia program known as Aktion T4, which officially began in 1939, upwards of 200,000 disabled people were murdered. Some died in the Reich's first gas chambers; many more were likely killed in acts of "wild euthanasia" performed by medical professionals who took it upon themselves to carry out the Nazi principle that care of the disabled was too great a financial strain for a country at war. Bodies were thrown into mass graves or incinerated. For the most part, families were told that their relatives had died of infectious disease.

In Vienna, almost eight hundred murders took place at the prominent children's clinic Am Spiegelgrund, where the atrocities continued even after death, with hundreds of children's brains preserved in jars of formaldehyde and used for experimentation. Research based on slides of victims' remains at Am Spiegelgrund continued long after the war, ending only in the 1980s.

One person who benefited from Austria's doppelganger flip was Hans Asperger, a young doctor who was appointed as director of the famed Heilpädagogik clinic where so many young people with autism and other developmental challenges had been treated. He had come up as a medical student in the idealistic heyday of Red Vienna and worked alongside Jewish psychiatrists like Georg Frankl, who helped develop progressive theories that we would now recognize as central to the understanding of neurodiversity—the idea that brains are wired in a range of ways and difference need not be equated with pathology. Up until the year before the Germans annexed Austria, Asperger echoed this analysis, writing of his young patients displaying autistic traits that they could not be neatly categorized under a diagnosis. "There are as many approaches [to child development] as there are different personalities. It is impossible to establish a rigid set of criteria for a diagnosis," he wrote in 1937. His view changed dramatically within months, as Asperger began to echo the Nazis' eugenicist discourse, now writing of the need to avoid "transmission of diseased hereditary material." Kids showing autistic traits that he had previously said defied diagnosis were recast as a "well-characterized group of children," whom he named "autistic psychopaths."

The diagnosis itself was imbued with Nazi ideology, under which every individual's value was measured, as Sheffer outlines, by their *Gemüt*—a tricky, hard-to-translate concept that referred, in this era, to a person's sense of group bonding within the broader *Volk*, the Aryan collective that was being engineered and militarized by the Nazi state. People with autism—because their gaze is inward rather than outward, and because many struggle to read social cues and tend to focus less on social approval than others do—had, according to Asperger, "poverty of *Gemüt*." They would not make good group players in the *Volk*. Most, he wrote, had no social value whatsoever: they would grow up to "roam the streets as 'originals,' grotesque and dilapidated, talking loudly to themselves or unconcernedly to passers-by." A small subset, however, who he called his "little professors," could play exceptional roles. In 1941, with the Nazis still solidly in control, he wrote, "We know how many of our former children, including very difficult cases, entirely fulfill their duties in their professions, in the armed forces, and in the [Nazi] party, not a few among them in eminent positions. This is how we know that the success of our work is worth the effort."

With the euthanasia program already murdering disabled people on a mass scale, he was effectively saying that most autistic people deserved to die—but the few who showed a special capacity for focus could be put to use by the Nazi Party (perhaps by becoming code breakers, or some other hyperconcentrated part of the fascist project). Recent research has shown that Asperger signed papers for children as young as two years old to go to the clinic Am Spiegelgrund, where they would be killed. Asperger, in other words, was a key node in the system of sorting who would live and who would be murdered, an apparatus that would soon be expanded into a murder machinery capable of killing millions of people who did not fit the Aryan ideal in other ways.

For Sheffer, this taints not only the diagnosis of Asperger's syndrome but also, potentially, the much broader autism spectrum diagnosis that Asperger did so much to shape. Based on these writings, it clearly had far less to do with medical science than with fascist thought: the Nazis required submission to a supremacist groupthink in order to build the Aryan race. Asperger's claim that autistic children were pathological because they lacked the capacity for *Gemüt* was less a medical diagnosis than a highly ideological one about what should constitute normal behavior: he was diagnosing them, quite literally, with a deficit of fascism. "It was up to Nazi child psychiatrists such as Asperger to diagnose a child's character against regime norms," Sheffer writes.

By setting his "little professors" apart from the rest of their autistic peers, and arguing that they alone were worth saving, Asperger created the controversial distinction between "high-functioning autism" and "low-functioning autism." This is Asperger's legacy: lifting up a small group of neuroatypical children as supposedly superior to all the others, while being part of an apparatus that sent children without that competitive edge to their deaths.

Asperger's jarring career trajectory demonstrates that, in just a handful of years, the same institutions and some of the very same people can shift from an ethos of care and curiosity toward a vulnerable group to one of callousness and genocidal cleansing. As if a switch has been flipped.

As one Covid year followed another and my doppelganger and the forces she helped incite spread new waves of panic about how all of us who have been vaccinated have lost our souls, like those changelings, or had impure blood, this was the form of doppelganging that increasingly preoccupied me: how, precisely, a society tips into its fascist double. Wolf had long argued that there are ten steps every tyrant follows to execute this shift. I don't think it's nearly so simple, nor is it all about the tyrant at the top. It's also about the hungers and appetites of everyday people—for those stirring feelings of superiority and purity. Though the doppelganger archetype has appeared across time to explore issues of life and death, the body versus the soul, the ego versus the id, the real child versus the false, this is something else that the figure of the double, or the "evil twin," has long been used to warn us about: the shadow tyrant who lives in us all and lies in wait in every nation.

Both This and That

Philip Roth has plenty to offer here as well. *Operation Shylock*, despite all the surface-level ridiculousness, ends up concerned with these broader and far more serious forms of doubling. The book is set in 1988 and unfolds against the backdrop of the real-world trial of John Demjanjuk, a Ukrainian-born autoworker in Cleveland, Ohio, who was arrested, extradited to Israel, and accused of being Ivan the Terrible, the notoriously sadistic Treblinka gas chamber guard who delighted in causing maximum suffering as he gassed hundreds of Jewish captives at a time. As I read the book, the realization slowly dawned on me that Roth's seemingly silly doppelganger caper is actually just a device to lead us into this more consequential territory.

So, even as Real Roth and Fake Roth wrestle over their petty ego struggles, the man accused of being Ivan the Terrible is in a Jerusalem courtroom facing a succession of traumatized Holocaust survivors. Real Roth sits in and listens to the accusers, and to the defense. Now in his late sixties, Demjanjuk insists that it was all a terrible case of mistaken identity, that his death camp identification card had been forged by the Soviets. He is not a monster; he is a pious family man, a loving father and grandfather, a prodigious gardener, and a pillar of his suburban community. Watching him on the stand, Real Roth imagines his defense: "My heart goes out to you for all you suffered, but the Ivan you want was never anybody as simple and innocent as good old Johnny the gardener from Cleveland, Ohio . . . All this innocuousness disproves a thousand times over these crazy accusations. How could I be both that and this?"

For Roth, the writer, Demjanjuk's ordinary homelife was no kind of alibi. The frightening thing was precisely that a person can be both that and this—the monstrous killing machine and the caring family man. The doubles coexist; they do not cancel each other out. "The Germans have proved definitively to all the world," Real Roth observes, "that to maintain two radically divergent personalities, one very nice and one not so nice, is no longer the prerogative of psychopaths only."

Asperger, too, maintained two seemingly divergent personalities—the man who patiently watched and drew up sensitive, humane profiles of his fascinating "little professors," making the case for their right to live, and the man who callously signed transfer orders for less verbal, less conventionally charming children. For Sheffer, the "double-sided character of Asperger's actions underscores the double-sided character of Nazism as a whole"—a system that committed depraved atrocities in the name of collective health and wellness.

The dual nature of Asperger's character now haunts the autism literature: Was he Jekyll or Hyde? Savior or Nazi? Light or shadow? The scholars continue to debate the point, but there is no need to choose: he can be both that and this; they are not in conflict. The autistic scholar Anna de Hooge writes this of the two faces of Asperger, the man whose name branded many people like her, until "Asperger's syndrome" was struck from the diagnostic manuals: "I am interested in the underlying ideology that made him decide which children were to be saved, and which were to be sent off to Spiegelgrund. What is more, I am interested in the way this ideology lives on."

I am interested in that too. Every night when I doomscroll, I encounter more people tossing around chilling language about their good genes and their strong immune systems and their "pureblood" and their perfect children as an argument against taking simple actions, like putting on a mask, that would protect people a little less strong and perfect than they imagine themselves to be. Largely unknowingly, they are the inheritors of the barbaric traditions that once sought to rid the world of children like mine. When glowing influencers spew fatphobic bile at people daring to ask them to consider their impacts on others, they are tapping into deep supremacist logics about which lives have value and which lives are disposable. When parents refuse to give their children vaccines that have controlled viruses like measles for generations because they are gripped with the terror of having the kind of child that the Nazis declared unworthy of life, they are feeding into these logics, too.

This is the lineage of today's anti-vaxxers. Yet in their pipiked Mirror World, many of them seem utterly convinced that they are the ones being forced to wear the modern equivalent of the yellow star, and that they are the ones heading for the concentration camps.

Does He Mirror?

I have no way of knowing whether my experience in the autism parent community is representative—after a random series of encounters on the edge of sports fields and in various therapeutic waiting rooms, I ran in the other direction. I can attest, though, that the vaccine misinformation industry is preying upon real suffering. Families of children with developmental disabilities live in the same world that we all do—the one that is very generous with diagnoses and awfully stingy with actual help. The one where talking about building palaces for poor children as a means of tearing down prison walls would reliably get you laughed out of any room where self-styled serious people gather. Caring for a child with severe disabilities can easily lead to bankruptcy, despite "good" health insurance. And even in places where the disability justice movement has won robust supports for school-age kids, many of those programs dry up as soon as children become young adults.

Even in those schools that have been forced to step up—which are overwhelmingly in whiter, wealthier districts where parents can afford to sue—the dominant teaching method is still ABA, often executed as a system of candies and consequences not unlike dog training. In New Jersey, after I got over my initial euphoria that we were no longer dealing with straight-up neglect in the school system, I often had the distinct feeling that the atypical kids were being hived away in special classes and bombarded with ABA training less to support their needs and more to show impressive results on the tests that never stopped coming. Those tests formed the basis for school rankings, which formed the basis for property values, which formed the basis for property taxes, which funded the schools. And from the moment the diagnosis process begins, children are put into a matrix of normalcy and deviance.

"Does he play with toys appropriately?" the first doctor asked.

Appropriately? Well, who's to say it's more appropriate to stage a race between toy cars than to pile them up against the wall and turn them into an abstract sculpture? Not I.

"Does he mirror?" one therapist, who came to our home, asked.

"What is mirroring?" I asked back.

"Does he mimic what you do, like Simon Says?"

Oh. I had never thought to notice. But that raised another question: Did I want him to mirror? If so, mirror whom? Me? Other kids? Cartoon characters? Isn't the reflexive impulse to copy what everyone else is doing part of what has landed us in such a mess? Sure, it would make life easier. But is it so bad to have a few kids in the mix who are tuned in to their own inner music?

Do we really need more mirrors? How about some portals to somewhere new?

So much of my family's experience with disability has been a conflict with the mindsets that seek to name, cure, and control. But there are—as always—other mindsets available, which is what we discovered, to our surprise, when we moved to the rock. In truth, it's the reason we have stayed. At first, I was sure that sending T. to regular school in the country, without the fancy supports we had in New Jersey, would be a disaster. It turned out to be the best experience of his young life, and for a simple reason: there is very little pushing, measuring, or testing.

There are no specialized autism therapists, but when he is stressed, he walks in the woods with a loving educational assistant, taking turns choosing topics to get used to the give-and-take of living in a world with other people. His endlessly creative teacher somehow makes time to build curricula about his latest predator interests. T. assures me that he has been blessed by a total absence of bullying. That could change, and probably will. I have met people who haven't been so lucky here. But for now, in this community, with more than its share of dropouts and misfits (and, sure, some odd political views floating around), he is experiencing something close to what all kids deserve: acceptance.

The Off-Ramp

Not long after Avi's campaign summer, I was standing in line at the drugstore waiting for a prescription when a young woman, who looked around eighteen, struck up a conversation about the merits of cloth masks versus disposable ones.

"I hate the blue masks," she offered. "They make too much garbage."

"Leave her alone," said the woman (mother? grandmother?) who was with her. She grabbed the teen's arm and pulled her away from me. "She"—meaning me—"doesn't want to talk to you."

I don't know what label a doctor had placed on this young person, but I suspect it wasn't that different from the one placed on my son.

"No, no I am happy to talk," I said. "What else am I doing? Just waiting."

And so we talked. About the benefits of cloth masks (softer, prettier, better for the environment). About how many brothers and sisters I have (one of each). About how old I am. And all the while, I watched her caregiver visibly relax and let her guard down.

I have had several such experiences, usually while waiting in line, and they always go the same way: first comes the friendliness of the neuroatypical person, piercing through my little bubble of public isolation (usually involving headphones), then the shame and panic of the parent or grandparent, and finally the relief at having permission not to feel those painful emotions about someone they love, finding a little safe harbor in a never-ending storm.

I know something of how they feel. When I was a teenager, my mother had a severe stroke and permanently lost many of her physical abilities, and some of her cognitive ones. As her caregiver, I learned quickly about our world of carelessness and grew to recognize the looks of disgust and impatience from people who clearly believed that disability should be hidden away. Even so, I carried my own shame and was not always able to see the beauty in the different ways that human brains and bodies meet and interact with the world.

I had a turning point when T. was in kindergarten and I was watching him struggle around a simple play structure outside our local school. A girl from his class showed up and started leaping and swinging like a professional gymnast, her long hair brushing the dusty ground as she hung upside down. What might it be like, I wondered, to have a child so able? And sweet, too! She paused and tried to help T. figure out how to cross the monkey bars. I have a very soft spot for confident girls with time for my son.

Around then her father showed up, and I complimented him on the awesomeness of his offspring and her kindness with a differently wired child. This precipitated an outburst of manic bragging, leading me to learn, in very short order, that in addition to her obvious proficiencies as a gymnast, his five-year-old could recite entire soliloquies from *Romeo and Juliet*, competed in chess tournaments, was a violin aficionado, and had never, ever ingested anything containing refined sugar.

I was so tired for him. The perfection Olympics in which this father-daughter duo were clearly excelling seemed like a terribly sad thing to do to childhood. This little one was already luminous—she did not need to be polished into a trophy. But if I was honest, I also could see how, if I had a child who navigated the world with such ease, it would be nearly impossible to resist the temptation to live through them and try to win all the prizes our brutal economic order has to offer the few deemed merit-worthy. It was in that moment that I realized the special gift of having a child whose innate differences meant that he was never going to be able to compete in that race. By then, he was already on his own field, making his own rules—cool rules, ones that might lead to some very interesting places when he is older—but rules that he alone could decode.

I looked at T. as he joyfully if clumsily slid down the plastic slide and blessed him for giving us both this off-ramp.

Secrets and Shadows

I have stressed over sharing even this much about T., this beautiful being who was born without the protective armor that so many of us take for granted. I hope, when he is older, that he agrees it was worth letting some light into the shadowy corners of autism parent world. I also deliberated over sharing that story about that very proud father, which may be painfully recognizable to him. Does he deserve that, as someone probably just a little too eager to impress a new acquaintance? Maybe not. Still, his attitude is worth considering, I think, because, unlike so much else I have been writing, it is not about the ludicrous goings on in the Mirror World. It's about what goes on in circles that pride themselves on reason and humanism and listening to the science, and caring for the less fortunate—circles that define themselves as not being like *them*.

It's well-off liberal parents who have turned childhood into an achievement arms race, one in which admittance to an elite university is the first of many finish lines, but one so important their children are pushed to turn their most intimate traumas into triumph-over-tragedy stories (while the wealthiest families simply bribe and cheat their way to access, as we all learned through recent scandals). I also worry that members of this same class of liberal parents will convince themselves, in a few years' time, that doing just a little bit of embryonic gene editing to enhance their future child's IQ or athletic prowess or height is not just their prerogative, but their duty.

The world is spiraling out of control, they will tell themselves. *Surely my kids deserve a competitive edge.* Or as Bill McKibben said to me recently, "Instead of figuring out how to have a world where everyone can thrive, they want their kids to thrive in a world that is falling apart."

This is what unsettles me most about the race for perfection at work in the interlocking worlds of wellness and parenting: the pervasive structural unwellness from which the hyperwell and insistently perfect are so clearly fleeing. The unwellness that is all around. At bottom, I suspect that much of the mirroring and doubling we are seeing comes down to who and what we cannot bear to see, to really look at—in our midst, in our past, and in the tumultuous future racing toward us. There are many different ways to try to outrun our shadows. Succumbing to conspiracy worlds is only one of them. And it was toward a confrontation with those shadows that this mapping was taking me, inexorably, next.

PART THREE

Shadow Lands

(Partition)

We have put up many flags,
they have put up many flags.
To make us think that they're happy.
To make them think that we're happy.

—Yehuda Amichai, "Jerusalem"

"It's gonna hurt, now," said Amy. "Anything dead coming back to life hurts."

—Toni Morrison, *Beloved*

11

CALM, CONSPIRACY . . . CAPITALISM

It was 2007, I was on a speaking tour for *The Shock Doctrine*, and the stop that day was Portland, Oregon. The kindly, gray-haired organizer who picked me up at the airport was vibrating with stress. She explained that there was a very active "truther" group in town and she had gotten wind of a plan to disrupt my event that evening.

Sure enough, they pulled it off. In the middle of my book talk at a local church, a couple of guys in hoodies in the balcony dropped a banner declaring 9/11 WAS AN INSIDE JOB.

The truther scene was thriving in those days, and some on the left tolerated or even cultivated it. Powered by the low-budget viral documentary *Loose Change*—the *Plandemic* of its time—the movement's strategy mainly involved trying to get high-profile critics of the Bush administration to "admit" that we all secretly knew that Dick Cheney and George W. Bush had conspired to blow up the Twin Towers and make it look like a terrorist attack. They hijacked the Q&As at many of my talks and did the same to my friend Jeremy Scahill when he was on tour with his book *Blackwater: The Rise of the World's Most Powerful Mercenary Army.*

Enough incidents like this over the years have led me to conclude that the line between unsupported conspiracy claims and reliable investigative research is neither as firm nor as stable as many of us would like to believe. It's clear that some people consume investigative journalism, fact-based analysis, and fact-free conspiracy interchangeably, drawing their own connections and mixing and matching between the three.

From the researcher's perspective, the differences between the genres should be glaring. Responsible investigators follow a set of shared standards: double- and triple-source, verify leaked documents, cite peer-reviewed studies, come clean about uncertainties, share sections of text with recognized experts to make sure technical terms and research methods are correctly understood, have fact-checkers comb through it all prepublication, then hand it all over to a libel lawyer (or in the case of my books, multiple lawyers in different territories). It's a slow, expensive, careful process, but it gets us as close as we know how to something we all used to agree was proof that something was true.

Conspiracy influencers perform what I have come to think of as a doppelganger of investigative journalism, imitating many of its stylistic conventions while hopping over its accuracy guardrails. Wolf is an impresario of the technique: repeatedly, she claims to have found a "smoking gun" or to have a "blockbuster scoop"; she makes references to tens of thousands of pages of scientific documents, as well as metadata, that no one is going to check to see if they say what she says they say (usually that "a genocide" has taken place through Covid vaccines—and no, the documents she cites that I've looked at most certainly do not show that).

Like the clutch of professional climate-change deniers who claim to "debunk" the avalanche of scientific evidence that the planet is warming by deploying entirely decontextualized temperature charts, along with outdated data and a steady flow of complex scientific terms, Wolf also engages in what we might think of as a pipiking of the science. She peppers her comments with medical terms that she abuses with abandon, rattling on about "lipid nanoparticles" and "spike proteins" and the "blood-brain barrier" so quickly and incomprehensibly that even Steve Bannon has to beg her, "Slow down! Slow down!"

The end result of being surrounded by this kind of discourse is a reflexive state of continuous disbelief that the Brazilian professor of philosophy Rodrigo Nunes calls "denialism." This in an upside-down state that, like everything else in the Mirror World, neatly serves the right and undercuts the left because, Nunes writes, it "displaces the real threats looming on the horizon into distorted, fun-house versions of themselves. Thus, the problem with democracy is not political elites everywhere who are beholden to the interests of corporations and financial markets, but a secret cabal of pedophiles planning to institute a world government." Just as "the problem with the environment is not climate change, but the weaponization of science by a political agenda bent on changing our lifestyles and preventing growth." To which we can now add that the problem of Covid was not a highly infectious disease being fought half-heartedly by for-profit drug companies and hollowed-out states, but an app that wanted to turn you into a slave.

This is surely why the Bannons of the world, bankrolled by a rotating cast of billionaires, love conspiracy theories, whether they personally believe them or not: they reliably shift attention away from the scandals we know about and that many have already painstakingly proved, and focus us, perennially, on something more explosive, something that is just on the verge of being proved (The election really was stolen! The vaccines really are killing babies! And doctors!), but never quite yet.

Since the Covid-19 global health crisis, we have been inundated with real examples of corporations profiteering off the virus, alongside cynical moves by political leaders to auction off our vital services under cover of the emergency. Trillions were spent to backstop markets and bail out multinationals, only to have workers laid off in droves; billionaires have increased their wealth at a blood-boiling rate, even as they have gouged customers and fueled a cost-of-living crisis. All of this is more than enough to justify a popular democratic revolt, without any embellishment (just as the illegal invasion of Iraq, and the hundreds of thousands of lives lost, should have been enough without talk of "inside jobs"). There was no need for histrionics about how unvaccinated people were experiencing "apartheid" when there was real vaccine apartheid between rich and poor countries; no need to cook up fantasies about Covid "internment camps" when the virus was being left to rip through prisons, meat-packing plants, and Amazon warehouses as if the people's lives inside had no value at all. In a just world, we would have been talking about these real and proven scandals around the clock; most of us didn't, in part because the clock was being run out with the fallout from made-up plots.

Calm as Shock Resistance

"Pattern recognition" is often how I describe the work of my life. I remember the moment, a true click, when I realized there was a connection between the increasing precarity of work, the consolidation of ownership in key industries, and the exponential increases in marketing budgets that characterized the hollow corporate structures of the first lifestyle brands. It wasn't a master plan that a cabal had cooked up, but there was a flow, a pattern, that wove seemingly disparate trends into a logical story about a new iteration of capitalism. That was the moment I decided to write *No Logo*, and the feeling was so powerful that more than a quarter century later, I remember where I was sitting and what I was doing when the pattern clicked into place (on the floor, on the landline speaking to a student journalist).

I wrote *The Shock Doctrine* in the hopes of providing a similar feeling of orientation. These were the years after the September 11 attacks had scrambled political signals and shaken the confidence of many friends and colleagues. I pursued a story, once again, of connections: this time between our moment of post-terror shock and the way other shocks have been used, over the last half century, to push policies that stripped other nations and peoples of rights, privacies, and wealth held in common.

In the torrent of disconnected facts that make up our "feeds," the role of the researcher-analyst is plain: to try to create some sense, some ordering of events, maps of power. The most meaningful response in my writing life came from the loveliest of literary mapmakers, John Berger, when I sent him *The Shock Doctrine* in galleys. Many people have said they found the book enraging, but his response was very different. He wrote that, for him, the book "provokes and instills a calm." When people and societies enter into a state of shock, they lose their identities and their footing, he observed. "Hence, calm is a form of resistance."

I think about those words often. Calm is not a replacement for righteous rage or fury at injustice, both of which are powerful drivers for necessary change. But calm is the precondition for focus, for the capacity to prioritize. If shock induced a loss of identity, then calm is the condition under which we return to ourselves. Berger helped me to see that the search for calm is why I write: to tame the chaos in my surroundings, in my own mind, and—I hope—in the minds of my readers as well. The information is almost always distressing and, to many, shocking—but in my view, the goal should never be to put readers into a state of shock. It should be to pull them out of it.

After immersing myself in the words and actions of my doppelganger through this protracted period, I am struck that she seems to have a very different goal. Wolf routinely describes her mental state as "terrified." She characterizes her own research into Covid vaccines as "shockingly shocking" and the public health measures she has chosen to wage war upon not as wrong, or even dangerous, but as "petrifying."

"I don't want to use inflated language," she told Steve Bannon about health officials dropping basic vaccination information on people's doorsteps. And then she went on, predicting, "They take your child away if you haven't vaccinated him or her, like that's the next step. Or they take you to a quarantine camp, if you can't show your vaccination papers. I mean, that may sound a tiny bit . . . anxious or inflated . . ." It does sound that way. It always sounds that way. It is supposed to. The effect of conspiracy culture is the opposite of calm; it is to spread panic.

The Conspiracy Is . . . Capitalism

Here is where things get more complicated, as they invariably do in the realm of doppelgangers. When radical and anti-establishment writers and scholars attempt to analyze the underlying systems that built and uphold power in our world, including the proven existence of covert operations to eliminate threats to those systems, it is common for them to be dismissed as conspiracy theorists. In truth, it is one of the most battle-worn tactics used to bury and marginalize ideas that are inconvenient to those who wield economic and political power, or who feel personally attacked by anti-corporate, anti-capitalist, or anti-racist analyses because the critiques implicate them. Every serious left-wing analyst of power has faced this smear, from Marx onward.

In their effort to counter spiraling Covid misinformation, many establishment institutions fell back on this tactic. For example, the European Commission published a guide that defined a conspiracy theory as "the belief that certain events or situations are secretly manipulated behind the scenes by powerful forces with negative intent." Okay, but that leaves out the most important factor: whether the theory in question is false or at least unproven. Because plenty of events and situations—financial crises, energy shortages, wars—are indeed "manipulated behind the scenes by powerful forces" and the effects of those manipulations on everyday people are intensely negative. Believing that does not make you a conspiracy theorist; it makes you a serious observer of politics and history.

For me, the reason to study and read and write about economic and social systems, and to attempt to identify their underlying patterns, is precisely because it is stabilizing. This kind of system-based work is akin to laying a strong foundation for a building: once it is in place, everything that follows will be sturdier; without it, nothing will be safe from a strong gust of wind. Yes, our world is still confusing after we understand this—but it is not incomprehensible. There are always systemic forces at play, and a great many of them have to do with the core capitalist imperative to expand and grow by seeking out new frontiers to enclose.

That imperative certainly explains a lot about the kinds of doubling discussed so far. The accelerated need for growth has made our economic lives more precarious, leading to the drive to brand and commodify our identities, to optimize our selves, our bodies, and our kids. That same imperative set the rules (or lack thereof) that allowed a group of profoundly underwhelming tech bros to take over our entire information ecology and build a new economy off our attention and outrage. It's also the logic behind the offloading of Covid response onto the individual (wear your mask, get your jab), to the exclusion of those bigger-ticket investments in strengthening public schools, hospitals, and transit systems. Elites who benefit greatly from these priorities are the same ones who bankroll political and media projects devoted to pitting nonrich people against one another based on race, ethnicity, and gender expression—making them less likely to unite based on common economic and class interests.

There is, of course, a difference between a system doing what it was designed to do, no matter the human costs, and secret cabals of nefarious individuals interfering with an otherwise fair and just democracy. That, I have always believed, is one of the core reasons for the left to exist: to provide a structural analysis of wealth and power that brings order and rigor to the prevailing (and correct) sense that society is rigged against the majority, and that important truths are being hidden behind pat political rhetoric. Because we cannot change what we do not understand. And because the system *is* rigged, and most people are indeed getting screwed—but without a firm understanding of capitalism's drive to find new profit sources to enclose and extract, many will imagine there is a cabal of uniquely nefarious individuals pulling the strings.

This certainly appears to be true of my doppelganger, going all the way back to her *Beauty Myth* days. "Somehow, somewhere, someone must have figured out that [women] will buy more things if they are kept in the self-hating, ever-failing, hungry, and sexually insecure state of being aspiring 'beauties,'" she wrote back then. A basic, underlying logic of the advertising industry, especially when targeting women, is that we buy more stuff when we feel insecure. But playing on those insecurities does not constitute a plot to keep us down, as Wolf was suggesting—it's just an example of plain old capitalism doing its thing, finding new and novel ways to commodify every aspect of life.

This is the same reason Wolf so completely misunderstood what was happening with police repression during Occupy Wall Street. When the parks were cleared, she saw a plot and a "war" on the American people at the highest level. In reality, police across the country shared tips on clearing the camps for the same reason they rained tear gas and pepper spray down on movements confronting the World Trade Organization and the International Monetary Fund a decade earlier and would do again against Black Lives Matter uprisings a few years later: because we live under a system structurally designed to protect the propertied classes against any and all challenges from below, sometimes through violent repression, sometimes through symbolic appropriation, often through a combination of the two.

Of my various differences with Wolf, this is the one that matters most to me, because I believe it to be at the heart of why she and so many others have come so unmoored. I am a leftist focused on capital's ravaging of our bodies, our democratic structures, and the living systems that support our collective existence. Wolf is a liberal who never had a critique of capital; she simply wanted women like her to be free from bias and discrimination in the system so that they could rise as individuals. "I believe in equipping women so that they're not disempowered in the market economy," she told *The Guardian*'s Katharine Viner many years ago.

Wolf believed strongly in the promise of the liberal meritocracy: giving people the tools to rise as individuals, not creating universal programs to guarantee a better life for all. She followed the meritocracy's rules and rode its elevator, floor by floor, to the top: high school debate club, Yale then Oxford, liberal media darling, advisor to some of the most powerful men in the world, dinner parties with the Davos set. She has described herself as "a child of the narrative" and a "darling of . . . northeastern or bi-coastal elite thought leaders." So what happened? Did she discover, at a certain point, that this elite liberal order, the one that had lifted her so high, was not what it seemed? That it was not actually fair, but rather rife with rigged rules and false promises and cruelties? Was it in the rubble of that collapsed worldview, with nothing to replace it, that she came to see a labyrinth of cabals and conspiracies?

Jack Bratich, a Rutgers University communications scholar with a focus on conspiracies, explained this possible trajectory to me like this: "Liberal investments in individualism result in thinking of power as residing in individuals and groups rather than structures. Without an analysis of capital or class they end up defaulting to the stories the West tells itself about the power of the individual to change the world. But hero narratives easily flip into villain narratives." This is a crucial point: conspiracy culture does not challenge the hyper-individualism that is at the heart of so many crises reaching their breaking points. Instead, it mirrors it, putting all the blame for society's ills on singularly powerful individuals: Fauci. Gates. Schwab. Soros.

Wolf claims that Covid health measures convinced her to believe in the existence of a satanic evil. It's unfortunate that it didn't persuade her to lose some of her faith in capitalism.

The Shock of Entanglement

This flip from hero to villain narratives goes some way toward explaining how so many seemingly apolitical people could have become obsessed with terrifying Covid conspiracy theories. Many, like Wolf, were people who had followed the rules of getting ahead in this broken system, and it had worked for them. They started their own business, saved some money, took out loans, maybe earned a little money on the side as a small-time landlord. They accepted the proposition that their job was to take care of themselves and their families and that nothing more would be asked of them (even as soaring housing, tuition, medical, and energy costs put the bare logistics of this kind of care increasingly out of reach). They had bought the story that their comforts and successes were the product of their ingenuity and hard work alone (not their workers, not their caregivers, not the trade policies that favor rich nations, and certainly not their race or class). And then, suddenly, we were all confronted with a crisis that required us to act as more than individuals, more than families, more than nations, because we are actually entangled with one another. And that was a shock bigger than Covid itself.

It's no good to only try to understand how things have gotten so strange—we also have to understand how strange they already were. In the neoliberal era that began in the 1970s and has not yet ended, every hardship and every difficulty—from poverty to student debt to home eviction to drug addiction—has been pathologized as a personal failing. Every success, meanwhile, is lauded as proof of the relative superiority of the supposedly self-made. And, of course, these delusions of rugged individualism go far deeper than the half century of neoliberal unmaking. We who live in settler colonial states like the United States, Canada, and

Australia have, for the most part, never truly reckoned with the fact that our nations exist only because of the twin thefts of stolen land and stolen people, that slavery and genocide were the bloody subsidies that allowed colonists, many of whom were themselves in debt peonage, to engage in their self-making adventures. And neither have the European nations that launched those colonial crusades in the first place.

We are now reaping the rotted harvest of decades of deliberately sown mistrust—mistrust of the very idea that we are members of communities and societies, mistrust of any expectation that governments can and should do anything positive for us. "There is no such thing as society," Margaret Thatcher once declared. Can we really be surprised that so many people believed her? This impoverished way of seeing the world and one another has gone on for so long, expressed itself in so many dialects (union busting, border cruelty, crumbling public hospitals and schools, etc.), that the very concept of a public good has now become foreign. Literally foreign, in the sense that policies that ask anything of individuals—whether in the face of Covid or the climate crisis or the inequality crisis—are now cast in the Mirror World as part of a Chinese plot to impose CCP values on the West.

Of course our societies—born out of the narrowest definitions of don't-tread-on-me liberty and a staunch commitment to not seeing what's right in front of us as a way of life—struggled to metabolize the Covid shock. This was a crisis that could *only* be met if we chose to truly see one another, even those laboring and living in the shadows, a crisis that could *only* be addressed with collective action and a willingness to make some individual sacrifices for the greater good. Who can forget those first tender weeks when everything froze. When so many of us were so alone, but at the same time alive with connections. Every intake of breath outside the home forced us to think: Who else exhaled into this air? Every time we touched anything—doorknob, elevator button, park bench, food carton, delivery box—we had to think about who else had touched it. Were they well? If they weren't, did they have the right to call in sick? Did they have access to health care? The illusion of our separateness fell away. We were not, and never were, self-made. We are made, and unmade, by one another.

Our governments didn't do nearly as much as they could have and should have to build a true infrastructure of care and solidarity during the pandemic—not compared with what we know is possible from the New Deal and the World War II mobilizations of the home front. Still, the period when many governments paid people to stay home, and offered Covid testing and vaccination for free, represented an extreme and historic deviation from every major public policy trend of the last half century, which has been a headlong flight from the very notion that we owe one another anything by right of our shared humanity. They had no choice: without these measures, millions more would have died needlessly and entire economies would have crashed.

It is worth remembering that it took decades to desocialize people to accept neoliberalism's cruelties. Anti-Black racism and anti-migrant hysteria played powerfully enabling roles, with a steady stream of politicians and media titans equating social programs designed to help everyone in need with Black "welfare queens," "super predators," and "illegals." There is no need to rehash the 1980s and '90s yet again. But in mapping the contours and happenings of the Mirror World, we do need to understand this: the legacy of generations of messages that pitted members of society against one another does not disappear overnight simply because there is a pandemic. And yet, strangely enough, when Covid hit, that was precisely the expectation among most centrist politicians. Which was itself a form of magical thinking.

With no warning, the message from much of our political and corporate classes changed diametrically. It turned out we were a society after all, that the young and healthy should make sacrifices for the old and ill; that we should wear masks as an act of solidarity with them, if not for ourselves; and that we all should applaud and thank the very people—many of them Black, many of them women, many of them born in poorer countries—whose lives and labor had been most systematically devalued, discounted, and demeaned before the pandemic.

Those expressions of solidarity were the real vertigo, the real upside-down world, since they bore no resemblance to the ways capitalism had taught us to unsee and neglect one another for so very long. Looking back now, it seems entirely unsurprising that a subset of the population said, *Fuck you: we won't mask or jab or stay home to protect people we have already chosen not to see.* It also makes perfect sense that the vaccines being free worked against them for many people—especially in the United States, a country that treats health care as a profit center and where many have come to equate good medicine with "gold-plated" private insurance plans. As Kevin Newman, a thirty-one-year-old estate agent in Arkansas reasoned, "If Covid was really serious, we'd have to pay for the vaccine. Everything else is expensive so why are they giving it out for free? It's suspicious."

It is notable also that the Covid protests took aim at symbols of collective action including, in both Italy and Australia, trade union headquarters, which were attacked and ransacked by diagonalist demonstrators. "FREEDOM," they bellowed in the streets. That empty, heavy word. Freedom to do what? Protests usually are expressions of collective power, based on the core principle that we are stronger when united. But this was something different: a temporary conglomeration of atomized individuals who saw anything collective as the enemy, set against their individual bodies and their individual families. It was, in a way, a revolt against connectedness, a howl against the lessons the virus had taught us all so jarringly: that we share the same air with people we don't know, the same hospitals, the same biome. That we are enmeshed with one another, like it or not. No, the demonstrators were saying, we are individual islands, shaped with our own hands alone; we answer to no one. We are "sovereign citizens" they declared, and you cannot force us to be in community or society.

None of this should have come as a shock. What *is* surprising, and frankly heartening, is that, after decades of frontal attacks on the idea that we live in a society, a critical mass of us had held on to enough of a civic and community spirit that we went along with these new rules for the better part of two years, and, moreover, that so many of us rejoiced at the sudden apparition of a social state. Yes, when our governments abandoned their Covid policies, we lapsed back to the crisis called "normal"—but for a time, we glimpsed another world, another kind of collective flip.

Some Conspiracies Are Real

Understanding how capitalism in its latest stage shapes and distorts our world can offer some stability. It does not, however, preclude the presence of real-world, provable conspiracies. If we define "conspiracy" as an agreement among members of a group to pull off some kind of nefarious plot in the shadows, then representatives of capital—in government and the corporate sector—engage in conspiracies as a matter of course. There most certainly was a CIA-backed conspiracy in the early 1970s to overthrow the democratically elected socialist president of Chile, Salvador Allende, after he nationalized the copper mines, as there was in 1953 to overthrow Iran's prime minister, Mohammad Mosaddegh, after he moved to nationalize the oil company that would become British Petroleum.

In *The Shock Doctrine* I told a counterhistory of the rise of neoliberalism through many such well-documented plots, and I have no doubt that there are other conspiracies that have managed to stay secret. We also know of many contemporary examples of powerful people conspiring against the public. The poisoned water system in Flint, Michigan, was covered up by state officials year after year. British Petroleum and Halliburton cut corners in the operation of the Deepwater Horizon offshore drilling rig, and the result was the largest accidental oil spill in history in the Gulf of Mexico, with the companies scrambling to cover up the full extent of the damage. Volkswagen ran a conspiracy for years to cover up how much polluting carbon its diesel vehicles were emitting (the cars were programmed to fool the testers). Most consequentially, Exxon and several other oil majors ran a conspiracy to spread doubt and confusion about the reality of climate change for decades, taking a page from the tobacco giants. These are just the barest of examples.

There were rooms in which these decisions were made; some of them may have been dimly lit. But unlike the satanic imaginings of QAnon, the motives for these conspiracies were rather banal: a U.S. mining company determined to maintain its control over a major source of lucrative metal, an oil giant looking to protect its foothold in a petro-rich nation.

Maximizing profit is just what capitalism does—even if it takes a conspiracy to do it. This points to another casualty of pipikism: the term "deep state." Originally, it was popularized by leftists in Turkey to describe the reality of covert activities carried out by a network of military and elite actors. But Bannon and Trump co-opted it to describe any form of power—economic, judicial, journalistic, intelligence—that posed a barrier to their unfettered and often unconstitutional exercise of power, while simultaneously deploying it as an easy scapegoat for their failures. Nothing was ever their responsibility; it was always the fault of the "deep state."

In *The Wealth of Nations*, published in 1776, Adam Smith wrote, "People of the same trade seldom meet together, even for merriment and diversion, but the conversation ends in a conspiracy against the public, or in some contrivance to raise prices." The English writer and publisher Mark Fisher went further, remarking in 2013 that much of what is packaged as conspiracies today is "the ruling class showing class solidarity"—by which he meant that it's mostly just ultrarich people, in business and government, having one another's back.

These kinds of conspiracies are real—and there are other conspiracies that are also real and distinctly seedier than those hatched in antiseptic boardrooms in New York and London to rig prices or fool regulators or sabotage a newly elected socialist government in the Global South. That's because the surface layers of markets that middle-class people in wealthy parts of the planet engage with directly—brightly lit grocery stores and gas stations, sleek websites and dull offices—are not the whole story of capitalism; they are its storefront. All of these operations require a level of extraction from their workers, shoppers, and users, but they also sit on top of more hidden parts of the supply chain, zones of hyper-exploitation, human containment, and ecosystem poisoning that are not glitches in the system but have always been integral parts of what makes our world run.

For the purposes of this map, we can call them the Shadow Lands. They are the mangled and dense understory of our supposedly frictionless global economy. Decades of wringing out every possible efficiency means that each link in the chain—the mines and industrial farms where raw materials are extracted; the factories and slaughterhouses that turn those inputs into parts and finished products; the trains and ships that carry them across continents and oceans; the warehouses that sort and store them to be ready at the click of a cursor; the trucks and cars that deliver them when the click arrives; the mountains of waste and poisoned waterways where the detritus from each stage ends up; the glimmering playgrounds where the ultrarich enjoy their spoils—carries a distinct yet numbingly familiar story of depredation.

What is shocking is less the stories themselves than the fact that they no longer seem to provoke much shock at all. A quarter of a century after I published *No Logo*, we seem to take it for granted that a piece of fast fashion worn by a young woman in New York or London or Toronto means that other young women have to risk being incinerated in their garment factories in Dhaka, Bangladesh. Or that suicide nets to catch desperate electronics workers are a normal part of the architecture in a factory making our cell phones in Shenzhen, China. Or that cities like Dubai and Doha are built and maintained by armies of migrants living and working in conditions so abject that when they are killed on the job, their employers face no consequences. Or that warehouse workers in New Jersey have to fight one of the three richest men on the planet to get breaks long enough to make it to the toilet. Or that content moderators in Manila must stare at beheadings and child rapes all day to keep our social media feeds "clean." Or that all of our frenetic consumption and energy use fuels wildfires in the swanky suburbs of Los Angeles and Sonoma that are battled by prison inmates who are paid just dollars a day for this perilous work, even as migrants from Central American nations battered by their own climate disasters pick avocados and strawberries in the toxic air—and if they fall ill or protest for fairer conditions are instantly sent home without pay, discarded like bruised fruit.

These, moreover, are the lucky denizens of the Shadow Lands, the relative winners. They have jobs that allow them to send money home to their families, or to pay for a few extras in prison. Countless others have been pushed into even more shadowy corners of our world—immigration detention facilities and holding zones, or boats that won't make it through a mild storm, or tent cities that grow in our gleaming cities as real estate becomes the site of ever more profitable speculation. Frictionlessness is the great promise of our age. But friction doesn't disappear just because we don't see it—it is simply displaced onto these lives of pure friction, in the Shadow Lands.

This dimness, too, is linked to real conspiracies. Not only are basic working and living conditions painfully difficult, but because they are deliberately kept in the shadows, to preserve the illusions of modernity, they also routinely tip into extreme sadism—the Shadow Lands are places where physical and sexual abuses committed by supervisors and guards and soldiers are routine. These abuses are built in because the lives of the people most affected—poor, undocumented, legally precarious, overwhelmingly Black and Brown—have already been discounted. Abuse thrives in the Shadow Lands because it can. And this, in turn, requires conspiratorial cover-ups to protect the perpetrators and to protect consumers who conspire to keep ourselves ignorant and innocent as we stroll through the more brightly lit parts of the supply chain.

And there is another, related kind of capitalist conspiracy that needs to be surfaced, this one simply flowing from the fact that when a tiny stratum of the population is permitted to grow wealthier than Victorian-era monarchs, as these Shadow Lands have allowed them to, some of the people who breathe that rarified air are going to get the idea that they are above the law. Which is simply to say: I think a great many secrets about powerful men died when Jeffrey Epstein died in prison, and I'm not sure we will ever know their full extent. Do you?

Power and wealth conspire to protect themselves. It happens in public, and it happens in private. It happens under the spotlight, and it happens in the shadows. So, in attempting to understand the ludicrous theories swirling in the Mirror World, we should be very careful not to be so reactive that we end up saying that sadism and depravity do not happen, that only a loony conspiracy theorist would believe something so out-there. Because an economic order that contains inequalities as extreme as ours—in which the vanity rocket ships of billionaires sail over seas of human misery—is its own kind of depravity, and that level of injustice reproduces more depravity as a matter of course.

The problem is no longer that we do not know these weighty truths—it is that too many of us do not know *how* to know them. We all know that our world sits on top of the Shadow Lands. But what do we do with that knowledge? Where does it go? Where is the outrage and shame and sadness diverted?

After two and half decades of covering the crimes of our oligarchic elites, I go through periods when the impunity of it all gets the better of me. The sweatshops and oil spills. The Iraq invasion. The 2008 financial crisis. The coups that threw a generation of idealists out of helicopters in Latin America. Washington's coordinated attack on Russia's nascent post-Soviet democracy that created the oligarchs and paved the way for Vladimir Putin. I simply cannot bear what these people have been able to get away with. No one paid. Everyone gets a reputational rebrand. Henry Kissinger keeps advising presidents. Dick Cheney is hailed as a reasonable Republican. Robert Rubin, one of the men who personally helped inflate the derivatives bubble that melted down the global economy in 2008, now gives advice about how we can't move too fast to prevent catastrophic climate change. My throat constricts. My breath becomes shallow. On bad days, I feel like I might explode. Impunity can drive a person mad. Maybe it can drive a whole society mad. "Abuse of power *begets* conspiracy allegations, and the men and women of conspiratorial capital at least partly have themselves to blame for the extreme and fictitious allegations made against them," Marcus Gilroy-Ware, a digital journalism scholar, writes in *After the Fact? The Truth About Fake News*. Sarah Kendzior, in her 2022 book *They Knew: How a Culture of Conspiracy Keeps America Complacent*, also explores the way impunity for real conspiracies helps fuel the rise of fantastical beliefs.

The conspiracy theories swirling about the Great Reset may well be a case in point. When they started showing up at the early anti-lockdown protests, they were presented as if a great secret was being revealed. What was strange, though, was that the Great Reset wasn't hidden—it was a branding campaign that the World Economic Forum had kicked off to repackage many of the ideas it has long advanced: biometric IDs, 3D printing, corporate green energy, the sharing economy. All were hastily positioned as a blueprint for reviving the global economy post-pandemic by "seeking a better form of capitalism." Through a series of videos, the Great Reset brought together heads of transnational oil giants to opine about the urgent need to tackle climate change, as well as politicians pledging to "build back better" and bring about a "fairer, greener, healthier planet." It was standard-issue Davos fare—arrogant, to be sure, and many parts were actively dangerous. But there was nothing new or hidden about it.

Yet over and over again, journalists and politicians on the right, and "independent researchers" on the left, acted as if they had uncovered a conspiracy that wily elites were trying to hide from them. If so, it was the first conspiracy with its own marketing agency and explainer videos.

A Fantasy of Justice

What is this strange drive to reveal the nonhidden? Maybe it's that, in liberal democracies that still pay lip service to social equality (or at least "equity"), there is something profoundly unsatisfying about how open our global elites are about the power they believe they have a right to wield over the rest of us. The mechanics of oligarchy are not hidden; they are flaunted with a level of pride that actively humiliates their spectators. Billionaires, heads of state, A-list celebrities, journalists, and members of various royal families gather every year at the World Economic Forum in Davos, Switzerland, just as they do in Aspen, Colorado, and just as they did in Manhattan at the Clinton Global Initiative—Google even runs an invitation-only annual "summer camp" in Sicily where you are as likely to bump into Mark Zuckerberg as Katy Perry. In every case, they take up the mantle of solving the world's problems—climate breakdown, infectious diseases, hunger—with no mandate and no public involvement and, most notably, no shame about their own central roles in creating and sustaining these crises.

Knowing that this kind of unmasked plutocracy can take root in democratic societies without so much as an effort to hide it is like being forced to watch your spouse cheat on you when that is not your kink. Maybe we should see conspiracy culture—with its theater of uncovering things that are not hidden—as some sort of twisted lunge for self-respect.

It might even be part of what's driving QAnon. At the heart of that conspiracy theory is a sensational fantasy of justice—the "great storm" or "great awakening" when the "white hats" suddenly arrest all the evil-doing pedophiles and satanists and thieves and send them to Gitmo. It's touchingly naïve, since, as Mark Fisher put it, "Does anyone really think, for instance, that things would improve if we replaced the whole managerial and banking class with a whole new set of ('better') people?" But you know what? *I get the appeal.* It sure beats having to watch Michelle Obama sharing candy with George W. Bush—or hearing the knowing laughs of the audience when the former president slips up and denounces the "wholly unjustified and brutal invasion of Iraq. I mean . . . of Ukraine," as he did in May 2022.

This raises an urgent question: Does anyone outside the Mirror World have a vision of justice and accountability? There is the persistent liberal dream that Donald Trump will finally be held legally accountable for one or more of his crimes while in or out of office. But beyond that, who is actively calling for our living war criminals to be brought before the International Criminal Court? What is the plan for seizing the assets of the companies fueling the climate crisis? It's pipikism in the extreme to hear MAGA Republicans describe the various show trials underway in the House as a new "Church Committee"—a reference to the Senate select committee convened in 1975, and chaired by Democratic senator Frank Church, to investigate some of the intelligence world's most notorious dirty tricks at home and abroad. But what did Democrats do, when they controlled the House, to investigate the ways that intelligence agencies have cooperated with tech giants to invade privacy and surveil us in countless ways? Or to pardon whistleblowers like Snowden? Have we given up on justice on this scale? If so, we can hardly be surprised to see the impulse resurface, in warped form, in the Mirror World. A vacuum has been created, and if my doppelganger has taught me anything, it is that vacuums tend to get filled.

There is something else that seems to be fueling conspiracy culture now. The extreme consolidation in the corporate world over the past three decades has produced a playing field so rigged against consumers that pursuing the basics of life can feel like navigating a never-ending series of scams. It's as if everyone is trying to trick us in the fine print of pages and pages of terms of service agreements they know we will never read. The black box is not just the algorithms running our communication networks—almost everything is a black box, an opaque system hiding something else. The housing market isn't about homes; it's about hedge funds and speculators. Universities aren't about education; they're about turning young people into lifelong debtors. Long-term care facilities aren't about care; they're about draining our elders in the last years of life and real estate plays. Many news sites aren't about news; they're about tricking us into clicking on autoplaying ads and advertorials that eat up the bottom half of nearly every site. Nothing is as it seems. This kind of predatory, extractive capitalism necessarily breeds mistrust and paranoia. In this context, it's not surprising that QAnon, a conspiracy theory that tells of elites harvesting the young for their lifeblood (adrenochrome), has gone viral. Elites are sucking us dry—our money, our labor, our time, our data. So dry that large parts of our planet are beginning to spontaneously combust. The Davos elite aren't eating our children, but they are eating our children's futures, and that is plenty bad. QAnon believers imagine secret tunnels underneath pizza parlors and Central Park, the better to traffic children. This is fantasy, but there are tunnels—literal Shadow Lands—under some major cities, and they do house and hide the poor, the sick, the drug-dependent, the discarded. Under the flashing lights of Las Vegas, hundreds or even thousands of people really do live in a sprawling network of storm tunnels.

Like my doppelganger projecting all of our surveillance fears on a vaccine app, conspiracy theorists get the facts wrong but often get the *feelings* right—the feeling of living in a world with Shadow Lands, the feeling that every human misery is someone else's profit, the feeling of being exhausted by predation and extraction, the feeling that important truths are being hidden. The word for the system driving those feelings starts with *c*, but if no one ever taught you how capitalism works, and instead told you it was all about freedom and sunshine and Big Macs and playing by the rules to get the life you deserve, then it's easy to see how you might confuse it with another *c*-word: conspiracy.

As Gilroy-Ware puts it, "Conspiracy theories are a misfiring of a healthy and justifiable political instinct: suspicion."

But suspicion directed at the wrong target is a very dangerous thing.

Outrunning Our Shadows

Jordan Peele's 2019 doppelganger horror film *Us* imagines a world much like our own sitting on top of a shadowy underworld, inhabited by doubles of everyone aboveground, with the doubles invisibly tethered to each other. Every move above must be mirrored below, in darkness and misery. The suffering of the underground people makes the ease aboveground possible, a dynamic many have interpreted as an analogy for the horrors of class under racial capitalism. But, in *Us*, the underworld people are tired of living distorted, shadow lives, so they come up to the light and wreak havoc.

Who are these shadow people?

"We're *Americans*," comes the gut punch.

The South Korean director Bong Joon-ho works with a similar under/over shadow world in his 2019 film, *Parasite*, with the working class, treated like bugs in their subterranean lairs, coming upstairs to occupy the gilded lives of the rich they are tired of serving. This is more than *Upstairs, Downstairs*; it's a metaphor for all the Shadow Lands of capitalism and imperialism: the teens in sweatshops in China, the kids in cobalt mines in Congo, the oil wars that fill our tanks, the migrants left to drown to protect the fantasy of a fortressed Europe. And now we can add the billions denied one shot of a Covid vaccine while those living in wealthy countries lined up for their third and fourth booster (that is, if they weren't squandering their privileges with manufactured threats of "tyranny").

The novelist Daisy Hildyard writes about the way we are entangled in these Shadow Lands as a form of doppelganging. In her 2017 book, *The Second Body*, she describes the human condition as one of having two bodies: the one we live in consciously—satiating our hunger, commuting to work, working out at the gym, making babies—and a shadow self that props up and supports those actions by traversing studiously denied parallel worlds on our behalf, extracting and manufacturing the resources and goods that make it all possible. She writes:

> You are stuck in your body right here, but in a technical way you could be said to be in India and Iraq, you are in the sky causing storms, and you are in the sea herding whales towards the beach. You probably don't feel your body in those places: it is as if you have two distinct bodies. You have an individual body in which you exist, eat, sleep and go about your day-to-day life. You also have a second body which has an impact on foreign countries and on whales . . . a body which is not so solid as the other one, but much larger.

In Hildyard's conception, our complicity in wars fought with our tax dollars to protect the oil and gas that likely warms our homes, cooks our food, and propels our vehicles, and in turn fuels extinction, is not separate from us; it's an extension of our physical beings. "This second body," she writes, "is your own literal and physical biological existence—it is a version of you." A less visible dimension of our embodied selves.

This is not just a pathology of the Mirror World, not just about *them*. It's about our world and every one of us. About a world that sits on top of the Shadow Lands—a world that always has. And this brings us to the dualism at the heart of our societies in the wealthy world—not the easy-to-spot goosestepping Nazi, but the exterminatory violence and ruthless exploitation that have always made up the underbelly of the project of "civilization." The great German philosopher Walter Benjamin wrote shortly before his death in 1940, "There is no document of civilization which is not at the same time a document of barbarism." Two decades later, the equally brilliant novelist, essayist, and playwright James Baldwin wrote, "It goes without saying, I believe, that if we understood ourselves better, we would damage ourselves less. But the barrier between oneself and one's knowledge of oneself is high indeed. There are so many things one would rather not know!"

The Covid era forced a reckoning with all kinds of truths that many of us would rather not know—about our present economic order, and the callous ways that our elders and so many who do the most critical work are treated. And about our collective past: the truth about the centrality of violently stolen African people and violently stolen Indigenous land to the creation of the modern world. It is this reckoning with the past, and its imprints on the present, that so many in my doppelganger's circle are trying hard to remove from textbooks and the shelves of school libraries. As if this weren't hard enough, we are also in a reckoning with the future, a future racing toward us after more than three decades of government and corporate leaders doing the precise oppose of what climate scientists pleaded with them to do: reduce greenhouse gas emissions. We feel the brutal futures that lurk behind the glow of our screens, the purr of our engines, the speed of our deliveries. We know the deadly prices that will be paid by our fellow humans both far and near, and by countless other-than-human beings and ecosystems as well. We glimpsed it in the fall of 2022, when floods in Pakistan displaced almost as many people as live in my entire country and drowned a season's worth of crops, and yet disappeared from our screens long before the waters receded.

In the relatively wealthy parts of this planet, these parallel Shadow Lands are our personal and planetary subconscious, and they haunt us. The ghosts of the past, present, and future, all racing toward us at once. We sense that the barriers that separate these worlds cannot hold for much longer. That, even for the most resourced among us, the curtain hiding the suffering and the ugliness is badly frayed. That just as societies can flip into their monstrous doppelgangers, so can the earth—from habitable to uninhabitable. That, as the Amazonian rain forest incinerates and Antarctica's ice cliffs heave into the sea, this process has already begun.

"When you are on a former battlefield or a mass grave, you know," writes Deena Metzger in her 2022 book, *La Vieja: A Journal of Fire*.

You do know. We all know. And we can sense that the shadows are closing in.

12

NO WAY OUT BUT BACK

Someday all of our kids and grandkids will ask each of us directly . . . 'Dad, Mom—Grandma, Grandpa—they will ask: What did you do in the war?'"

When Naomi Wolf published those words in her newsletter on March 2, 2022, there was a war raging, the most catastrophic assault on a European country since the Second World War. For a week, Russia had been pounding Ukraine's capital, Kyiv, and the surrounding suburbs, and the siege on the port of Mariupol had just begun; a million Ukrainians had fled their besieged country, according to United Nations estimates at the time. But Wolf was not referring to that war when she imagined children and grandchildren interrogating their elders. Nor was she referring to the war on our planet, though the Intergovernmental Panel on Climate Change had finalized a report three days earlier that read, in the words of UN secretary-general António Guterres, like an "atlas of human suffering and a damning indictment of failed climate leadership."

No, my doppelganger, in a post that she headlined "I'm Not 'Brave'; You're Just a P—y," was referring to a war unfolding at the Walker Hotel in the affluent Manhattan neighborhood of Tribeca, a war in which Wolf herself, according to this account, played nothing short of a heroic role.

The Case of the Overnight Oats

Wolf explained that she had been staying at the hotel and had noticed that its coffee shop had a sign stating that seating was for "vaccinated only." The coffee shop was a Blue Bottle, a boutique chain where a cup of coffee sells for $4 and overnight oats for $6. Wolf decided to put her body on the line to stand up to this tyranny:

> So on Day 3 of my stay, I politely informed the staff at the Blue Bottle Cafe that I was unvaccinated, and that I would now take my small coffee and my overnight oats to the forbidden lunch counter, and I would sit there peacefully, but that I would not comply with the NYC directive for the cafe to discriminate against me.
>
> The staff informed me stertorously—doing their job—that my doing so was against NYC "mandate." I said that I understood, but that I was nonetheless choosing not to comply . . . I then sat down at the illegal lunch counter, texted my lawyer to be on standby, posted publicly to Gov [Kathy] Hochul and to Mayor [Eric] Adams that I was currently intentionally violating the discriminatory NYC mandate that prevented unvaccinated people from being seated in cafes and restaurants, and that I was at the Walker Hotel Tribeca cafe lunch counter at that very moment if they wished to arrest me.
>
> Then I waited for an hour, heart pounding, to be arrested.
>
> Do you know what happened?
>
> *Nothing.*

Yup. Absolutely nothing. The police did not get involved, and it would seem that both the governor and the mayor were otherwise occupied.

Undeterred, and with her social media feeds now on high alert, Wolf proceeded to Grand Central Station and pulled the exact same stunt in a waiting area with a vaccination requirement. This time "two cops appeared at once." According to Wolf's account, they politely directed her to a different waiting area, reserved for unvaccinated people:

> I explained that the strength of New York City, and of America for that matter, was its diversity and its equal treatment of all, and that if people had refused to comply with other forms of discrimination and forced separate accommodations, discriminatory rules would have ended sooner. I stated for the second time that day I intended peacefully not to comply.

Wolf waited to get arrested for her second courageous stand of the day. "I was braced for the handcuffs again," she wrote. "Once again my heart was racing." But just like at the Blue Bottle, nothing happened. Zero. "When I asked if I could now walk away and take my train—no one stopped me."

From these rather mundane experiences grabbing a coffee and taking the train, Wolf drew some very big conclusions:

> When I refused to comply with these unlawful "mandates" that have burnt out the soul of a once-great city, *nothing happened* . . . But it took those awful, frightening moments of pressing against those terrifying-sounding "mandates" to prove, at least to myself, that they were meaningless.
>
> Other people's courage builds possibilities in this world.

That, Wolf wrote, is "the takeaway."

That is not the only possible takeaway from my doppelganger's inability to get arrested in New York City. Another is that, despite her continuous claims to the contrary, a coup d'état never had taken place to end freedom under the cover of a pandemic, and that she never was living under a biofascist regime. In fact, as she must have known when Wolf staged her protest, New York mayor Eric Adams had already announced that the city would be lifting vaccine mandates for indoor dining as long as Covid levels remained low. Just a few days later, that happened. Despite some real instances of overreach, a temporary health measure was, in fact, temporary.

As I have said, I was conflicted on the vaccine apps: increased digitization of daily life deepens preexisting inequalities, but so does letting a virus run rampant as the bodies pile up. Once the virus mutated and it became clear that vaccines were becoming less effective in preventing infection, continuing the vaccine mandates began to make less sense, which is why they were being lifted in places like New York. (Masks and rapid tests were still pretty effective at limiting infection and transmission, but requirements related to them, unfortunately, were lifted, too.)

Setting those matters aside, what struck me most in Wolf's overwrought account of an ultimately uneventful day in the city was her odd choice of words. Blue Bottle is mainly a grab-and-go chain; it has some eclectic seating, but it doesn't have a "lunch counter," words Wolf used three times. Her use of that anachronistic term was, quite obviously, designed to recall the bloody and courageous sit-ins at actual lunch counters in the early 1960s, most prominently at the Woolworths five-and-dime store in Greensboro, North Carolina, when four Black civil rights activists insisted on their right to be served despite the whites-only policy. The acts of the Greensboro Four inspired more acts of civil disobedience throughout the segregated South; many were beaten and arrested for their courage.

Jim Crow was indeed a tyrannical system designed to maintain Black people's status as second-class citizens. By invoking lunch counters, and referencing earlier moments in U.S. history with "forced separate accommodations" and "discriminatory rules," Wolf was brashly putting herself in the same league as the Greensboro Four, as well as Rosa Parks, who in 1955 famously refused to give up her seat to a white passenger on a bus in Montgomery, Alabama. (Wolf is enough of an admirer that she named her daughter after her.) Later she would write that living in New York State during Covid had been "as if we were all living under Jim Crow laws."

Racial Role-Playing

These historical invocations were not anomalies. In her interviews, alongside her promiscuous Nazi references, Wolf repeatedly draws parallels between vaccine mandates and very real structures of racial oppression. The broader anti-vaccine, anti-mask, anti-lockdown movement, meanwhile, has consistently analogized itself to Black liberation movements and draws liberally from their lexicons. Steve Bannon has taken to telling his activist audience that by storming school board meetings and taking over local Republican Party chapters, they are "bending the arc." Whether in New York or Sydney, Paris or Rome, white people—overwhelmingly in the majority as protesters and protest leaders—pronounced themselves to be part of "a new civil rights movement" because they were victims of a new human hierarchy in which they were "second-class citizens" and faced "medical apartheid." Some held signs that said MANDATE = SLAVERY. In September 2021, a teaching assistant at an elementary school in Newberg, Oregon, went so far as to protest her district's vaccine mandate by showing up for work in blackface. "I am representing Rosa Parks," she told a talk-show host. Taken together, this movement has claimed, at various times, to be standing up to pretty much all the crimes that have been perpetrated against racial and religious minorities since the Crusades: slavery, genocide, the Holocaust, Jim Crow, apartheid, and more.

One of the glowing influencers who I follow, for instance, said she is tired of fighting for her "right to breathe"—a reference to her refusal to wear a mask in stores when they were mandated. A group of mothers in San Diego who didn't want their kids to have to wear masks in school called their organization Let Them Breathe. It is difficult to imagine that these educated, upper-middle-class white mothers were unaware that their slogan echoed another—the cries of "I can't breathe" that rose up from the streets in 2014 after a New York City police officer put Eric Garner in a chokehold and, after Garner uttered those fateful words, ended his life. They must have known that those same words roared up from the streets again in 2020, when George Floyd said them before he was murdered by a Minneapolis police officer. Yet less than a year after the country was rocked by protests sparked by Floyd's killing—and Ahmaud Arbery's, and Breonna Taylor's, and so many others before and after—here were those three words again, in only slightly altered form, being directed at public health policies designed to reduce transmission of Covid-19, which was still disproportionately ravaging Black communities.

This kind of racial role-playing is ubiquitous among the diagonalists.

In the spring of 2021, Wolf was scheduled to speak about her "Five Freedoms" campaign at an anti-vax event that was planned for Juneteenth, the day that commemorates the end of slavery in the United States. The journalist Eoin Higgins questioned the organizer about the appropriateness of co-opting a holiday so central to Black liberation for these purposes. The response: "We have been enslaved by our government."

The event appears to have been canceled, but the original plan points to something that has often struck me about Wolf's ceaseless claims that Covid measures have ushered in a new era of political obedience she and her fellow travelers alone have had the courage to resist. Their story completely ignores the fact that in that summer of 2020, despite mask mandates and social distancing rules, millions of people took to the streets, day after day, night after night, to rise up against police murders of Black people, and to demand a radical reallocation of resources away from mass incarceration and militarized policing and toward educational, housing, and health infrastructure and services that would begin to close the wealth and investment gaps that treat Black communities as de facto second class, even if legalized segregation has ended.

If you were a person concerned that Covid marked the dawn of a new age of CCP-inspired mass obedience, surely it would be worth mentioning that the largest protests in the history of the United States happened in the Covid era, with millions of people willing to face clouds of tear gas and streams of pepper spray to exercise their rights to speech, assembly, and dissent. Come to think of it, if you were a person concerned with tyrannical state actions, you would also be concerned about the murders and mass denials of freedom to incarcerated people that drove that uprising. Yet in all the videos Wolf has put out issuing her dire warnings about how the United States was turning into a nation of sheeple, I have seen her acknowledge neither the existence of this racial justice reckoning nor the reality that if a Black person had pulled the same stunt that she did at the Blue Bottle or Grand Central Station, they very likely would have ended up face down in cuffs—not because vaccine rules were tyrannical, but because of systemic anti-Black racism in policing, the issue that sparked the protests she has so studiously ignored.

Things grew only more ridiculous/serious when, in June 2022, three months after the Battle of Little Blue Bottle, Wolf staged a more successful publicity-seeking stunt while in Salem, Oregon. She found one of the only restaurants in the city that still required proof of vaccination for indoor dining—Epilogue Kitchen and Cocktails, a Black-owned business whose windows displayed portraits of George Floyd and Breonna Taylor as well as signs saying BLACK LIVES MATTER and NO PLACE FOR HATE. Despite having all the rest of Salem's restaurants to choose from, and despite having a reservation elsewhere, Wolf strolled into Epilogue and staged a confrontation until she was asked to leave. She then filmed herself lecturing the restaurant's Black manager, saying, "A lot of people in this nation's history pushed boundaries like that. And it turned out to be the right thing to do because people do have, you know, equal rights in this country." She also claimed that the vaccine requirement was "absolutely discrimination."

This went on for a painfully long time, with Wolf declaring her treatment "an important moment in this nation's history." After she proudly posted the videos on Gettr, the restaurant was, entirely predictably, inundated with racist abuse from her followers—by phone and email and over social media. Many took it upon themselves to make fake reservations (some under Donald Trump's name) and deliberately drove down the restaurant's ratings. "We've had over 150 fake one-star reviews," Epilogue co-owner Jonathan Jones reported one week later. "Most of them dive pretty quickly into racism. Pretty unbridled, gross racism." Indeed, many of the responses combined themes that have recurred on this journey so far: fatphobia, anti-Black racism, conspiracy, and claims of genetic superiority, with special hatred reserved for the Black Lives Matter posters in the window.

All of this raises the question of what the relationship is between the diagonalists and the other major movements of our time. Are they running on non-intersecting tracks? Do we see, as many diagonalists claim, evidence of rampant double standards, with anti-lockdown protests condemned by liberal elites while racial justice uprisings were celebrated? Or is the dynamic more complex, with one movement engaged in some kind of warped-mirror dialectic with the other?

I have no doubt that, while vaccine passports were in effect, people who had not gotten the shot felt like victims of discrimination or even, for a time, like social pariahs. And there could and should have been clearer exceptions available for people with medical conditions that made mask-wearing and vaccines higher risk. Yet witnessing how many of the loudest voices laying claim to this treacherous form of discrimination were, like me, well-off white women, I couldn't shake the feeling that part of the reason why they were making these choices was that they believed that being outside the Covid health consensus conferred on them a powerful kind of victim status—this at a time when the spotlight on racialized violence was causing plenty of white women to question ourselves and our roles. Did being a white woman count as a basis for discrimination at a time when everyone was railing against the archetypal Karen? Well, maybe, if a Karen can convince herself she is actually a Rosa in disguise, denied access to restaurants and transportation and shunned by friends and family. Surely, by laying claim to that abrupt loss of status, that would raise her status—which, let's face it, is not an entirely outlandish thing to believe at this stage of neoliberal capitalism, which has done a fine job of transforming identity-based oppression from a basis for solidarity and shared analysis (the original intention of identity politics) to its own form of currency.

In a particularly revealing moment, while Wolf is lecturing the Black manager of that Salem restaurant about the irony of opposing anti-Black violence while discriminating against the unvaccinated, the manager replies calmly, "I'm sorry that you're centering yourself." The restaurant owner and manager said afterward that they had no clue who Wolf was at the time of the encounter. But on another level, they knew exactly who she was.

In nations whose economies were built on the back of enslaved Black people's labor, and whose very existences are owed to the stealing of lands from Indigenous peoples through campaigns of horrific violence, torture, famine, and forced relocation, the past is our collective, unshakable, omnipresent shadow. Only in spasms of reckonings like the one that followed George Floyd's murder does the dominant culture manage to look with anything more than furtive glances at these foundational crimes—or at the present-day realities of continued racial segregation in our neighborhoods, schools, health-care, and justice systems. Not to mention the highly racialized fault lines that separated who got to stay at home and complain about it during the pandemic and who was expected to brave the virus without proper protective gear in hospitals, care homes, warehouses, waste facilities, and so many other underpaid workplaces that hold up the infrastructure of contemporary life.

As conservatives and liberals mirror one another, each claiming the mantle of truth and righteousness, this unreckoned-with history and present are a large part of whiteness's shadow world, the truth that is simultaneously known and repressed. In *Between the World and Me*, Ta-Nehisi Coates calls white people's denial of this shadow "the Dream," an abbreviation of the American Dream that de-emphasizes the American part in favor of the reverie part. Crucially, the Dream knows it's a dream, knows it's not real, knows that reality is pounding at the door, threatening an awakening from slumber. And so huge efforts must be made to keep the curtains drawn so that the light does not stream in.

That is the cruelest irony of Wolf's antics at eateries in both Manhattan and Salem. At the same time as she was absorbing and appropriating the language of the civil rights movement, many of her fellow travelers in the Mirror World were actively fighting to suppress all attempts to tell a truer story of America's past, claiming that, like masks and vaccines, teaching students about the reality of racism in their country is a form of child abuse. They are the ones pushing for laws calling for only "patriotic" history to be taught and for books to be banned—because, as the historian Keeanga-Yamahtta Taylor writes, knowing history demands doing something about its legacies in the present:

> These collective efforts have made a mockery of public conversations about the history of American racism and xenophobia—and, in some contexts, have made them all but impossible. Discussions of America's racist history lend important insights into the patterns of poverty, unemployment, and social deprivation that exist today. They underlie the arguments for the creation or expansion of public programs intended to alleviate racial exclusion.

Those conversations are obviously anathema on the right, Taylor notes, but they are also "evaded even by some liberals afraid of being tagged as favoring 'big government.'"

And so, while Wolf was cosplaying Rosa Parks, some of her newfound fellow warriors in the fight for "freedom" were busily banning books about the precise history they were all pilfering, including a little illustrated book called *I Am Rosa Parks*, which made it onto a Pennsylvania school board's banned book list. In her dozens and dozens of media appearances on right-wing outlets that I have listened to, I have never heard Wolf speak out against the escalating book bans around the country, even as she laments her own deplatforming as a member of the "shadow banned."

It's as if by absorbing the language and postures of the oppressed, the diagonalists are attempting to outrun the long shadow of the past. Including the fact that our young countries are built on top of burned villages and graveyards, whose spirits have never been put to rest.

A Tale of Two Truck Convoys

In May 2021, the Tk'emlúps te Secwépemc First Nation, an Indigenous community in the interior of British Columbia, issued a statement that would reverberate around the world. It said that it had located the probable graves of as many as 215 children on the grounds of the former Kamloops Indian Residential School, which had been in operation for nearly a century. Some of the children appeared to have been as young as three years old when they were buried. Indigenous students had been sent there from across the province and beyond.

The residential schools were but one relatively modern weapon of the genocide that collectively decimated the Indigenous population of the Americas by more than 90 percent after European contact. Survivors of the schools had long shared memories about secret burial grounds. About children who disappeared in the night, never to return. About babies who went mysteriously missing after having been fathered by priests. It was such an open secret that an official Truth and Reconciliation Commission report, issued in 2015, called on the government of Canada to launch a full investigation into deaths and possible murders in the schools.

The report meticulously examined what it categorized as a "cultural genocide": between the 1880s and the late 1990s, at least 150,000 First Nations, Métis, and Inuit children from across Canada had been removed from their families and culture and forced to attend these so-called residential schools, which were run by the Catholic Church and other organizations at the behest of the federal and provincial governments. After conducting thousands of interviews, the TRC identified the names of 3,201 children who died in residential schools, a number that has since been updated to 4,117. Justice Murray Sinclair, chairman of the TRC, later estimated that the true number may be closer to 25,000, and he consistently urged the government to investigate the grounds of the former institutions.

But Ottawa dragged its feet. It was in this context that some First Nations undertook their own searches, which proceeded even under the eerie quiet of Covid isolation. And now, with the aid of ground-penetrating radar, the soil was giving up its secrets, confirming with Western science the bitter truths that survivors and their descendants already knew. The schools didn't only set out to deliberately kill Indigenous culture; they killed Indigenous children. Many of them. By medical neglect, malnutrition, physical abuse, and sometimes, it seems, murder. "Apocalypse," in its original Greek, means an uncovering, a disclosing, a revelation. This was that.

The confirmation of buried children in Kamloops—a material surfacing of the collective subconscious through radar "reflections"—stripped the last vestiges of deniability from the genocidal violence that made Canada possible. And it was just the beginning. The Tk'emlúps te Secwépemc First Nation would eventually adjust the number from 215 to 200, but in the weeks that followed, hundreds more unmarked graves would be found at the sites of other former schools; as I type, an investigation of possible graves is being carried out just a few minutes away from where I live. Already, dozens of shallow graves have been found. To date, over two thousand suspected unmarked graves have been identified on former school grounds in Canada. There is little doubt that more such macabre confirmations are in store.

The underlying goal of those institutions was not education. It was ending Indigeneity as an identity. Officially, Canada's objective for the schools was to "kill the Indian in the child"—to sever all connections between Indigenous peoples and their land-based traditions, ceremonies, languages, and kinship relations. Sometimes this is attributed exclusively to racism, but that is only half the story: the white and Christian supremacy that underpinned the residential school system also served national economic and political interests. Canada, which began as a cluster of fur-trading companies and other extractive industries, needed those schools because its hunger for land was voracious, and those severed connections—the uprooted and traumatized relationships between parents and children, between land and people—helped make it possible to seize unceded Indigenous land for unfettered resource extraction and settlement by colonists.

As in the reckonings sparked by the murder of George Floyd in 2020, the truth about the unmarked graves that surfaced in 2021 sparked waves of rage, grief, and solidarity across Canada. Statues of colonial figures who helped design these twisted institutions were toppled; a major university changed its name; churches were burned. Eventually, Pope Francis would come to Canada in what he termed a "penitential pilgrimage," after which he concluded, "Yes, it's a genocide." Canada's Parliament then unanimously passed a motion stating that the residential school system met the United Nations' definition of genocide.

A symbol of the movement seeking justice for these crimes, which predates the radar confirmations of the graves, is an orange shirt and the slogan EVERY CHILD MATTERS. That spring, orange flags with those words began flapping in the wind outside thousands of homes and businesses, institutions from banks to universities had "orange shirt days," and orange ribbons—215 of them—were tied to chain-link fences outside nearly every school and playground. Public squares filled up with memorials made of little shoes and teddy bears. Newspapers ran articles debating the white supremacist legal fictions that provided the cover story for tearing families apart and stealing land—absurd, unilateral edicts like "Manifest Destiny" and the "Doctrine of Discovery," under which European monarchs and popes declared that they had a divine right to plunder already-inhabited but newly "discovered" lands.

Here in so-called British Columbia (a province whose very name is a humiliating colonial mash-up of the British Crown and Christopher Columbus), it seemed as if the buried worlds upon which our settler state was built were rushing to the surface. The deaths of these children and the subsequent cover-ups were true conspiracies, and now they could no longer be denied. Grand Chief George Manuel, who helped found the modern Indigenous rights movement, attended the Kamloops school. "Hunger is both the first and last thing I can remember about that school," he wrote in his memoir. "Not just me. Every Indian student smelled of hunger." Weakened bodies made Indigenous youth more vulnerable to disease; Manuel himself contracted tuberculosis at age twelve and lived with disability for the rest of his life.

His granddaughter, Kanahus Manuel, one of the leaders of a movement that has been trying for years to stop the expansion of an oil pipeline through BC's interior, described the purpose of the schools that had abused so many members of her family: "They stole the children to steal the land." When I interviewed Kanahus shortly after the graves were located, she told me that justice could come only with meaningful redress. She was demanding "land back," the rallying cry around which large parts of the Indigenous rights movement is now galvanized. Difficult conversations were finally happening about what that might mean.

As the foundational crimes of the colonial project were escaping the Shadow Lands and coming to light, one thing was clear to many: The comforting mythologies of official history simply would not do any longer. Coming just one year after the racial reckonings that followed George Floyd's killing, reckonings that had also shaken Canadian institutions in virtually every sector and profession, these monstrous, long-buried crimes inflicted on young bodies and minds by church and state demanded of Canadians a new story of who we are, how we got here, and who we want to be going forward.

The announcement about the graves happened in late May. Canada normally celebrates its national holiday on July 1, on the anniversary of its colonies forming a confederation. In 2021, with searches still underway, a sober consensus emerged that the usual prideful displays of red-and-white maple-leaf flags and fireworks were not appropriate, not this year. The capital city of British Columbia, Victoria, canceled Canada Day altogether. Other cities marked the day with Every Child Matters murals and official expressions of grief and contrition, including from Prime Minister Justin Trudeau, who called on the country to "be honest with ourselves about our history." Here on the coast where I live, the Canada Day crowd was a sea of orange, without a red-and-white flag in sight.

"Nations themselves *are* narrations," Edward Said wrote in *Culture and Imperialism*. Our narration wasn't holding. That spring and early summer was like a national excavation, digging deeper than ever before in my lifetime. Interestingly, I experienced it as the opposite of vertigo. In place of the ephemera and boosterism of national mythmaking and official histories, a solid idea seemed to be forming about where we live and how this land came to be available to settlers like me—and what it might take to finally be good guests and neighbors, without all the denial required of lives built on not-seeing and not-knowing. "An invented past can never be used; it cracks and crumbles under the pressures of life like clay in a season of drought," James Baldwin wrote. However, "to accept one's past—one's history—is not the same thing as drowning in it; it is learning how to use it."

Many Indigenous friends and neighbors I spoke with, though raw with grief and rage, expressed cautious hope that this kind of deep learning might actually be afoot. In an interview with *The Globe and Mail*, Norman Retasket, a survivor of the Kamloops school, observed, "If I told the same story three years ago," about what happened at the school, it would have been seen as "fiction." Now his stories are believed. "The story hasn't changed," he said. "The listener has changed."

One person who felt changed by what he was learning was Mike Otto, a white trucker, small-business owner, and father who lives a couple of hours down Highway 97 from those first graves. Otto found himself imagining what Indigenous families must have been going through all these years, the ones who never knew what happened to "those little ones that had gone missing." Witnessing the pain of his Indigenous neighbors, Otto decided he needed to do something to show that non-Indigenous Canadians like him stood in solidarity with their efforts to seek justice from the government, the court system, and the church.

The pandemic was still raging, and the community where the graves were found had made it clear that they did not want crowds of strangers traipsing through their territory. Otto had an idea for something powerful that would respect the community's need for physical distance: a trucker convoy, one that would pass in front of the burial grounds, make some offerings, then leave. He called it the We Stand in Solidarity Convoy.

Otto posted invitations to various trucker Facebook groups and reached out to influential people in the industry. His goal was for the convoy to grow to 215 trucks; in the end, closer to 400 trucks joined up, along with many motorcycles and cars. Drivers decorated their vehicles with messages of love, hung orange shirts on their grilles, and waved EVERY CHILD MATTERS flags. The convoy was met with cheers all along the way, and in some cases whole towns came to greet them and share food. When the trucks made it to the former residential school, honking their airhorns as they passed, many members of the Secwépemc Nation greeted them with ceremonial drumming, warrior songs, and burning sage. Fists were raised in resolve, and faces were washed in tears.

I mention these events because they were meaningful in the part of the world where I live, a too-rare example of non-Indigenous people taking on Indigenous death as a true collective crisis, rather than shunting off the quest for justice and reparation to those who are already carrying so much. But I also mention the four-hundred-vehicle convoy of June 2021 because it has been largely forgotten, even in Canada, with Mike Otto and his feat of bighearted organizing entirely displaced in the public imagination by a far noisier convoy of Canadian truckers that took place a mere eight months later.

Honks Heard Around the World

Perhaps you remember it from the winter of 2022. International media couldn't get enough of the images of burly Canadians, their big rigs festooned with FUCK TRUDEAU signs, shutting down the center of Ottawa, our capital city, for the better part of a month. Or of the blockades on bridges that turned key trade routes between Canada and the United States into parking lots. This second convoy was sparked by a new requirement that truckers show proof of Covid vaccination in order to cross the border, though it quickly grew into a more generalized call for an end to "the mandates," including mask mandates and any other public health restrictions.

Most Canadian truckers were fully vaccinated and had no problem with the health measures. But a minority of them, steeped in diagonalist rhetoric, claimed that the vaccine requirement constituted a new form of tyranny, and so they teamed up with a mix-and-match of aggrieved small-business owners, ex-cops and ex-soldiers, the author of *Oh She Glows* vegan cookbooks, and a great many evangelical Christians—all banding together to "shut the country down," with a stretch goal of convincing the governor general, the Queen's representative in Canada, to dissolve Trudeau's newly reelected government.

The convoy had plenty of fans. Donald Trump and Elon Musk celebrated the "Canadian truckers" as working-class heroes; Steve Bannon and Tucker Carlson gave them blanket coverage; my doppelganger cheered them on as modern-day freedom fighters. Soon enough, copycat convoys were on the move from Washington, D.C., to Wellington, New Zealand. After taking a remarkably passive approach to the occupation for weeks, the Trudeau government made an abrupt about-face and invoked, for the first time in our history, the Emergencies Act, which cleared the way for a range of repressive tactics like freezing supporters' bank accounts. The rationale for invoking the act was so loose that it set a dangerous precedent for any future action that disrupts major economic activity, whether a strike or an Indigenous blockade. And the heavy-handed crackdown made the convoyers even more popular with the likes of Bannon and the podcast giant Joe Rogan, who featured them repeatedly.

The protests certainly served up good visuals. There were snowball fights, beer kegs, pot in the air, and a sea of Canadian flags. There were Jericho Marchers and street sermons and many people claiming to be taking orders directly from God. There were hugs for strangers and epithets for passersby wearing masks. There really was an inflatable hot tub. And there were also all the unmistakable signs of political discombobulation that mark the diagonalist world: someone earnestly waving a giant swastika-festooned Nazi flag and others waving Confederate flags, alongside anti-vax demonstrators wearing their yellow stars and holding signs declaring themselves to be living under apartheid or Jim Crow. Were these people Nazis or anti-Nazis? Segregationists or anti-segregationists? Were they proud patriots or insurrectionists determined to overturn the results of our recent election? It hardly seemed to matter—the convoy was pipiked to its core, a knot of seriousness and ridiculousness that would never be untangled.

Many convoy supporters attempted to portray the obviously racist elements as isolated, likely a covert op by the secret police or antifa demonstrators, designed to discredit them. Inconveniently for these theories, the connections run deep. One of the convoy's most outspoken leaders was a man named Pat King, who offered logistical support for protesters via his Facebook page, which had around 350,000 followers at the time. King is an open racist who has referred to Indigenous culture as "a disgrace" and who, in 2019, organized a similar though smaller convoy to oppose immigration and climate action, which were positioned as twin threats to the Canadian way of life. "It's called depopulation of the Caucasian race, or the Anglo-Saxon," King claimed. "And, that's what the goal is, is to depopulate the Anglo-Saxon race, because they are the ones with the strongest bloodlines." He also spoke of a plan to "not only infiltrate by flooding with refugees, [but also] to infiltrate the education systems to manipulate it."

King was, of course, parroting the "Great Replacement" theory, which has been at the heart of so much white supremacist carnage. And he was far from the only convoy leader with openly racist views and affiliations. The Canadian Anti-Hate Network reported that virtually every group it monitors was playing a leadership role, including a network that seeks to carve out a new country called Diagolon, which would run from Alaska, through the Canadian prairies and Alberta, and all the way to Florida. According to the Anti-Hate Network, "Diagolon is increasingly becoming a militia network. Their goals are ultimately fascist: to use violence to take power and strip rights away from people who do not meet their purity tests based on ideology, race, and gender . . . Their motto is 'gun or rope.'"

It is worth pausing over these facts. The revelation of the unmarked graves less than a year earlier had forced a conversation about the fact that those schools were part of an official state policy to actively replace Indigenous nations, languages, and cultures with English- and French-speaking Christian culture. The residential schools were machines expressly designed to eradicate cosmologies that knew the natural world to be sacred, alive, and interdependent—teachings that are deeply relevant to our moment of planetary crisis. Now there was a convoy led by a man who claimed it was his Christian Caucasian culture that was under threat of being replaced by darker, inferior others through the so-called Great Replacement. For Jesse Wente, a prominent Ojibwe writer and chair of the Canada Council for the Arts, the mirroring was glaring. It's "not a coincidence this occurs as more truths of history are revealed," Wente wrote about the convoy, which he described as "a desire to reassert colonial dominance in the face of actually having to face [those truths] and to provide a sense of community where the pandemic has shown there is little."

One Conservative MP, in an attempt to paint the Ottawa occupation as just a bunch of patriotic Everymen, described the mood on the streets as "Canada Day times a thousand." In a way, the description fit. It definitely seemed that all those red-and-white flags that were left at home on our mournful, contemplative Canada Day were back with a vengeance, flying off every truck, often merged, oddly, with the U.S. Stars and Stripes, as if after two years of racial reckonings our two countries had melded in a single project of collective forgetting.

Integrating the Shadow Lands on which the modern world was built holds out the potential for reaching something resembling solid ground. As Baldwin wrote, only when we confront the terrors of the past can history become something we can all use, perhaps even to forge a new basis for unity. But no one said that integration was going to be painless. So, one way of seeing the convoy of eighteen-wheelers that made its way to Ottawa is as an angry reassertion of innocence, an attempt to stuff down these difficult truths ever deeper in the shadows, while trying to reanimate that comforting dream of righteousness and dominance—as individuals and as a nation.

The convoy that shut down Ottawa made for a stark contrast with the lesser-known convoy that occurred eight months earlier. Where Mike Otto's demonstration had been marked by a rare willingness to look honestly at the genocide that birthed our nation, this new convoy embodied an aggressive presentism—a refusal to contemplate any uncomfortable truths, whether Canada's violent history, or the reality that Covid was still surging (many convoyers got sick), or the planetary warming they were helping along by idling their massive trucks for a month (the convoy's unofficial symbol was the smuggled-in jerry can filled with gas). In less than a year, we had gone from the We Stand in Solidarity Convoy, a recognition and embrace of enmeshment, to the Freedom Convoy, a rejection of interdependence in favor of hyper-individual independence. Clearly, a subset of my country wanted their guilt-free fantasies back—and they would hold the rest of us hostage to get them.

I, Too, Am a Victim, the Biggest Victim!

Because ours is a doppelganger politics, a simple rejection of what is feared is insufficient—there has to be a mirroring, a mimicking, a pipiking. So, in addition to the snow forts and airhorns in Ottawa, the Freedom Convoy also had a peace pipe and a tepee (denounced by three local Algonquin chiefs). Some of the convoyers waved orange EVERY CHILD MATTERS flags off their trucks—seemingly not in recognition of the Indigenous children who were raped, tortured, and killed in residential schools and whose remains were still being uncovered, but rather in reference to their own children, who, in the ever-escalating diagonalist discourse, were facing what some demonstrators called a "second genocide" as a result of having to wear face masks and being expected to get vaccinated. This Mirror World equivalency had been building for months: within two weeks of the discovery of the first unmarked graves, a group of white anti-vax moms started selling orange sweatshirts and other items declaring COVID 19 IS CANADA'S SECOND GENOCIDE.

Did the truckers intend to upstage, blot out, and co-opt the Indigenous and Black racial justice reckonings that have so deeply challenged our national stories and so many of our self-conceptions during these pandemic years? Surely not in any conscious way. There was no shadowy room where Steve Bannon and the Proud Boys met with my doppelganger and Pat King to cook up that devious scheme. Rather, I think what we are seeing may be more like a reflex, an instinct for what feels, to its participants, like self-preservation.

It's tough to live in a moment when so many truths that had been sold as settled suddenly become wobbly and wavy under our feet. It's especially tough at a time when a great deal else feels uncertain: the possibility of owning a home, or scraping together enough money for soaring rents, or holding on to any given job, or even knowing how much the basics of life are going to cost week to week. It's all tilting and rolling, and so much, like the assumed predictability of seasons, will never be stable again, at least not for several generations, and that is in a best-case scenario. All of this destabilization places demands on us: to change, to reassess, and to reimagine who we need to become. It should not be a surprise that a moment this demanding is conjuring up some extreme behaviors and apparitions. It should not be a surprise that, instead of looking squarely at what has been revealed in wave after wave of unveiling—the nurses forced to wear garbage bags instead of proper protective gear; the cool hatred in Derek Chauvin's eyes as he pressed his weight onto George Floyd's neck; the perversion of the priests; the skies stained orange from wildfires—many are opting for some rather spectacular distractions. Including the distraction of casting themselves as cosmic victims of every crime against humanity of the past five hundred years combined.

This might explain why the conspiratorial claims in the Mirror World so often seem to contradict one another. For this new political configuration, convincing people of their unproven theories was never the real point—it was only ever a tool. The point, consciously or not, is to foster denial and avoidance. The point is not to have to do hard and uncomfortable things in the face of hard and uncomfortable realities, whether Covid, or climate change, or the fact that our nations were forged in genocide and have never engaged in a remotely serious process of making repair. Denial is so much easier than looking inward, or backward, or forward; so much easier than change. But denial needs narratives, cover stories, and that is what conspiracy culture is providing.

Still, I'm troubled by the comfort this analysis implies, the fact that it places the denial all on those who inhabit the Mirror World. It's similar to the problem of climate change denial: There are the hard deniers, who are easy to spot, saying it's all a hoax. But the bigger obstacle may always have been the soft deniers, the rest of us who know it's real but act like it's not, who keep forgetting, in myriad ways, both large and small.

As I noted earlier, Bannon pounds relentlessly at what he calls the Big Steal—the claim that Biden stole the 2020 election—while the Democrats call that the Big Lie. And it is a big lie, a dangerous one. But is it *the* Big Lie? Bigger, say, than trickle-down economics? Bigger than "tax cuts create jobs"? Bigger than infinite growth on a finite planet? Bigger than Thatcher's double whammy of "There is no alternative" and "There is no such thing as society"? Bigger, for that matter, than Manifest Destiny, Terra Nullius, and the Doctrine of Discovery—the lies that form the basis of the United States, Canada, Australia, and every other settler colonial state? If we can stand to look at the Shadow Lands even for a moment, it becomes clear that we are ensnared in a web of life-annihilating lies and that whatever the Mirror World is on about this week is neither the biggest lie nor the one with the highest stakes. It's entirely possible that Bannon and Wolf's war on reality is just what happens when so many of the big lies that built the modern world visibly crumble. As the house collapses, some people choose to take flight into full-blown fantasy, sure—but that doesn't mean that the rest of us who were also born and raised in that house are guardians of the truth.

What, then, are many of us still not seeing, still avoiding, in these shadow-laden woods?

13

THE NAZI IN THE MIRROR

One night, while the truckers were having their snowball fights on the other side of the country, I decided to watch something that I hoped might help me make some sense of these strange happenings: the four-part HBO miniseries *Exterminate All the Brutes*, from the Haitian filmmaker Raoul Peck. Slow and deliberate, it leaves lots of time to think. At one point in the voice-over, Peck says, "The very existence of this film is a miracle." It is certainly a sign that more cracks are opening up to the Shadow Lands, and more secrets and ghosts are escaping their burial grounds.

Peck's earlier films—including *Lumumba*, about the assassination of the Congolese liberation leader and prime minister Patrice Lumumba; *I Am Not Your Negro*, about the life and thought of James Baldwin; and *The Young Karl Marx*—had, he explained, each told a piece of the violent story of how our world was born. Now Peck was reaching for a unifying theory that runs through these and other chapters, attempting to identify a worldview that could stitch together the various massacres and holocausts and political assassinations that cleared land for European settlers in the Americas and made it possible to pillage Africa and build racial apartheid in the United States.

"The foundation of it all," Peck says, is embedded in the title he chose, inspired by the 1992 book *"Exterminate All the Brutes,"* by the Swedish writer Sven Lindqvist, who took it from a fateful line in Joseph Conrad's *Heart of Darkness*, first published in 1899, which tells the story of a colonial ivory-trading mission in central Africa. Conrad drew on numerous examples of Europeans setting out to "civilize the savages" as a high-minded excuse for asserting a right to their lands, wealth, and bodies. Inevitably, that civilizing urge tipped into a blinding drive to wipe out the natives—a conclusion foretold as soon as one group of people set themselves up as biologically superior to all others.

That sentence—"exterminate all the brutes"—is the murderous annihilatory impulse to pursue one's interests at all costs. It is the supremacist mindset that casts the extinguishments of entire peoples and cultures not merely as an unavoidable element of the march of progress but also as a salutary stage in the evolution of the human species. "And if the inferior race must perish, it is a gain, a step toward the perfecting of society which is the aim of progress," Mr. Travers explains in Conrad's novel *The Rescue*, a distillation of the mindset that drowned whole continents in blood, and that was certainly at work here in Canada, in those so-called schools with secret cemeteries. Within this mindset, genocide is not a crime; it's merely a difficult but necessary stage, one blessed (for the believers) by God or (for the rationalists) by Charles Darwin, who wrote in *The Descent of Man*, "At some future period, not very distant as measured by centuries, the civilised races of man will almost certainly exterminate, and replace, the savage races throughout the world." A "great replacement" theory if ever there was one.

What I did not expect was to discover that Peck's opus was a doppelganger story. His thesis is that the dominant story we tell about Hitler and the Holocaust—which treats that frenzy of death as so extreme that it is without historical precedents or antecedents—is flat wrong. Peck argues instead that the Holocaust was an intensified and compacted expression of the very same violent colonial ideology that ravaged other continents at other times. The Nazis then applied that ideology within Europe itself. At the heart of *Exterminate All the Brutes* is the claim that Hitler—the twentieth century's most despised villain, and rightly so—was not the civilized, democratic West's evil "other," but its shadow, its doppelganger. This draws on Lindqvist's argument that the exterminatory mindset lies at "the core of European thought . . . summing up the history of our continent, our humanity, our biosphere, from Holocene to Holocaust."

The story Peck and Lindqvist tell begins not in the Americas, but in Europe in the centuries leading up to the Spanish Inquisition and the burnings at the stake and the bloody expulsions of Jews and Muslims. Then it crosses the Atlantic and plays out on a vastly larger scale in the genocide of Native Americans, as well as the so-called Scramble for Africa, before looping back to Europe during the Holocaust. This challenges how the story of the Second World War is so often told: as one of heroic anti-fascist Allies united against the monstrous Nazis. Certainly, defeating Hitler and freeing the camps, however belatedly, was the most righteous victory of the modern age. Complicating this story is the fact that Hitler spoke and wrote extensively about the many ways in which he drew inspiration for his genocidal regime from British colonialism and from the various structures of racial hierarchy pioneered inside North America.

For instance, in 1941, Hitler remarked, "Concentration camps were not invented in Germany. It is the English who are their inventors, using this institution to gradually break the backs of other nations." He was speaking for propaganda purposes, but with an element of truth. Concentration camps had, in fact, been used in many colonial contexts—by the Spanish in Cuba; by German colonists in Southwest Africa, against the Herero and Nama people; by the British in what is now South Africa, during the Anglo-Boer War, with tens of thousands of captives dying in the disease-ridden enclosures. Before Hitler began casting the mass murder of genetic "inferiors" as an act of health care for the race, the British Royal Navy commander Bedford Pim explained to the Anthropological Society of London in 1866 that, when it comes to killing Indigenous peoples, there was "mercy in a massacre."

The influences were more recent and contemporary as well. When Hans Asperger and other doctors in Germany and Austria began deciding which disabled people would live and which were "unworthy of life," they were heavily influenced by the United States, where the world's first eugenics-based law to mandate involuntary sterilization was passed in Indiana in 1907 and soon spread to other states. Through laws like these, the U.S. eugenics movement had already provided a pseudoscientific rationale for the forced sterilization of tens of thousands of would-be parents whose genes were deemed threats to the overall pool—a project riddled with built-in biases about the relative intelligence of those of Anglo and Nordic stock. The Nazis took this precedent and radically expanded it, with an estimated 400,000 people sterilized during their rule, but their innovations in this realm were a matter of scale and speed, not kind.

James Q. Whitman, author of *Hitler's American Model: The United States and the Making of Nazi Race Law*, published in 2017, documents many of the Nazis' American debts in chilling detail. A professor of law at Yale University, Whitman makes the case that the legal contortions the United States had developed to deny full citizenship rights based on race helped inspire the 1935 Nuremberg Laws, which would legalize stripping German Jews of their citizenship and denying them political rights, while banning sex, marriage, and reproduction between Aryans and Jews (the Reich Citizenship Law and the Law on the Protection of German Blood and German Honor). They found templates for the new Jewish ghettos they created partly by studying the systems of legalized segregation developed under Jim Crow laws and those for Native reservations; South Africa's apartheid system also provided key inspiration.

Most foundationally, many Nazis were students and fans of the American frontier mythology—the presumed right to push westward to claim ever more territory for settlement. The German analogy was *Lebensraum*, or space required to live and grow, which Hitler adopted and translated into an imperative to conquer and seize lands to the east of Germany. As in the America West, this territory was occupied by many who were considered obstacles to the project—by Slavs and Jews. Praising European settlers for having "gunned down the millions of redskins to a few hundred thousand," Hitler claimed it was now Germany's turn to engage in cleansings and mass relocations on its own frontier.

"There is only one task: To set about the Germanization of the land by bringing in Germans and to regard the indigenous inhabitants as

Indians," Hitler said in 1941. He said at another point that year, "In this business I shall go straight ahead, cold-bloodedly . . . I don't see why a German who eats a piece of bread should torment himself with the idea that the soil that produces this bread has been won by the sword. When we eat wheat from Canada, we don't think about the despoiled Indians." On his right to lay claim to Ukraine's grain, Hitler joked, "We'll supply the Ukrainians with scarves, glass beads and everything that colonial peoples like."

The Nazis saw some of the residents of the lands they usurped as fit for slave labor, but the Jews were considered beyond redemption and therefore faced eradication, in part to make room for German settlers. As the war went on, the scale and speed of death was unprecedented—no one had previously built gas ovens or crematoria and put them to use day after day to eliminate a vast population. But though the Nazis' killing spree took state-sponsored hate to new extremes, extermination for the purposes of land theft was not Hitler's innovation. "Auschwitz was the modern industrial application of a policy of extermination on which European world domination had long since rested," Lindqvist writes. However, he continues, "when what had been done in the heart of darkness was repeated in the heart of Europe, no one recognized it. No one wished to admit what everyone knew."

That is incorrect. Several leading Black intellectuals saw the parallels with great clarity at the time. W. E. B. Du Bois, in *The World and Africa*, published soon after the end of the Second World War, wrote, "There was no Nazi atrocity—concentration camps, wholesale maiming and murder, defilement of women or ghastly blasphemy of childhood—which Christian civilization of Europe had not long been practicing against colored folk in all parts of the world in the name of and for the defense of a Superior Race born to rule the world." What *was* new: it was now fellow Europeans who were being cast as the inferior race.

In *Discourse on Colonialism*, the Martinican author and politician Aimé Césaire charged that Europeans tolerated "Nazism before it was inflicted on them." Until these methods came home to European soil, "they absolved it . . . shut their eyes to it, legitimized it, because, until then, it had been applied only to non-European peoples." Hitler's crime for the Allies, Césaire believed, was that he did to Jews and Slavs what "until then had been reserved exclusively for" the nonwhite colonized in foreign lands. But seen from the perspective of the Caribbean, it was all one long, continuous, snaking story.

Césaire was explicit that, in his view, Hitler was not merely the enemy of the United States and the United Kingdom—he was their shadow, their twin, their twisted doppelganger: "Yes, it would be worthwhile to study clinically, in detail, the steps taken by Hitler and Hitlerism and to reveal to the very distinguished, very humanistic, very Christian bourgeois of the twentieth century that without his being aware of it, he has a Hitler inside him, that Hitler *inhabits* him, that Hitler is his *demon*."

The Mirror Shatters

This analysis destabilizes pretty much all the stories that I grew up with, which taught us that the Holocaust was a singular event without precedent, so far outside the bounds of human history that it was essentially impossible to comprehend. We learned, in myriad ways, that there was something sacrilegious about even speaking of the Nazi Holocaust in the same breath as any other crime, that to do so made it less horrific, less shocking, somehow ordinary. But what if ordinary is horrific? What if that's the point: that Nazism is not an aberration from an otherwise uplifting story of enlightenment and modernity, but its not-so-distant double, its other face?

Referencing Germany's great scribe, Johann Wolfgang von Goethe, Lindqvist writes, "The idea of extermination lies no farther from the heart of humanism than Buchenwald lies from the Goethehaus in Weimar. That insight has been almost completely repressed, even by the Germans, who have been made sole scapegoats for ideas of extermination that are actually a common European heritage."

There are many well-known arguments for why the Holocaust perpetrated by the Nazis was different. It was higher tech. Death came faster. It was industrial in its scale. All true. But it's also true that every holocaust is different. Every genocide has its own particular characteristics, and every hated group is hated in its own special way. By sheer numbers of dead, the genocide of Indigenous peoples in the Americas surpasses all others. In terms of modern technologies, the transatlantic trade in kidnapped and enslaved Africans, and the plantations the trade served in the antebellum South and the Caribbean, were highly modern for their times. So cutting-edge, scholars have shown, that the systems developed to transport, insure, depreciate, track, control, and extract maximum wealth from this coerced labor shaped many aspects of modern accounting and human resources management. And as Rinaldo Walcott, a scholar of race and gender, writes in his manifesto *On Property*, "The ideas forged in the plantation economy continue to shape our social relations." Among those social relations are modern policing, mass surveillance, and mass incarceration.

On what else does the claim to exceptionalism rest? The fact that European Jewry was so deeply assimilated and embedded in European culture, so committed to being "civilized," as it was defined on the continent at the time. Many of those killed were even rich. But what of the established Japanese families sent to internment camps in the United States and Canada in this same period? What of the arson and massacre of "Black Wall Street" in Tulsa, Oklahoma, in 1921, well before the war? Different scales of crimes, to be sure, yet all show the limits of assimilation as protection. The refusal to believe that they could be the targets of Nazi slaughter was the undoing for many Jews in Germany and Austria: for far too long, they told themselves they were too cultured and too educated to ever be cast as brutes. What Du Bois and Césaire tried to tell us is that culture, language, science, and economy are no protection against genocide—all it takes is sufficient military force wielded by a power willing to denounce your culture as savage and declare you brutes. That is the story of colonial violence the world over. Casting people as unattached to land—because they practice a different form of agriculture, because they move with the seasons, whatever story served the end goal—has always been a precursor to genocide. Jews were declared "rootless" before they were slaughtered, much as colonial powers had declared Indigenous peoples nomadic and therefore uncivilized as a prelude to stealing their land on pain of annihilation on every continent on the planet.

Many people whose cultures, lands, and bodies had been targeted in these ways recognized the logic behind Hitler's political project precisely because it was familiar. After Kristallnacht in 1938, for instance, a delegation from the Australian Aborigines League wrote a protest letter condemning "the cruel persecution of the Jewish people by the Nazi Government of Germany" and, in a little-known historical chapter, hand-delivered it to the German consulate in Melbourne (the consulate refused to accept it). This was well before Western governments were willing to confront Hitler; yet these Indigenous leaders, who were still fighting for basic rights of their own, clearly saw the gravity of the threat. The Nazis' industrial killing was new, and the Jewish case is different. *But so is every case.* And some things are all too similar.

The flip side of the post–World War II cries of "Never again" was an unspoken "Never before." The insistence on lifting the Holocaust out of history, the failure to recognize these patterns, and the refusal to see where the Nazis fit inside the arc of colonial genocides have all come at a high cost. The countries that defeated Hitler did not have to confront the uncomfortable fact that Hitler had taken pointers and inspiration on race-making and on human containment from them, leaving their innocence not only undisturbed but also significantly strengthened by what was indeed a righteous victory.

This is Lindqvist's point: "Two events need not be identical for one of them to facilitate the other. European world expansion, accompanied as it was by shameless defense of extermination, created habits of thought and political precedents that made way for new outrages, finally culminating in the most horrendous of them all: the Holocaust." And one of the hardest habits of thought to shake is the reflex to look away, to not see what is in front of us, and to not know what we know.

When Lindqvist wrote *"Exterminate All the Brutes,"* it was the early 1990s, and the climate crisis was barely in his sightlines. He did not yet know that European powers and their settler colonial states would spend the next three decades effectively deciding to let continents where those "inferior races" reside burn and drown because, once again, the alternative interrupted the flow of limitless wealth accumulation. We must now ask this: What if full-blown fascism is not the monster at the door, but the monster inside the house, the monster inside us—even we whose ancestors have been victims of genocide?

This, I fear, is the deepest danger posed by the Mirror World and its increasingly belligerent war on history. The door to the Shadow Lands was cracked open; truths were flying out that would no longer be contained. The most abused shadow workers in our economy—immigrant women and men on temporary work visas laboring in four care homes in a single day, or packing chicken parts in impossibly cold and bloody facilities—were finally on our television screens. Not because they were being cheered as heroes, but because they were the ones in the so-called hot spots: the ones whose bodies were piling up in morgues and refrigerated trucks. We had no choice but to see and to reckon with what had been so long hidden and repressed. Then, when so many of us streamed into the streets that first Covid spring and shouted the names of the murdered and, then, one year after that, when we bowed our heads in grief for the little ones who never returned, more truths were escaping.

Like that couple in the Pre-Raphaelite painting, more and more of us were beginning, just beginning, just barely, to see ourselves and our place in a larger world crowded with spectral presences. For some, it made us faint. For others, it made us mad. For a great many, it made us want to change: to expel the monster inside the collective unconscious, or at least try. Try to be the kind of people whose daily lives do not require the annihilation of other lives and other ways of life.

"Forces opposed to justice stand ready to reverse the gains of yesterday's struggles entirely, should the opportunity present itself," writes Olúfẹ́mi O. Táíwò in *Reconsidering Reparations*, published in 2022. By then, the forces of forgetting were already roaring back—to slam that door, and to shroud our countries in innocence and righteousness once again. "There is a resistance to memory inside memory itself," writes the historian of psychoanalysis Jacqueline Rose.

One year after the announcement about unmarked school burial grounds in Kamloops, the *New York Post* ran a piece quoting an influential conservative ideologue and a longtime opponent of Indigenous rights, Tom Flanagan, who called the revelation of the graves "the biggest fake news story in Canadian history" and a case of "moral panic." It seems that to many people, a truthful telling of history feels like treachery—and must be stamped out. But if those truths are stuffed back away, they will keep haunting us and keep reemerging in the Mirror World in distorted, twisted form.

On May 14, 2022, an eighteen-year-old white supremacist obsessed with the Great Replacement theory and low birth rates among whites drove to a Tops supermarket in Buffalo, New York, with the aim of killing as many Black people as possible. He murdered ten people with a legally purchased AR-15-style rifle. He livestreamed the massacre, as others had before him, performing himself as his generation had been taught to do. He left a long, rambling manifesto behind, praising Nazis and calling himself, among other things, an "ecofascist." Julian Brave NoiseCat, a writer and colleague from the climate justice movement, noticed some uncanny parallels at work:

> I'm struck by the similarity of right-wing conspiracy theories to actual policies towards Indigenous peoples.
>
> 'replacement theory'—Manifest Destiny
>
> QAnon (mass institutionalized child abuse)—boarding and residential schools
>
> 'plandemic'—smallpox, alcohol, bioterrorism
>
> It's all so Freudian. The fear that it will happen to them stems from an implicit admission that they did it to others.
>
> As though the Black, Brown and Indigenous downtrodden are just as hateful as they are and are going to turn around and do to them what they did to us.

Is that part of what we are seeing? Are increasingly violent conspiracy theorists in the Mirror World afraid of being rounded up, treated as second-class, occupied, and culled because on some level they know that these are the genocidal behaviors that created and sustain their relative but increasingly precarious privileges? Are they terrified that if the truths of the Shadow Lands—past, present, and future—are ever fully revealed and reckoned with, then it can only result in a dramatic role reversal, with the victims becoming the victimizers?

Well, it has happened before. In fact, it's happening right now, in a place where everything is doubled, where doppelganger politics govern every aspect of life. It's happening in Israel, and in its partitioned shadow land, Palestine. Our last stop, and the place where so many forces we have encountered on this winding journey converge and collide.

14

THE UNSHAKABLE ETHNIC DOUBLE

"It's anti-Semitism."

The power is out for the fifth time in this winter of record-breaking windstorms and mudslides, and I have decamped to my parents' place to siphon electricity for my laptop. Mom is taking advantage of this rare alone time to caution me against dwelling on the Wolf issue. (A bit late for that!)

"They see you both as a type," she says over a bowl of defrosted vegetable soup. "Why draw attention to it?"

She seems sad when she tells me this, deflated. Focusing on my doppelganger trouble—using it to spin out this web of theories about digital doubles and personal brands and the Mirror World and the Shadow Land—will only, she feels certain, attract more of the kind of dangerous attention that is the real reason behind the confusion in the first place. Which, for her, is obvious. It's the Jew thing.

Others have made points that back her up. Jeet Heer, a columnist for *The Nation* and an avid Wolf watcher, wrote after one of her more egregious streaks of Covid misinformation, "At this point, confusing Naomi Klein with Naomi Wolf is just anti-Semitism. I'm sorry, I don't make the rules. Your brain should be able to handle more than one Naomi."

I don't make the rules, either. Hannah Arendt had a rule, though. "If one is attacked as a Jew, one must defend oneself as a Jew," she wrote. "Not as a German, not as a world-citizen, not as an upholder of the Rights of Man." So is that what I have to do? What I have been putting off doing all this time? Do I have to defend myself from all this *as a Jew*?

Join the club, White Lady, I hear some of you saying.

This is fair. Countless people on this planet riven with racial hierarchies contend with far more heinous forms of ethnic and racial projection, forced to represent only their skin color to white eyes. They also log on to social media to find themselves blamed and credited for the words and actions of others. The Australian poet Omar Sakr regularly shares outrageous stories about TV bookers and random readers confusing him with a parade of other public figures with brown skin. Once, he was even sent a complete travel itinerary so that he could arrive for his guest appearance on a home improvement show with which he had no prior contact. And the show made the *same* error with another writer, Osman Faruqi.

"WHY ARE YOU SENDING US OTHER PEOPLE'S TRAVEL ITINERARY?" Sakr demanded. "ARE YOU TRULY INCAPABLE OF TELLING BROWN MEN APART?"

Or think of all of the people who have to contend with the daily wince of having a "work twin"—another person of color from a vaguely similar ethnic background (or a wholly dissimilar one) with whom they are constantly confused by their colleagues. To state the obvious: these are not doppelgangers. There are no uncanny similarities between the people involved—it's just the way race continues to break so many of our brains.

In truth, I have mostly been free to tell myself that this kind of doubling was not my cross to bear. I moved through the world blithely assuming the people I met would easily decode the distinctiveness in my particular arrangement of features and correctly identify me as me—and not project a presumed identity onto me based on a haze of my skin tone, hair texture, and eye shape. What my mother was saying over lunch, though, was that I have been badly fooling myself, that Wolf and I had always been lumped together inside a very particular cultural stereotype—that of the striving Jewess.

"Some reproach me with being a Jew, some praise me because of it, some pardon me for it, but all think of it," fretted the German political writer Ludwig Börne in 1832. (Changing his name from Loeb Baruch and converting to Protestantism wasn't enough to protect him.) This is another theme that emerges in Roth's *Operation Shylock*: the supposedly eternal nature of Jew-hatred. By the end of the book, Roth's real double turns out not to be Fake Roth at all. We learn that, in a way, there is no Real Roth, a man of letters and intellect, just as there is no Fake Roth, a zealous activist and evangelist of Diasporism. Both, within the world of the novel, end up being cast as Philip Roth the Jew. And that means that both are Shylock, the moneylending mutilator in Shakespeare's *Merchant of Venice*, determined to get his pound of flesh. For Roth, Shylock is the Jews' eternal doppelganger.

This is how prejudice works. The person holding it unconsciously creates a double of every person who is part of the despised group, and that twisted twin looms over all who meet the criteria, always threatening to swallow them up. Having one of these doubles means that whoever you are, whatever identity you have fashioned for yourself, however fresh and unique your personal brand, and however much you distinguish yourself from the stereotypes associated with your kind, for the hater you will always stand in as a representative of your despised group. You are not you; you are your ethnic/racial/religious double, and you can't shake that double because you did not create it.

"The Jew is one whom other men consider a Jew . . . for it is the anti-Semite who *makes* the Jew." Jean-Paul Sartre wrote those words in his book-length essay *The Anti-Semite and Jew*. This was a deliberately provocative remark, since of course many Jews make their own Jewishness through the positive practice of their culture and faith—not other people's hatred. But Sartre wrote that in the immediate aftermath of Paris's liberation from the Nazis, with memories still fresh of a time when France's Jews—many of whom were so assimilated they barely identified as Jews or even knew that their parents or grandparents were Jewish—were being systematically investigated and inspected for telltale Semitic signs. This is the premise of Joseph Losey's creepy 1976 doppelganger film, *Mr. Klein*, which tells the story of a wealthy Parisian art dealer who is mistaken for a Jew with the same name and gradually becomes ensnared with his own unshakable ethnic double. The film begins in a medical clinic, with an emotionless doctor examining a middle-aged woman: gums, nostrils, jaw, gait—each meticulously and humiliatingly measured and probed to check for a Jew lurking within. The anti-Semite making the Jew, creating the deadly doppelganger with clinical precision.

All members of historically hated groups lug around versions of this invisible double, and some doublings are far more dangerous than others. To be Black in the United States, W. E. B. Du Bois wrote in 1897, required a "double-consciousness," a constant feeling of "two-ness," which generated a longing "to merge his double self into a better and truer self," one that did not require this partition. To this day, Blackness generates a double that is so treacherous to those it is projected upon, and so unremitting in its persistence through the centuries, that no activity is safe from being overtaken by the lethal racial double—not driving, not going for a run, not walking home from the store, not struggling with the lock on your own jammed front door. ("I plan to give you reasons for your jumpy fits / and facial tics," wrote June Jordan in her 1976 poem "I Must Become a Menace to My Enemies.") Facial recognition software, originally marketed as a way to remove these kinds of biased doublings from policing, has automated them instead, with artificial intelligence repeatedly misidentifying Black faces, often leading to wrongful arrests and upended lives. In Europe, meanwhile, boat after boat of Black migrants continue to be left to drown, the dangerous doubles of their passengers overtaking them before they even reach dry land.

François Brunelle, the Montreal artist who has made portraits of hundreds of doppelgangers, explains why he is drawn to photographing uncannily similar faces: "The face is the ultimate communication tool that we have to establish and maintain relationships between us as human beings." Yes. And for a great many people, the face's ability to communicate is sabotaged by other people's warped receptors *all the time.*

Other forms of racial doubling ebb and flow on the geopolitical tides. After the September 11 attacks in New York and Washington, the figure of the Muslim terrorist loomed so large as a double for all Muslim men that everything from studying engineering to going to the airport became suddenly perilous. For what is a racial profile if not a doppelganger made by the state? In practice, that meant that passengers with common names like Mohammed (never mind Osama) had to contend with the very real possibility that they had landed on some top secret, error-riddled no-fly list, which could get them pulled off a plane for special questioning or, worse, hooded and "rendered" to one of the Bush administration's new "black sites." The anti-Chinese scapegoating drummed up in the Covid era (with my doppelganger and her relentless spinning of CCP bioweapon plots playing no small role) has cast such an ominous shadow over Asian life that roughly one-third of Asian Americans polled by Pew Research in the spring of 2022 reported changing their daily routines to avoid being targeted by hate crimes.

Where does the Jewish double fit into this landscape of malevolent twinning? Hasidic Jews, conspicuous in black hats and long coats, are easy targets for street violence. But a secular Jew like me? Frankly, I'm battling the feeling that it is slightly fraudulent to even mention it in the same breath. Thanks to the timing and location of my birth, which coincided with a high point in Holocaust education and collective contrition, I have been largely protected from direct encounters with Jew-hatred. A notable exception was a year spent in Oxford, England, when I was ten, where "Jew" was such a frequent schoolyard taunt that I hid my religious identity and muddled my way through morning hymns ("Shine, Jesus, shine! Fill this land with the Father's glory!"). Still, I never thought anti-Semitism had the power to hurt much more than my feelings: my biggest concern was that discovery would cost me my friendship with Katie Bennett, the vicar's daughter. (It didn't. "Happy Hannukah, Naomi!" her dad said to me casually that December—turns out I made a lousy undercover Jew.)

It's a little different for Avi. He has more classically Jewish features and mannerisms than I do, and after a quarter century of living with him, I have come to recognize the visceral reaction he occasionally inspires. I recognized this same doubling at work when I was on the campaign trail with Bernie Sanders in 2020: some people just couldn't get past the pushy, angry, uncouth Jew they imagined him to be based on his style of speech and mannerisms—never mind the abiding compassion and gentleness of the man himself.

But me? I had smoothed out my ethnic edges, surely; I had protected myself from triggering others in that visceral way. Yet, even as I write these words, I am suddenly unsure I ever believed them. Isn't fear of my Jewish shadow the real reason I complained so bitterly about my too-Jewish name, with its built-in whiny drawl? Isn't it the same reason I obsessively straighten my wavy hair, priding myself on it not being as conspicuous as, say, that of the person I have referred to more than once as "my big-haired doppelganger"? Does this not betray a self-hating desire to avoid the persistent smear directed at Jewish women by Jews and non-Jews alike—that of the Jewish American princess? Isn't biblical Naomi—so driven, doing whatever it took for her people to survive—the ethnic double I was afraid of being confused/conflated with all along? These are all distinct possibilities.

It's also possible that the post-Holocaust lull in open Jew-hatred is coming to a close. Since Trump, anti-Jewish hate crimes have been on the rise. Jews figure prominently in the Great Replacement theory—we eternal Shylocks are apparently the reason so many immigrants are allowed in: so that we can make more coin exploiting them. This was the belief system espoused by the gunman who killed eleven people during Saturday morning services at the Tree of Life synagogue in Pittsburgh, Pennsylvania, in 2018. Kanye West's threat to go "death con 3 On JEWISH PEOPLE" who supposedly control his world may have helped open the floodgates further. Many differences remain between the various forms of racial and gender doubling that are surging right now. People don't quicken their steps or lock their car doors because of my Jewish shadow; doctors don't discount my body's capacity to feel pain, and assailants don't calculate that no one with power will come looking for me if they do me harm. And yet, as we have seen, the need for perfect likenesses can easily obscure commonalities—and, as importantly, short-circuit potential solidarities.

Satan's Army of Evil Twins

Scholars of anti-Semitism trace Jew-hatred back to antiquity, to Hellenistic resentments of Jewish self-segregation, a perceived clannishness. But it was in the Christian world that it became inescapable. The New Testament is a powerful cosmology of doubles: God/Satan, Christ/Antichrist, angels/demons, heaven/hell. Since Jews are associated with Satan in the gospels, Jews and Christians were placed in a twinned relationship from the start, with Jews perennially cast as the demonic doppelgangers of the faithful followers of Christ. Not only did we fail to recognize the true messiah when we had the chance, but we are perennially blamed for Jesus's death. (So, to correct my earlier statement: this is exactly our cross to bear.) It's a story that set the stage for centuries of smears and libels.

Many of those libels involve grisly claims of Jews kidnapping Christian children to drain their blood and use it in secret rituals, accusations that served as pretexts for anti-Jewish mob violence. There are frescoes that still hang in Polish cathedrals showing plump perforated babies at the feet of hunched-over Jews. This old form of Jew-hatred peaked with the Reconquest of Spain and the expulsion of Jews and Muslims in 1492, which followed massacres, Jew burnings, and mass forced conversion to Catholicism (which offered little protection from being exposed as a closet Jew during the Inquisition). In response to the 1492 expulsion, many Jewish and Muslim refugees—allies at the time—were given safe passage to the Ottoman Empire.

That spasm of violence was not the first time groups of humans slaughtered groups of other humans in battles over land and resources. But this is the period, argue Sven Lindqvist and Raoul Peck, that gave birth to the impulse, which would repeat again and again in the subsequent centuries, to "exterminate all the brutes" in the name of civilization, progress, and piety. And, not coincidentally perhaps, 1492 was the same year that Christopher Columbus's ships set sail to cross the Atlantic, bringing with them a globalization of these tools of pious annihilation.

The association of Jews with satanism provided justification throughout the Middle Ages and well beyond for constraining Jews as second-class citizens, corralled in ghettos and excluded from owning agricultural land and from participating in key trades. Jews were therefore street peddlers and merchants, as well as moneylenders, a profession they were permitted largely because it allowed the Christian ruling class to keep this ungodly activity at arm's length. By the 1700s, small lenders grew into larger banks, and it was this development—itself born of anti-Semitism—that would sustain the more modern and ongoing forms of anti-Semitism, those focused on the figure of the money-grubbing Jewish banker, responsible for all the woes and hardships of working people—and plotting, in an international cabal of similarly scheming Jews, to do far worse.

From the Illuminati to *The Protocols of the Elders of Zion*, from the Rothschild banking family to George Soros's philanthropy, Jews have been the subjects and targets of the most persistent conspiracy theory of the last two and half centuries. Despite shifting names and players, the script has stayed remarkably similar: an international Jewish conspiracy stands accused of colluding in the shadows to undermine Christian values, weaken Christian states, seize Christian property, and, in later versions, control the media. From revolutions to pandemics to terrorist attacks, it always seems to be our fault.

QAnon stands out not for the originality of its plotlines, but for its ability to mash up the more modern trope of a Jewish cabal running the world with the more ancient blood libel involving kidnapped and drained Christian children. In QAnon's version, an international conspiracy that includes many prominent Jews, but is not restricted to Jews, kidnaps children to drain them of adrenochrome, apparently in the hopes of prolonging the conspirators' own lives. These stories are currently coursing and combining and morphing in our culture, lending an ancient and sinister energy to the invisible ethnic double that we Jews lug around.

Look Over There!

In the Mirror World, conspiracy theories detract attention from the billionaires who fund the networks of misinformation and away from the economic policies—deregulation, privatization, austerity—that have stratified wealth so cataclysmically in the neoliberal era. They rile up anger about the Davos elites, at Big Tech and Big Pharma—but the rage never seems to reach those targets. Instead it gets diverted into culture wars about anti-racist education, all-gender bathrooms, and Great Replacement panic directed at Black people, nonwhite immigrants, and Jews.

Meanwhile, the billionaires who bankroll the whole charade are safe in the knowledge that the fury coursing through our culture isn't coming for them. Neither Steve Bannon nor Tucker Carlson invented this play.

Over the centuries, anti-Jewish conspiracy has played a very specific purpose for elite power: it acts as a buffer, a shock absorber. Before popular rage could reach the kings, queens, tsars, and old landed money, the conspiracies absorbed it, directing anger to the middle managers—to the court Jew, to the scheming Jew, possibly with horns hidden under his skullcap. To Shylock.

This is why anti-Semitism is sometimes referred to as "the socialism of fools," a phrase coined by the Austrian democrat Ferdinand Kronawetter and popularized by Social Democrats in Germany in the 1890s. Where a socialist analysis, grounded in material realities, explains that capitalism is a system guided by internal logics that require dispossession and exploitation, peddlers of anti-Semitic conspiracy theories offer juicy tales of satanic evildoers acting outside the normal boundaries of societies and economies. And if they exist outside these structures, then they can simply be excised from the body politic—run out of town or, per Lindqvist and Peck, exterminated like brutes.

In Europe, whenever multiethnic groups of workers and peasants started to build power from below, threatening to challenge entrenched wealth, spasms of anti-Semitic propaganda soon followed. Again and again, rootless Jewish devils were pitted against the rooted, ethnically pure Christian citizens of the nation-states in which Jews were never fully accepted, from Spain to France to Poland. The perennial evil twin.

These methods have recurred through the centuries for a simple reason: they work. They were a reliable means of blasting apart nascent alliances and coalitions of working people and safeguarding the interests of the wealthy and powerful.

The failed Russian Revolution of 1905 was a particularly tragic case. In January of that year, workers and peasants across the Russian empire staged a wave of strikes and revolts, including inside the military, challenging the monarchy and the rule of Nicholas II. The revolution was led by a multiethnic and diverse alliance, with one of its key factions being the Jewish Labor Bund, a socialist party with tens of thousands of members and hundreds of local councils and defense militias that was particularly powerful in Poland and Ukraine. One of the Bund's core principles was *doi'kayt*, or "hereness"—the idea that Jews belonged where they lived, in what was known as "the pale of settlement," and should fight for greater rights and increased justice as Jews and as workers, alongside non-Jewish members of their class. They should not have to place their hopes in a far-off Jewish homeland, as the early Zionists had begun to argue in that same period. Nor should they have to flee to North America, as hundreds of thousands of German and Eastern European Jews had already felt forced to do. *Doi'kayt* proclaimed that Bundists would stay here—and make here better.

In response to the surging revolutionary coalition, Russia's elites, including the tsar, fought back in two ways: first, by offering concessions, including the creation of a weak multiparty parliamentary system, and second, and simultaneously, by unleashing a virulent campaign of anti-Semitic hate that painted the 1905 revolt as a plot by seditious Jews to rule over Christians. This combination of minor reforms with a major distraction did the trick. Immediately after the reforms were announced, anti-Jewish mobs staged bloody pogroms in 660 towns and cities, with the worst taking place in Odessa. An estimated eight hundred Jewish people were killed in the rampage. The historian Robert Weinberg described some of the atrocities in *The Russian Review*: "They hurled Jews out of windows, raped and cut open the stomachs of pregnant women, and slaughtered infants in front of their parents. In one particularly gruesome incident, pogromists hung a woman upside down by her legs and arranged the bodies of her six dead children on the floor below her."

It is an image eerily reminiscent of the oil paintings from two centuries earlier depicting the Jewish blood libel—except now made real, and committed *against* Jews. According to Weinberg, "Ethnic divisiveness was a centrifugal force that diminished the capacity of Odessa workers to act in a unified fashion." A lesson for the tsar, and a lesson for the ages: if you want to crush a revolutionary movement coming at you from below, nothing works quite like an anti-Semitic conspiracy that calls up hatreds older than Jesus Christ.

In truth, any number of identity-based divisions can be marshaled to perform this function: Jews versus Blacks, Blacks versus Asians, Muslims versus Christians, "gender critical" feminists versus transgender people, migrants versus citizens. This is the playbook used by Trump and the other pseudo-populist strongmen the world over: throw some minor economic concessions to the base (or at least claim to do so), unleash the dogs of race and gender-based hatreds, and preside over a rapid upward transfer of wealth, alongside an authoritarian concentration of power.

The Socialism of Facts

One of the interesting things about digging into the history of Jew-hatred is how contradictory the theories are: Are Jews greedy bankers scheming to get Christian property so we can pocket the money? Or are we rabble-rousing communists scheming to do away with capitalism altogether? A widely circulated Nazi caricature depicts the "eternal Jew"—a hunched man with gold coins in one hand and a map of Germany with a hammer and sickle on it in the other, somehow managing to be an arch capitalist and a revolutionary Marxist at the same time. Conspiracy theories don't require internal consistency to find traction (see: Covid is a mild cold—chill out! Covid is a bioweapon—freak out!). Still, it's striking that the two most tenacious lines of attack that Jews have faced over the generations—the scheming Jewish bankers and the scheming Jewish Marxists—are perennially on a logical collision course with each other.

As always, there are seeds of truth to fertilize the fantasies. Just as Jews, because they were barred from so many other industries, were overrepresented in finance, Jews were also overrepresented among revolutionary socialists and communists. Like, *really* overrepresented. Their ranks included, but were by no means restricted to, Leon Trotsky and much of the Menshevik and Bolshevik leadership at the heart of the Russian Revolution; Rosa Luxemburg and many of her comrades in the Spartacus League who hoped to bring a more democratic version of the revolution to Germany; Vladimir Medem and the entire leadership of the Bund; Emma Goldman and the New York anarchist left; and Walter Benjamin, Theodor Adorno, and others in the Frankfurt School. And, of course, the man himself. Karl Marx was not raised Jewish, but he was descended from rabbis on both sides of his family; Marx's father converted to Lutheranism, changing his name from Hershel to Heinrich.

One way to understand Jewish attraction to communist and socialist ideology might be "Wow, the left really is a Jewish conspiracy!" Another could be that, because Jews have been the targets of so much hatred and discrimination, they are preternaturally concerned with tackling injustice in its many forms (one of the flattering lefty stories I grew up with). But there is another, related possibility: that Jewish interest in the theoretical side of what we now call Marxism—with its sweeping and scientific explications and analyses of global capitalism—is an attempt to compete with those conspiracy theories that have dogged our people through the ages. That all the thousands of pages of theories and manifestos are, partly at least, a long procession of Jews banging their heads up against the brick wall of history and saying: No, your money problems are not the result of Jewish "shysters" ripping off hardworking "goyim"—they flow from a system that was designed to extract maximum wealth from working people. And that system is not called the "Illuminati" or the "Elders of Zion"—it's called capitalism. And only unity among members of the working classes—regardless of race, ethnicity, gender, or religion—will ever stand a chance of winning a fairer world. And also: Please don't kill us.

These theorists were hardly mere spectators, after all. To one degree or another, all the Jewish socialists and communists writing and organizing in the nineteenth and early twentieth centuries had skin in the game. Marxism sprouted in the same soil that fertilized *The Protocols of the Elders of Zion* and that would eventually produce Weimar and then Nazi Germany. No one's life was unaffected; no one was safe from their Shylock doubles, not even the converts and atheists. Marx's father converted not out of faith, but because he was a lawyer and a new Prussian decree had barred Jews from occupying legal positions or state offices.

Eleanor Marx, Karl's daughter, chose to reclaim their family heritage and taught herself Yiddish so she could better organize Jewish garment workers in London's East End, unequivocally declaring, amid a spasm of European anti-Semitism, "I am a Jewess." Rosa Luxemburg's political party was a target of what she described as "an all-out orgy of anti-Semitism" in the press. Trotsky, in his early career as a journalist, was shaped by covering outbreaks of anti-Semitic mob violence, describing scenes of gangs "drunk on vodka and the smell of blood." He was himself routinely portrayed as a Jewish devil (horns and all) by his political adversaries. And, in 1940, the year of his death, Trotsky vividly observed that "in the epoch of its rise, capitalism took the Jewish people out of the ghetto and utilized them as an instrument in its commercial expansion. Today decaying capitalist society is striving to squeeze the Jewish people from all its pores."

These revolutionaries had grander aims than simply denying their enemies the potent weapon of the anti-Semitic conspiracy theory. They dedicated their lives to enacting socialism in the real world. Still, in their fierce dedication to making political education accessible to working people, I think it's fair to see the battle against Jewish conspiracy as subtext, if not text. A quest to swap out the irrational hatreds of the vulnerable with worthier targets—economic systems, ideologies, structural inequities. To replace the socialism of fools with the socialism of facts.

A Debate Cut Down Midsentence

None of this is to say that, among the Jewish intellectuals of these tumultuous times, there was any kind of agreement on what to do about the persistence of anti-Semitism. In the decades before Hitler synonymized Judaism with trauma, and before dissent was supplanted, in many corners, with terrified conformity, Jewish intellectual life roared with drag-down debates over what was then euphemistically called "the Jewish Question." (Today's equivalent might be called "the Identity Politics Question" or "the Race Versus Class Question.") The Cornell University professor Enzo Traverso, who has extensively researched this intellectual history, describes the Jewish Question as "a set of problems related to emancipation and anti-Semitism, cultural assimilation and Zionism"—and among Jewish Marxists and socialists, there was nothing approaching consensus about the possible answers.

Should Jews strive for full equality in Christian societies—voting rights, access to all industries (the position of the Social Democrats)? Or should the goal be revolutionary transformation of those societies accompanied by full Jewish assimilation into the liberated proletariat since religion would be less necessary as a source of solace ("Religion is the sigh of the oppressed creature, the heart of a heartless world, and the soul of soulless conditions. It is the opium of the people," Marx wrote, a position pursued by Trotsky and Luxemburg)? Was Judaism a prison from which the revolution would offer liberation (as the Bolsheviks claimed, though many conceded that there was a need to protect the right to religious practice in private life)? Or was Jewish assimilation, even in a socialist society, a trap, eliding the need for European Jews' distinct culture and language to be protected within a multiethnic, multinational workers' society (the Bund's "hereness" position)? Or was Jew-hatred simply too deep on the continent, too primal, for any of this to work, so that Jewish liberation could be found only in the working-class movements of the amnesiac Americas (the position held by many of my family members as they crossed the Atlantic)? Or was even that mere fantasy, especially under the harsh, overtly racist, and anti-Semitic immigration laws introduced by the United States and Canada in the 1920s and '30s, making the only hope for Jewish safety a nation-state of their own, where wandering would end and socialism could become a reality (the view of the Labor Zionists)?

So the Bundists, with their tens of thousands of working-class members devoted to "hereness," regularly debated the Zionists, mocking them for their "thereness." The Bund held fast to the belief that Jews would be free when everyone was free, and not by building what amounted to a militarized ghetto on Palestinian land. "Your liberation can only be a by-product of the universal freeing of oppressed people," wrote the Bundist leader Victor Alter in 1937. Besides, argued Walter Benjamin, "things will go very badly in Europe if the intellectual energies of the Jews abandon it."

Rosa Luxemburg, years earlier, had sparred with the Bund and advocated a universalism unbound by her Jewish identity. "What do you want with this theme of the 'special suffering of the Jews'?" a friend asked in 1917. She replied, "I am just as much concerned with the poor victims on the rubber plantations of Putumayo, the black people in Africa with whose corpses the Europeans play catch . . . I have no special place in my heart for the [Jewish] ghetto. I feel at home in the entire world wherever there are clouds and birds and human tears." Those lines led her detractors to claim that she minimized Jewish suffering at a time of great hardship. I prefer to see her reaching, however idealistically, for a vision of human solidarity that transcended identity and national borders.

The tumultuous debates over the Jewish Question did not end because one faction won the argument due to the greater force of their ideas, or because they captured the hearts and minds of the majority of Jewish people. The debates died out because, like Red Vienna, the whole terrain on which the debate was happening was crushed by terror, with betrayal and abandonment foreclosing on one possibility after another. Jews were annihilated in the lands where the Nazis gained control and where Jewish workers' movements, filled with revolutionary swagger, had staged strikes and organized self-defense leagues. When Stalin took command of the Soviet Union, he further centralized power, waging ruthless war on his rivals and attempting to cover over his atrocities by unleashing the hounds of anti-Semitism once again (even, according to Trotsky, calling up the ancient blood libel to accuse his son Sergei of plotting the mass poisoning of workers). Meanwhile, the United States and Canada, like so many other nations, offered little safe harbor to boats filled with desperate Jewish refugees coming from Europe. (In the infamous words of one Canadian bureaucrat: "None is too many.") So much for safety being found amid the optimism and amnesia of New York and Montreal.

Revisiting the raucous debates over the Jewish Question within the European Jewish left, I am struck by the fact that so many of the key players advancing a different vision for our people died violently. Rosa Luxemburg was shot by German paramilitary officers and thrown into Berlin's Landwehr Canal in 1919—and the officer who orchestrated her death would become an ally of Hitler's. Countless leaders of the Bund were murdered in Hitler's camps, others in Stalin's purges. Trotsky was stabbed with an ice ax by one of Stalin's agents, but not before he conceded that assimilation as a solution to the Jewish problem had failed, though he remained a critic of Zionism. Walter Benjamin took his own life in the seaside Catalan town of Portbou, Spain, unable to secure passage out of Europe after being forced to flee Vichy France.

The one who haunts me most is a Belgian leftist named Abram Leon. Still in his twenties during the war, he could have passed for a young Trotsky himself: a round baby face topped with wavy black hair and heavy black-framed glasses. As a teen, he had lived in Palestine with his family. Back in Belgium, he grew disillusioned with Zionism and became a staunch Trotskyist. During the Nazi occupation, he was forced underground but continued to organize clandestine meetings and publish illegal pamphlets and newspapers. He also worked on a project that might be described as an attempt to understand his own Jewish double: during the war, Leon researched and wrote a scholarly treatise about the uses of anti-Semitism to the global capitalist project, reaching back to the Roman Empire and continuing to the Nazi era. It's hard to imagine how he was able to conduct this kind of deep research while underground, but he managed, drawing on a wide range of sources.

Leon's analysis of the Nazis' use of anti-Semitic conspiracy theories feels particularly relevant to our historical moment. He describes how Hitler harnessed the economic suffering of the lower and middle classes—impoverished by the First World War, pounded by the sanctions afterward, then hit with the Great Depression—and directed that discontent at a chimera the Nazis called "Jewish capitalism." Cast as distinct from the rest of supposedly healthy and decent capitalism, Jewish capitalism was a mythic structure, a bogeyman, with a familiar purpose: "Big business," Leon wrote, "endeavored to divert and control the anti-capitalist hatred of the masses for its own exclusive profit." Very much as the internationally networked Bannonite right rages at "globalists" to divert popular rage away from capitalism as a system and toward an imaginary cabal that can be cut out, leaving the structures that created and protect the global billionaire class intact.

Leon also explained how the Nazi Party, having witnessed the successful workers' revolution in Russia, and seeing communism gaining political power in Germany, set out to deliberately weaken the importance of class in the minds of German workers. This was done by replacing class solidarity with racial solidarity, supplanting the common interests shared by all workers with the pleasures and rewards that flowed from belonging to the Aryan race, a bond that claimed to unite the poorest Christian workers with the wealthiest industrialists. But because workers and owners actually have starkly different interests under capitalism, that maneuver required a shadow, an evil twin. "Just as it is necessary to cast the different classes [of Aryans] into *one single race*," Leon wrote, "so is it also necessary that this 'race' have only a single enemy: 'the international Jew.' The myth of race is necessarily accompanied by its 'negative'—the antirace, the Jew." This was a highly incisive analysis of the dialectical relationship between race and class within a white supremacist regime—Leon was arguing that class solidarity between workers, across ethnic lines, was the primary competition and threat to the Nazi project.

He compiled his insights and research into an important, if little-known, book, *The Jewish Question: A Marxist Interpretation*, first published in French in 1946. But Leon never got to see the culmination of his efforts, because the very dynamics he was analyzing came for him. In 1944, as a member of the self-styled master race's "antirace," he was captured, tortured by the Gestapo, and sent to Auschwitz, where he was murdered in the gas chambers. He was twenty-six.

In this time of great pipiking, what moves me most about Leon's short life is his faith in ideas. Even surrounded on all sides by mass slaughter, even under such extreme personal circumstances, he still managed to believe that words and analysis and research mattered, that they still had the power to break an evil spell. Even if those words were too late to matter for him.

Leon's story encapsulates the fate of the debate over the Jewish

Question within the Jewish left: it was murdered midsentence. Traverso writes that "the war and the Holocaust . . . by exterminating most of [the debate's] actors, destroyed the conditions for such a debate." It was more than that, too. For many of those who survived, Stalin went on to kill their confidence in the possibility—even the *desirability*—of revolutionary change. Unlike the beacon of Red Vienna, the more brutal and totalitarian the Soviet experiment became, the less socialism seemed able to offer a moral alternative to barbarism. Stalin's greatest betrayal of all.

Twins Battling for All Eternity

Though members of each tendency survived, in the rubble, only one answer to the Jewish Question continued to assert itself with great confidence: Zionism. Israel as a territorial homeland for the Jews, a nation that could be armed and protected from all possible threats, positioned itself as the only option left. The only one not crushed by one form of totalitarianism or another.

And so, in the now very real battle over land and borders, a great many of those earlier debates appeared to fall away. Inside the young nation, and especially after the 1967 war and the protracted occupation of the West Bank and Gaza, anti-Semitism came to be treated not as a question in need of historically informed answers, but rather as something eternal, outside the bounds of history. In this pessimistic telling, Jew-hatred was cast as so potent, so deeply rooted in the collective understory of humanity, that attempts to fight it by advancing principles of universal human equality, and by joining forces with the many other groups of people who have been terrorized and slaughtered in the name of racial or religious purity and/or superiority, were treated by Israeli leaders and many Jews in positions of leadership as not just naïve but also actively dangerous.

Zionism's offer after its ideological competitors were drastically weakened was simple: rather than trying to defeat anti-Semitism by getting at its roots, we will hold a gun to its head and force it into submission. And in the face of the spectral Shylock, the eternal Jew that is the shadow-double of all Jews, Israel will respond with a doppelganger of its own: the sunbaked, muscle-bound, land-hungry, machine-gun-toting New Jew—that unbound alter ego of the pale, studious, melancholic Old Jew.

This was the doubling that preoccupied Roth, but it didn't end there, of course. Just as the Old Jews were trapped in a fraternal battle with European Christians, cast as devils onto which all evil was projected, so the New Jews required their own anti-self: the Palestinian, a locus of perpetual threat inside Israel and on its borders.

To explain how we got to this seemingly intractable place, a little history is required—never a simple proposition in a part of the world where rivaling versions of the past are a dense thicket. The 1930s saw a series of Arab revolts against the influx of Jewish migrants to Palestine, which was then under British control. This wave of Jewish immigration was regarded by many Palestinians as a colonial imposition, a perception that was further cemented when British troops and local police put down the Arab uprising with tremendous force, fueling further resentment. When Palestine was partitioned in 1947, a move with overwhelming Arab opposition, and Israel declared statehood the next year, the first Arab-Israeli war was locked in. These were the years that Palestinians call the Nakba, or catastrophe: roughly 750,000 Palestinians were expelled, hundreds of Palestinian villages were destroyed, and thousands were killed, with many of the horrifying truths about these atrocities finally escaping Israel's own Shadow Lands in recent years.

Of course Palestinians would resist such ethnic cleaning with violence of their own. Yet rather than seeing Arab resistance for what it was—a nationalist, anti-colonial battle over land and self-determination (with some anti-Semitic elements, to be sure)—many influential Zionist leaders portrayed the entire Palestinian cause as nothing but more irrational Jew-hatred, a seamless continuation of the very same anti-Semitism that had resulted in the Holocaust, and that therefore needed to be crushed with the kind of militarized force that Jews had not been able to marshal in Nazi-controlled Europe. Within this imaginary, the Palestinian, as the Jew's new eternal enemy, was treated as so illegitimate, so irrational, so other, that Israelis believed themselves to be justified in reenacting many of the forms of violence, dehumanizing propaganda, and forced displacement that had targeted and uprooted the Jewish people throughout Europe for centuries, a process that continues to this day with ongoing home demolitions, Israeli settlement expansions, targeted assassinations, settler rampages through Palestinian communities, openly discriminatory laws, and walled ghettos into which Palestinians are corralled.

At my Hebrew day school in Montreal, as in so many schools like it, the facts of the Nazi genocide were drummed into us like arithmetic tables: the numbers of dead, the twisted forms of torture, the gas chambers, the cruelly closed borders. This was the late 1970s and early '80s—before the immersive Holocaust museums with walk-in cattle cars were constructed, before the March of the Living tours took hundreds of thousands of young Jews on trips to Auschwitz—but we received lo-fi versions of the same experiences, and our terrified imaginations filled in the blanks.

Looking back as the parent of a child older than we were then, I am struck by what wasn't a part of these strangely mechanical retellings. There was space for the surface-level emotions: horror at the atrocities, rage at the Nazis, a desire for revenge. But not for the more complex and troubling emotions of shame or guilt, or for reflection on what duties the survivors of genocide may have to oppose genocidal logics in all of their forms. I am struck that we never actually grieved, nor were we invited to seize our anger and turn it into an instrument for solidarity.

Many years later, my friend Cecilie Surasky, then one of the leaders of Jewish Voice for Peace, observed of these kinds of educational methods: "It's re-traumatization, not remembering. There is a difference." When she said it, I knew it was true. Remembering puts the shattered pieces of our selves back together again (re-member-ing); it is a quest for wholeness. At its best, it allows us to be changed and transmuted by grief and loss. But re-traumatization is about freezing us in a shattered state; it's a regime of ritualistic reenactments designed to keep the losses as fresh and painful as possible. Our education did not ask us to probe the parts of ourselves that might be capable of inflicting great harm on others, and to figure out how to resist them. It asked us to be as outraged and indignant at what happened to our ancestors as if it had happened to us—and to stay in that state.

The reason for this frozen quality to our education, I now see, was that the Holocaust was a plot point in a larger, prewritten story we not only were being told but also were trapped inside: a phoenix-from-the-flames narrative that began in the gas chambers of Nazi-controlled Europe and ended on the hilltops around Jerusalem. Though there were certainly exceptions, for the most part, the goal of this teaching was not to turn us into people who would fight the next genocide wherever it occurred. The goal was to turn us into Zionists.

The line between the terrifying stories of our people being hunted and exterminated and the existence of this state on the other side of the world, was, we were told, a straight one. It went like this: If fascist fervor ever surged again, and men in jackboots got it into their heads to purge their national bodies of Jewish genes, we would not be left helpless and unarmed once again, not be left to plead for our survival, not be locked out of every nation that might have saved us, not be devoured by the specter of our Shylock doppelganger. Why? Because next time we would have Israel—the white-and-blue flag that flew at every school assembly, the place where the trees we had donated our allowances to buy were standing tall, planted over the Palestinian villages we were never told existed.

As was the case in many left-wing Jewish homes, I learned a different version of "Never again"—that it was a directive, a sacred duty, to oppose hate and discrimination in all its forms, no matter who was the target. But, for the same reasons that she selected my biblical name, my mother insisted that I go to Hebrew day school to cement the bond to our tribe, to learn the songs, rituals, and languages (both Hebrew and Yiddish) that our adversaries had been trying to annihilate since before the Inquisition. And at that school, "Never again" did not mean "Never again to anyone," as it did in our home—it meant "Never again to the Jews." It meant "Never again because of Israel." It meant "Never again because we who have been haunted by Shylock forever have our own double now—and he has a great many guns."

Doppelganger Nation

"Doppelgänger politics." That is how Caroline Rooney, professor of African and Middle Eastern Studies at the University of Kent, describes the state of Israel and the complex psychological space it occupies as both victim and perpetrator. The doppelganger nature of the country's identity is embedded in the dualistic language used to describe it, in which everything is double and never singular: Israel-Palestine, Arab and Jew, Two States, The Conflict. Based on a fantasy of symmetrical power, this suturing together of two peoples implies conjoined twins in a state of unending struggle, an irresolvable sibling rivalry between the two peoples, both descended from Abraham.

For Rooney, Israel as doppelganger exists on two levels. First, it is a doppelganger of the forms of chauvinistic European nationalisms that turned Jews into pariahs on the continent since well before the Inquisition. That was Zionism's win-win pitch to anti-Semitic European powers: you get rid of your "Jewish problem" (i.e., Jews, who will leave your countries and migrate to Palestine), and Jews get a state of their own to mimic/twin the very forms of militant nationalism that had oppressed them for centuries. (This is why Zionism was so fiercely opposed by the members of the Bund, who believed that nationalism itself was their enemy and the wellspring of race hatred.)

Israel also became a doppelganger of the colonial project, specifically settler colonialism. Many of Zionism's basic rationales were thinly veiled Judaizations of core Christian colonial conceptions: Terra Nullius, the claim that continents like Australia were effectively empty because their Indigenous inhabitants were categorized as less than fully human, became "A land without a people for a people without a land"—a phrase adopted by many Zionists and that originated with nineteenth-century Christians. Manifest Destiny became "land bequeathed to the Jews by divine right." "Taming the wild frontier" became "making the desert bloom."

As in all colonial projects, Israel's settlers needed to engage in various kinds of active unseeing. The legendary U.S. investigative journalist

I. F. Stone supported the creation of a Jewish homeland in Palestine, even embedding himself on one of the clandestine boats, crowded with Holocaust survivors, that eventually made it to safety in "stucco-colored Haifa" in 1946. But after the 1967 war, he conceded, "For the Zionists, the Arab was the Invisible Man. Psychologically he was not there." Or as the Israeli prime minister Golda Meir put it, "There was no such thing as Palestinians . . . They did not exist." The great Palestinian poet Mahmoud Darwish maps this spectral status—of being a "present-absentee"—in his book *In the Presence of Absence*. The lie of Indigenous absence, familiar to all settler colonial projects, required a great deal of effort to maintain. The Jewish National Fund planted pine trees on top of Palestinian villages and centuries-old agricultural terrace systems. Hebrew place names replaced Arabic ones. Olive trees, some millennia old, were, and still are, uprooted. As the journalist Yousef Al Jamal writes, "Israeli settlers continue their unbated campaign of uprooting Palestinian olive trees because this tree reminds them of the Palestinian existence."

There were notable differences in this doppelganger version of settler colonialism, however. One was timing. After World War II, anti-colonial movements surged in the Global South, with wave after wave of national movements rising up to reject colonial mandates and assert the right to self-determination. In the years after the war, all around what would become the state of Israel, former colonies were declaring their independence: the French were forced to definitively release their mandate over Syria and Lebanon and withdraw troops in 1946; Jordan won its independence from Britain that same year; Egyptians were in open revolt against the continued presence of the British. Israel, which became a state in 1948, was both a product of those forces and a glaring exception to them. Britain lifted its colonial mandate as part of a broader contraction of its once-global empire. Because a small population of Jews had lived in Palestine continuously, Zionists framed their movement as one of national liberation: like other oppressed people, Jews were getting a state of their own. Of course, from the perspective of the much larger population of Palestinians, who were being evicted from their homes, lands, and communities to make way for a brand-new country, Israel was very far from an anti-colonial project. It was the opposite: a settler colony being established at a time when the rest of the world was going in the opposite direction. This could only have been incendiary.

Israel's settler colonialism differed from its predecessors' in another way. Where European powers colonized from a position of strength and a claim to God-given superiority, the post-Holocaust Zionist claim to Palestine was based on the reverse: on Jewish victimization and vulnerability. The tacit argument many Zionists were making at the time was that Jews had earned the right to an exception from the decolonial consensus—an exception born of their very recent near extermination. The Zionist version of justice said to Western powers: If you could establish your empires and your settler colonial nations through ethnic cleansing, massacres, and land theft, then it is discrimination to say that we cannot. If you cleared your land of its Indigenous inhabitants, or did so in your colonies, then it is anti-Semitic to say that we cannot. It was as if the quest for equality were being reframed not as the right to be free from discrimination, but as *the right to discriminate*. Colonialism framed as reparations for genocide.

Except if Hitler had been inspired by settler colonialism in North America—and he clearly was—then this was anything but reparations. It was a continuation of the colonial logic, but with broken and traumatized people let loose on a people even less powerful than themselves. Palestinians, under this arrangement, became, as the anti-colonial scholar Edward Said put it, "the victims of the victims," or, in the words of the scholar Joseph Massad, "the new Jews."

To do onto others the same othering that has been done onto you is, of course, psychologically intolerable. Indeed, such actions are so antithetical to Jewish values that they demand extreme repression and projection. Doppelgangers in literature often embody a partitioned self, and, as Rooney writes, "doppelgänger politics is first of all a politics of self-partition," with everything we cannot bear to see projected onto the other. If Israel practices doppelganger politics by imitating European nationalisms, it also enacts it in this second way: by projecting all criminality and violence onto the Palestinian other, lest the state's own foundational crimes be confronted. Meanwhile, the colonial nature of the project only grows more naked with time, with openly racist and Jewish supremacist political players consolidating their power at every level. When it formed at the end of 2022, Israel's new far-right government called not just for continued occupation of the West Bank but for its annexation, explicitly stating in its coalition agreement that "the Jewish people has an exclusive and unquestionable right to all areas of the Land of Israel. The government will promote and develop settlement in all parts of the Land of Israel—in the Galilee, the Negev, the Golan, Judea and Samaria." The frontier was moving, as all frontiers do.

Unseeing the Other

It's not hard to see why many were drawn to Zionism's promise at the start. After so much trauma, it must have felt irresistible to be offered a flag, a uniform, and a gun—to have more choices than whether to be a target or a charity case. If I had been on one of those boats full of refugees no one wanted, would I have had the strength and forethought to resist the promise of a fortressed state of our own? I have no confidence that I could have.

Rendered invisible and unseeable by Israelis, many Palestinians respond by refusing to see the state that refuses to see them. "The Zionist entity," some still call it, seven decades after its formation. "Will you or won't you acknowledge that Israel has a right to exist?" demand Israel's leaders and defenders, insisting that a refusal to make this acknowledgment proves that Palestinians favor a second Holocaust. But many Palestinians and their supporters refuse to budge, knowing that conceding Israel's right to exist would change nothing about its actions, and would uphold an idea of an exclusively Jewish homeland that they contest on principle. I understand this refusal—it is one of the few tools available to an occupied and vastly outgunned people. But it also seems worth acknowledging that for Jewish people who have been treated as inhuman for so much of our history, being called an "entity" is a wounding thing, and wounding in a way that may not be particularly constructive.

As for those not directly affected by this struggle, it would help if more conversations could hold greater complexity—the ability to acknowledge that the Israelis who came to Palestine in the 1940s were survivors of genocide, desperate refugees, many of whom had no other options, *and* that they were settler colonists who participated in the ethnic cleansing of another people. That they were victims of white supremacy in Europe being passed the mantle of whiteness in Palestine. That Israelis are nationalists in their own right and that their country has long been enlisted by the United States to act as a kind of subcontracted military base in the region. All of this is true all at once. Contradictions like these don't fit comfortably within the usual binaries of anti-imperialism (colonizer/colonized) or the binaries of identity politics (white/racialized)—but if Israel-Palestine teaches us anything, it might be that binary thinking will never get us beyond partitioned selves, or partitioned nations. None of this is intended as an apologia for Israeli settler colonialism. Rather, it is an attempt, as the British scholar Jacqueline Rose put it regarding her book *The Question of Zion*, to "go into the mindset of Zionism without blocking the exit."

In China Miéville's eerie novel *The City & The City*, two metropolises occupy the same physical location, but residents are not permitted to acknowledge each other's existence. When this carefully guarded delusion is punctured, and a resident of one city recognizes or interacts with the doppelganger city, this is known as a "breach" and it is very serious. Many have read the book as an allegory for Israel-Palestine, even though the refusal to see the other in the day-to-day is overwhelmingly on the Israeli side. (Palestinians cannot avoid seeing the walls and soldiers that keep them confined and surveilled.) Still, the novel does help conceptualize the strangeness of the daily spatial terrain, particularly in the West Bank, dotted with fast-expanding illegal Israeli settlements.

Like all segregated societies that are layered on top of each other, Israel and Palestine are not two distinct geographies. Instead, they make up a singular doppelganger society, requiring a doubling of everything: schools, roads, laws, courts. It's a psychological prison for Jewish Israelis, locked inside a fortress of fear and denial, and it's a very literal prison for Palestinians, entrapped in a warren of walls and checkpoints in the West Bank, in the open-air prison that is Gaza, and in the sprawling jail cells that have made incarceration such a routinized part of daily life that around 20 percent of the Palestinian population in the occupied territories has experienced some form of arrest and/or detention by Israeli forces—some 800,000 people, according to a study by the Palestinian prisoner support group Addameer.

In interviews, Miéville expresses discomfort with the idea of his book as an allegory, saying that such a reading is too literal and that the novel explores the arbitrary logics of borders more generally, between nations and even inside them. Israelis are certainly not the only people on this brutally divided planet trying to lead carefree lives without having to think about the unmarked graves, stolen land, packed prisons, and spectral presences that make their nation possible. It is not the only nation trying to achieve "security" by penning other people in and pointing guns at them. It is hardly the only nation with Shadow Lands that refuse to stay in the shadows. Yet in the crowding of these two, twinned peoples onto this tiny sliver of territory—the wrenching intimacy of the home invasions and demolitions, the ritualistic regularity of the pummeling of Gaza, the spectacle of once-stateless refugees exiling other people into the sea of statelessness—we see in hyper concentrated form the dead end of this project that dared to call itself "civilization."

Because, though it may be tempting, Israel-Palestine cannot be written off as a confounding ethnic conflict between a set of intransigent Semitic twins. It is, instead, the latest chapter in that story of the construction of the modern world, a world that is now on fire. A world that was born in fire. A story in which we are all implicated, wherever we live. It began in the lead-up to the Inquisition, with the burnings, torture, and then expulsion of Muslims and Jews; continued with the bloody conquest of the Americas and the ransacking of Africa for riches and human fuel to power the new colonies; wreaked colonial havoc in Asia; and then returned to Europe for Hitler to distill all of the methods forged in these earlier chapters—scientific racism, concentration camps, frontier genocide—into his Final Solution.

But the story didn't end there. Because the Allies, who finally saw fit to stop Hitler, decided that they did not want to open their borders to his surviving victims, and instead offloaded their Jewish problem, along with their collective shame and guilt about the Holocaust, onto the Arab world and said: "You take it."

Engaging with the form of Zionism that created the state of Israel in 1948 means accepting that a people, just like a person, can be victim and victimizer at the same time; that they can be both traumatized and traumatizer. So much of modern history is a story of pools of trauma being spatially moved around the globe like chess pieces made of human misery, with yesterday's victims enlisted as today's occupying army. The story we are trapped in is not about a people, or two people, or twins. It's a story about a logic, *the* logic that has been ravaging our world for so very long.

I think that's why, after all of this mapping of mirrored selves and mirror worlds and fascist doubles, I find myself drawn to this place that for so much of my life has been my own Shadow Land—a place I have struggled with in public and in private and in my own highly divided family (which runs the gamut from staunch anti-Zionists to orthodox settlers). Because for me, while Israel is a place, it has also always been a warning. A warning about the perils of building identity based on retraumatization rather than confronting our collective grief; about the dangers of building a group identity around insiders and outsiders; about what happens when once vibrant debate gives way to fiercely policed speech.

When Wolf Was Right

Which brings us back to . . . her.

For a brief period, before she fully surrendered to conspiracy world, before the *Outrages* debacle, before all the pictures of clouds, my doppelganger did something I admired. I might not have chosen the exact same words that she chose, or said them in exactly the same way, but I remember seeing a few people confusing me with her at the time, and being just fine with that.

It was 2014 and Israel had launched a particularly deadly assault on Gaza, carried out in the name of destroying the tunnel systems that brought weapons (and much else) over the borders and stopping Palestinian rocket fire. The casualty toll tells the story of appalling asymmetry between occupier and occupied. According to a United Nations report, 1,462 Palestinian civilians were killed that summer, compared with 6 Israeli civilians; 789 Palestinian fighters were killed, compared with 67 Israeli soldiers. The Israeli human rights organization B'Tselem reported that of those who did not take part in the hostilities, "526—a quarter of all Palestinians killed in the operation—were children under eighteen years of age."

Before this, I had not noticed Wolf speaking out about Israeli crimes. Like many North American liberal Jews, she had lived in Israel, spoke Hebrew, believed in a two-state solution. But something wasn't adding up for her about this latest attack. She was shocked by the civilian deaths, particularly the children. Wolf wrote that the assault was a violation of Jewish values and the lessons of the Holocaust. Then she did something quite remarkable: she turned her Facebook page into a clearinghouse for "citizen journalists" to show the human face of the attack on Gaza. For a time, it became a vital source of information. She also wrote a widely circulated post:

> People are asking why I am taking this 'side'. There are no sides. I mourn all victims. But every law of war and international law is being broken in the targeting of civilians in Gaza. I stand with the people of Gaza exactly because things might have turned out differently if more people had stood with the Jews in Germany.

She went on to describe going to synagogue, hoping in vain that what she saw as a profound moral crisis might be addressed by her spiritual community. "I . . . had to leave," she wrote, "because I kept waiting for the massacre of Gaza to be addressed . . . nothing. where is god? God is only ever where we stand with our neighbor in trouble and against injustice. I turn in my card of faith as of now because of our overwhelming silence as Jews . . . about the genocide now in Gaza."

The word "genocide" set off a fury, but Wolf isn't known for understatement. And she made her case for why the word fit: the targeting of civilian infrastructure, the absence of a humanitarian corridor, the clear collective punishment. She also gave a series of high-profile speeches on the topic, including a particularly notable one at the Oxford Union. What stood out most when I watched it recently was that it contained none of the swaggering overconfidence that she displays to such disastrous effect about epidemiology. Instead, her voice trembles, and she confesses to being terrified to be entering this fraught conflict. Yet, unlike other subject areas, where she seems to be mostly bluffing, Wolf knows her Old Testament and makes a convincing biblical case that Genesis never promised Israel to the Jews exclusively, that it was always conditional on behaving justly, including being kind to strangers.

All of this went very badly for Wolf. "Naomi Wolf's Allegations of an Israeli Genocide Fuel Anti-Semitism" was a typical headline in the Israeli press. In the United States, one prominent rabbi in particular, Shmuley Boteach, seemed to make it his mission to take her down. Wolf told *The Guardian* she lost her university position over the issue. "I was [teaching] at Barnard, and the trustees said they were not comfortable with my politics being the face of the university," she said. "All I ever wanted was to teach and do this kind of research." She also received "some serious threats online"—enough that she consulted a private security company, and that's where she met her husband, a former U.S. special forces officer who founded Striker Pierce Investigations.

Having run afoul of many of the same guardians of official Jewry over the past three decades, I have no doubt that these events were both frightening and painful for Wolf. These were her friends, family members, and colleagues turning on her. Zionism, moreover, had always been a plank in her political home. Now that plank was giving way. Which raises a possible question: Did that experience—followed by the public excommunications—contribute to how unmoored she became in subsequent years? Does losing her political home partially explain how far she would stray to find a new home?

Wolf's experience of being harshly attacked, threatened, and professionally penalized for questioning Zionist orthodoxy is far from unique. It's part of a much larger story about how a culture that once coursed with debate about these very questions—from our duties to universal rights to the possibilities for multiracial solidarity—had become its mirror opposite. There used to be so many ways to be Jewish and to battle anti-Semitism; it was a question, one with many possible answers. And then we were told that there was just one answer.

That consensus was always an illusion, and the façade has, in recent years, been shattered by a new generation of Jewish writers and organizers gathered around publications like *Jewish Currents*, and organizations like IfNotNow and Jewish Voice for Peace, who are returning to old Bundist notions of "hereness," while joining with Palestinians to challenge Israel's colonial violence. But they are still small—at least compared with the groups that claim to speak on behalf of all Jews: the ones that have, for a very long time, been dealing with our community's collective, intergenerational trauma by drawing up enemies lists, by demanding loyalty oaths, by getting lectures and plays and films by Palestinians and their supporters canceled and articles retracted and job offers revoked. These self-appointed spokespeople have claimed that honest political disagreements are existential crises for our entire identity group, and now many champion laws that punish individuals and businesses for supporting the indispensable political tool of peaceful boycotts.

This reality lies at the root of my own discomfort with those progressive tendencies that cheer the censoring of our political opponents, or that offer blank deference to people claiming victim status: I have seen too often how both can go terribly wrong.

The Missing Chapter

Philip Roth, unsurprisingly, had a lot to say about all this. He was interested in imperfect victims, and the way trauma can be misused. "The Nazis are an excuse for everything that happens in this house!" Portnoy says to his sister in the book that made Roth famous. And as the political scientist Corey Robin observed in a 2021 essay, Roth "isn't speaking only of his family; he's talking about the house of Israel."

Roth was acutely uncomfortable with the ways Israeli militarism threatened to engulf cultural Judaism. Throughout *The Counterlife*, and then *Operation Shylock*, a procession of characters flagellate themselves over the country's moral decay. In *Shylock*, a character who turns out to be a Mossad agent describes Israel as "a Jewish country without a Jewish soul." Fake Roth accuses Israel of, "in many, many terrible ways, deforming and disfiguring Jews as only our anti-Semitic enemies once had the power to do." Yet another character, this one an old Palestinian friend of Roth's (who some critics presumed to be based on the Palestinian American scholar Edward Said), describes diasporic Jewish culture as "all human, elastic, adaptable, humorous, creative" but declares that, in Israel, "all this they have replaced here with a stick!"

Did that make Roth an anti-Zionist? He kept us guessing. After having revived so many of the Bund's old arguments for Diasporism, the book ends with Real Roth succumbing to his primal ethnic fear. He accepts an undercover assignment for the Mossad to collect intelligence about "Jewish anti-Zionist elements threatening the security of Israel." When the Mossad offers him a bribe to delete the last chapter of the book, which tells the story of this top secret operation, Real Roth complies. The book ends abruptly, leaving the reader to imagine its final pages in a shredder.

After all of that anti-Zionist venting, Roth's final message seemed clear. Yes, he had been a critic of Israel and an irreverent provocateur his whole life. But when it was all on the line, he, too, was willing to set his personal beliefs aside and do his duty for his fortressed, militarized tribe. His proxy character, the Real Roth, acted not as a writer, not as a committed loner and nose-thumber, but as a true Jew as defined by the Mossad, stepping into the generalized collective identity beneath his specific individual identity, the collective identity rooted not in what any one Jewish person may or may not want to be or do, but in the deep and abiding fear of what non-Jewish people will do to us. In the face of his unshakable ethnic doppelganger, Roth accepted Israel's offer and became a different kind of double: a New Jew. ("I am a tribesman who stood with his tribe," the Mossad agent character says.)

In a blazing 1963 *Commentary* essay, "Writing About Jews," Roth had said that it was the job of a novelist neither to perform propaganda for his ethnic group nor to concern himself with parochial questions like "What will the *goyim* think?" Thirty years later, was he letting us know that he had changed his mind, that he was ready to do his tribal duty? Or was the entire ending parody—Roth toying with his Jewish critics by saying: *Look, Rabbi, I'm doing state propaganda, like you always wanted me to—even letting the Mossad hack apart my book! Am I a good Jew now?* Or maybe he didn't want to choose: maybe he was telling us that he was both that and this.

Armed and Dangerous

And what of her? Other Naomi? Which is she?

Well, for a week in mid-May 2022, my doppelganger posted a series of photographs of her new long gun, spaced out to win maximum engagement from her fans on Gettr. To kick things off, she posted a photo of the gun in a large box: "It finally happened; I purchased my first firearm today. I am the proud if slightly nervous owner of a 22 Rimfire Rifle. Starting ladylike and manageable." Next, she posted a picture of her husband, putting it together: "Who knew that the perfect husband for a feminist is a man who will help assemble his wife's first rifle." Finally, she posted a picture of the fully assembled firearm on her writing table. "Maybe every writer and dissident critic should have a bipod at home in such times as these. The pen may be mightier than the sword, but perhaps these days, with the Ministry of Truth about to take aim at us, writers need both the pen and the (defensive) sword."

That was the same day when, in Buffalo, New York, an eighteen-year-old white supremacist murdered ten people at a supermarket with a legally purchased AR-15-style rifle.

The following week, Wolf shared a video in which she said that the only reason the United States "is not entirely enslaved like Australia or Shanghai or Canada . . . is that we have millions of owners of guns . . . it is harder to subjugate an armed population. This is why our founders gave us the Second Amendment. For exactly times like these."

There was a mass shooting on that day too, this one at an elementary school in Uvalde, Texas. The killer, also eighteen, murdered nineteen children and two teachers with a legally purchased assault rifle.

In her newsletter, Wolf went deeper, writing a kind of feminist love letter to her new firearm: "How had this issue escaped me so long, as a rape survivor myself, and as a feminist? The rape survivor in me longed, on an animal level, for a weapon. Longed, on an animal level, to deter any future attacker. The rape survivor in me wanted a weapon the way an injured creature wants teeth and claws." She wondered, "Could it always have been this easy? Could women resist and deter victimization—by simply owning, and knowing how to use, firearms?" Her answer? "Obviously."

Wolf is certainly not the first former victim to have succumbed to the promise of the gun, though she used to know that it rarely ends well, for either victim or victimizer. Still, it strikes me that it must be liberating, after living so long in opposition, then so long in humiliation, to finally be on the side with so few facts and so very many guns.

She doesn't talk or write about Palestinian rights anymore; they aren't a top concern for her new friends on the *War Room*. And her definition of God no longer seems to involve standing "with our neighbor in trouble and against injustice." On the contrary, she is fully enlisted in the trenches of Bannon's "Border War," echoing his lie about "fully open borders presided over by President Biden." This, she says, is "a tyrant's dream," and, she claims, "Traitors are dissolving the boundaries of our nation."

Civil war is here, she darkly warns: "I am a peaceful person. I do not want war. But war is being waged upon us." And like so many others, she is getting ready with more than words.

Erez from Erez

I have had my own encounters with Israel's doppelganger politics, too many to share at this late stage on our journey. But perhaps there is time for just one.

It was 2009 and I had just published the Hebrew and Arabic editions of *The Shock Doctrine*. A few months earlier, the Israeli military had launched a horrific attack on the Gaza Strip, killing an estimated 1,400 Palestinians and destroying critical infrastructure. I decided that year that I had no choice but to respect the call for boycott, divestment, and sanctions (BDS) that came from a broad coalition of Palestinian civil society groups—but I also wanted the book to come out in Israel and Palestine, because it had a chapter on the thriving disaster capitalism industry there. In collaboration with activists in Ramallah and Jerusalem, I found a way to publish that respected the call, which involved working with an activist Israeli press that had a long history of supporting Palestinian rights.

Before the book's launch in Israel, I went to Gaza to see the aftermath of the attacks for myself. I was traveling with Avi and our friend Cecilie Surasky from Jewish Voice for Peace. We weren't sure it would be possible to get in—Israel tightly controls access to Gaza through the Erez checkpoint, and getting a press pass as a foreign journalist required going through the Israeli press agency. Any one of us could have raised a security flag. But probably because of our Jewish names, the person staffing the office didn't bother looking into us, and we got the necessary accreditation. At the Erez checkpoint, our Jewish names activated our ethnic doubles once again and we were assumed to be sympathetic to Israel's occupation. So while Palestinians stood in long interrogation lines, we sailed through with just a quick ID check, along with bag and body X-rays. Then, jarringly, we were on the other side of the concrete wall, surrounded by watchtowers.

Once in Gaza, the three of us spoke with dozens of Palestinians from different sectors to try to learn as much as we could about life under siege. We met with farmers, a beekeeper, and a doctor, all of whom had lost children in the recent air attack. We saw young bodies burned by white phosphorous. We waded through the rubble of apartment buildings that could not be rebuilt because basic building supplies like cement were being blocked by the siege. We met Mona Al Shawa, a Palestinian women's rights activist, who told me, "We had more hope during the attacks; at least then we believed things would change." Now, she said, outside attention had moved on and Gazans once again felt abandoned by the world. The idea that there was more hope when they were under active air assault still haunts me.

On our last afternoon, we sat on plastic chairs in the shaded backyard of a prominent Palestinian family who insisted on feeding us a sumptuous meal of food from their garden—immense-hearted people who refused to hate us because of our ethnic doubles. The father, a doctor, told us that he was happy for his young children to meet Jewish people who wanted peace and justice, since the only Jews they get the chance to interact with are the soldiers at the checkpoints.

"I don't want them to grow up hating Jews," he told us. "But what can I do if the only Jews he sees are pointing guns?"

By late afternoon it was time to head back to Jerusalem, and that's when our trouble started. A human rights group in Gaza City had organized a press conference about my trip, and the news had clearly made its way up the chain of command at the Erez checkpoint; this time, they were ready for us.

Rather than letting us return, the Israelis kept us waiting, just the three of us, on the Gaza side of the wall for hours. As night fell and the curfew passed, we were left wondering whether we would get through at all. The checkpoint is in a buffer zone, with a long, desolate outdoor corridor dotted with Hamas security details, so being stranded there without a vehicle and no friends around wasn't ideal.

Finally, a remote door in the wall opened and, once we had been fully searched and scanned, we were approached by a stocky, muscular officer with a short black brush cut who identified himself as Erez.

"Erez from Erez," I said, trying to keep it light. He didn't smile; he simply looked past me to Avi and instructed him to follow upstairs for additional screening. Cecilie and I waited while he was interrogated. When Avi emerged, he was walking quickly and motioning us to move fast and get the hell away from all the Erezes.

Back at the Jerusalem Colony Hotel, we learned that he had been taken to a corner office to meet a senior Israeli Defense Force commander. The commander took Avi to the window and pointed at a battalion of tanks doing some kind of exercise nearby.

"You see that? I was minutes away of sending them in to rescue you. Do you have any idea of how much danger you were in? Any idea what Hamas was planning to do to you? We see and hear everything that goes on there." (This is the flip side of the unseeing of Palestinians that is central to a doppelganger society: the all-seeing eye of the surveillance state.)

Erez then joined in to tell Avi that he had heard some of what I had been saying about BDS, and he had some man-to-man advice: "Tell your wife what happened. Tell her what Hamas wanted to do to you. Get your woman under control."

With the aid of many beers, the three of us deconstructed the levels of gaslighting that Erez from Erez appeared to have orchestrated. No, we did not buy that the Israeli military was about to open a ground war in Gaza to rescue three Jews who were not lost. Nor did we believe we had been in imminent danger from Hamas. They had questioned Avi in a makeshift checkpoint inside a shipping container for about fifteen minutes, mainly to find out why he had an Israeli first name if he was Canadian (his mother's youthful labor Zionism). But they were satisfied with his press credentials—and it was the Israelis who had left us on the Gazan side for hours before allowing us through the checkpoint.

It seemed clear that they wanted us to sweat, to wonder if we were being abandoned behind "enemy" lines. And then they wanted to send a very clear message: that whoever we thought we were and whatever we thought we were doing, here, on these blood-soaked lands, we were nothing but our ethnic doubles, nothing but our Jewishness. That Jewishness would get us kidnapped or killed by Hamas in Gaza, never mind my foolish support for Palestinian rights, and then it would only be the Israeli army that would ride to our rescue, its soldiers risking their lives to save ours, even though they hold us in utter contempt. Because, like Hamas, they don't care about who we think we are as individuals; they care about our Jewish doubles. So, when Hamas attacked us as Jews, Israel would be there to save us as Jews.

That was the piece of theater that was supposed to get me under control, and it is a snapshot of the seedy bargain Israel offers to all Jews, now more than ever. Sure, you might not like the look of what we do—the Palestinian teenagers in prison, the killing of journalists, the openly racist, anti-Arab parties that have moved from the fringes to some of the most powerful offices in Israel's government. But you will accept it because when the world turns against Jews once again—and it will, because Shylock is eternal—you will come running here, with our tanks, our fighter jets, and the nuclear arsenal we will neither confirm nor deny, as your only safe place in the world.

I understand the primal terror that leads many of my people to cosign that contract, because the same trauma has been passed down through the generations to me. But I still can't do it; the price is too high. And not just for Palestinians and Jews. Because the deal Erez offered us is a version of the same poisonous deal all who are relatively fortunate on this partitioned planet are being offered. Take the gun. Accept the cages. Fortress your escape pod, and your borders. Perfect your kids. Protect your brand. Ignore the Shadow Lands. Play the victim.

But partitioning and performing and projecting are no longer working. The borders and walls don't protect us from rising temperatures or surging viruses or raging wars. And the walls around ourselves and our kids won't hold, either. Because we are porous and connected, as so many doppelganger stories have attempted to teach us.

So there has to be another way. Another portal, to another story of us.

PART FOUR

Facing the Real

(Integration)

If the word integration means anything, this is what it means: that we, with love, shall force our brothers to see themselves as they are, to cease fleeing from reality and begin to change it.

—James Baldwin, *The Fire Next Time*

Haunt the dreams of your comrades, and the nightmares of your enemies; live in a future that never came—be a specter, a memory, and a herald. Remind them that the current state was not inevitable until it came to be. Do not occupy yourself with the question of why this very possible future failed, leave the victorious to grope for answers. Be the question, and do not heed your impotence. A ghost has no need for material presence or action, you just need to shimmer.

—Alaa Abd el-Fattah, *You Have Not Yet Been Defeated*

15

UNSELFING

I have passed out a few times in my life—from fever, hunger, drink. But I have fainted only once.

I was seventeen, and it was a few weeks after my mother's first stroke. I arrived at the hospital straight from school to find her out of bed for the first time. A physical therapist was helping her take her first steps with a walker (soon, when the second stroke hit, she would lose this ability and much more). Through a pane of glass in the waiting area, I watched her as if she were somebody else's mother: the shaky, irregular steps, the lopsided face, the IV and feeding tube. The next thing I knew, I was facedown on the cold vinyl floor.

Vertigo invades when the world we thought we knew no longer holds.

The world is not holding. The living systems that support all of our lives are sick. Staggering. Trembling. In need of our urgent care.

A confession. In the period of time I have spent writing about my double and the Mirror World, I had originally planned to write about a different kind of vertigo, one related to my real work, whatever "real" is these days. For nearly two decades, ever since the levees in New Orleans broke in the wake of Hurricane Katrina, my research, writing, filmmaking, organizing, and public speaking had focused almost exclusively on aspects of the deepening climate crisis. And most of it followed a very particular narrative arc, one to which I had grown quite attached. The story went like this: Things are bad. They are about to get a lot worse. But we can avert that "a lot worse" if we embrace a Marshall Plan/New Deal/World War II–scale mobilization that will transform our entire economy so that it is largely powered by the wind and the sun, while giving us a historic opportunity to battle pretty much every form of inequality under that sun.

The catch was that we had to do it fast. "Decade Zero" was what they were calling it when I first went to a United Nations climate conference in 2009. By 2014, when *This Changes Everything* came out, we were already nearly halfway through it. Then Decade Zero came and went. In 2020, based on the best available science, we said that, while it was too late to stop dangerous warming, there was still time to avert catastrophic climate change, but, once again, we would need to cut global pollution in half in a decade. The good news was that, by then, there was a surging, intergenerational climate movement, along with a rapidly expanding understanding that system-scale change was the only credible path forward.

That same year, before the pandemic hit, I had been working with manic intensity on the campaign to make Bernie Sanders the Democratic nominee for U.S. president, in large part because Sanders was running on a disruptive platform that recognized the urgency for transformational climate action—and because he was clearly ready for the necessary battles with big polluters. In the months leading up to, and slamming into, the outbreak of Covid-19, I went to five states as a campaign surrogate for his climate policies, revving up the troops at dozens of rallies and volunteer meetings. On the exhilarating days—like when glitzy, Trumpy Las Vegas voted overwhelmingly for Bernie—part of me thought we might actually pull it off and get Bernie into the Oval Office, as improbable as that seemed even to us.

We didn't pull it off (obviously). And now another "last decade to save the world" is rapidly slipping away.

In the early months of the pandemic, when I was still living in New

Jersey, I went for one of those eerie, empty-road walks and saw a neighbor having a protracted conversation with a squirrel. She looked happy out there on her porch in her bathrobe, not at all self-conscious about being witnessed in the act of cross-species communion. Like so many of us, I let myself hope, in those hallucinatory days, that despite everything we had messed up, we might be getting another chance to reassess our collective priorities, along with our frenetic and depleting ways of living. That we might come through the pandemic's portal transformed.

Something shifted in me one year into that wretched disease, though. Maybe it was sparked by news that emissions were already rebounding in China, as they soon would everywhere else. Or maybe it was when Joe Biden started handing out thousands of new oil and gas drilling permits. Or when the cruise ships filled with tourists wanting to see Alaska's glaciers before they are gone started showing up again off the coast where I now live.

The greatest cause of my mounting despair, though, was none of this. It was when the mass movements that had grown so rapidly in recent years—staging climate strikes, supporting Sanders and other insurgent candidates, filling the streets with calls for racial justice—started dividing and devouring themselves from the inside, often with people who were clearly building their personal brands at the forefront of the divisions. With online clout too often determining movement leadership, and few ways to hold those leaders accountable, conflict and mistrust easily spread, supercharged by algorithms hooked on rage and egged on by fake accounts and Russian bots that heaped salt on all our open wounds. The predatory corporate logics that earlier iterations of the left recognized as our enemies were clearly deep inside us now: in the arteries that connected us, in our habits of mind, in our very cells. It felt like nothing could be trusted, least of all one another.

For me, it meant that I had run out of halfway-credible pathways away from disaster to offer. I no longer saw how we could avoid the social and ecological outcomes that so many of us most fear. That was the deepest source of my vertigo. Who was I without that story of possible salvation to share?

That's when I made the odd decision to follow my doppelganger down her various rabbit holes. More than anything, I think it was to distract myself from having to write about what I could no longer deny: that we appeared to be blowing our last best chance to change. I couldn't face writing that, not me. And so I found something else.

Yet, the further along I have gone on this journey into a world of doubles, the more it led me back to where I began. The more I looked at doppelgangers and the messages they carry, both personally and politically, the more relevant that knowledge seemed to our prospects of becoming the kinds of people capable of getting off our treacherous path.

The self as perfected brand, the self as digital avatar, the self as data mine, the self as idealized body, the self as racist and anti-Semitic projection, the child as mirror of the self, the self as eternal victim. These doubles share one thing in common: all are ways of not seeing. Not seeing ourselves clearly (because we are so busy performing an idealized version of ourselves), not seeing one another clearly (because we are so busy projecting what we cannot bear to see about ourselves onto others), and not seeing the world and the connections among us clearly (because we have partitioned ourselves and blocked our vision). I think this, more than anything else, explains the uncanny feeling of our moment in history—with all of its mirrorings, synthetic selves, and manufactured realities. At bottom, it comes down to who and what we cannot bear to see—in our past, in our present, and in the future racing toward us.

Performing and partitioning and projecting are the individual steps that make up the dance of avoidance. What is being avoided? I think it's our true doppelganger. What Daisy Hildyard calls our "second body," the one enmeshed with wars and whales, the one benefiting from the genocides of the past and adding our little drops of poison to the great die-offs of the future. The second body that perpetually mines the Shadow Lands for its comforts and conveniences.

We avoid because we do not want to be bodies like that. We do not want our bodies to participate in mass extinction. We do not want our bodies to be wrapped in garments made by other bodies that are degraded, abused, and worked to exhaustion. We do not want to ingest foods marred by memories of human and nonhuman suffering. We do not want the lands we live on to be stolen and haunted. We do not want the children we love to live in a world that is less alive, less wonderous, more frightening.

How could we? It is all so unbearable. No wonder we work so hard to look away. No wonder we erect those walls, literal and psychological. No wonder we would rather gaze at our reflections, or get lost in our avatars, than confront our shadows.

James Baldwin, speaking about the double projected onto him as a Black man in the United States, observed that it had everything to do with the person doing the projecting. What was a white man seeing when he saw Baldwin? "It wasn't me," he said, "it was something he didn't want to see. And you know what that was? It was ultimately, yes, his own death. Or call it trouble. Trouble is an excellent metaphor for death."

So many forms of doubling are ways of not looking at death/trouble. And death feels awfully close these days—as close as a fentanyl-laced pill, a heat dome, a hate crime, an intake of virally loaded breath. Much closer for some than for others, as usual—but not far enough, I suspect, for anyone's comfort. So how do we stop averting our gaze? How do we face our second bodies and our mortal bodies in a sustained way, rather than throwing up partitions, performances, and projections to hide from them? What would it take to stop running? To know—really know—what we already know?

Feel Like Coral, Like Fish

The director and screenwriter Adam McKay's thinly veiled climate allegory *Don't Look Up* (2021) is very much about not looking. While monitoring the night sky, Jennifer Lawrence's character, the Michigan State doctoral candidate Kate Dibiasky, discovers a comet hurtling toward Earth. As a result, the comet is named after her, and her colleagues applaud this peak personal-branding success in their corner of the academy. The trouble, of course, is that the comet in question turns out to be a "planet killer," which means Comet Dibiasky is the last kind of brand anyone would want (or, indeed, the last brand anyone will have).

Watching this from inside my own personal-branding meltdown, it occurred to me that Kate's plight perfectly mirrors the bizarre contradictions of our high-stakes moment in planetary history: we are all trapped inside economic and social structures that encourage us to obsessively perfect our minuscule selves even as we know, if only on a subconscious level, that we are in the very last years when it might still be possible to avert an existential planetary crisis. The canvas of change shrinks ever smaller just as our problems grow ever larger.

Some of the climate scientists whose work I most respect have come around to an understanding that there is an intimate relationship between our overinflated selves and our under-cared-for planet. David Bowman, professor of fire science at the University of Tasmania, where blazes and drought have devoured unique and magical forest ecologies, says humans most urgently need to learn a simple lesson: "We're not just the center of the universe. This world wasn't made just for us." Charlie Veron, a legendary coral scientist who has spent a lifetime studying the Great Barrier Reef, now in its death throes, describes the journey of his life as one of de-centering himself so that he has the headspace to truly see other life-forms, human and nonhuman alike. It was a hard-won lesson, which began with losing his young daughter Fiona, or Noni, to drowning, a tragedy that made him realize that her life was more important to him than his own. Leveled by personal and ecological grief, he aspires to dissolve into the reef he studies, to "feel like a coral or a fish." This recalls the novelist and philosopher Iris Murdoch's description of observing something beautiful—whether a bird or a painting—as "an occasion for 'unselfing.'"

There is an urgency to this, as Veron points out. Because "the people who are the exploiters of this planet are people who put themselves first"—unable to unself even for a moment. Put a little differently, the climate crisis can be understood as a surplus of heat-trapping gases in the atmosphere; it can also be understood as a surplus of self—a result of all the literal and figurative energy it takes to perform and perfect the selves fortunate enough to live outside the Shadow Lands.

If Comet Dibiasky symbolizes the mindset that is keeping us trapped in this cycle, Veron's humbling journey to unselfing may well hold the key to our collective survival. Because it means that our role here on earth is not simply to maximize the advantage in our lives (or to try to extend our selves beyond our life with "grief tech" avatars). It's to maximize (protect, regenerate) all of life. We are here not just to make sure we as individuals survive, but to make sure that life survives; not to chase clout, but to chase life.

This is something else we might choose to learn from our double walkers. The idea that each one of us has a look-alike walking around somewhere means that no one is quite as special or unique as we might have imagined ourselves to be. Within capitalism's hall of mirrors, this revelation tends to be told as a horror story, as embodied by Jesse Eisenberg's character in *The Double*, the one who whimpers, "I'd like to think I'm pretty unique." This is the must-kill-must-stab-must-be-the-last-me-standing response to doppelgangers that threads its way through Western literature, film, and monotheistic religion. But there is also the option of viewing our doubles the way Fake Roth does: *Hurray! I'm not alone in this cruel world!*

That is what I see when I look at François Brunelle's doppelganger art project, *I'm Not a Look-Alike!*, with its photographs of hundreds of pairs of people who have been confused with each other. The most captivating aspect of the work is not that the pairs look so much alike but that they seem the opposite of horrified about that revelation. Brunelle's images are touchingly intimate, with the identical strangers utterly at ease: some of their bodies drape over the others', some gaze into each other's eyes, some are playful. They are comfortable in their lack of individuality, interested in this other person who looks like a mirror of themselves. It reminds me of something I read by the philosopher Helena de Bres, who has a twin sister. She expressed "pity for those who suffer the almost unimaginable misfortune of being born into this world alone."

Yet we are not alone, at least not as alone as it can feel. Most of us lack the intimacy of twindom, sure, but connections and solidarities and kinships are available to all of us should we choose to guard the boundaries of our selves less jealously. We have kin everywhere. Some of them look like us, lots of them look nothing like us and yet are still connected to us. Some aren't even human. Some are coral. Some are whales. And they are there to connect with, if we can get out of our own way for long enough.

To be clear, I am not planning to embrace my doppelganger as a long-lost relative. But doppelgangers, by messing with our heads and our illusions of sovereignty, can help teach us this lesson: that we are not as separate from one another as we might think. Not as individuals, and perhaps not even as groups of individuals who have been born into various kinds of seemingly eternal fratricidal duels.

What I see in the photographs in *I'm Not a Look-Alike!* is a model for surrender, not to sameness but to interconnection and enmeshment—the same lesson the pandemic tried to teach us in those early days. No one makes themselves; we all make and unmake one another. Reject that truth for long enough, and you will end up in the Mirror World, shouting "FREEDOM" into the freezing winter air while you honk an airhorn and declare yourself a "sovereign citizen," accountable to no one and nothing.

Speaking of which, I have noticed, of late, that the confusion with Other Naomi has died down. It would seem that gun-toting, Bannon-joining, commie-bashing Naomi Wolf is now an unmistakable phenomenon unto herself. A relief, to be sure, but, perhaps oddly, I'm not sorry the confusion ever happened. Looking back at my period of intense doppelganger trouble, I realize that, despite its moments of undeniable self-involvement, in the end it has helped me achieve a measure of freedom from the tyranny of my own self. What began as a form of self-defense (I *will* reassert myself as the owner of my ideas, my identity, my name!) became, gradually, a form of self-release. By creating a crisis in my personal brand (the one I always denied I had), and by introducing a hefty dose of ridiculousness into the seriousness with which I once took my public persona, and by showing me how terribly grim it is to spend your life chasing clout, Other Naomi has left me with no choice but to loosen the grip on that performed and partitioned version of me. Doing so has left me feeling significantly calmer. And as John Berger taught me long ago, "calm is a form of resistance."

Self-involvement, however it manifests—my doppelganger's megalomania, my various neuroses, your fill-in-the-blank—is a story in which the self takes up too much space, just as the story of Judeo-Christian Western civilization puts the human (read: white, male, powerful human) at the center of the story of life on this planet, with all of it created for our species. None of it is true. Whether we are loving ourselves too much or loathing ourselves too much—or, more likely, doing both—we're still at the center of every story. We're still blotting out the sun.

All of which is why, over the course of this now concluding journey, I have come to embrace Naomi confusion as an unconventional Buddhist exercise in annihilating the ego. I could never quite get the hang of nonattachment before this; but I think, thanks to her, I have.

That, I concede, is far too neat an ending to this story. If performing and partitioning and projecting are all techniques of avoiding the Shadow Lands, then neither Buddhist detachment nor Freudian integration of the unconscious is enough to help us confront that which we have been avoiding. Our crises are material and profoundly collective, and so, ultimately, we will be able to bear unbearable realities only if we also work to change them. That means we must take action (Action! Action!) to make the world different from the way it is now. We must attempt, with great urgency, to imagine a world *that does not require Shadow Lands*, that is not predicated on sacrificial people and sacrificial ecologies and sacrificial continents. More than imagine it, we must begin, at once, to build it.

This starts with naming, as bell hooks always did, the systems that have carved out the Shadow Lands, deemed them erasable, disposable: capitalism, imperialism, white supremacy, patriarchy. It requires teaching those words, and their true meanings, to the people in our lives, so that the next time someone tells them that their suffering and burdens are all the fault of child-stealing globalists, or job-stealing immigrants, or well-meaning teachers, or the Jews or the Chinese or the drag queens at the library, they will know better. And they will be able to fight better. "We can be hard and critical on structures, but soft on people," says the civil rights scholar john a. powell. That is the opposite of the discourse that dominates today, the one that is so very hard on people and far too soft on structures.

The shift to confronting and reimagining structures requires something else: a recognition that this work is not something we can do on our own, as individuals, with a charity donation or an equity and diversity training, or a performance of virtue on social media. Indeed, a central reason why so many of us cannot bear to look at the Shadow Lands is that we live in a culture that tells us to fix massive crises on our own, through self improvement. Support labor rights by ordering from a different store. End racism by battling your personal white fragility—or by representing your marginalized identity group in elite spaces. Solve climate change with an electric car. Transcend your ego with a meditation app.

Some of it will help—a bit. But the truth is that nothing of much consequence in the face of our rigged systems can be accomplished on our own—whether by our own small selves or even by our own identity groups. Change requires collaboration and coalition, even (especially) uncomfortable coalition. Mariame Kaba, a longtime prison abolitionist who has done as much as anyone to imagine what it would take to live in a world that does not equate safety with police and cages, puts the lesson succinctly, one passed on to her by her father: "Everything worthwhile is done with other people."

If our situation seems uniquely challenging (and on bad days, borderline hopeless), it likely has to do with how much we have come to expect from our individual selves combined with the brokenness of structures—trade unions, close-knit neighborhoods, functioning local media, and so on—that once made it easier to do things together. It's our fragmentation that daunts us, as much as the challenges themselves.

And yet even in these unstable times, I do think it's possible to overcome some of that fragmentation, and to weave ourselves together in new ways. The wave of unconventional union organizing at corporations like Amazon and Starbucks shows that many young workers are already figuring out those new ways. Same goes for the movements organizing debtors into quasi-unions, like the Debt Collective, as well as the unions for tenants and unhoused people that have formed in many gentrified cities that have allowed rents to soar to impossible heights. Elon Musk's overnight transformation of Twitter into his personal vendetta machine did wonders to make the case for why we cannot leave our vital information ecology to the whims of billionaires and must, instead, invest in communal alternatives, ones that are not based on mining our data by encouraging our worst selves. These are all good signs. But none of these changes will happen fast enough until more of us figure out how to soften the borders around our individual selves and around our various identity groups to allow for a coming together in common cause.

Are we capable of it? Doppelgangers, by eliciting such contradictory emotions, warn us that it will be a struggle. On the one hand, there is the horror at a lack of uniqueness and singularity; on the other, the deep desire to connect, to merge into others, to feel the edges of the self dissolve. With or without doppelgangers, most of us experience the push and pull of these emotions, as individuals and as members of groups: we want separation and distinctness, and we want unity and community. The tension is fruitful and does not need to be resolved. The problem lies in the fact that our culture is so biased toward one tendency over the other. It's the scramble for separateness that is richly rewarded and encouraged in our zero-sum economy, while the urge to act in solidarity and mutual aid with others is discounted and disappeared, when not being actively punished.

This bias against solidarity is particularly dangerous in our present moment, as our various fascist doppelgangers grow bolder by the day. The supremacist, annihilatory logic was never truly confronted, and now supermarkets and Walmarts and mosques and synagogues are being turned into slaughterhouses by young men with guns who are convinced that someone is trying to "replace" them. And it's surging along the diagonal lines that connect the people with ideas about the supremacy of their race to the people with fixations about the supremacy of their immune systems and the perfection of their kids.

In the face of these very tangible threats, fiercely defending the borders of our identities, and the borders of our broader ethnic/racial/gender identity groups, is serving us all poorly. Indeed, if history is any guide, it will be our undoing. Because every story of triumph for the fascist right is also a story of fragmentation, sectarianism, and stubborn refusal to make strategic alliances on the anti-fascist left.

Conspiracy theories, as we have seen, are both symptoms of confusion and powerlessness *and* tools of division and distraction that benefit elites. But conspiracy theories are far from the only things that keep us divided; so, at times, are the ways we have learned to understand our own victimization, and the way it may or may not relate to the victimization of others. Arielle Angel, editor in chief of *Jewish Currents* and a descendent of Holocaust survivors, wrote powerfully about this recently:

> These days, I feel the threat of fascism humming in my body like a once-broken bone before the rain. It is a bequest from the pain of my grandparents, for better or worse, and perhaps from further ancestors, who fled the fanatical Spanish monarchs and priests. In living rooms and pitch meetings, as the protest or party winds down, my comrades and I debate the relative merit of one strategy over another, while conceding that none look particularly promising. But what is clear is this: We are going to need each other. This means staying attuned to the possibility of a collective power, instead of attached to a proprietary pain.

That is one overarching message I choose to take at the end of my doppelganger journey: time to loosen the grip on various forms of proprietary pain and selfhood, and reach toward many different forms of possible connection and kin, toward anyone who shares a desire to confront the forces of annihilation and extermination and their mindsets of purity and perfection. Faced with the ultimate doppelganger threat—the flip into fascism that is already well underway in many parts of the world—this ability to melt some of the hard, icy edges of identity, however well earned those defenses may be, will be important to any hope we have of success. It will not be enough to protect "our" people; we will need to have the stamina of true solidarity, which defines "our people" as "all people."

This kind of universalism is hard. There are so many perfectly good reasons for people on the broadly defined left to be fed up, angry, and disappointed with one another, and to latch onto those disappointments to rationalize splintering into smaller and smaller groups. But when power and wealth and weaponry and information technology are concentrated in so few hands, and those hands are willing to deploy them for the most venal and reckless of ends, splintering is tantamount to surrender. Up against oligarchy, all we have is the power latent in our capacity to unite. Race, gender, sexual orientation, class, and nationality shape our distinct needs, experiences, and historical debts. We must hold on to those realities *and* build on a shared interest in challenging concentrated power and wealth, while constructing new structures that are infinitely more fair, and more fun.

Most tasks are easier said than done. In the case of coming together across seemingly intractable barriers, however, the reverse may be true: this one is easier done than said. Stuck in the realm of words, we will never run out of reasons to fracture. But when we take action to change material circumstances—whether trying to unionize our workplaces, or halt evictions, or free political prisoners, or build alternatives to policing, or stop a pipeline, or get an insurgent candidate elected—those tensions do not disappear, but they are often balanced by the recognition of shared interests, the pleasures of camaraderie, and, occasionally, the thrill of victory.

It's more than that, too, as Keeanga-Yamahtta Taylor said to me recently. Drawing on her research as a historian, as well her own experiences as an activist, she pointed out that movements change the people who participate in them. "Struggle helps us see each other," she said. "It helps us break from our individualism and the particularities of our identities." When individuals organize toward a goal, they discover not only that they share interests with people who might look (and vote) very differently from them but also that a new sense of power flows from this alliance. "The struggles we engage in create the potential and possibilities of uniting because it clarifies what's at stake and how we might overcome it," Taylor explained.

This echoes a point made by John Berger in a 1968 essay about the alchemy of large protests, strikes, rallies, and sit-ins. These demonstrations, Berger wrote, don't just demonstrate something to those in power (that people are angry, say, and have the power to disrupt the smooth flow of business). They also demonstrate something to the people gathered on the streets. Those people come to realize that they are not merely individuals, with the limited power of their individual selves, but that "they belong to a class. Belonging to that class ceases to imply a common fate, and implies a common opportunity." Those opportunities manifest in different ways: when individual renters or debtors or workers can't pay the bills, it's a crisis for them and their families. When groups of renters or debtors or workers refuse to pay the bills, or decide to jointly withhold their labor, it's a crisis for their creditors, their landlords, and their bosses.

This is the power of collective organizing: it expands the sense of the possible by expanding the possible "we." It persuades participants that, contrary to what they have been told, their pain is not the result of a failure of character or insufficient hard work. Rather, it is the consequence of economic and social systems precisely designed to produce cruel outcomes, systems that can be changed only if people drop the shame and unite toward a shared goal. When enough people start believing that, it is an awakening in the truest sense of the word—a new group identity is constructed in real time, one wider and more spacious than what existed before.

Freud observed that when a person is confronted by their doppelganger, they become unfamiliar to themselves. On an individual level, that is deeply destabilizing, as I have learned. But I also know, as an activist who has lost herself in causes and crowds, that becoming unfamiliar to oneself need not be a horrifying experience; I have felt it to be transcendent. When we come together in movements working for the scale of change demanded by our times (which is less green juice than Global Green New Deal), it changes us, and we become people who are, if not unfamiliar, then certainly unexpected. Braver. More hopeful. More connected. More able to feel love toward people we barely know.

Something else changes, too: when our actions begin to integrate with our beliefs, when we are doing some of the work that we know needs to be done, we have less need for the various doubles our culture offers up disguised as a good life. The allure of disappearing into our digital avatars wanes—whether Bannon's idea of Ajax embodying himself in real life or the various glowing influencers performing themselves into the ether. As Marx said of religion, doubles are our opiates; we have less need for them when there is less pain and dissonance to escape.

Though rare, I have seen this happen. I have been in factories taken over by their workers and squares occupied by the people and cities in the grips of revolutionary fervor—moments when everyone you meet is your political comrade and lifelong friend rolled into one. And it was there, too, in that U.S. presidential campaign that united millions with three words that began as a slogan and became a kind of social justice prayer: "Not me. *Us.*" The campaign's pivotal moment took place at a rally in Queens, New York, in October 2019. That's when Sanders, in front of a crowd of twenty-five thousand people, did something he hadn't done before. He exhorted everyone there to look to someone in their midst, someone they did not know, "maybe somebody who doesn't look kinda like you, maybe somebody who might be of a different religion than you, maybe they come from a different country . . . My question now to you is are you willing to fight for that person who you don't even know as much as you're willing to fight for yourself?"

Would they fight to end student debt, even if they had no debt? Would they fight for the rights of immigrants, even if they were a citizen themselves? Would they fight for the rights of people who hadn't been born yet to live a life safe from climate breakdown? In the roar of the crowd, people were more than moved—they were altered. Altered by the power represented by the idea of standing up and fighting beyond the narrowest conception of self and identity.

The trouble is, a presidential campaign isn't capable of making good on a promise like that. By definition, an electoral campaign has a finite life span, and it ends when the candidate wins or loses. When Bernie lost and that end arrived, the unselfing we felt so powerfully on the campaign trail seemed to end right along with it. Shut in our homes by the first wave of strict lockdowns, severed from the movement that had held us together, so many of us who had been overcome by the power of "us" felt as if we had just been summarily dropped into a deep sea of "me."

Still, we glimpsed what was possible, and we learned a critical lesson: An election is too fleeting and unstable a container to hold a message as important as "Not me. *Us.*" But that doesn't mean the message was wrong.

Rebuilding the Roads Not Taken

This brings us to one last way of understanding doppelgangers and the messages they carry, one that may be useful in thinking about the difficult collective work that lies ahead. Freud speculated that the figure of the doppelganger recurs in the culture in part because the idea of there being duplicate selves stands in for the vast potentialities that our lives hold. We are the product of choices—made by us, and made by others. But, Freud wrote, those never are the only choices available. There are also "all the possibilities which, had they been realized, might have shaped our destiny, and to which our imagination still clings, all the strivings of the ego that were frustrated by adverse circumstances, all the suppressed acts of volition that fostered the illusion of free will."

Seen in this way, the idea of our duplicates walking around stands in for the roads not taken. Who might we be if the choices that determined our lives had been slightly—or radically—different? What latent versions of ourselves exist but never got the chance to be realized because we took one road rather than another? Or lived in one type of society rather than another?

This is the kind of doppelganger explored in multiverse stories like *Everything Everywhere All at Once*. In the film, Michelle Yeoh plays an overburdened immigrant to the United States who is juggling a husband serving her with divorce papers, a daughter she doesn't know how to love, a father she is disappointing, and a laundry business facing a government audit. But then this downtrodden woman turns out to be a multiverse-traveling superhero who, in one universe, is a glamorous film star, much like Yeoh herself (the directors used real footage of Yeoh on the red carpet for earlier films). The movie, and particularly that footage, underlines how thin the membrane is between the lives any of us end up with and the lives we might have had if circumstances had been different. Having a child is a decision to close off some potential lives and open others. So is taking a job, or not taking one.

Yet we all know (or should know) that the choices available to us are hardly random. They radically expand and contract based on which countries we happened to be born into, which bodies, which genders, which races, which families. It's not only individual lives that hold doppelganger potentialities—so, too, do whole societies. Because we all embody Philip Roth's that-and-this-ness. Kind and callous. Compassionate and out for our narrowest self-interest. Open to one another and harrowingly closed.

My dive into doppelganger culture helped attune me to many examples of that-and-thisness, in myself and in others. Extreme cases, like Hans Asperger, who went from a doctor who was curious and caring toward people like my son, to a man who sent kids who were a little different to their deaths. Or even my own Jewish culture—the way it flipped from a place of such bold and elastic debate to the rigid orthodoxies of with-Israel-or-against-us that are only now beginning to crack. Or the way many people joined the 2020 racial justice uprisings, full of revolutionary hope at the prospects for transforming a society based on principles of equality and care—and then, one year later, some of those very same people seemed unreachable, lost to despair and, at times, conspiracy. "If you have never believed yourself to be entitled to anything, you are less likely to turn against others than you are to turn against yourself," Keeanga-Yamahtta Taylor told me. Each flip is different, but we are all surrounded by evidence of the different people we might have been, and might still become, under slightly different circumstances.

Take those two trucker convoys: the noisy one and the quieter one eight months earlier, which was organized in solidarity with Indigenous communities grieving their stolen children. They made such a stark contrast. So, one way of seeing the two convoys is that one was good and the other bad. One was progress, the other a white-lash. That would be a comforting binary to choose between, and, in way, that's how I told the story. But here is where the ground starts moving: some truckers participated in *both* convoys. In June 2021, they felt sorrow and solidarity; in

February 2022, rage and self-righteousness. They were, like everyone, both that and this. And marginally different circumstances—social, political, economic—brought out different sides of them.

When I try to understand Other Naomi, I see something similar. She, too, is both that and this. As a young writer, she helped inspire countless women to become feminists. In middle age, she took stands that required real moral courage—as when she walked out of that synagogue or shared her platform with people being pounded by missiles. She has also, especially lately, done a great many things that are extremely harmful, and I think many of the reasons behind them are pretty uninteresting: a desire for attention, for ego gratification, for cash; perhaps a drive to prove that she was right and that every person who ever attacked her was wrong. But all of those baser impulses have been greatly exacerbated by a culture that places limitless value on attention and money, while creating information tools that seem designed to turn every person's screwup into an opportunity for public shaming, mockery, abandonment, and humiliation on a scale previously unimaginable.

Which, I suppose, is another way of saying that my doppelganger doesn't just look like me. To borrow from Jordan Peele, she looks like *Us*.

A Struggle Between Care and Uncare

The question I am left with is not the one I hear so frequently about her: How did a person like *that* turn into a person like *this*? But: What kind of system is most likely to light up the best parts of all of us—and sustain the fire beyond a protest, or a summer uprising, or a presidential campaign?

"I believe the starting point for building a more caring society," writes Sally Weintrobe, a psychoanalyst who specializes in the climate crisis, "is never forgetting that care and uncare are inherent parts of us all, and that each seeks expression and dominance over the other." In other words, we (not just those evil *others*) are all in a perpetual struggle with our that-and-thisness. The trouble is, we live in a society that encourages and rewards the uncaring parts of ourselves, while making it hard to care for others outside our immediate family (and often within it) in any sustained way. So, Weintrobe, argues, if we want more people to make better choices—not to shop for useless stuff as a source of solace, not to spread disinformation for clicks and clout, not to see other people's vulnerability and need as a threat to our own interests—we need better structures and systems.

Personally, and to no one's surprise, I think the jury is in on capitalism: it lights up our most uncaring, competitive parts and is failing us on every front that matters. What we need are systems that light up our better selves, the parts of ourselves that want to look outward at a world in crisis and join the work of repair. Systems that make it easier, in ways big and small, for care to win the battle over uncare.

Where do we find models for a society like that? If doppelgangers remind us of the lives we might have lived, the people we might have been, perhaps we could look to the roads not taken.

Red Vienna Lives

Here, then, is one possible portal out of doppelganger world: those ways of organizing societies that were once on the table, that were even tried, and that we could try again. Dig deep enough into any culture, and we will find alternative ways of resisting and living, and even some models that have been carefully protected from the steamroller that calls itself "progress" and "civilization." In this book, I have tried to excavate some of those often forgotten roads-not-taken within my own (Jewish, leftist) tradition. Models like the Jewish Labor Bund and its commitment to being part of a multiethnic alliance of workers. As well as the Bundists' commitment to "hereness," to fighting for justice wherever they were—an idea that has great applicability to our time, when so many millions are being forced to move and find new homes and need a framework to claim their right to "here," wherever that is. Or the democratic socialism that Rosa Luxemburg imagined as the only alternative to barbarism. The ideas that built our world are failing us, but there are always other logics and ideas that can be picked up. Ideas about how to protect distinct cultures, languages, and identities without building fortressed state borders around them. About unity and solidarity among all the peoples forced to carry treacherous shadow doubles. A new story drawing on a patchwork of older stories.

I think about Abram Leon, writing his book *The Jewish Question* as the Nazis closed in, carefully explaining how racist conspiracies change the subject from capitalism to cabals. He wrote those words in his midtwenties knowing that millions of his people had already died and that his ideas might soon be all that was left of him. But he believed in ideas enough to write them down—and that means they are still available to be picked up.

This is not about what-ifs: What if the understanding of Hitler as a doppelganger to the colonial project—as expressed by W. E. B. Du Bois and Aimé Césaire and Walter Benjamin and Abram Leon—had been heeded eight decades ago? It wasn't. But it's not too late to listen now, and to have what we hear inform what we do next. We are told that the way things are is the only way they can be, because every other model has supposedly already been tried, and all have failed. But these ideas about different ways of being and thinking and living did not all fail; rather, many of them fell, crushed by political violence and racial terror. Being crushed is not the same as failing, because what was crushed can be revived, reimagined anew. For Freud, doppelgangers represented paths not taken, choices not made. We could also choose to see them as reminders of roads that can *still* be taken, of pasts that are still pertinent to our present.

The one I think about most is Red Vienna, and the extraordinary child-centered society it built in the rubble of the First World War. That experiment fell under the boot of fascist force—but the spirit that built metaphorical palaces for children in order to tear down prisons was an enormous success. Democratic socialists organized at every level—from the workplace to the neighborhood to elected office—and enacted policies that were staggeringly popular and effective. The armies of care workers. The free diapers and clothing for babies. The light-filled social housing for workers, much of which still stands today. The parks and the swimming pools. The right to nature. The artistic and creative approaches to children's education. The refusal to write off poor or neurodiverse children. The insistent welcoming of refugees and victims of ethnic hatred. The commitment to providing an alternative to the evils of nationalism that were sweeping the continent.

The First World War maimed a generation of soldiers on the field of battle and left them disabled, while also creating countless orphans. It was in that context that Red Vienna's soaring vision transformed an impoverished, disease-ridden city into a beacon of another way of living, of relating, despite imperfections and impairments. Or, more precisely, *because* of imperfections and impairments.

Leanne Betasamosake Simpson, a Michi Saagiig Nishnaabeg writer and artist, said something to me more than a decade ago that I still think of often. She was talking about living in a part of Ontario that has been a site of intense industrial pollution, and the draw of moving to more "pristine" wilderness. But, she said, "when I think of the land as my mother or if I think of it as a familial relationship, I don't hate my mother because she's sick, or because she's been abused. I don't stop visiting her because she's been in an abusive relationship and she has scars and bruises. If anything, you need to intensify that relationship." You visit her even more. I related to this on many levels, as the daughter of a mother who became severely disabled and as the mother of a child with what is officially classified as a disability (though we prefer to see it as a different way of being human). Simpson's formulation calls on us to reckon with the sickened and impaired state of our world, but not to use that as an excuse to walk away in search of perfection. On the contrary, when we are surrounded by need, we are called upon to become better caretakers.

The disability rights theorist Sunaura Taylor has thought and written a lot about what a care-based society might mean in our time of planetary shocks and layered disasters. For Taylor, there are many parallels between the state of our natural world and the states of so many disabled bodies and minds trying to figure out how to live in that world. The ecological crisis is not a simple binary of health and death, she argues. Yes, some species are going extinct and some ecologies no longer support life. But the most prevalent state of our depleted soils and drought-struck riverbeds and diminished wild creatures and overlogged forests is chronic impairment, and the impaired environment is "precarious, dependent, filled with loss and struggle, requiring assistance, accommodation, and creative forms of care." She goes on:

> As a disabled person I recognize this as disability . . . What we live with in the present and will for decades to come, even under the best-case scenarios, is mass ecological disablement of the more than human world, a disablement that is utterly entangled with the disablement of human beings. Given this, it seems vital to consider what forms of care, treatment, and assistance this age of disability will require.

Her challenge is the antithesis of the quest for individual perfection and optimized strength that has done so much damage in the Covid era. It is also markedly different from the ways that pain and trauma are so often performed as currency in the attention economy—as points of separation between us rather than possible connection. Taylor's approach seems particularly urgent, given that long Covid, especially after multiple reinfections, may well play out as a mass disabling event, with a great many formerly healthy, able-bodied people struggling with new limitations for which there is no quick fix.

Taylor does not deny that disability can represent real loss—for both humans and nonhumans—but she calls for an "environmentalism of the injured: the insistence on fighting for a world in which the injured can flourish." This is not charity or good deeds; none of us stand apart from injury. We are all, in some way, damaged by this world, soon to be damaged by it, and/or causing damage. Like everything else we project onto the other, injury and disability will not stay "over there"; they will eventually come for us—our bodies, our families, our beloved places. If we fail to build infrastructures of care, the cruelties and derangements of the Covid era will be only the barest glimpse of the barbarism to come. Taylor is offering a vision for the other side of the portal out of doppelganger culture: a society without sacrificial people and places, a world that no longer requires Shadow Lands. An end to running away from our second bodies. True integration.

Double Vision

I have written about settler colonialism in these pages as a violent and annihilatory practice, which it is. It also strikes me that it must have been frightening for the early European settlers of these lands to come to places they did not know or understand, places that, for them, had no stories, no myths, no sacredness. One of the ways that they attempted to orient themselves was by giving these places that were so new to them the names of other, more familiar places, or giving the new places their own names. The towns in the part of the world where I live mainly bear the names of men who happened to arrive with their families in the mid-1800s and had the audacity to name the land after themselves. Gibsons. Roberts Creek. Wilson Creek.

Gradually, the real names of these places are becoming visible, the names behind and beneath those names. Now the green road signs along the highway often have two names: they will read TS'UKW'UM (WILSON CREEK) or XWESAM (ROBERTS CREEK); the two worlds occupy the same space. It makes for a challenging twinning, holding in one's consciousness the names colonists gave places they barely knew and the names the shíshálh Nation had and never stopped having for these same places. The signs invite those of us who are not Indigenous to have a double consciousness—to remember that we are living in a nation that imposed itself onto other nations and tried to relegate those nations—their people, languages, cultures, ways of knowing—to the Shadow Lands.

The green road signs are supposedly evidence of what our government calls "reconciliation," a small consequence of the Truth and Reconciliation Commission's wrenching investigation into the crimes of the so-called residential schools. These realities are very far from reconciled, but what the signs do is make the absence of reconciliation visible. It's the barest of beginnings, but it gently suggests how we might face some of the hardest and strenuously avoided truths.

◈

As I was concluding the writing of this book, Queen Elizabeth II died at age ninety-six; hers was a good death, an inevitable death, a nontragic death. Much of the English-speaking world went into a strange kind of heart-thumping mourning, the kind of collective mourning our culture has not engaged in for so many other deaths: bad deaths, preventable deaths, premature deaths, tragic deaths. I joked in poor taste with friends in London that at least we in Canada still had a queen—the so-called QAnon Queen who lives not far from me and issues all kinds of ludicrous edicts.

It wasn't really a joke. I'm honestly not sure why anyone should see one queen as absurd and the other as perfectly reasonable. It seems to me that fantasy is at work anytime anyone dares to put on a crown, or draw a line on the earth and declare a new country (especially if it's someone else's country, which it always is). In these lands designed to be doppelgangers of other lands (*New* York, *New* England, *New* France, *New* South Wales, and so on), created by decree by men in various kinds of robes far away, when we start trying to clear away the fact from fiction, fantasy from reality, it will be a good long time before we find something solid. If there is one thing I admire about the diagonalists and other denizens of the Mirror World, it's that they still believe in the idea of changing reality, an ambition that I fear too many on this side of the glass have lost. We shouldn't make up facts like they do, but we should stop treating a great many human-made systems—like monarchies and supreme courts and borders and billionaires—as immutable and unchangeable. Because everything some humans created can be changed by other humans. And if our present systems threaten life to its very core, and they do, then they must be changed.

Vertigo invades when the world we thought we knew no longer holds. The known world is crumbling. That's okay. It was an edifice stitched together with denial and disavowal, with unseeing and unknowing, with mirrors and shadows. It needed to crash. Now, in the rubble, we can make something more reliable, more worthy of our trust, more able to survive the coming shocks.

EPILOGUE: WHO IS THE DOUBLE?

I found myself shaken by a metaphysical doubt. Had *I* been the imposter all the time? Was I the Other?

—Graham Greene, *Ways of Escape*

I have questions for my doppelganger, many of them. About her alliance with Steve Bannon and about his alliances with outright fascists. About the thousands of people who have died of Covid because they feared vaccines would kill them, or kill their babies, or keep them from having babies. About her gun and where she sees it fitting in with all the other guns. About what her followers did to that Black-owned restaurant in Oregon. About why she doesn't appear to be concerned about the repeal of *Roe v. Wade*. About what really happened after she started speaking out about Palestine—and then stopped.

I very much wanted to put these questions to Wolf. I made a list and put in a request for an interview. I followed up with emails to her website, her publisher, and her personal account. I enlisted the help of a mutual friend, one of the few who had not cut her off. I wrote that though we had political disagreements, I could promise a respectful debate. I told her we could air it at *The Intercept*, hoping she would see the advantage while she was promoting a book.

I heard nothing back. At the time, she was appearing on dozens of far-right shows where she was treated the way she seems to see herself: as a prophet, a Cassandra, a persecuted victim of powerful forces, a hero for nonetheless being willing to speak her truth. I didn't seem to have anything she needed.

It's too bad. If she had agreed to the interview, I would have asked her all of those questions, and one more besides. I would have asked her if she remembers me.

It was January 1991; I was twenty, she twenty-eight. *The Beauty Myth* had just come out and made a big splash in the United Kingdom. A faculty member at my college had been impressed and invited this up-and-coming young feminist to speak in the common room of one of our dorms, months before her book would go supernova in North America. As a baby feminist on campus, I got a call asking if I would like to interview Wolf for the campus newspaper, *The Varsity*. I had never interviewed an author before. I said yes.

There were just thirty of us there in the room; that's how early it was in her fame. We sat cross-legged on cheap broadloom carpet listening as Wolf told us that powerful forces had developed unattainable beauty ideals at the precise moment when young women like us were finally on the cusp of breaking through glass ceilings that had held our mothers back. That was why so many of us starved ourselves, gagged ourselves, wasted valuable brain cells hating our bodies or dreaming of plastic surgery instead of doing the work we were there to do. It was exhausting us, distracting us, robbing us of our rightful power and place in the world.

I sat in the front row, transfixed. It wasn't the content, on which I barely focused. There was nothing in my quick read of *The Beauty Myth* that was new or revelatory to someone raised by a second-wave feminist who had made a documentary film about pornography eleven years before. Earlier that year, my friends and I had organized screenings of the documentary *Killing Us Softly*, which carefully deconstructed representations of female beauty and docility in advertising, the same ground covered in *The Beauty Myth*. In the question period, a friend of mine gently challenged Wolf on why she had so little to say about the particular pressures on Black and Asian women to bleach their skin and surgically lift their eyelids in order to conform to Eurocentric beauty ideals. We were already way ahead of her.

None of this took away from her magnetism, though. Because what *was* revelatory was Wolf's person. The fact that these words about beauty were coming from someone so young, confident, and conventionally beautiful. She was like a pot-smoking older sister who had come of age in the freewheeling 1970s, whereas we had been teens in the glossy and suffocating 1980s. It might seem like a small thing, but Wolf didn't dress like a power author. Back then, she wore faded jeans and T-shirts. She had a leather jacket on in her author photo. All of this, and she had written a book that people were paying attention to. A Big Book about Big Ideas.

It had never occurred to me that such a thing was possible. I wasn't one of those kids who mapped out their career paths at puberty. I joined no clubs, had no goals. I got kicked out of high school once, and I flunked out of junior college when my mom got sick, before finally making it to university, where I would drop out again. I had no picture of what my adult life could be beyond a vague sense that I wanted to do something with words that would let me travel and afford a loft of the kind I had seen on the television show *Moonlighting*. But what Wolf had done—write a book of ideas, command an international audience before hitting thirty, all by calling bullshit on patriarchy? That felt like something worth aspiring to.

After the Q&A wrapped up and the mingling began, I introduced myself as the student journalist with a shared first name who was scheduled to interview her.

Wolf locked her eyes on mine. "I knew it was you," she said. "You look like you've just been raped."

I can still feel the jolt her words sent through my body. It was a wildly inappropriate thing to say, I see that now. In retrospect, it was also an early flag about a propensity for jumping to conclusions before having all, or any, of the facts. Thinking back to the certainty with which she spoke those words, I can feel her hunger for intimacy, as well as her compulsion to be in the know, to be the expert in every interaction. Having learned a little since then about the techniques of charismatic leaders in the commingling worlds of spirituality, women's wellness, and conspiracy, I now see it as a textbook power move: I think Wolf was asserting her access to some special vein of knowledge to gain my instant trust.

Absolutely none of this occurred to me at the time, however. Because at the time what it felt like was that Naomi Wolf was seeing directly into my soul.

I did interview her about *The Beauty Myth*, in a vestibule off the common room, and the article took up a full page in *The Varsity*, right across from a piece denouncing the first Gulf War ("U.S. Out of the Gulf: No More Vietnams!"). And we talked about more than the book as well. Her instant-intimacy stunt worked, and I spilled my guts. No, I had not just been raped, not recently. But I was in the middle of a different kind of assault. The first Intifada was raging, and one week earlier I had published an angry article in our campus newspaper about Israeli human rights abuses. As Wolf's writing would do two and half decades later, it had caused a firestorm. There had been furious excommunications and death threats, and thousands of copies of the student newspaper were thrown in the dumpster outside our offices. There was a campaign to get university donors to threaten to withdraw funding unless the paper was sanctioned, and at least one tried, without success. I suppose it was my first experience with what today is called cancel culture.

So Wolf could well have picked up a trauma vibe from me; she just guessed the wrong source. When I explained the situation, she was reassuring. She said I had a story to tell and encouraged me to write it. She said she would help me place it in *The New York Times*; her boyfriend was an editor there. I did write it, and it was rejected by the *Times* (obviously), but it was published in a small feminist journal called *Fireweed*, in a special issue opposing Israel's occupation and colonization of Palestine. It was my first professional publication; I stroked the journal's smooth glossy cover, amazed.

For a little while after we met, Wolf and I stayed in touch. I remember a late-night conversation with her in which I confessed an inability to ever shed my own self-consciousness. It was as if I hovered over myself watching, even in the most intimate situations, like there was a double of me, always criticizing, correcting my flaws. ("I don't know how to be myself. It's like I'm permanently outside myself," Simon tells his doppelganger in *The Double*.) Wolf had an explanation for me, one that seemed to make sense of my guardedness. "That is the male gaze," she said, and I was sure she was right.

We lost touch soon after, and I kept only hazy track of her work—the power-feminism manifesto *Fire with Fire*, the advice to Al Gore on being more alpha. I couldn't relate to this shoulder-pad person she had become, a woman who seemed to want so much of the wrong kind of power.

Wolf may well not remember any of this. Provoking emotional reactions from undergrads was apparently not unusual for her. According to a 2005 article in the *San Francisco Chronicle*, "Her intense energy, deepened with high expectations for her students, can bring young women to tears." I wonder if she used that just-raped line on any of them.

Yet even as I outgrew Wolf as a feminist role model, the feeling I had in that campus common room endured—the revelation about what, and when, an author could be. When I was twenty-six, I dropped out of university (for the second time) to write a book about anti-democratic corporate power and the nascent movements springing up in opposition. My father was horrified that I was giving up on my degree (again), but I was convinced that if I wrote that book in that moment, it would leave a mark on the world, just as I had seen happen with *The Beauty Myth*.

That belief did not waver, even when I racked up a stack of rejection letters from U.S. publishers. Even when an editor in a glass corner office overlooking the Hudson River leaned back in her chair and explained, "I want to read this book, but readers want memoirs of eating disorders." I was enraged by the idea that the only acceptable realm of expertise for young women writers was our own bodies. On my way out, she handed me galleys for just such an eating-disorder memoir, a book she clearly hoped would be the next *Beauty Myth*. It wasn't—but I suppose *No Logo* kind of was.

I sometimes wonder what gave me the idea that I had a right to take up so much space, to make such big and bold claims, so young. Where did that audacity come from? My mother deserves more credit than I ever give her: I grew up surrounded by courageous, creative feminists, even if they didn't think much about reaching beyond the movement. There were teachers, a couple of really good ones. But, if I'm honest, Wolf played a role, too—that accident of finding myself in her intense orbit just at the point when I was ready to imagine a different kind of future for myself.

When I look at my first author photo on the inside back flap of *No Logo*, in which I had long, wavy brown hair, I wince at how much I must have subconsciously tried to resemble the press photo of her that ran in *The Varsity* a decade earlier. I guess that means that, when she reads these words, she would be fully within her rights to react as Fake Roth does when he claims of Real Roth, "*He's* the fake, *that's* the irony—*he's the fucking double*, a dishonest impostor and fucking hypocritical fake."

I have interrogated this, tried to pry apart my gratitude for the role she played then from my feelings—fear, revulsion, fascination, anger, concern—for the role she plays today. If she did act as a very different kind of mirror all those years ago, one that helped me see what I could become, what do I owe her now? Silence? Respect? Lifelong loyalty?

I don't think so. If there is anything this journey has taught me, it's that identity is not fixed. Not mine. Not Wolf's. Not even the barrier between our two identities. It's all fluid, shifting around and doubling constantly. Negotiating that doubling—between our younger selves and our older selves, between our public selves and our private selves, between our living selves and our dying selves—is a part of what it means to be human. A bigger part of being human, though, and certainly of living a good life, is not about how we make ourselves in those shifting sands of self. It's about what we make together.

Besides, I'm not named after Ruth, the loyal one, worth seven sons. I'm named after Naomi, the one who did what it took to survive.

NOTES

More extensive endnotes, along with direct links to online sources, can be found at naomiklein.org.

Introduction: Off-Brand Me

4 *More than six hundred people died*: Michael Egilson, "Extreme Heat and Human Mortality: A Review of Heat-Related Deaths in B.C. in Summer 2021," Report to the Chief Coroner of British Columbia, June 7, 2022, 4; Stefan Labbé, "Heat Dome Primed B.C. Coastlines to Resemble Subtropical East Asia, Says Researcher," *North Shore News*, April 29, 2022.

6 *"that species of the frightening"*: Sigmund Freud, "The Uncanny," in *The Uncanny*, trans. David McLintock (London: Penguin, 2003), 124. Freud's essay was originally published in 1919.

6 *"may identify himself with another"*: Freud, "The Uncanny," 142.

9 *"a mode of being"*: *Emilio Uranga's* Analysis of Mexican Being*: A Translation and Critical Introduction*, trans. Carlos Alberto Sánchez (1952; repr. London: Bloomsbury Academic, 2021), 180.

10 *"It's too ridiculous"*: Philip Roth, *Operation Shylock: A Confession* (New York: Simon & Schuster, 1993), 55.

13 *"Chaos is merely order"*: José Saramago, *The Double*, trans. Margaret Jull Costa (Orlando, Fla.: Harcourt Books, 2004), vii.

Part One: Double Life

15 *"I have found a way"*: Jules Gleeson, "Judith Butler: 'We Need to Rethink the Category of Woman,'" *The Guardian*, September 7, 2021.

1. Occupied

18 *You could look it up*: Naomi Klein, "Occupy Wall Street: The Most Important Thing in the World Now," *The Nation*, October 6, 2011.

19 *"I found out what it was"*: Naomi Wolf, "The Shocking Truth About the Crackdown on Occupy," *The Guardian*, November 25, 2011.

19 *"they had a first amendment right"*: Naomi Wolf, "Naomi Wolf: How I Was Arrested at Occupy Wall Street," *The Guardian*, October 19, 2011.

20 *"When you connect the dots"*: Wolf, "The Shocking Truth About the Crackdown on Occupy."

20 *"Sadly, Americans this week"*: Wolf, "The Shocking Truth About the Crackdown on Occupy."

21 *"Her partner, the film producer Avram Ludwig"*: Matt Wells, "Occupy Wall St: Naomi Wolf Condemns 'Stalinist' Erosion of Protest Rights," *The Guardian*, October 19, 2011.

21 *"not who he purports to be"*: Joe Coscarelli, "Naomi Wolf Thinks Edward Snowden and His Sexy Girlfriend Might Be Government Plants," *New York Magazine*, June 14, 2013; Naomi Wolf, "My Creeping Concern That the NSA Leaker Is Not Who He Purports to Be . . . ," Facebook Notes, posted June 15, 2013, updated March 14, 2021.

21 *"mass lockdowns"*: Naomi Wolf, Facebook post, September 30, 2014.

21 *possibly not real murders*: Max Fisher, "The Insane Conspiracy Theories of Naomi Wolf," *Vox*, October 5, 2014.

21 *"intelligence service"*: Naomi Wolf, "A Tale of Two Rape Charges," *The Great Debate* (blog), Reuters, May 23, 2011.

21 *potentially fraudulent*: "Naomi Wolf Compiles Ballot Paper Complaints," *The (Glasgow) Herald*, September 27, 2014.

21 *not the demands*: "Progressive Feminist Naomi Wolf Rips the Green New Deal as 'Fascism'—'I WANT a Green New Deal' but 'This One Is a Straight Up Power Grab,'" *Climate Depot*, February 21, 2021.

22 *"aluminum on a global level"*: Tim Skillet @Gurdur, tweet, March 24, 2018, Twitter.

22 *"It was amazing to go to Belfast"*: Naomi Wolf @naomirwolf, tweet, July 5, 2019, 1:13 a.m., in Séamas O'Reilly @shockproofbeats, tweet, April 5, 2020, 4:27 a.m., Twitter.

22 *"What little girls learn"*: Naomi Wolf, *The Beauty Myth: How Images of Beauty Are Used Against Women* (1990; repr. New York: Perennial, 2002), 157–158.

22 *There were major statistical errors*: Casper Schoemaker, "A Critical Appraisal of the Anorexia Statistics in the Beauty Myth: Introducing Wolf's Overdo and Lie Factor (WOLF)," *Eating Disorders* 12, no. 2 (2004): 97–102.

22 *"the most important feminist publication"*: Alice Steinbach, "WOLF VS. 'BEAUTY MYTH' Feminist Sees Conspiracy in Stress on Appearance," *Baltimore Sun*, June 23, 1991.

23 *"The ruling elite"*: Wolf, *The Beauty Myth*, 25.

23 *"will to power"*: Naomi Wolf, *Fire with Fire: The New Female Power and How to Use It* (London: Chatto & Windus, 1993), xviii.

24 "Seventeen *magazine level of thinker"*: Camille Paglia, "Hillary, Naomi, Susan and Rush. Sheesh!," *Salon*, November 17, 1999.

25 *from a "beta male" to an "alpha male"*: Michael Duffy and Karen Tumulty, "Campaign 2000: Gore's Secret Guru," *Time*, November 8, 1999.

25 *"Ms. Wolf is the moral equivalent"*: Maureen Dowd, "Liberties; The Alpha-Beta Macarena," *New York Times*, November 3, 1999.

25 *"a year of chaos"*: Naomi Wolf, *The Treehouse: Eccentric Wisdom from My Father on How to Live, Love, and See* (New York: Simon & Schuster, 2005), 13.

25 *"My father had raised me"*: Wolf, *The Treehouse*, 25.

25 *"heart" mattered "over facts, numbers, and laws"*: Wolf, *The Treehouse*, 27.

25 *given the creative way*: Naomi Wolf, "Dr. Naomi Wolf Confronts Yale for Crimes Against Students," *DailyClout* (video), December 5, 2022.

26 *"Destroy the box"*: Wolf, *The Treehouse*, 9.

26 *"Before you can even think about"*: Wolf, *The Treehouse*, 72.

26 *"Wolf is a cloud truther"*: Eve Andrews, "The Real Fear Behind Climate Conspiracy Theories," *Grist*, April 6, 2018.

27 *"If the Naomi be Klein"*: See, for example @markpopham, tweet, October 23, 2019, 6:18 a.m., Twitter. The origins of this poem are unclear and there are several versions of it, so it is not necessarily attributable to the above handle.

28 *"Someone, out in this world"*: Grace Ebert, "I'm Not a Look-Alike: Hundreds of Unrelated Doppelgängers Sit for François Brunelle's Uncanny Portraits," *Colossal*, February 9, 2022.

28 *"detestable coincidence"*: Edgar Allan Poe, "William Wilson," *Burton Gentleman's Magazine & American Monthly Review* 5, no. 4 (October 1839): 208.

28 *"above a very low whisper" . . . "arch-enemy and evil genius"*: Poe, "William Wilson," 207, 212.

2. Enter Covid, the Threat Multiplier

31 *"vaccinated people's urine/feces"*: Naomi Wolf @naomirwolf, tweet, June 4, 2021, Twitter.

32 *"conspiracy without the theory"*: Russell Muirhead and Nancy L. Rosenblum, *A Lot of People Are Saying: The New Conspiracism and the Assault on Democracy* (Princeton, N.J.: Princeton University Press, 2019), 19.

32 *"a genocide"*: Naomi Wolf, "Dear Friends, Sorry to Announce a Genocide," *Outspoken with Dr Naomi Wolf*, Substack, May 29, 2022.

32 *nearly doubling her following*: Before Covid, Wolf had around 70,000 followers; by May 2021, when she was deplatformed, she had 138,000. Naomi Wolf @naomirwolf, web capture of Twitter account, May 15, 2021.

32 *"local leaders are dying too"*: Naomi Wolf @DrNaomiRWolf, Gettr post, May 16, 2022.

33 *"demonic"*: Steve Bannon, host, "Chris Wray Lies on 60 Minutes," *War Room: Pandemic* (podcast), episode 1,808, April 25, 2022, at 33:59–34:06, posted on Apple Podcasts.

33 *"transnational group of bad actors"*: Naomi Wolf, "Facing the Beast," *Outspoken with Dr Naomi Wolf*, Substack, July 17, 2022.

33 *"hundreds of women"*: Geoff Brumfiel, "The Life Cycle of a Covid-19 Vaccine Lie," National Public Radio, July 20, 2021.

34 *"a very highly followed influencer"*: Brumfiel, "The Life Cycle of a Covid-19 Vaccine Lie."

34 *"bleeding between [her] period"*: Morgan Yew @weynagrom, tweet, May 23, 2021, Twitter, video 9 of 25, at 0:24.

34 *"They are sterilizing an entire generation"*: Yew, tweet, May 23, 2021.

34 *"one foot in the grave"*: Yew, tweet, May 23, 2021.

35 *"autocratic tyrants"*: "Naomi Wolf Sounds Alarm at Growing Power of 'Autocratic Tyrants,'" *Tucker Carlson Tonight*, Fox News, February 22, 2021.

35 *"This is your periodic reminder"*: Naomi Klein @NaomiAKlein, tweet, February 23, 2021, Twitter.

35 *"Still here, sadly"*: Naomi Klein @NaomiAKlein, tweet, June 5, 2021, Twitter.

36 *"a much-hyped medical crisis"*: Naomi Wolf, 2021 introduction to *The End of America: Letter of Warning to a Young Patriot* (White River Junction, Vt.: Chelsea Green Publishing, 2021), xv.

36 *the "guise" of a medical emergency*: "Naomi Wolf Sounds Alarm at Growing Power of 'Autocratic Tyrants.'"

36 *"I have relegated"*: Richard Gillard @RickyBaby321, Gettr post, February 26, 2022.

36 *"We can't have two of you"*: *Dual*, directed by Michael Ragen (RLJE Films, 2022).

37 *"An uncanny effect"*: Sigmund Freud, *The Uncanny*, trans. David McLintock (London: Penguin, 2003), 150.

38 *"I'm not myself, you see"*: Lewis Carroll, *Alice's Adventures in Wonderland* (1865; repr. Vancouver: Engage Classic, 2020), 35.

38 *"Those fears distract people"*: Benedict Carey, "A Theory About Conspiracy Theories," *New York Times*, September 28, 2020.

40 *"Oh Jesus"*: Tahar @laseptiemewilay, tweet, March 30, 2021, 7:12 p.m., Twitter.

41 *"our friends, professional colleagues"*: Richard Seymour, *The Twittering Machine* (London: Indigo Press, 2019), chapter 1, part III.

41 *"When a human being becomes"*: Zadie Smith, "Generation Why?," *New York Review*, November 25, 2010.

45 *"Don't call me Naomi"*: Ruth 1:20 (New International Version).

45 *"Where you go, I will go"*: Ruth 1:16 (New International Version).

3. My Failed Brand, or Call Me by Her Name

46 *"Naomi Klein should sue"*: Dan Hon @hondanhon, tweet, May 8, 2021, Twitter.

46 *"Stretching Capacity Too Thin"*: "Brand Dilution: Definition, Causes and Examples," *MediaValet*, March 2, 2021.

47 *"likely to cause confusion and dilution"*: "'Satan Shoes' to Be Recalled as Nike Agrees to Settle Lawsuit," BBC News, April 9, 2021.

48 *"Regardless of age"*: Tom Peters, "The Brand Called You," *Fast Company*, August 31, 1997.

48 *the magazine even published a mea culpa*: David Lidsky, "Me Inc.: The Rethink," *Fast Company*, March 1, 2005.

48 *"a full flight of TV and print ads"*: Peters, "The Brand Called You."

50 *"historically anachronistic"*: Stuart Hall, *The Hard Road to Renewal: Thatcherism and the Crisis of the Left* (London: Verso, 1988), 276.

50 *"caught in a structure"*: Wendy Brown, "Resisting Left Melancholy," *boundary 2* 26, no. 3 (Autumn 1999): 26.

54 *"The (Safe for Work) Self"*: Alice Marwick, *Status Update: Celebrity, Publicity, and Branding in the Social Media Age* (New Haven, Conn.: Yale University Press, 2013), 163.

55 *"a wish defense"*: Otto Rank, *The Double: A Psychoanalytic Study* (Chapel Hill: University of North Carolina Press, 1971), 86.

55–56 *"The double was originally an insurance"*: Sigmund Freud, "The Uncanny," in *The Uncanny*, trans. David McLintock (London: Penguin, 2003), 142. Freud's essay was originally published in 1919.

56 *"becomes the uncanny harbinger of death"*: Freud, "The Uncanny," 142.

57 *"There is a fake 'Naomirwolf' on Telegram"*: Naomi Wolf, "Pixels, Bots and Human Cruelty," *Outspoken with Dr Naomi Wolf*, Substack, January 13, 2023.

59 *"Now who's more real"*: *American Dharma*, directed by Errol Morris (Utopia, 2018).

59 *"People take on these digital selves"*: *American Dharma*.

59 *"I want Dave in Accounting to be Ajax"*: Jennifer Senior, "American Rasputin," *The Atlantic*, June 6, 2022.

59 *"Lee Seong-yoon"*: Timothy W. Martin and Dasl Yoon, "These Campaigns Hope 'Deepfake' Candidates Help Get Out the Vote," *Wall Street Journal*, March 8, 2022.

60 *"a bit creepy"*: Martin and Yoon, "These Campaigns Hope 'Deepfake' Candidates Help Get Out the Vote."

60 *"These digital doppelgangers"*: Mark Sutherland, "ABBA's 'Voyage' CGI Extravaganza Is Everything It's Cracked Up to Be, and More: 'Concert' Review," *Variety*, May 27, 2022.

60 *"to take the sting out"*: Anjana Ahuja, "'Grief Tech' Avatars Aim to Take the Sting Out of Death," *Financial Times*, December 20, 2022.

61 *landmark 2015 book*: Simone Browne, *Dark Matters: On the Surveillance of Blackness* (Durham, N.C.: Duke University Press, 2015).

61 *"This is a difficult archive to write about"*: Browne, *Dark Matters*, 91–92.

61 *"a biometric technology"*: Browne, *Dark Matters*, 91.

61 *"Branding in the transatlantic slave trade"*: Browne, *Dark Matters*, 91.

61 *"an object among other objects"*: Frantz Fanon, *Black Skin, White Masks*, trans. Richard Philcox (New York: Grove Press, 2008), 89.

61 *"relate to our self in the third person"*: Nancy Colier, "The Branding of the Self," *Psychology Today*, August 15, 2012.

62 *"A foolish consistency"*: Ralph Waldo Emerson, "Self-Reliance," in *Ralph Waldo Emerson: Essays and Journals*, ed. Lewis Mumford (New York: Doubleday, 1968), 95.

63 *"is a machine"*: Lilly Singh, "I'll See You Soon . . . ," YouTube, November 12, 2018, at 2:43.

64 *"Come for the nectar of approval"*: Richard Seymour, *The Twittering Machine* (London: Indigo Press, 2019), chapter 2, part IX.

64 *"several dozen executions"*: Alison Flood, "Naomi Wolf Accused of Confusing Child Abuse with Gay Persecution in Outrages," *The Guardian*, February 8, 2021.

65 *University courses, seeking to instill*: Matthew Sweet, "Blind to Bestiality and Paedophilia: Why Naomi Wolf's Latest Book Is Its Own Outrage," *The Telegraph*, February 5, 2021.

65 *"off the chessboard"*: Ankita Mukhopadhyay, "Naomi Wolf Talks Homophobia, Feminism and 'Outrages,'" *Fair Observer*, January 8, 2020.

65 *"dialogue between me and myself"*: Hannah Arendt, *The Origins of Totalitarianism* (1951; repr. Cleveland, Ohio: Meridian Books, 1962), 476.

66 *"making present to my mind"*: Hannah Arendt, "Truth and Politics," in *The Portable Hannah Arendt*, ed. Peter Baehr (New York: Penguin, 2000), 556.

4. Meeting Myself in the Woods

68 *It depicts a couple*: There have been multiple versions of *How They Met Themselves*: a drawing dated 1851 (which purportedly was lost or destroyed), a pen-and-ink re-creation of the 1851 design dated 1860, and a watercolor replica of the 1860 drawing dated 1864. Here I'm referencing the 1864 watercolor version. See Ford Madox Hueffer, *Rossetti: A Critical Essay on His Art* (London: Duckworth, 1902).

69 *"People with healthy self-esteem"*: bell hooks, *Rock My Soul: Black People and Self-Esteem* (New York: Atria Books, 2003), 92.

69 *"I'm walking around"*: George Yancy and bell hooks, "bell hooks: Buddhism, the Beats and Loving Blackness", *New York Times*, December 10, 2015.

69 *"substance of books"*: Heather Williams, "bell hooks Speaks Up" *The Sandspur* (Rollins College, Winter Park, Fla.), March 26, 2013, 1.

69 *"white supremacist capitalist patriarchy"*: bell hooks, *Feminist Theory: From Margin to Center* (Boston: South End Press, 1984), 51.

69 *"avoid using the phrase"*: bell hooks, *Feminist Theory: From Margin to Center* (Boston: South End Press, 1984), 29.

70 *"what happens if we don't take care of ourselves"*: "bell hooks & john a. powell: Belonging Through Connection," interview at the Othering & Belonging Conference, April 2015, YouTube, at 6:00–6:40.

71 *"too ridiculous"*: Philip Roth, *Operation Shylock: A Confession* (New York: Simon & Schuster, 1993), 55.

71 *"the state penetrating their body against their will"*: Jeffrey Tucker, "The Pathogenic Excuse for Attacking Liberty: An Interview with Naomi Wolf," *Brownstone Institute* (video/podcast), May 9, 2022, at 10:31–11:21.

71 *Charlie Chaplin's daring satire*: *The Great Dictator*, directed by Charles Chaplin (United Artists, 1940).

5. They Know About Cell Phones

75 *children had lost the reflex to smile*: Matthew Gertz, "Fox Keeps Hosting Pandemic Conspiracy Theorist Naomi Wolf," Media Matters for America, April 20, 2021.

75 *"vaccines w nanopatticles"*: Matthew Gertz @MattGertz, tweet, February 26, 2021, Twitter.

75 *quarantining the feces*: David Connett, "Naomi Wolf Banned from Twitter for Spreading Vaccine Myth," *The Guardian*, June 5, 2021.

76 *"Whatever Happened to Naomi Wolf?" articles*: Liza Featherstone, "The

Madness of Naomi Wolf," *New Republic*, June 10, 2021; Ian Burrell, "Naomi Wolf's Slide from Feminist, Democratic Party Icon to the 'Conspiracist Whirlpool,'" *Business Insider*, June 5, 2021; Rebecca Onion, "A Modern Feminist Classic Changed My Life. Was It Actually Garbage?," *Slate*, March 30, 2021.

76 *"Great Reset" campaign*: "CommonPass—Travelling the World in the Covid Era," World Economic Forum, video, August 24, 2020.

76 *approaching a "cliff"*: "Watch Dr Naomi Wolf Discuss 'Why Vaccine Passports Equal Slavery Forever,'" DailyClout channel on YouTube, March 30, 2021, at 15:30.

76 *Great Replacement theory*: Brian Stelter, "ADL Calls on Fox News to Fire Tucker Carlson Over Racist Comments About 'Replacement' Theory," CNN, April 9, 2021.

77 *extreme rhetoric*: "Naomi Wolf on the New American Coup," Big Think channel on YouTube, April 23, 2012; Naomi Wolf, "Fascist America, in 10 Easy Steps," *The Guardian*, April 24, 2007.

77 *"a tyrannical totalitarian platform"*: "Watch Dr Naomi Wolf Discuss 'Why Vaccine Passports Equal Slavery Forever,'" at 15:22.

77 *"most serious warning"*: "Watch Dr Naomi Wolf Discuss 'Why Vaccine Passports Equal Slavery Forever,'" at 0:53; Paul Vallely, host, "The Stand Up America US Show," *Don Smith Show* (podcast), episode 35, May 16, 2022, at 40:01, posted on Rumble.

77 *"enslaves a billion people"*: "Watch Dr Naomi Wolf Discuss 'Why Vaccine Passports Equal Slavery Forever,'" at 4:23.

77 *allow a "tyrannical" state*: "Watch Dr Naomi Wolf Discuss 'Why Vaccine Passports Equal Slavery Forever,'" at 1:58, 2:58, and 15:21.

78 *"If you're talking about staging a protest"*: "Watch Dr Naomi Wolf Discuss 'Why Vaccine Passports Equal Slavery Forever,'" at 7:57.

78 *"two-tiered society"*: Tim Hains, "Naomi Wolf: Mandatory Vaccine Passport Could Lead to the End of Human Liberty in the West," *RealClearPolitics*, March 29, 2021, at 2:45; "Watch Dr Naomi Wolf Discuss 'Why Vaccine Passports Equal Slavery Forever,'" at 7:57.

78 *"a dissident"*: "Watch Dr Naomi Wolf Discuss 'Why Vaccine Passports Equal Slavery Forever,'" at 6:55.

78 *"bioweapon"*: "His Glory Presents: Take FiVe w/ Dr. Naomi Wolf," *His Glory*, July 28, 2022, at 28:54.

78 *"It's not about the vaccine"*: Hains, "Naomi Wolf: Mandatory Vaccine Passport," at 2:06.

78 *"machine reading assesses"*: "Watch Dr Naomi Wolf Discuss 'Why Vaccine Passports Equal Slavery Forever,'" at 5:37–5:58.

78 *tracking your search histories*: "Watch Dr Naomi Wolf Discuss 'Why Vaccine Passports Equal Slavery Forever,'" at 8:27.

78 *"has the power to turn off your life"*: Hains, "Naomi Wolf: Mandatory Vaccine Passport," at 3:05.

79 *"IBM has a horrible history"*: Hains, "Naomi Wolf: Mandatory Vaccine Passport," at 3:12.

79 *"a tweak of the back end"*: "Watch Dr Naomi Wolf Discuss 'Why Vaccine Passports Equal Slavery Forever,'" at 5:26.

79 *"geolocate you"*: "Watch Dr Naomi Wolf Discuss 'Why Vaccine Passports Equal Slavery Forever,'" at 8:23.

79 *"the technology itself"*: Alexis Hancock, email to author, August 26, 2022.

79 *a couple of instances*: Kenith Png, "Police Would Not Agree to Stop Accessing COVID SafeWA App Data, Premier Mark McGowan Says," ABC News, June 15, 2021.

80 *"We cannot rely on pharmaceutical technology alone"*: Beatrice Adler-Bolton and Death Panel, "Mask Off," *New Inquiry*, April 28, 2022.

81 *entire world could have been vaccinated*: William Horobin, "It Would Cost $50 Billion to Vaccinate the World, OECD Says," *Bloomberg*, December 1, 2021.

81 *$37 billion from the Covid vaccine in 2021*: Julia Kollewe, "Pfizer Accused of Pandemic Profiteering as Profits Double," *The Guardian*, February 8, 2022.

81 *just 7.5 percent of Africans*: Maggie Fick and Edward McAllister, "COVID Shots Are Finally Arriving, but Africa Can't Get Them All into Arms," Reuters, December 6, 2021.

82 *"a failure of catastrophic proportions"*: "COVID-19: Pfizer Reports Massive Revenues Whilst Failing to Vaccinate Billions," Amnesty International, November 2, 2021.

82 *"It's not going to work"*: Stephanie Nebehay and Josephine Mason, "WHO Warns Against Vaccine Hoarding as Poorer Countries Go Without," Reuters, December 9, 2021.

82 *"the viral underclass"*: Steven W. Thrasher, *The Viral Underclass: The Human Toll When Inequality and Disease Collide* (New York: Celadon Books, 2022).

83 *IBM's collaboration*: Hains, "Naomi Wolf: Mandatory Vaccine Passport," at 3:12.

83 *"Speaking as a tech CEO"*: "Watch Dr Naomi Wolf Discuss 'Why Vaccine Passports Equal Slavery Forever,'" at 5:06; Hains, "Naomi Wolf: Mandatory Vaccine Passport," at 2:01.

83 *the site averaged*: Domain overview for DailyClout, January 2017–April 2021, Semrush, accessed July 2022.

83 *"The founders did not create liberty for America"*: Naomi Wolf, "Fake Patriotism," *Huffington Post*, November 2, 2008.

84 *referenced "the CCP"*: "Watch Dr Naomi Wolf Discuss 'Why Vaccine Passports Equal Slavery Forever.'"

84 *"This is literally the end of human liberty"*: Hains, "Naomi Wolf: Mandatory Vaccine Passport," at 1:47.

84 *"there won't be capitalism"*: "Watch Dr Naomi Wolf Discuss 'Why Vaccine Passports Equal Slavery Forever,'" at 13:35.

84 *"CCP-type conditioning"*: "Watch Dr Naomi Wolf Discuss 'Why Vaccine Passports Equal Slavery Forever,'" at 12:57.

84 *"weakening the West"*: "Watch Dr Naomi Wolf Discuss 'Why Vaccine Passports Equal Slavery Forever,'" at 10:22.

84 *"un-American"*: "Robert Kennedy Jr Slams the Corrupt System of Big Pharma, Dr Fauci and the F.D.A.—Video," DailyClout, May 26, 2022, at 9:36.

84 *"model legislation"*: Steve Bannon, host, "The Dirty Dozen: 12 Most Dangerous People in America," *War Room: Pandemic* (podcast), episode 1,120, July 24, 2021, at 18:32.

84 *urged me to "study" it*: Correspondence with author, April 3, 2021.

85 *"warrior" and her "courage"*: Multiple commenters, "Watch Dr Naomi Wolf Discuss 'Why Vaccine Passports Equal Slavery Forever.'"

85 *"the mark of the beast"*: Multiple commenters, "Watch Dr Naomi Wolf Discuss 'Why Vaccine Passports Equal Slavery Forever."

85 *"the vaccine passport is NOT"*: Matthew Giffin, comment, "Watch Dr Naomi Wolf Discuss 'Why Vaccine Passports Equal Slavery Forever.'"

85 *"It is obvious to me"*: Matthew Giffin, comment, "Watch Dr Naomi Wolf Discuss 'Why Vaccine Passports Equal Slavery Forever.'"

85 *"Go to China and stay"*: @Scipio, comment, "Watch Dr Naomi Wolf Discuss 'Why Vaccine Passports Equal Slavery Forever.'"

85 *In the Maine House of Representatives*: Representative Shelley Rudnicki, Facebook post (image), May 10, 2021; Associated Press, "Republican Barred from Inviting Guests into State House," *Associated Press News*, May 11, 2021.

85 *one of the leading states . . . vaccine passports were akin*: Craig Mauger, "Michigan Leads the Nation in New COVID Cases, According to CDC Data," *Detroit News*, November 16, 2021; Bruce Walker, "Michigan House Oversight Committee Considers Legislation to Ban Vaccine Passports," *Center Square*, May 6, 2021; Dave Boucher, "Michigan Lawmakers Invite COVID-19 Conspiracy Theorist to Testify on Bill to Ban Vaccine Passports," *PolitiFact*, May 6, 2021.

86 *"the infrastructure, globally"*: Jason Horowitz, "Steve Bannon Is Done Wrecking the American Establishment. Now He Wants to Destroy Europe's," *New York Times*, March 9, 2018.

86 *"good enough"*: Jennifer Senior, "American Rasputin," *The Atlantic*, June 6, 2022.

87 *"surveillance capitalism"*: Shoshana Zuboff, *The Age of Surveillance Capitalism: The Fight for a Human Future at the New Frontier of Power* (London: Profile Books, 2019).

87 *Israeli-designed spyware*: Stephanie Kirchgaessner et al., "Revealed: Leak Uncovers Global Abuse of Cyber-surveillance Weapon," *The Guardian*, July 18, 2021.

87–88 *"nanny cams" . . . Ring doorbell footage . . . "God View" . . . personal photos . . . period-tracking apps*: Allyson Chiu, "She Installed a Ring Camera in Her Children's Room for 'Peace of Mind.' A Hacker Accessed It and Harassed Her 8-Year-Old Daughter," *Washington Post*, December 12, 2019; Alfred Ng, "Amazon Gave Ring Videos to Police Without Owners' Permission," *Politico*, July 13, 2022; Alex Hern, "Uber Employees 'Spied on Ex-partners, Politicians and Beyoncé,'" *The Guardian*, December 13, 2016; Johana Bhuiyan and Charlie Warzel, "'God View': Uber Investigates Its Top New York Executive for Privacy Violations," *BuzzFeed News*, November 18, 2014; Kashmir Hill, "The Secretive Company That Might End Privacy as We Know It," *New York Times*, January 18, 2020; Rina Torchinsky, "How Period Tracking Apps and Data Privacy Fit into a Post-Roe v. Wade Climate," National Public Radio, June 24, 2022.

89 *"replication as travesty"*: The Red Hand Files, Nick Cave, Issue #218, January 2023.

90 *"CCP-style social credit score system"*: Paul Vallely, host, "The Stand Up America US Show," *Don Smith Show* (podcast), episode 35, May 16, 2022, at 40:01, posted on Rumble.

91 *"they start purging your enemies"*: Adam Creighton, "The Plague Afflicting Liberal Democracy," *The Australian*, June 5, 2021.

91 *"deprivatization"*: Ben Tarnoff, *Internet for the People: The Fight for Our Digital Future* (London: Verso Books, 2022).

91 *"To build a better internet" . . . "What is at stake"*: Tarnoff, *Internet for the People*, xv, 33.

92 *"the digital town square"*: Jean Burgess, "The 'Digital Town Square'? What Does It Mean When Billionaires Own the Online Spaces Where We Gather?," *The Conversation*, April 27, 2022.

92 *"From the edges to the core"*: Tarnoff, *Internet for the People*, 58.

93 *"stay ahead of the censors"*: Steve Bannon, host, "Breaking Down the Data That the Establishment Fears," *War Room: Pandemic* (podcast), episode 143, September 22, 2022, posted on Amazon Music.

6. Diagonal Lines

96 *"better . . . than seven sons"*: Ruth 4:15 (New International Version).

96 *"uncover his feet and lie down"*: Ruth 3:4 (New International Version).

98 *"a horrible human being"*: Adam Creighton, "The Plague Afflicting Liberal Democracy," *The Australian*, June 5, 2021.

98 *"Ding dong the witch is dead"*: Jet @Jet0o, tweet, June 5, 2021, Twitter.

99 *"the Twitter killer"*: Steve Bannon @SteveBannon, Gettr post, July 4, 2021.

99 *soldiers in his "cavalry"*: Steve Bannon @SteveBannon, Gettr post, October 29, 2022.

99 *"profoundly" disagree with Trump "ideologically"*: Adam Rawnsley, "Anti Vaxxer Naomi Wolf Joins Trump's Doomed Tech Suit," *Daily Beast*, July 28, 2021 (updated July 30, 2021).

100 *"going to school with Jews"*: Nancy Dillon, "Anti-Semitic Trump Campaign CEO Stephen Bannon Not a Big Fan of 'Whiny Brat' Jews, Ex-wife Says," *New York Daily News*, August 27, 2016.

101 *"conspiracy singularity"*: Anna Merlan, "The Conspiracy Singularity Has Arrived," *Vice News*, July 17, 2020.

102 *"Born in part from transformations"*: William Callison and Quinn Slobodian, "Coronapolitics from the Reichstag to the Capitol," *Boston Review*, January 12, 2021.

103 *"media darling"*: Naomi Wolf, "The Last Stage of a Tyrannical Takeover—Interview with Naomi Wolf," interview by Joseph Mercola, June 1, 2022.

103 *"I never thought I would be talking to you"*: Tucker Carlson, "Naomi Wolf Sounds Alarm at Growing Power of 'Autocratic Tyrants.'"

103 *one of Britain's most vocal climate change deniers*: James Delingpole, "'Climategate Was Fake News,' Lies the BBC . . . ," *Breitbart*, July 11, 2019, posted on the Internet Archive's Wayback Machine.

103 *"This is so unlikely"*: James Delingpole, "Naomi Wolf," *The James Delingpole Podcast*, May 3, 2021, 0:25–1:04.

103 *"I spent years thinking you were the devil"*: Steve Bannon, host, "Not Science Fiction . . . Dr. Naomi Wolf Reveals Dangers of Vaccine Passports," *War Room: Pandemic* (podcast), episode 874, April 14, 2021, at 13:43–14:03, posted on Rumble.

104 *comparing Covid health measures*: Joseph Mercola, host, "Best of Series—Ten Tyrannical Steps," *Take Control of Your Health* (podcast), May 4, 2022; Bannon, "Not Science Fiction . . . Dr. Naomi Wolf Reveals Dangers of Vaccine Passports."

105 *"a cautionary tale"*: Rachel Cooke, "Naomi Wolf: 'We're in a Fight for Our Lives and for Democracy,'" *The Guardian*, May 19, 2019.

105 *"Some writers take to drink"*: Michiko Kakutani, "Vidal: 'I'm at the Top of a Very Tiny Heap,'" *New York Times*, March 12, 1981.

106 *"premium" membership*: "Become a DailyClout Member," DailyClout (website), accessed November 2, 2022.

107 *"the first viral pandemic"*: Steven W. Thrasher, *The Viral Underclass: The Human Toll When Inequality and Disease Collide* (New York: Celadon Books, 2022), 4.

107 *"We knew the branding was conspiratorial"*: Josh Rottenberg and Stacy Perman, "Meet the Ojai Dad Who Made the Most Notorious Piece of Coronavirus Disinformation Yet," *Los Angeles Times*, May 13, 2020.

107 *"capitalizable conspiracy"*: Callison and Slobodian, "Coronapolitics from the Reichstag to the Capitol."

108 *"the most comprehensive edition"*: Leonard Wolf, ed., *The Essential Dr. Jekyll & Mr. Hyde: The Definitive Annotated Edition of Robert Louis Stevenson's Classic Novel* (New York: Plume, 1995), back cover.

109 *"she had to find a new world"*: Ian Burrell, "Naomi Wolf's Slide from Feminist, Democratic Party Icon to the 'Conspiracist Whirlpool,'" *Business Insider*, June 5, 2021.

110 *"left the country"*: Naomi Wolf, "A Lost Small Town," *Outspoken with Dr Naomi Wolf*, Substack, October 26, 2022.

110 *"Unlike the Silicon Valley oligarchs"*: Gettr @GETTRofficial, tweet, September 23, 2021, Twitter.

110 *"Speak freely"*: "Parler: About This App," Google Play, updated August 28, 2022.

111 *"crushing you every day"*: Steve Bannon, host, "Independence Day!!; Naomi Wolf's Coup," *War Room: Pandemic* (podcast), episode 1,506, December 23, 2021, at 24:55, posted on Rumble.

111 *"mass formation psychosis"*: "No Evidence of Pandemic 'Mass Formation Psychosis,' Say Experts Speaking to Reuters," Reuters Fact Check, January 7, 2022.

111 *"My job . . . is to wake people up from the Truman Show"*: James Pogue, "Inside the New Right, Where Peter Thiel Is Placing His Biggest Bets," *Vanity Fair*, April 20, 2022.

111 *"becalmed . . . like Stepford kids"*: Naomi Wolf, @DrNaomiRWolf, Gettr, April 16, 2022.

111 *"latest thinking"*: "Dr Naomi Wolf on Kristina Borjesson Show," *Today's News Talk* (audio), July 24, 2022, at 26:46.

112 *"You can't pick up human energy"*: "Dr Naomi Wolf on Kristina Borjesson Show," at 26:58–28:26.

112 *"lipid nanoparticles"*: "Dr Naomi Wolf on Kristina Borjesson Show," at 30:23, 29:30.

112 *"That's how these lipid nanoparticles work"*: "Dr Naomi Wolf on Kristina Borjesson Show," at 30:21.

113 *the discovery of the syndrome*: Paul Meehan, *The Ghost of One's Self: Doppelgangers in Mystery, Horror and Science Fiction Films* (Jefferson, N.C.: McFarland, 2017), 28.

113 *"better to reign in Hell"*: John Milton, *Paradise Lost* (London: 1677), line 263.

7. MAGA's Plus-One

116 *Trump fomented . . . Democrats enabled*: Patricia Zengerle, Richard Cowan, and Doina Chiacu, "Trump Incited Jan. 6 Attack After 'Unhinged' White House Meeting, Panel Told," Reuters, July 12, 2022; Dan Friedman and Abigail Weinberg, "Here's the Whole Transcript of That Leaked Steve Bannon Tape, Annotated," *Mother Jones*, August 17, 2022.

117 *Russia accused Ukraine . . . "mirror imaging"*: "Putin Accuses Ukraine of 'Dirty Bomb' Plans, Says Risks of World Conflict High," Reuters, October 26, 2022; "Ukraine Says Russian Troops Will Fight for Key City as Proxy Government Flees," *New York Times*, October 24, 2022.

117 *feigning outrage . . . gloves-off U.S. interference*: Julian Barnes, "Russian Interference in 2020 Included Influencing Trump Associates, Report Says," March 16, 2021; Elaine Sciolino, "U.S. to Back Yeltsin If He Suspends Congress," *New York Times*, March 13, 1993.

118 *"lab leak theory"*: Rob Kuznia et al., "Weird Science: How a 'Shoddy' Bannon-Backed Paper on Coronavirus Origins Made Its Way to an Audience of Millions," CNN Politics, October 21, 2020; "His Glory Presents: Take FiVe w/ Dr. Naomi Wolf," *His Glory*, July 28, 2022, at 28:54.

118 *Monsanto lobbies ceaselessly . . . linked with cancer*: Zach Boren and Arthur Neslen, "How Lobbyists for Monsanto Led a 'Grassroots Farmers' Movement Against an EU Glyphosate Ban," *Unearthed*, October 17, 2018; "IARC Monograph on Glyphosate," WHO International Agency for Research on Cancer; "Roundup Weedkiller 'Probably' Causes Cancer, Says WHO Study," *The Guardian*, March 21, 2015.

118 *Johnson & Johnson*: Edward Helmore, "Lawsuits, Payouts, Opioids Crisis: What Happened to Johnson & Johnson?," *The Guardian*, October 18, 2019.

119 *rare cases of heart inflammation*: "Myocarditis and Pericarditis After mRNA COVID-19 Vaccination," Centers for Disease Control and Prevention, September 27, 2022, https://www.cdc.gov/coronavirus/2019-ncov/vaccines/safety/myocarditis.html.

119 *possible small uptick in strokes*: "CDC & FDA Identify Preliminary COVID-19 Vaccine Safety Signal for Persons Aged 65 Years and Older," Centers for Disease Control and Prevention, January 13, 2023, https://www.cdc.gov/coronavirus/2019-ncov/vaccines/safety/bivalent-boosters.html.

120 *"genocide"*: Naomi Wolf, "Dear Friends, Sorry to Announce a Genocide," *Outspoken with Dr Naomi Wolf*, Substack, May 29, 2022.

120 *"could have been prevented with primary series vaccination"*: Krutika Amin et al., "COVID-19 Mortality Preventable by Vaccines," Health System Tracker, April 21, 2022.

121 *unvaccinated people were not full citizens*: Jon Henley, "Macron Declares His Covid Strategy Is to 'Piss Off' the Unvaccinated," *The Guardian*, January 4, 2022.

123 *"transhumanism" correspondent*: Steve Bannon, host, "The Transhumanist Revolution," *War Room: Pandemic* (podcast), episode 1,394, November 6, 2021; Charlie Kirk, host, "Transgenderism to Transhumanism with 'Detransitioner' Ritchie Herron and Tech Writer Joe Allen," *Charlie Kirk Show* (podcast), September 15, 2022.

125 *"I am a woman, I am a mother"*: Benjamin Dodman, "'Mother, Italian, Christian': Giorgia Meloni, Italy's Far-Right Leader on the Cusp of Power," France24, September 24, 2022.

125 *"perfect consumer slaves"*: Ian Schwartz, "Italy's Giorgia Meloni: We Are the Enemy to Those Who Would Like Us to Have No Identity, Be the Perfect Consumer Slaves," *RealClearPolitics*, September 26, 2022.

125 *"big financial speculators"*: Amy Kazmin, "Giorgia Meloni Faces Economic Storm as She Prepares to Take Helm in Italy," *Financial Times*, October 18, 2022.

125 *"The* War Room *is a cash machine"*: Jennifer Senior, "American Rasputin," *The Atlantic*, June 6, 2022.

127 *"Speak in the vernacular"*: Mike Davis, "Ten Immodest Commandments: Lessons from a Fumbling-and-Bungling Lifetime of Activism," *Truthout*, November 20, 2011.

128 *"deplorables"*: Steve Bannon, host, "Biden Chaos; Easy Money Destroys the Deplorable's," *War Room: Pandemic* (podcast), episode 1,517, December 28, 2021, posted on Rumble.

128 *"Never again will they be able to other you"*: Steve Bannon, host, "Independence Day!!; Naomi Wolf's Coup," *War Room: Pandemic* (podcast), episode 1,506, December 23, 2021, at 17:30, posted on Rumble.

128 *his "community"*: Bannon, "Independence Day!!," at 19:53.

128 *"heads on pikes"*: Dan Mangan, "Steve Bannon's Podcast Barred from Twitter After He Made Beheading Comment About Fauci, FBI Director Wray," CNBC, November 5, 2020.

128 *"border warfare" . . . "inclusive nationalism"*: Screen capture from *War Room* posted on the Internet Archive's Wayback Machine, October 22, 2022; Steve Bannon @SteveBannon, post, Gettr, June 9, 2022.

128 *polling supports this claim*: Joshua Jamerson and Aaron Zitner, "GOP Gaining Support Among Black and Latino Voters, WSJ Poll Finds," *Wall Street Journal*, November 7, 2022.

129 *"run this country for one hundred years"*: Steve Bannon, host, deleted episode, *War Room: Pandemic* (podcast); Bannon, "Biden Chaos," at 13:56.

129 *"true American patriots"*: "Competing Visions of America: An Evolving Identity or a Culture Under Attack? Findings from the 2021 American Values Survey," Public Religion Research Institute, November 1, 2021.

129 *"muscle memory"*: Steve Bannon, host, deleted episode, *War Room: Pandemic* (podcast).

129 *"Step 3. Develop a thug caste"*: Naomi Wolf, "Fascist America, in 10 Easy Steps," *The Guardian*, April 24, 2007.

130 *"Warrior Moms" . . . "Army of Moms"*: Steve Bannon, host, "Parents Are Still Taking to the Streets," *War Room: Pandemic* (podcast), episode 1,387, November 3, 2021, posted on Rumble; Steve Bannon, host, "Army of Moms Have Been Mobilized," *War Room: Pandemic* (video), October 29, 2021, at 0:45.

131 *She warns him gravely . . . a president who forcibly separated*: Bannon, "Independence Day!!," at 43:50; Myah Ward, "At Least 3,900 Children Separated from Families Under Trump 'Zero Tolerance' Policy, Task Force Finds," *Politico*, August 6, 2021.

131 *"shortlist for woman of the year"*: Steve Bannon, host, *War Room: Pandemic* (podcast), May 21, 2021, clip posted on Media Matters for America.

131 *does not seem to like being referred to as a "mercenary"*: Brian W. O'Shea, comments, Dr Naomi Wolf, Facebook post, November 22, 2014.

131 *"Greetings"*: Naomi Wolf @naomirwolf, tweet, December 20, 2022, Twitter.

132 *"does something that's needed"*: "US Abortion: Best Selling Author Dr Naomi Wolf Discusses Leaked US Supreme Court Documents," GB News channel on YouTube, May 3, 2022, at 4:14–4:27.

132 *"Gosh darn I am TIRED"*: Naomi Wolf @DrNaomiRWolf, Gettr post, May 13, 2022.

132 *"an historic day"*: Bannon, "Parents Are Still Taking to the Streets," at 24:58.

132 *Wolf had strongly pushed back*: Rachel Savage, "INTERVIEW—U.S. Author Naomi Wolf Condemns UK's 'Moral Panic' on Trans Issues," Reuters, November 27, 2020.

132 *"huge victory"*: Bannon, "Parents Are Still Taking to the Streets," at 20:50–24:58.

133 *"You did so much"*: Bannon, "Parents Are Still Taking to the Streets," at 20:50.

133 *"a full-throated apology"*: Naomi Wolf, "Dear Conservatives, I Apologize," *Outspoken with Dr Naomi Wolf*, Substack, March 9, 2023.

133 *"that species of the frightening"*: Sigmund Freud, "The Uncanny," in *The Uncanny*, trans. David McLintock (London: Penguin, 2003), 124. Freud's essay was originally published in 1919.

134 *"Each is a distorting mirror"*: "Two Birthdays," *The Spectator*, April 12, 1939, 5.

135 *"Soldiers! Don't give yourselves to brutes"*: *The Great Dictator*, directed by Charles Chaplin (United Artists, 1940), at 2:00:00–2:01:30.

135 *resist the "slavery"*: "Watch Dr Naomi Wolf Discuss 'Why Vaccine Passports Equal Slavery Forever,'" DailyClout channel on YouTube, March 30, 2021.

135 *"reason" and "democracy"*: *The Great Dictator*, at 2:02:40.

8. Ridiculously Serious, Seriously Speechless

136 *cache of leaked Carlyle Group documents*: Naomi Klein, "James Baker's Double Life," *The Nation*, October 12, 2004.

137 *"They tried to implement this doctrine of shock"*: Alexis Tsipras and Slavoj Žižek, "The Role of the European Left," Subversive Festival, Zagreb, Croatia, SkriptaTV channel on YouTube, May 15, 2013, at 9:16.

140 *"In Bailey, Roth found"*: Laura Marsh, "Philip Roth's Revenge Fantasy," *New Republic*, March 22, 2021.

141 *"Where's Philip?"*: Philip Roth, *Operation Shylock: A Confession* (New York: Simon & Schuster, 1993), 22.

142 *"'I'm looking at myself'"*: Roth, *Operation Shylock*, 71.

142 *"Your name! Your name!"*: Roth, *Operation Shylock*, 99.

143 *"Philip, I feel that I'm reading"*: Roth, *Operation Shylock*, 31.

144 *"all of them in one"*: Roth, *Operation Shylock*, 34.

144 *"It's too ridiculous to take seriously"*: Roth, *Operation Shylock*, 55.

144 *"preposterous proxy"*: Roth, *Operation Shylock*, 115.

145 *"the antitragic force"*: Roth, *Operation Shylock*, 389.

146 *"open race hate" . . . "genocidal talk"*: Tucker Carlson, "Open Race Hate Forms Much of MSNBC's Substance," October 20, 2022.

146 *"Some time in the last five years"*: Sarah Ditum, "Naomi Wolf Is Not a Feminist Who Became a Conspiracy Theorist—She's a Conspiracist Who Was Once Right," *New Statesman*, October 7, 2014.

148 *"There has been a distinct warming up"*: Naomi Klein, "Screen New Deal," *The Intercept*, May 8, 2020.

149 *"CEO of a tech company"*: "Watch Dr Naomi Wolf Discuss 'Why Vaccine Passports Equal Slavery Forever,'" DailyClout channel on YouTube, March 30, 2021.

149 *imagining that a global calamity*: Arundhati Roy, "The Pandemic Is a Portal," *Financial Times*, April 3, 2020.

150 *"the ones who want us eating insects"*: Ben Blanchet, "Newsmax TV Bans Reporter over Wacky Rant About Satan, Insects and Drinking Blood," *HuffPost*, October 20, 2022.

152 *"I AM THE YOU THAT IS NOT WORDS"*: Roth, *Operation Shylock*, 87.

153 *world's ten richest men*: Nabil Ahmed et al., "Inequality Kills: The Unparalleled Action Needed to Combat Unprecedented Inequality in the Wake of COVID-19," Oxfam International, January 2022.

153 *almost certainly fired by an Israeli soldier*: Agence France-Presse, "Shireen Abu Aqleh Killed by 'Seemingly Well-Aimed' Israeli Bullet, UN Says," *The Guardian*, June 24, 2022.

153 *"In many ways, nothing has really changed"*: Angela Davis, interview by Alonzo King (audio recording), *City Arts & Lectures*, May 24, 2022.

154 *"Build back better. Blah, blah, blah"*: "Greta Thunberg Mocks World Leaders in 'Blah, Blah, Blah' Speech," BBC News channel on YouTube, September 28, 2021, at 0:06–0:52.

154 *"They even succeeded in watering down"*: "Greta Thunberg: 'COP26 Even Watered Down the Blah, Blah, Blah,'" BBC News, November 15, 2021.

155 *"At some point you'd have to live"*: Tamara Lindeman, "Loss," on the album *Ignorance* (Fat Possum Records, 2021).

9. The Far Right Meets the Far-Out

163 *"World Wide Walkout"*: Naomi Wolf, @DrNaomiRWolf, "#walkoutwednesday," Gettr post, November 3, 2021.

165 *"I feel like a vaccination"*: "Newsmax Host Suggests Vaccines Are 'Against Nature,' and Some Diseases Are 'Supposed to Wipe Out a Certain Amount of People,'" Media Matters for America, July 12, 2021 (video and transcript of *Rob Schmitt Tonight*, Newsmax, July 9, 2021).

166 *"A wonderful plague"*: "The Charter of New England: 1620," *The Avalon Project: Documents in Law, History, and Diplomacy*, Yale Law School. Note: I have modernized the language for clarity of reading.

166 *"But for the natives in these parts"*: Howard Simpson, *Invisible Armies: The Impact of Disease on American History* (New York: Bobbs-Merrill, 1980), 7. Note: I have modernized the language for clarity of reading.

166 *writing of "the Indians"*: "A New Description of That Fertile and Pleasant Province of Carolina, by John Archdale, 1707," in *Original Narratives of Early American History: Narratives of Early Carolina 1650–1708*, ed. Alexander Salley Jr. (New York: Charles Scribner's Sons, 1911), 282–311.

169 *"conspirituality"*: Charlotte Ward and David Voas, "The Emergence of Conspirituality," *Journal of Contemporary Religion* 26, no. 1 (2011): 103–121.

169 *"the Disinformation Dozen"*: "The Disinformation Dozen: Why Platforms Must Act on Twelve Leading Online Anti-Vaxxers," Center for Countering Digital Hate, March 24, 2021.

170 *Christiane Northrup*: Sam Kestenbaum, "Christiane Northrup, Once a New Age Health Guru, Now Spreads Covid Disinformation," *Washington Post*, May 3, 2022 (updated May 9, 2022).

171 *"You can go eat deep-fried pickles"*: Jessica Wallace, "Kamloops Gym Owners Explain Why They Remain Open Despite Public Health Order Mandating They Close," *Kamloops This Week*, December 23, 2021.

172 *"Third Shift [added] to their leisure time"*: Naomi Wolf, *The Beauty Myth: How Images of Beauty Are Used Against Women* (1990; repr. New York: Perennial, 2002), 26–27.

172 *"part of a larger withdrawal"*: Barbara Ehrenreich, *Natural Causes: An Epidemic of Wellness, the Certainty of Dying, and Killing Ourselves to Live Longer* (New York: Hachette Book Group, 2018), 54–56.

172 *"I may not be able to do much"*: Ehrenreich, *Natural Causes*, 56–57.

173 *"I was tired of flat, unforgiving dressing room lights"*: Carmen Maria Machado, *Her Body and Other Parties* (Minneapolis: Graywolf Press, 2017), 153.

173 *"I kneel down next to it"*: Machado, *Her Body and Other Parties*, 165.

174 *"Old age isn't a battle"*: Philip Roth, *Everyman* (London: Vintage, 2007), 156.

175 *"Black women are three times more likely" . . . infant mortality rates*: "Working Together to Reduce Black Maternal Mortality," Centers for Disease Control and Prevention, April 3, 2023; Danielle M. Ely and Anne K. Driscoll, "Infant Mortality in the United States, 2019: Data from the Period Linked Birth/Infant Death File," *National Vital Statistics Reports* 70, no. 14 (December 8, 2021): 1–17.

175 *"Let me show you how simple"*: "About: A Note from Steph," Glowing Mama (website), accessed October 13, 2022.

176 *"medicine's sexism"*: Michelle Cohen, "Goop Has Exploited the Medical Establishment's Failures on Women's Health," CBC News, August 27, 2018.

177 *"a leading cause of death"*: Rupa Marya @DrRupaMarya, tweet, May 15, 2022, Twitter.

179 *an estimated $155 billion*: "Dietary Supplements Market Report till 2027," MarketsandMarkets, April 2022.

180 *"If you don't support us"*: Alex Jones, "The Alex Jones Show," *Infowars*, May 11, 2022.

180 *states like Wyoming and Mississippi*: John Elflein, "Percentage of U.S. Population Who Had Been Given a COVID-19 Vaccination as of October 5, 2022, by State or Territory," Statista, October 2022.

181 *"Health is NOT THE GOAL of the medical establishment"*: "Homepage," Christiane Northrup M.D. (website), accessed January 3, 2023.

183 *"Do you hate my body, Mom?"*: Machado, *Her Body and Other Parties*, 164.

183 *obesity, diabetes, and some forms of addiction*: "People with Certain Medical Conditions," Covid-19, Centers for Disease Control and Prevention, updated February 10, 2023.

184 *"Go fucking eat a carrot and jump on a treadmill"*: @glowingmamafit, Instagram Reel, September 13, 2021.

184 *"Thousands of white Americans"*: Keeanga-Yamahtta Taylor, "The Black Plague," *New Yorker*, April 16, 2020.

184 *changed as the pandemic wore on*: Akilah Johnson and Dan Keating, "Whites Now More Likely to Die from Covid Than Blacks," *Washington Post*, October 19, 2022.

186 *"they turned out great!"*: "Nashville Hat Shop Faces Backlash for Selling Anti-vaccine Nazi Jewish Star," BBC News, May 30, 2021.

186 *"The Slavs are to work for us"*: Branko Marcetic, "You Know Who Else Opposed Vaccine Mandates? Hitler," *Jacobin*, September 18, 2021.

187 *"deaths pulled from the future"*: Beatrice Adler-Bolton, "Deaths Pulled from the Future," *Blind Archive*, Substack, January 3, 2022.

187 *"you may roughly divide the nations"*: "Living and Dying Nations: From Lord Salisbury's Speech to the Primrose League, May 4," *New York Times*, May 18, 1898.

188 *Of the first 800,000 people . . . people living in poor U.S. counties*: Julie Bosman, Amy Harmon, and Albert Sun, "As U.S. Nears 800,000 Virus Deaths, 1 of Every 100 Older Americans Has Perished," *New York Times*, December 13, 2021; "A Poor People's Pandemic Report: Mapping the Intersections of Poverty, Race and COVID-19," Executive Summary, Poor People's Campaign, April 2022.

189 "Leute, die sich selber sehen": Andrew J. Webber, *The Doppelgänger: Double Visions in German Literature* (New York: Oxford University Press, 1996), 3.

190 *Vancouver is the third most expensive*: Tom Huddleston Jr., "These Are the 5 Most Expensive Cities in the U.S. and Canada—and Los Angeles Isn't One of Them," CNBC News, July 6, 2022.

190 *Many commentators speculated*: Jen St. Denis, "The Billionaire and the Mayor," *The Tyee*, October 24, 2022.

190 *"They don't work for some women's bodies"*: Harry Bradford, "Lululemon's Founder Blames Yoga Pants Problem on Women's Bodies," *HuffPost*, November 6, 2013.

191 *"Are Erections Important?"*: Bob Kronbauer, "Here's the Weird Essay Chip Wilson Just Wrote About Erections," *Vancouver Is Awesome*, May 29, 2019.

191 *fund right-wing politicians*: Marc Fawcett-Atkinson, "Right-Wing Populist Group Fined for Ads Targeting Left-Leaning Politicians," *National Observer*, October 7, 2022; Dan Fumano, "Lululemon Founder Gives $380,000 to Boost B.C.'s Right-Leaning Candidates, Asks Others to Donate," *Vancouver Sun*, August 3, 2022.

191 *"The election was about fear of crime"*: Garth Mullins @garthmullins, tweet, October 16, 2022, Twitter.

10. Autism and the Anti-Vax Prequel

193 *chlorine dioxide*: See, for example, Kerri Rivera with Kimberly McDaniel and Daniel Bender, *Healing the Symptoms Known as Autism*, 2nd ed., e-book (Kerri Rivera, self-published, 2014), 81.

195 *"proven to be false"*: "Retraction—Ileal-Lymphoid-Nodular Hyperplasia, Non-Specific Colitis, and Pervasive Developmental Disorder in Children," *The Lancet* 375, no. 9713 (February 6, 2010): 455.

195 *faulty "interpretation"*: Simon H. Murch et al., "Retraction of an Interpretation," *The Lancet* 363, no. 9411 (March 6, 2004): 750. Of the twelve original coauthors who could be contacted, ten retracted the paper. The journal was unable to contact the thirteenth coauthor, John Linnell. The two who did not sign off on the retraction were Andrew Wakefield and Peter Harvey.

195 *"callous disregard"*: "Fitness to Practise Panel Hearing," General Medical Council (UK), January 28, 2010.

195 *a resurgence of diseases including measles*: Manisha Patel et al., "Increase in Measles Cases: United States, January 1–April 26, 2019," *Morbidity and Mortality Weekly Report*, Centers for Disease Control and Prevention, May 3, 2019. "Elimination" defined as the "absence of sustained measles transmission that is continuous for ≥12 months in a defined geographic area."

196 *"reaching [the] highest number of reported cases in 23 years"*: "Worldwide Measles Deaths Climb 50% from 2016 to 2019 Claiming over 207,500 Lives in 2019," news release, World Health Organization, November 12, 2020.

196 *"I respect all the research"*: Naomi Wolf, "'TRUTH' with Robert F. Kennedy, Jr. Featuring Naomi Wolf—Season 2 Episode 21," Children's Health Defense (video), March 8, 2021, at 06:20.

196 *"This Christmas, give"*: "The Real Anthony Fauci and The Bodies of Others Boxed Set," All Seasons Press, https://www.allseasonspress.com/store/p/the-real-anthony-fauci-and-the-bodies-of-others-boxed-set, accessed January 12, 2023.

196 *"Asperger's-like" . . . "a kind of Asperger's quality"*: Naomi Wolf, *The Bodies of Others: The New Authoritarians, COVID-19 and the War Against the Human* (Fort Lauderdale, Fla.: All Seasons Press, 2022), 97; Naomi Wolf, "Global Predators and the Assault on Human Freedom: The Naomi Wolf Interview," *The Monica Crowley Podcast*, May 25, 2022, at 27:42–29:12, posted on Apple Podcasts.

197 *"Don't you tell me"*: @glowingmamafit, Instagram reel, September 13, 2021.

197 *masks and vaccines . . . anti-racist education . . . gender expressions*: "'This Is Rape': Protesters Yell at Parents Walking with Masked Kids at School Event," CNN News (video), October 8, 2021; Andrew Guttman, "Dad Who Decried Antiracism Initiatives at Brearley Urges Parents to Join Fight," *New York Post,* May 8, 2021; "Digital Hate: Social Media's Role in Amplifying Dangerous Lies About LGBTQ+ People," Center for Countering Digital Hate and Human Rights Campaign, August 10, 2022.

198 *"extinguish" behaviors*: "Extinction in a basic principle of behavior, and its purpose is to extinguish or put an end to unwanted behaviors. Simply put, when a behavior is reinforced, it continues, so extinction removes the reinforcer and the behavior stops." Lizzy Engelman, "A Crash Course on Extinction," *ABA Solutions* (blog), July 15, 2019.

199 *"his intense fear of indoor spaces"*: Whitney Ellenby, "Bystanders Were Horrified. But My Son Has Autism, and I Was Desperate," *Washington Post*, February 27, 2018.

199 *"Many, many autistic children"*: Aaden Friday, "When You're Autistic, Abuse Is Considered Love," *The Establishment*, March 21, 2018.

199 *"precious moments"*: Ellenby, "Bystanders Were Horrified."

199 *"indistinguishable from their normal friends"*: Ole Ivar Lovaas, "Behavioral Treatment and Normal Educational and Intellectual Functioning in Young Autistic Children," *Journal of Consulting and Clinical Psychology* 55, no. 1 (1987): 8.

200 *billions spent on autism research*: "Research Funding for Autism in the United States from 2008 to 2023," Statista, September 8, 2022.

200 *1 in every 44 . . . 1 in 150*: "Community Report on Autism 2021," Autism and Developmental Disabilities Monitoring Network, Centers for Disease Control and Prevention; "Prevalence of Autism Spectrum Disorders," Autism and Developmental Disabilities Monitoring Network, Centers for Disease Control and Prevention, March 30, 2012.

200 *the clinical definition of autism expanded*: Lorna Wing, *The Autistic Spectrum*, new updated ed. (London: Constable & Robinson, 2002), 23.

200 *many more people deciding to get tested*: Steve Silberman, *Neurotribes: The Legacy of Autism and the Future of Neurodiversity* (New York: Penguin Random House, 2015), 41–43, 421.

200 *better at recognizing autism in girls . . . Black, Indigenous, and Latino boys*: Laura Hull, K. V. Petrides, and William Mandy, "The Female Autism Phenotype and Camouflaging: A Narrative Review," *Review Journal of Autism and Developmental Disorders* 7, no. 4 (2020): 306–317; Terra Vance, "What's in a Word: Autism and White Privilege," *Neuroclastic: The Autism Spectrum According to Autistic People*, June 2, 2019; David S. Mandell et al., "Race Differences in the Age at Diagnosis Among Medicaid-Eligible Children with Autism," *Journal of the American Academy of Child & Adolescent Psychiatry* 41, no. 12 (2002): 1447–1453.

200 *children born to older parents*: Kristen Lyall et al., "The Changing Epidemiology of Autism Spectrum Disorders," *Annual Review of Public Health* 38, no. 1 (2017): 81–102.

201 *"anti-vax capital" . . . 66.8 percent of one-year-olds . . . diphtheria*: Ben Smee, "When Covid Came to the Anti-Vax Capital of Australia," *The Guardian*, August 13, 2021; "Children Fully Immunised in NSW by Local Government Area 2020–21," NSW Government Health, updated September 3, 2021; Jennifer King, "Now Diphtheria: Is Northern NSW Incubating Another Australian Health Crisis?," *The Guardian*, July 8, 2022.

201 *"I died in that moment"*: Jenny McCarthy, *Mother Warriors: A Nation of Parents Healing Autism Against All Odds* (New York: Penguin, 2009), 7.

201 *"If you ask 99.9 percent of parents"*: Jenny McCarthy, "We're Not an Anti-Vaccine Movement . . . We're Pro-Safe Vaccine," *Frontline*, PBS, March 23, 2015.

201 *hawking her book*: McCarthy, *Mother Warriors*.

202 *"the world we live in"*: Eric Garcia, "Tracing America's Covid Vaccine Conspiracies to Autism Fearmongering," MSNBC Opinion, December 8, 2021.

202 *"the ideas" were "lying around"*: Milton Friedman with Rose D. Friedman, *Capitalism and Freedom*, 40th anniversary ed. (Chicago: University of Chicago Press, 2002), xiv.

202 *The grift goes back*: "Fitness to Practise Panel Hearing," General Medical Council.

203 *"Boom—the soul's gone from his eyes"*: "Jenny McCarthy and Holly Robinson Peete Discuss Their Battles with Autism on Oprah," *People*, September 18, 2007.

203 *two to four in ten thousand*: Lorna Wing and David Potter, "The Epidemiology of Autistic Spectrum Disorders: Is the Prevalence Rising?," *Mental Retardation and Developmental Disabilities Research Reviews* 8, no. 3 (2002): 151–161.

203 *"unquestionably endowed"*: Leo Kanner, "Autistic Disturbances of Affective Contact," *Nervous Child* 2 (1943): 247.

203 *"spectrum disorder"*: Wing, *The Autistic Spectrum.*

203 *"high-functioning" autism*: *Diagnostic and Statistical Manual of Mental Disorders*, 4th ed. (Washington, D.C.: American Psychiatric Association, 1994), 954–955.

204 *"the myth of changeling children"*: Lorna Wing, "The History of Ideas on Autism: Legends, Myths and Reality," *Autism* 1, no. 1 (1997): 13–14.

204 *"In some versions"*: Wing and Potter, "The Epidemiology of Autistic Spectrum Disorders," 151.

204 *entice the fairy parents*: Kristen L. Bone, "Murders Most Foul: Changeling Myths," in *Women and the Abuse of Power: Interdisciplinary Perspectives*, ed. Helen Gavin (Bingley, UK: Emerald, 2022), 31–42.

204 *"[The changeling] must be beaten"*: Carl Haffter, "The Changeling: History and Psychodynamics of Attitudes to Handicapped Children in European Folklore," *Journal of the History of the Behavioral Sciences* 4, no. 1 (1968): 57.

205 *"There is ample evidence"*: D. L. Ashliman, "Changelings: An Essay," section 6, 1997.

205 *"Stories with these fantasy endings"*: Ashliman, "Changelings," section 6.

205 *"stories began to circulate"*: Silberman, *Neurotribes*, 42.

207 *11 percent of Vienna's population at the time*: Mario Holzner and Michael Huberman, "Red Vienna: A Social Housing Experiment, 1923–1933," *Journal of Interdisciplinary History* 53, no. 1 (2022): 49–88.

207 *"The Viennese socialists"*: Tamara Kamatovic, "How Vienna's Socialist City Hall Put Children at the Heart of the Welfare State," *Jacobin*, June 22, 2020.

207 *"No longer subjugated"*: Quoted in Kamatovic.

207 *"No Viennese child"*: Quoted in Kamatovic.

208 *"He who builds children palaces"*: Quoted in Kamatovic.

208 *"Vienna had become a crucible of ideas"*: Edith Sheffer, *Asperger's Children: The Origins of Autism in Nazi Vienna* (New York: W. W. Norton, 2018), 38.

209 *As Silberman documents*: Silberman, *Neurotribes*, 87–88.

210 *"'family welfare' under the Nazis"*: Kamatovic, "How Vienna's Socialist City Hall Put Children at the Heart of the Welfare State."

210 *"unworthy of life"*: This phrase is commonly attributed to the Nazi Party,

which probably borrowed it from the German attorney Karl Binding and the psychiatrist Alfred Hoche. See Karl Binding and Alfred Hoche, *Permitting the Destruction of Life Unworthy of Life: Its Measure and Form*, trans. Cristina Modak (Greenwood, Wis.: Suzeteo Enterprises, 2012), originally published in German in 1920. See also Howard Brody and M. Wayne Cooper, "Binding and Hoche's 'Life Unworthy of Life': A Historical and Ethical Analysis," *Perspectives in Biology and Medicine* 57, no. 4 (2014): 500–511.

211 *"There are as many approaches"*: Quoted in Sheffer, *Asperger's Children*, 214.

211 *"transmission of diseased hereditary material"*: Quoted in Herwig Czech, "Hans Asperger, National Socialism, and 'Race Hygiene' in Nazi-Era Vienna," *Molecular Autism* 9, no. 1 (2018): 13.

211 *"autistic psychopaths"*: Quoted in Sheffer, *Asperger's Children*, 214.

211 *"poverty of* Gemüt*"*: Quoted in Sheffer, 157.

211 *"roam the streets as 'originals'"*: Quoted in Sheffer, 179.

211 *"little professors"*: Silberman, *Neurotribes*, 6.

211 *"We know how many of our former children"*: Quoted in Czech, "Hans Asperger, National Socialism, and 'Race Hygiene' in Nazi-Era Vienna," 16.

212 *Recent research has shown*: Czech, 20.

212 *"It was up to Nazi child psychiatrists"*: Sheffer, *Asperger's Children*, 67.

213–214 *"My heart goes out to you"*: Philip Roth, *Operation Shylock: A Confession* (New York: Simon & Schuster, 1993), 62–63.

214 *"The Germans have proved"*: Roth, *Operation Shylock*, 63.

214 *"double-sided character of Asperger's actions"*: Sheffer, *Asperger's Children*, 17.

214 *"I am interested in the underlying ideology"*: Anna N. de Hooge, "Binary Boys: Autism, Aspie Supremacy and Post/Humanist Normativity," *Disability Studies Quarterly* 39, no. 1 (2019).

11. Calm, Conspiracy . . . Capitalism

225 *"displaces the real threats"*: Rodrigo Nunes, "Are We in Denial About Denial?," *Public Books*, November 25, 2020.

226 *"Hence, calm is a form of resistance"*: John Berger, blurb, "Advance Praise," *The Shock Doctrine: The Rise of Disaster Capitalism* (website), accessed November 8, 2022.

227 *"shockingly shocking"* . . . *"petrifying"*: Steve Bannon, host, "Naomi Wolf: The Lies of Pfizer," *War Room: Pandemic* (podcast), May 4, 2022, at 0:41, posted on Rumble; Paul Elias Alexander, "Dr. Wolf: Twitter Ban—Menstrual Dysregualtion [*sic*] and Serious Fertility Issues After COVID Injection," July 30, 2022, at 11:42, posted on Rumble.

227 *"I don't want to use inflated language"*: Naomi Wolf, interview by Steve Bannon, *War Room: Pandemic* (podcast), episode 1,076, July 6, 2021, at 27:17–27:35.

228 *"the belief that certain events"*: "Identifying Conspiracy Theories," European Commission, accessed November 8, 2022.

229 *"Somehow, somewhere, someone"*: Naomi Wolf, *The Beauty Myth: How Images of Beauty Are Used Against Women* (1990; repr. New York: Perennial, 2002), 66.

229 *she saw a plot and a "war"*: Naomi Wolf, "The Shocking Truth About the Crackdown on Occupy," *The Guardian*, November 25, 2011.

230 *"I believe in equipping women"*: Katharine Viner, "Stitched Up," *The Guardian*, September 1, 2001.

230 *"a child of the narrative"*: Alexander, "Dr. Wolf: Twitter Ban," at 16:29.

230 *"Liberal investments in individualism"*: Jack Bratich, email to author, October 26, 2022.

232 *"There is no such thing as society"*: Margaret Thatcher, September 23, 1987, transcript of an interview by Douglas Key for *Woman's Own*, Margaret Thatcher Foundation.

234 *"If Covid was really serious"*: Nikou Asgari, "'A Form of Brainwashing': Why Trump Voters Are Refusing to Have a Vaccine," *Financial Times*, July 20 2021.

234 *"sovereign citizens"*: "Sovereign Citizens Movement," Southern Poverty Law Center, accessed November 8, 2022.

236 *popularized by leftists in Turkey*: Ryan Gingeras, "How the Deep State Came to America," *War on the Rocks*, February 4, 2019.

236 *"People of the same trade"*: Adam Smith, *The Wealth of Nations* (1776; repr. London: David Campbell Publishers, 1991), 116.

236 *"the ruling class showing class solidarity"*: Mark Fisher, "Exiting the Vampire Castle," *Open Democracy*, November 24, 2013. Republished with permission from *The North Star* (original publication date November 22, 2013).

239 *"Abuse of power* begets *conspiracy"*: Marcus Gilroy-Ware, *After the Fact? The Truth About Fake News* (London: Repeater Books, 2020), 169. Italics in the original.

239 *impunity for real conspiracies*: Sarah Kendzior, *They Knew: How a Culture of Conspiracy Keeps America Complacent* (New York: Flatiron Books, 2022).

241 *"Does anyone really think"*: Mark Fisher, *Capitalist Realism: Is There No Alternative?* (Zero Books, 2009), 68.

241 *"wholly unjustified and brutal invasion"*: "George W. Bush Confuses Iraq with Ukraine in Gaffe," Associated Press channel on YouTube, May 19, 2022.

243 *"Conspiracy theories are a misfiring"*: Gilroy-Ware, *After the Fact?*, 169.

244 *"You are stuck in your body"*: Daisy Hildyard, "The Second Body," *The Learned Pig*, November 15, 2017. Excerpt from Daisy Hildyard, *The Second Body* (London: Fitzcarraldo Editions, 2017).

244 *"There is no document of civilization"*: Walter Benjamin, "Theses on the Philosophy of History," in *Illuminations: Essays and Reflections*, ed. Hannah Arendt (London: Bodley Head, 2015), 248.

244 *"It goes without saying"*: James Baldwin, "The Creative Process," in *The Price of the Ticket: Collected Nonfiction 1948–1985* (New York: St. Martin's/Marek, 1985), 317.

245 *"When you are on a former battlefield"*: Deena Metzger, *La Vieja: A Journal of Fire* (Topanga, Calif.: Hand to Hand, 2022), 1.

12. No Way Out but Back

246 *"Someday all of our kids"*: Naomi Wolf, "I'm Not 'Brave'; You're Just a P—y," *Outspoken with Dr Naomi Wolf*, Substack, March 2, 2022.

246 *"atlas of human suffering"*: "IPCC Adaptation Report 'a Damning Indictment of Failed Global Leadership on Climate,'" *UN News*, February 28, 2022.

247 *"So on Day 3"*: Wolf, "I'm Not 'Brave.'"

248 *"the takeaway"*: Wolf, "I'm Not 'Brave.'"

248 *had already announced*: Eric Adams @NYCMayor, tweet, February 27, 2022, Twitter.

248 *Just a few days later*: "As COVID Cases Plummet and Vaccination Rates Reach New Heights, Mayor Adams Announces Next Phase of Pandemic Response," NYC: Official Website of the City of New York, March 4, 2022.

249 *"forced separate accommodations"*: Wolf, "I'm Not 'Brave.'"

249 *enough of an admirer*: Ann Gerhart, "Who's Afraid of Naomi Wolf? The List Is Growing Fast Since the 'Promiscuities' Author Turned Gore Adviser," *Washington Post*, November 5, 1999.

249 *"as if we were all living"*: Naomi Wolf, "A Lost Small Town," *Outspoken with Dr Naomi Wolf*, Substack, October 26, 2022.

250 *a teaching assistant . . . "I am representing Rosa Parks"*: Ryan Clarke, "Newberg School Staffer Shows Up in Blackface, Fired from Position," *Newberg Graphic*, September 20, 2021; Lars Larson, host, "Lauren Pefferle—NW School Worker Shows Up to Protest Vaccine Mandate . . . in Blackface," *The Lars Larson Show*, September 23, 2021, at 3:18, posted on SoundCloud.

250 *Let Them Breathe*: Tania Thorne, "The Woman Behind Let Them Breathe; the Fight Against School Mask Mandates," KPBS, October 20, 2021.

251 *"We have been enslaved by our government"*: Eoin Higgins, "Fresh Off Twitter Ban, Naomi Wolf to Headline Anti-Vax 'Juneteenth' Event," *The Flashpoint*, Substack, June 8, 2021.

252 *"A lot of people in this nation's history" . . . "absolutely discrimination"*: Naomi Wolf @DrNaomiRWolf, Gettr post (video), June 30, 2022, at 2:01 and 3:58.

252 *"an important moment in this nation's history"*: Wolf, Gettr post, June 30, 2022, at 3:11.

252 *"We've had over 150 fake one-star reviews"*: April Ehrlich, "Salem Restaurant Buried in Fake Reviews, Hateful Comments Following Naomi Wolf Incident," Oregon Public Broadcasting, August 1, 2022.

253 *"I'm sorry that you're centering yourself"*: Wolf, Gettr post, June 30, 2022, at 3:32.

254 *"the Dream"*: Ta-Nehisi Coates, *Between the World and Me* (New York: Spiegel & Grau, 2015).

254 *"These collective efforts"*: Keeanga-Yamahtta Taylor, "American Racism and the Buffalo Shooting," *New Yorker*, May 15, 2022.

255 *"shadow banned"*: Naomi Wolf @DrNaomiRWolf, Gettr post, April 14, 2022.

255 *three years old*: "Remains of Children of Kamloops Residential School Discovered," press release, Kamloops Indian Band, May 21, 2021.

256 *"cultural genocide"*: *Honouring the Truth, Reconciling for the Future: Summary of the Final Report of the Truth and Reconciliation Commission of Canada* (Truth and Reconciliation Commission of Canada, 2015), 1.

256 *at least 150,000*: *Honouring the Truth, Reconciling for the Future*, 3.

256 *forced to attend*: *Honouring the Truth, Reconciling for the Future*, 53.

256 *the names of 3,201 children . . . updated to 4,117*: *Canada's Residential Schools: Missing Children and Unmarked Burials: The Final Report of the Truth and Reconciliation Commission of Canada*, vol. 4 (Montreal: McGill-Queen's

University Press, 2015), 15; "Concerted National Action Overdue for All the Children Who Never Came Home from Residential Schools," joint news release, National Centre for Truth and Reconciliation and Indian Residential School History and Dialogue Centre at UBC, June 2, 2021.

256 *closer to 25,000*: "Murray Sinclair on the Deaths of Children in Residential Schools, and What Must Be Done to Help Survivors," *The Current*, CBC Radio, June 2, 2021, at 5:57–6:23.

256 *over two thousand suspected unmarked graves*: Carina Xue Luo, "Missing Children of Indian Residential Schools," Academic Data Centre, Leddy Library, University of Windsor, September 6, 2022.

257 *"kill the Indian in the child"*: "Residential Schools in Canada: Education Guide," *Historica Canada*, 9, accessed January 3, 2023.

257 *"Yes, it's a genocide"*: Ka'nhehsí:io Deer, "Pope Says Genocide Took Place at Canada's Residential Schools," CBC News, July 30, 2022.

257 *unanimously passed*: Sean Kilpatrick, "Motion to Call Residential Schools Genocide Backed Unanimously," *Globe and Mail*, October 28, 2022.

258 *"Hunger is both the first and last thing"*: George Manuel and Michael Posluns, *The Fourth World: An Indian Reality* (Don Mills, Ontario: Collier-Macmillan Canada, 1974), 65.

258 *"They stole the children"*: Naomi Klein, "Stealing Children to Steal the Land," *The Intercept*, June 16, 2021.

259 *"be honest with ourselves about our history"*: Justin Trudeau, "Trudeau Says Canadians 'Must Be Honest' About Country's History in Canada Day Message," Global News channel on YouTube, July 1, 2021, at 1:15.

259 *"Nations themselves* are *narrations"*: Edward Said, *Culture and Imperialism* (New York: Alfred A. Knopf, 1993), xiii.

259 *"An invented past can never be used"*: James Baldwin, *The Fire Next Time* (New York: Franklin Watts, 1963), 95.

259 *"If I told the same story"*: Melissa Tait, "Healing Through Drums," *Globe and Mail*, September 29, 2022.

259 *"those little ones that had gone missing"*: Mike Otto, "An Idea Turned into a Trucking Convoy for a Cause," *Over the Road Legend* (podcast), July 14, 2021, at 7:16.

262 *King is an open racist*: Shannon Proudfoot, "Tamara Lich vs. Pat King: A Tale of Two Convoy Protest Leaders," *Globe and Mail*, November 4, 2022.

262 *"It's called depopulation"*: Pat King, "Trudeau Is Going to Catch a Bullet . . . Only Way This Ends Is with Bullets," video posted on Streamable, at 0:56.

262 *"not only infiltrate"*: David Bauder, "What Is White Replacement Theory? Police Probe Conspiracy's Role in Buffalo Shooting," Global News, May 16, 2022.

262 *reported that virtually every*: "The 'Freedom Convoy' Is Nothing but a Vehicle for the Far Right," Canadian Anti-Hate Network, January 27, 2022.

262–263 *"Diagolon is increasingly becoming"*: Peter Smith, "A Holocaust Denier Is Travelling Across Canada Building Up the Country's Newest Far-Right Militia Movement," Canadian Anti-Hate Network, January 11, 2022.

263 *"not a coincidence"*: Jesse Wente @JesseWente, tweet, February 17, 2022. Account has been deleted. Quoted with permission.

263 *"Canada Day times a thousand"*: "Ottawa Occupation Was 'Canada Day Times 1000': Lianne Rood Conservative MP," Women in Canadian Politics channel on YouTube, March 2, 2022, at 0:18.

265 *orange sweatshirts*: Matthew Remski, "Oppression Fantasies of White Anti-Vax Moms," *The Conspirituality Report*, Medium, June 1, 2021.

13. The Nazi in the Mirror

267 *"The very existence of this film"*: *Exterminate All the Brutes*, directed by Raoul Peck (HBO Original, April 7, 2021).

267 *"The foundation of it all"*: "*Exterminate All the Brutes*: Raoul Peck's Statement of Intent," HBO channel on YouTube, April 6, 2021.

268 *"And if the inferior race must perish"*: Joseph Conrad, *The Rescue* (New York: W. W. Norton, 1968), 148.

268 *"At some future period"*: Charles Darwin, *The Descent of Man, and Selection in Relation to Sex* (London: John Murray, 1896), 1:156.

269 *"the core of European thought"*: Sven Lindqvist, *"Exterminate All the Brutes": One Man's Odyssey into the Heart of Darkness and the Origins of European Genocide* (London: Granta, 1997), 3.

269 *"Concentration camps were not invented in Germany"*: Quoted in Nikolaus Wachsmann, *KL: A History of the Nazi Concentration Camps* (London: Little Brown, 2016), 6–7.

269 *"mercy in a massacre"*: Bedford Pim, *The Negro and Jamaica* (London: Trübner, 1866), 63.

269–270 *world's first eugenics-based law*: Phillip Reilly, *The Surgical Solution: A History of Involuntary Sterilization in the United States* (Baltimore: Johns Hopkins University Press, 1991).

270 *"gunned down the millions"*: Quoted in James Q. Whitman, *Hitler's American Model: The United States and the Making of Nazi Race Law* (Princeton, N.J.: Princeton University Press, 2017), 9.

270 *"There is only one task"*: Quoted in David Blackbourn, *The Conquest of Nature: Water, Landscape, and the Making of Modern Germany* (New York: W. W. Norton, 2006), 303.

271 *"In this business I shall go straight ahead"*: *Hitler's Table Talk 1941–1944: His Private Conversations*, trans. Norman Cameron and R. H. Stevens (New York: Enigma, 2000), 69.

271 *"We'll supply the Ukrainians with scarves"*: *Hitler's Table Talk 1941–1944*, 34.

271 *"Auschwitz was the modern industrial application"*: Lindqvist, *"Exterminate All the Brutes,"* 160.

271 *"when what had been done in the heart of darkness"*: Lindqvist, *"Exterminate All the Brutes,"* 172.

271 *"There was no Nazi atrocity"*: W. E. B. Du Bois, *The World and Africa: An Inquiry into the Part Which Africa Has Played in World History* (New York: International Publishers, 1965), 23.

271 *"Nazism before it was inflicted on them"*: Aimé Césaire, *Discourse on Colonialism*, trans. Joan Pinkham (New York: Monthly Review Press, 2000), 36.

272 *"Yes, it would be worthwhile"*: Césaire, *Discourse on Colonialism*, 36.

272 *"The idea of extermination"*: Lindqvist, *"Exterminate All the Brutes,"* 9.

273 *"The ideas forged in the plantation economy"*: Rinaldo Walcott, *On Property: Policing, Prisons, and the Call for Abolition* (Windsor: Biblioasis, 2021), 13.

274 *"the cruel persecution"*: Nomi Kaltmann, "The Courage of William Cooper," *Tablet*, January 26, 2021.

274 *"Two events need not be identical"*: Lindqvist, *"Exterminate All the Brutes,"* x.

275 *"Forces opposed to justice"*: Olúfẹ́mi O. Táíwò, *Reconsidering Reparations* (New York: Oxford University Press, 2022), 199.

275 *"There is a resistance to memory"*: Jacqueline Rose, *Proust Among the Nations: From Dreyfus to the Middle East* (Chicago: University of Chicago Press, 2011), 120.

275 *"the biggest fake news story"*: Dana Kennedy, "'Biggest Fake News Story in Canada': Kamloops Mass Grave Debunked by Academics," *New York Post*, May 27, 2022.

276 *He left a long, rambling manifesto*: Maxine Joselow, "Suspect in Buffalo Rampage Cited 'Ecofascism' to Justify Actions," *Washington Post*, May 17, 2022.

276 *"I'm struck by the similarity"*: Julian Brave NoiseCat @jnoisecat, tweet, May 16, 2022, Twitter.

14. The Unshakable Ethnic Double

278 *"At this point"*: Jeet Heer @HeerJeet, tweet, March 20, 2021, Twitter.

278 *"If one is attacked as a Jew"*: Hannah Arendt, *Essays in Understanding, 1930–1945*, ed. Jerome Kohn (New York: Harcourt, Brace, 1994), 12.

279 *"WHY ARE YOU SENDING"*: Omar Sakr @omarsakrpoet, tweet, March 29, 2022, Twitter.

279 *"Some reproach me with being a Jew"*: Quoted in Hannah Arendt, *The Origins of Totalitarianism* (New York: Harcourt, Brace, 1951), 64.

280 *"The Jew is one whom"*: Jean-Paul Sartre, *Anti-Semite and Jew*, trans. George J. Becker (1948; repr. New York: Schocken Books, 1995), 49. The original, in French, was written in 1944 and published in book form in 1946.

281 *"double-consciousness"*: W. E. B. Du Bois, "Strivings of the Negro People," *The Atlantic*, August 1897.

281 *"I plan to give you reasons for your jumpy fits"*: June Jordan, "I Must Become a Menace to My Enemies," in *Things That I Do in the Dark: Selected Poetry* (1977; repr. Boston: Beacon Press, 1981), 144.

281 *"The face is the ultimate communication tool"*: Grace Ebert, "I'm Not a Look-Alike: Hundreds of Unrelated Doppelgängers Sit for François Brunelle's Uncanny Portraits," *Colossal*, February 9, 2022.

286 *"the socialism of fools"*: Richard Evans, *The Coming of the Third Reich* (New York: Penguin Press, 2004), 173.

287 *bloody pogroms in 660 towns and cities*: Robert Weinberg, "Workers, Pogroms, and the 1905 Revolution in Odessa," *Russian Review* 46, no. 1 (January 1987): 53.

287 *"They hurled Jews out of windows"*: Weinberg, 63–64.

287 *"Ethnic divisiveness was a centrifugal force"*: Weinberg, " 75.

290 *"I am a Jewess"*: Henry Rosenthal, "Eleanor Marx: 'I Am a Jewess,'" Jews, Marxism and the Workers Movement, Marxists Internet Archive.

290 *"an all-out orgy of anti-Semitism"*: Georg Adler, Peter Hudis, and Annelies Laschitza, eds., *The Letters of Rosa Luxemburg* (London: Verso, 2011), 295.

290 *"drunk on vodka"*: Quoted in Alan Johnson, "Leon Trotsky's Long War Against Antisemitism," *Fathom*, March 2019.

290 *"in the epoch of its rise"*: Quoted in Johnson.

291 *"a set of problems"*: Enzo Traverso, *The Jewish Question: History of a Marxist Debate*, trans. Bernard Gibbons (Leiden: Brill, 2019).

291 *"Religion is the sigh"*: Karl Marx, *Critique of Hegel's "Philosophy of Right,"* trans. Anette Jolin and Joseph O'Malley (Cambridge: Cambridge University Press, 1970), 131.

291 *"Your liberation"*: Antony Polonsky, "The Bund in Polish Political Life, 1935–1939," in *Essential Papers on Jews and the Left*, ed. Ezra Mendelsohn (New York: New York University Press, 1997), 172.

292 *"things will go very badly"*: Walter Benjamin, *Gesammelte Schriften*, ed. Rolf Tiedemann and Hermann Schweppenhäuser (Frankfurt: Suhrkamp, 1991), 838.

292 *"What do you want with this theme"*: Dana Mills, "Lessons from the Life of Rosa Luxemburg," Verso Blog, March 5, 2021.

292 *"None is too many"*: Irving Abella and Harold Troper, *None Is Too Many: Canada and the Jews of Europe, 1939–1948* (Toronto: University of Toronto, 2017).

293 *"Jewish capitalism"*: Abram Leon, *The Jewish Question: A Marxist Interpretation* (1946; repr. New York: Pathfinder Press, 1970), 239.

293 *"Big business"*: Leon, *The Jewish Question*, 234.

294 *"Just as it is necessary"*: Leon, *The Jewish Question*, 239.

295 *"the war and the Holocaust"*: Traverso, *The Jewish Question*, xv.

299 *"Doppelgänger politics"*: Caroline Rooney, "Prison Israel-Palestine: Literalities of Criminalization and Imaginative Resistance," *Journal of Postcolonial Writing* 50, no. 2 (2014): 134.

299 *"A land without a people for a people without a land"*: Diana Muir, "A Land Without a People for a People Without a Land," *Middle East Quarterly* 15, no. 2 (Spring 2008): 55–62.

299 *"making the desert bloom"*: Alan George, "'Making the Desert Bloom': A Myth Examined," *Journal of Palestine Studies* 8, no. 2 (Winter 1979): 88.

300 *"stucco-colored Haifa"*: I. F. Stone, *Underground to Palestine* (New York: Boni & Gaer, 1946), 221.

300 *"For the Zionists, the Arab was the Invisible Man"*: I. F. Stone, "Holy War," in *The Best of I. F. Stone*, ed. Karl Weber (New York: Public Affairs, 2006), 235.

300 *"There was no such thing as Palestinians"*: Quoted in Rashid Khalidi, *Palestinian Identity: The Construction of Modern National Consciousness* (New York: Columbia University Press, 1997), 147.

300 *"present-absentee"*: Mahmoud Darwish, *In the Presence of Absence*, trans. Sinan Antoon (New York: Archipelago Books, 2011).

300 *"Israeli settlers continue their unbated campaign"*: Yousef Al Jamal, "JNF Greenwashing as a Means to Hide Ethnic Cleansing in Palestine," *Politics Today*, February 14, 2022.

301 *"the victims of the victims"*: Edward Said, *The Pen and the Sword: Conversations*

with David Barsamian (Monroe, Maine: Common Courage Press, 1994), 53; Bryan Cheyette, "A Glorious Achievement: Edward Said and the Last Jewish Intellectual," in *Edward Said's Translocations*, ed. Tobias Doring and Mark U. Stein (New York: Routledge, 2012), 78.

301 *"the new Jews"*: Joseph Massad, "Affiliating with Edward Said," in *Edward Said: A Legacy of Emancipation and Representation*, ed. Adel Iskandar and Hakem Rustom (Berkeley: University of California Press, 2010), 33.

301 *"doppelgänger politics is first of all"*: Rooney, "Prison Israel-Palestine," 134.

302 *"the Jewish people has an exclusive"*: Natasha Roth-Rowland, "Land Grabs. Homophobia. Radicalized Police: What to Expect from Israel's Far-Right Government," *+972 Magazine*, December 29, 2022.

303 *"go into the mindset of Zionism"*: Jacqueline Rose, "Nation as Trauma, Zionism as Question: Jacqueline Rose Interviewed," *openDemocracy*, August 17, 2005.

303 *around 20 percent of the Palestinian population*: "General Briefing: Palestinian Political Prisoners in Israeli Prisons," Addameer Prisoner Support and Human Rights Association.

306 *According to a United Nations report*: "Key Figures on the 2014 Hostilities," United Nations Office for the Coordination of Humanitarian Affairs, June 23, 2015.

306 *"526"*: "50 Days: More Than 500 Children: Facts and Figures on Fatalities in Gaza, Summer 2014," B'Tselem, July 20, 2016.

306 *"citizen journalists"*: L. Finch, "How a Jewish-American Author's Facebook Page Became a Hub for Citizen Reporting on Gaza," *Global Voices*, August 5, 2014.

306 *"People are asking"*: Naomi Wolf, Facebook post, July 21, 2014.

307 *a typical headline*: Shmuley Boteach, "Naomi Wolf's Allegations of an Israeli Genocide Fuel Anti-Semitism," *Jerusalem Post*, September 10, 2014.

307 *"I was [teaching] at Barnard"*: Rachel Cooke, "Naomi Wolf: 'We're in a Fight for Our Lives and for Democracy," *The Guardian*, May 19, 2019.

307 *a former U.S. special forces officer . . . Striker Pierce Investigations*: "Security Consultant Shares Insider Tips on Self-Defense," DailyClout channel on YouTube, May 19, 2022, at 6:32–6:43; Vincent M. Mallozzi, "An Author and Investigator Find Comfort in Each Other," *New York Times*, November 24, 2018.

308 *"The Nazis are an excuse for everything"*: Philip Roth, *Portnoy's Complaint* (New York: Bantam Books, 1969), 86.

308 *"isn't speaking only of his family"*: Corey Robin, "Arendt and Roth: An Uncanny Convergence," *New York Review*, May 12, 2021.

309 *"a Jewish country without a Jewish soul"*: Philip Roth, *Operation Shylock* (New York: Simon & Schuster, 1993), 109.

309 *"in many, many terrible ways"*: Roth, *Operation Shylock*, 81.

309 *"all human, elastic, adaptable, humorous, creative"*: Roth, *Operation Shylock*, 126.

309 *"Jewish anti-Zionist elements"*: Roth, *Operation Shylock*, 358.

309 *"I am a tribesman"*: Roth, *Operation Shylock*, 351.

309 *"What will the* goyim *think?"*: Philip Roth, "Writing About Jews," *Commentary*, December 1963.

310 *"It finally happened"*: Naomi Wolf @DrNaomiRWolf, Gettr post, May 13, 2022.

310 *"Who knew that the perfect husband for a feminist"*: Naomi Wolf @DrNaomiRWolf, Gettr post, May 13, 2022.

310 *"Maybe every writer and dissident critic should have"*: Naomi Wolf @DrNaomiRWolf, Gettr post, May 14, 2022.

310 *"is not entirely enslaved like Australia"*: Naomi Wolf @DrNaomiRWolf, Gettr post (video), May 24, 2022.

311 *"How had this issue escaped me"*: Naomi Wolf, "Rethinking the Second Amendment," *Outspoken with Dr Naomi Wolf*, Substack, June 4, 2022.

311 *"with our neighbor in trouble"*: Naomi Wolf, Facebook post, July 21, 2014.

311 *"fully open borders"* . . . *"a tyrant's dream"* . . . *"Traitors are dissolving"*: Naomi Wolf, *The Bodies of Others: The New Authoritarians, COVID-19 and the War Against the Human* (Fort Lauderdale, Fla.: All Seasons Press, 2022), 47; Joseph Mercola, "The Last Stage of a Tyrannical Takeover—Interview with Naomi Wolf," *Bitchute* (video), June 1, 2022, at 13:56.

311 *"I am a peaceful person"*: Steve Bannon, host, "'We Are at War': Naomi Wolf Breaks Down the WHO's Plan to Seize Power," *War Room: Pandemic* (podcast), May 12, 2022, at 5:13, posted on Rumble.

15. Unselfing

320 *cut global pollution in half in a decade*: "Special Report: Global Warming of 1.5°C," Intergovernmental Panel on Climate Change, 2018; Jonathan Watts, "We Have 12 Years to Limit Climate Change Catastrophe, Warns UN," *The Guardian*, October 8, 2018.

320 *glitzy, Trumpy Las Vegas*: "Nevada Caucuses 2020: Live Election Results," *New York Times*, February 24, 2020.

321 *new oil and gas drilling permits*: Matthew Brown, "US Drilling Approvals Increase Despite Biden Climate Pledge," Associated Press, July 12, 2021; "New Data: Biden's First Year Drilling Permitting Stomps Trump's by 34%," press release, Center for Biological Diversity, January 21, 2022.

322 *"second body"*: Daisy Hildyard, "The Second Body," *The Learned Pig*, November 15, 2017, excerpt from Daisy Hildyard, *The Second Body* (London: Fitzcarraldo Editions, 2017).

323 *"It wasn't me"*: Eve Auchincloss and Nancy Lynch, "Disturber of the Peace: James Baldwin—an Interview/1969," in *Conversations with James Baldwin*, ed. Fred L. Standley and Louis H. Pratt (Jackson: University Press of Mississippi, 1989), 73.

324 *"We're not just the center"*: *The Magnitude of All Things*, directed by Jennifer Abbott (National Film Board of Canada, 2020), at 55:11.

324 *"feel like a coral or a fish"*: *The Magnitude of All Things*, at 48:38.

324 *"an occasion for 'unselfing'"*: Iris Murdoch, *The Sovereignty of Good* (New York: Schocken Books, 1971), 84.

324 *"the people who are the exploiters"*: *The Magnitude of All Things*, at 43:13.

325 *"I'd like to think"*: *The Double*, directed by Richard Ayoade (Magnolia Pictures, 2014), at 1:26:52.

325 *"pity for those who suffer"*: Helena de Bres, "It's Not You, It's Me," *The Point*, September 23, 2019.

327 *"We can be hard and critical"*: john a. powell, interview by Ivan Natividad,

"To End White Supremacy, Attack Racist Policy, Not People," *Berkeley News*, January 25, 2021.

328 *"Everything worthwhile"*: Eve L. Ewing, "Mariame Kaba: Everything Worthwhile Is Done with Other People," *Adi Magazine*, Fall 2019.

330 *"These days, I feel the threat"*: Arielle Angel, "Beyond Grievance," *Jewish Currents*, Summer 2022.

331 *"Struggle helps us see each other"*: Keeanga-Yamahtta Taylor, conversation with author, October 17, 2022.

332 *"they belong to a class"*: John Berger, "The Nature of Mass Demonstrations," *International Socialism* 1st series, no. 34 (Autumn 1968): 11–12.

333 *"maybe somebody who doesn't look kinda like you"*: Bridget Read, "The Bernie Rally Felt So Much Bigger Than Bernie," *The Cut*, October 21, 2019; Bernie Sanders, "Bernie's Back Rally with AOC in New York," Bernie Sanders channel on YouTube video, October 19, 2019, at 2:47:27.

334 *"all the possibilities"*: Sigmund Freud, "The Uncanny," in *The Uncanny*, trans. David McLintock (London: Penguin, 2003), 143. Freud's essay was originally published in 1919.

335 *"If you have never believed"*: Keeanga-Yamahtta Taylor, conversation with author, October 17, 2022.

336 *"I believe the starting point"*: Sally Weintrobe, *Psychological Roots of the Climate Crisis: Neoliberal Exceptionalism and the Culture of Uncare* (New York: Bloomsbury Academic, 2021), 13.

337 *the only alternative to barbarism*: Rosa Luxemburg, *Socialism or Barbarism: Selected Writings*, ed. Paul Le Blanc and Helen C. Scott (London: Pluto, 2010).

339 *"when I think of the land as my mother"*: Naomi Klein, "Dancing the World into Being: A Conversation with Idle No More's Leanne Simpson," *Yes Magazine*, March 6, 2013.

340 *"precarious, dependent"*: Sunaura Taylor, "Age of Disability," *Orion*, November 9, 2021.

340 *"environmentalism of the injured"*: Taylor, "Age of Disability."

Epilogue: Who Is the Double?

344 *carefully deconstructed*: *Killing Us Softly: Advertising's Image of Women*, featuring Jean Kilbourne (Media Education Foundation, 1979).

347 *"I don't know how to be myself"*: *The Double*, directed by Richard Ayoade (Magnolia Pictures, 2014), at 41:23.

347 *"Her intense energy"*: Lisa Hix, "Did Father Know Best? In Her New Book, Third Wave Feminist Naomi Wolf Reconsiders Her Bohemian Upbringing," *San Francisco Chronicle*, June 19, 2005, via SFGate.

348 "He's *the fake*": Philip Roth, *Operation Shylock* (New York: Simon & Schuster, 1993), 367.

ACKNOWLEDGMENTS

After a quarter century writing books in a particular political and editorial style, it can be tough to shift gears. I was so fortunate to work with a brilliant editorial team that greeted this change in direction with excitement. Kimberly Witherspoon of Inkwell Management, now my agent, was on board for all the right reasons from our first phone call. She jumped in with commanding confidence, and we have collaborated with a rare warmth and collegiality ever since. I will always be grateful to Sue Halpern for introducing us.

Kim was determined to find an editor and a house that would break as many rules of corporate publishing as required to let this book become what it wanted to be. We found that and more in Alexander Star and the whole team at Farrar, Straus and Giroux. After an hour talking literary doubles and conspiracy theories with Alex, I knew I had found someone who would fall down the rabbit hole with me—and yank me out when needed. On the best days, the work felt like play. Alex sharpened and deepened the text in countless ways, while closely collaborating with and drawing wisdom from my longtime Canadian editor, Louise Dennys, now publisher emerita of Penguin Random House Canada, as well as Martha Kanya-Forstner, Publisher of Knopf Canada, and Thomas Penn, publishing director at Penguin Books UK. I am deeply grateful to Mitzi Angel and Stefan McGrath for placing their faith in me.

Before there were agents and editors, there was Harriet Clark. At a moment of particularly acute pandemic vertigo, I decided to use the restrictions on travel, and the wonders of Zoom, to go to the writing school I had never attended. Harriet was my school. After only a couple of months of feeling like a clumsy undergrad, the idea for this project took root. As it grew, Harriet never stopped teaching me, and my debt to this literary doula is immense.

Another great debt is to Kendra Jewell, lead researcher on this project. While completing their anthropology PhD at the University of British Columbia, Kendra made time to dig into everything from theories of doppelgangers in psychoanalysis to charter schools in Florida. Kendra's mind is a marvel, and thinking with them has been one of the joys of my professional life. We were fortunate to work closely with two other top-notch research assistants, Isabella Pojuner and JJ Mazzucotelli, both completing master's degrees at UBC. This research team worked with tremendous dedication for months, conducting literature reviews, checking and rechecking facts, combing over endnotes—and they all deserve danger pay for the number of *War Room* episodes they had to transcribe. I am also grateful to Nicole Weber, my former research assistant at Rutgers University, who was a wonderful colleague in this book's earliest stage.

I gave drafts to several friends, colleagues, and family members for feedback: Bill McKibben, Alex Kelly, Harsha Walia, Cecilie Surasky, Jacqueline Rose, Johann Hari, Katharine Viner, Rajiv Sicora, Celeste Lecesne, Larry Zuckerman, Nancy Friedland, MJ Shaw, Christine Boyle, Michele Landsberg, and Stephen Lewis, as well as Seth, Bonnie, Michael, and Misha Klein. All came back with sharp and useful insights. The results of my never-ending conversations with Kyo Maclear and V can be felt on every page, as can my Thursday forest hikes with Kara Stanley.

I owe a particular debt to two extremely busy writers and intellectuals: Keeanga-Yamahtta Taylor and China Miéville. Both engaged substantively with early versions of this manuscript and influenced it in ways both large and small. A conversation with Molly Crabapple about the Jewish Labor Bund had a profound impact on the text at a crucial point, as did her smaller interventions later on. I am intensely grateful to my dear friend and comrade Anthony Arnove, who continues to represent various titles on my backlist. Anthony gave feedback on this manuscript and was very helpful in steering me to key texts about "the Jewish question" in Marxist thought. Roger Hodge at *The Intercept* carefully edited several articles that are mentioned in this text, and supported this project even when it meant long disappearances, as did Betsy Reed.

I am always at a loss for how to thank the magnificent Jackie Joiner, who has been managing my professional and personal life since 2005. All I can say is that she makes everything possible and does so with unfailing kindness and good humor—while being a publishing savant.

In the very early stages of researching this book, I had a conversation with Gage Averill, now provost of UBC, that changed my life. I am so grateful to him for bringing me to UBC and to all my colleagues in the Geography Department and the Centre for Climate Justice, particularly Geraldine Pratt and Jessica Dempsey (both early readers), as well as Mohammed Rafi Arefin, Sara Nelson, Alec Blair, and Jarrett Martineau. My seminar students at Rutgers and UBC have been a steadying force in tumultuous times: our weekly three-hour discussions never fail to renew my faith in the possible. I am also grateful to the remarkable Barbara Ransby for including me as a fellow in the University of Illinois's Social Justice Portal Project, a space for cross-disciplinary conversations between activists and scholars that challenged and inspired me.

There were periods when I needed to run away from home for a few weeks to write and I had some truly wonderful hosts: the Indigo cottage in Pender Harbour, Jane Walker in Squamish, Nancy and Craig in Sechelt. But nothing could have been more nourishing than being temporary springtime housemates with V and Celeste in the Hudson Valley. In these pages, I wrote about the teachers and education assistants who support and celebrate neurodivergence. They also made my writing life possible:

Jeannette Lewis, Erin Wilson, Nikki Underwood, Robin Hansen, and Tania Obalek. Care labor truly is the foundation of the next world.

What richness it is to live inside a web shimmering with so much creativity, commitment, and generosity. And all of this is on top of the more private support and replenishment that is my immediate family: Avi, my forever rock on the rock, and T., my northern light. This is a book about the instability of the self, but the truth is that as long as I have you two, I will always know who I am.

INDEX